A Reader's Guide to
the Contemporary English Novel
REVISED EDITION

arlos

A READER'S GUIDE TO
The Contemporary
English Novel

revised edition

Frederick R. Karl

THAMES AND HUDSON · LONDON

Acknowledgments for copyright material used in the first edition will be found on page 365. The author gratefully offers these additional acknowledgments for copyright material used in this revised edition for the first time: From Doris Lessing's *The Four-Gated City*, copyright © 1969 by Doris Lessing Productions Ltd.; reprinted by permission of Alfred A. Knopf. From Doris Lessing's *The Golden Notebook*, copyright © 1962 by Doris Lessing; reprinted by permission of Simon & Schuster. From Anthony Powell's series *A Dance to the Music of Time: Casanova's Chinese Restaurant*, © 1960 by Anthony Powell; *The Soldier's Art*, copyright © 1966 by Anthony Powell; *The Military Philosophers,* copyright © 1968 by Anthony Powell; all reprinted by permission of Little, Brown and Company. From Angus Wilson's *The Old Men at the Zoo,* copyright © 1961 by Angus Wilson, all rights reserved; reprinted by permission of The Viking Press and Martin Secker & Warburg Ltd.

Portions of this book appeared earlier in different form in *The Sewanee Review, Twentieth Century Literature, Prism, Mosaic,* and *Contemporary Literature.*

© 1961, 1962, 1971, 1972 by Frederick R. Karl
Revised edition, 1972

Printed Offset Litho in Great Britain by
Cox & Wyman Ltd, London, Fakenham and Reading

ISBN 0 500 14019 7 CLOTHBOUND
ISBN 0 500 15014 1 PAPERBOUND

Contents

A Reader's Guide to
the Contemporary English Novel
REVISED EDITION

I

The Contemporary English Novel

WE HAVE BEEN REMINDED with alarming frequency that
the English novel of the last thirty years has diminished in scale:
that no writer has the moral urgency of a Conrad, the verbal gifts
and wit of a Joyce, the vitality and all-consuming obsession
of a Lawrence; further, that the novel has forsaken its traditional
role of delineating manners and morals, and, finally, that the
novel is in a decline from which rescue is virtually impossible.
Granted that these claims do have partial substance, nevertheless
one must insist that the novel of the last three decades or so—the
post-*Ulysses* novel—contains the vitality and vigor worthy of a
major genre. Granted also that recent years have not turned up
another Joyce, Lawrence, or Conrad; they have, however, seen
distinguished work by established writers like Graham Greene,
Samuel Beckett, Henry Green, Elizabeth Bowen, C. P. Snow, Ivy
Compton-Burnett, and Evelyn Waugh, as well as promising novels
by their younger contemporaries, Lawrence Durrell, Iris Murdoch, William Golding, Doris Lessing, Angus Wilson, and Philip
Toynbee, among several others.

The English literary response to the severe international crises
of the second third of this century has been curious. The novelists
of the *first* third were concerned with major problems and major
conflicts. Forsaking direct political comment, they were neverthe-

less involved in the larger world. The novelists' intentions were realistic as well as impressionistic, and the fictional world that resulted was varied, many-hued, occasionally profound, and often exciting. This heritage of intellectual excitement has passed to the poets and not to the novelists of the second third of the century, while the novel has become something else. In the hands of Graham Greene, Elizabeth Bowen, Evelyn Waugh, C. P. Snow, George Orwell, and Joyce Cary, the novel has generally tended to become restrictive rather than extensive, to bring back traditional character and plot rather than to seek the inexpressible; in brief, to return to more self-contained matter while retaining, however, many of the technical developments of the major moderns. The contemporary novel is clearly no longer "modern."

The second group of novelists, several of whom had begun to write in the early 1930's, skipped the immediate influences of their older contemporaries and with few exceptions returned to the narrative manner of the late Victorians. C. P. Snow is closer to George Eliot, Galsworthy, and Bennett than he is to Joyce or Lawrence, or any of the major continental writers; while Joyce Cary seems to be following Sterne, Fielding, and Dickens; and Graham Greene appears akin to Wilkie Collins, Robert Louis Stevenson, Rider Haggard, and early Conrad. Ivy Compton-Burnett does not trespass this side of 1910, and George Orwell returned to Gissing and Zola for his method. In common, these writers agree that the experimental novel—especially its treatment of plot—is no longer viable and that retreat is perhaps expedient.

In many ways, of course, this realization is healthy. Experimentation is always to be encouraged, but it can easily lead to disastrous results, as many of the less successful attempts at "modernity" have demonstrated. The drawbacks to this failure to experiment, however, are as obvious as the virtues. While the contemporary writer gains directness, he forgoes paradox, irony, density, significance of theme—elements that enabled the impressionists and symbolists to go beyond the stated and the defined. The earlier novelists skillfully manipulated an audience which had accepted the Victorian and late Victorian novel and showed it the possibilities that the genre still offered. Conrad, Lawrence, and

Joyce pumped new life into a genre that had been declared dead and created new readers for new novels. The second group of realists has not sought so broad an audience and through retreat has limited the novel's horizons. Technique, experimentation, method—these terms are now hardly mentioned. C. P. Snow, for example, has voiced his disdain for those who create "artistic novels," like Plato apparently desiring to banish the poet from scientific society.

If there is a difference in the creations of the two groups, part of this difference is due to the backgrounds of the various writers. The contemporary novelists represent England and English ideals more closely than did their predecessors. Of the three major novelists in the older group, only Lawrence, it will be recalled, was native-born. The foreigners Conrad and Joyce introduced several ideas into the novel that do not derive from any English tradition; while C. P. Snow, Elizabeth Bowen, Joyce Cary and Evelyn Waugh, to name only four contemporaries, clearly are, whether for good or ill, English. The novel in Joyce's hands was internationalized; in Cary's and Waugh's Anglicized.

The earlier novel, despite its ostensible anti-intellectuality, moved into the realms of psychology, sociology, anthropology; its methodology had the jaggedness of contemporary life. The younger novelists, with some few exceptions, have far less grandiose plans; they do not deride intellect in intellectual terms, nor do they incorporate strange knowledge into their work. Their novels are, generally, shorter than those of their predecessors. We communicate now in communiqués, Camus said in *The Stranger*. One of the most successful and knotty of contemporary novelists, Graham Greene, writes novels that rarely extend beyond 75,000 words; and yet he, more than most of his contemporaries, is concerned with such weighty subjects as man's relation to himself and to his God. Greene is satisfied to make his point specifically: his characters are few, his architectonic is simple, his language direct.

The tremendous pressure of outside events in the last thirty years has resulted in withdrawal; and while the first group of novelists *included,* the second has *excluded.* As outside pressures increased, the retreat became more apparent, the novel attaining chance moments of intensity but at the expense of scope. By some curious psychological and social process which defies precise analysis, the contemporary novelist has sensed that a total immersion in life would destroy him and that to survive he must retreat from major issues. After Lawrence, no novelist can fully believe that man, like the phoenix, will rise from his own ashes. After Conrad, few have accepted the temporary saving nature of illusions. After E. M. Forster, not many optimistically claimed that men will ultimately survive through "connecting." After Joyce, who will agree with Molly Bloom's ringing "yes I said yes I will Yes"?

Among major contemporary novelists, only C. P. Snow has sought realistic explanations of the social and political conflicts of the period, and Snow has lost in intensity of characterization and situation what he has gained in range. If Snow, to achieve his aims, has sacrificed the interior, which was the forte of the first group of novelists, then, conversely, Elizabeth Bowen, Ivy Compton-Burnett, Lawrence Durrell, Henry Green, and Evelyn Waugh have renounced the larger world in favor of the inner man. Only Graham Greene and Samuel Beckett have attempted both. The great events of the thirties, with changing alliances and growing world tensions; the tumultuous war years, with their despair, frustration, and qualified victory; the post-war years, with their increasing anxieties and the sense of possible world destruction have been neglected by the contemporary novelist, as if the tremendous complexity of the modern world leaves him no choice but to retreat to the individual. This evasion becomes even more difficult to explain when we recognize that the contemporary novelists are for the most part not symbolists or avant-garde experimenters. On the contrary, they are often close to Naturalism, and we would expect contemporary events to enter directly into the flow of their narratives.

It is doubly curious that class structure—perhaps *the* staple of the English novel—has almost disappeared from the world of the major contemporary novelists, as though class distinctions had themselves vanished completely from English life. Certainly for Beckett and Durrell, class counts little; Beckett's anti-heroes are *déclassé,* and Durrell's sensualists are completely outside the restrictions of English social life. In Snow's novels, class conflicts are of course present, particularly in Lewis Eliot's early life, but these restrictions can be overcome by intelligence and perseverance. Snow is less interested in the class struggle itself than in individual power struggles. Orwell's novels are infused with class, but he reacts here less as an artist than as a journalist or social historian. Class has assumed a large importance only in a number of the humorists, Waugh and Powell, for example, or in several less influential novelists like L. P. Hartley, Olivia Manning, V. S. Pritchett, Angus Wilson, and William Sansom. However, these writers either use class differences strictly for comic purposes (unlike Dickens and the other major nineteenth-century novelists), or else lack at least at this stage in their development the artistic intensity to make class conflicts meaningful. When class is a serious factor —as in the novels of the "Angries"—it loses its substance in adolescent pranks and outrageous parodies. It rarely comes to us as an ever-present and disturbing aspect of life—as in Gissing, Wells, and Lawrence—something which cannot be eliminated by a funny face or witty remark.

Comedy itself, although it predominates in contemporary English fiction as much as in the nineteenth century, lacks size and vitality. Evelyn Waugh, certainly one of the most trenchant humorists of the era, is not an effective satirist; sentimentality and incoherent belief lie beneath his work's brilliant surface. Another writer of Waugh's generation, Henry Green (different though he is in kind and degree), has nevertheless insulated his comic characters from the world. Carrying on the tradition of the Dickensian eccentric, Green derives his comic effects simply from what people are. Green's view is not of course rosy (to use his word), but one suspects his calculated confusion and chaos hide the comforting belief that the world would be a better place could people only get together and be themselves.

A less well known comic novelist who has attempted to convey the shifting quality of reality as it passes back and forth before a mirror is Nigel Dennis, whose *Cards of Identity* is a novelistic tour de force. Dennis has found that man literally needs a role cut out for him. As in a Pirandello "comedy," a character's "card of identity" is no longer his own sign of personal identification but one invented by a novelist who keeps his character alive through illusions. The "gimmick" provides moments of brilliance, but the disadvantage is that the novelist seems to be playing a game and that the methodology squeezes out all other aspects of life.

Only Samuel Beckett, among the comedians, is sufficiently mature to generate works which are philosophic critiques of society. Beckett is a contemporary Thoreau gone sour over the inability of the individual to create his own world. As an Irishman living in France and England and writing in English and French, Beckett finds the implausible more real than the plausible and the impossible more significant than the possible. Confusion for him becomes cosmic: his rebellion is against both heaven and earth.

Unlike Beckett's work, the novels of the "Angry Young Men" —most of whom are not very angry—indicate how comedy has lost its bite. From Amis's famous Jim Dixon to Donleavy's less well-known Sebastian Dangerfield (*The Ginger Man,* 1958), the heroes of these novelists are angry at hypocrisy, sham, and class restrictions; they do not, however, seek to put the world right but adapt themselves to those aspects of existence they can tolerate. Neo-Rousseauists, Hemingway he-men, they seek the primitive, the pure, the natural.

The real rebel is of another sort, protesting not only against the personally disagreeable but against the entire order of the universe. When the rebel is authentic and not a *poseur,* he knows there is little basis for a *rapprochement* with society. The real protestant is never at rest. Part of what made Conrad, Joyce, and Lawrence effective was their awareness that the individual gains uniqueness by his struggle against what both sustains him and destroys him. It is precisely this voice of protest that has been hushed to a whisper in the contemporary novel. When young novelists like Amis, Wain, and Braine do attempt the novel of protest, their voices are often too weak and diluted to be audible.

The real rebel, if we continue our search, is not Colin Wilson's "Outsider," a creature whom many English critics mistook for the Messiah. Wilson's man is rebellious only in the dubious sense of being possessed; he is anxious to impose his views upon the world. This attitude is of course antithetical to the real rebel, who even disdains what will come of his own efforts.

Perhaps the true English rebel in our day is the sensualist, Durrell's Alexandrians or Isherwood's perverted Mr. Norris. Durrell seeks to make the strange familiar and the familiar strange and through this device to gain distance. The insider and outsider are seen in a new perspective. He succeeds in conveying a curious asexual sensuality—his people aspire to sensuality because they believe it is expected of them, but their effort fails. Durrell's Alexandria must dwarf its people, and yet these people must be capable of accepting what Alexandria offers, a virtual paradise for the sensualist. They are not, however, of sufficient stature to do what is expected of them. Isherwood's Mr. Norris is almost too familiar for comment. He rebels by seeking sexual satisfaction under a booted whore's whip. But after Proust's Charlus, such perversions seem minor indeed, merely the exhausted devices of a depleted sensuality, not an obsession that must be satisfied. Charlus would give anything for the chains and whips and young men; he is the closest thing we have to a genuine Don Juan in the twentieth century. Compared with him, Mr. Norris is puny and seedy.

Only Beckett carries on the great tradition, and yet how curiously he has had to shape his material to create a rebel, that is, a person who functions by virtue of what he is rather than by what is expected of him. The rebel is not a criminal and not a force for evil, although he may commit anti-social acts. He is, fundamentally, a person for whom society does not offer a testing ground: he seeks his philosophy in himself, not in God or his environment. He is, at best, true to himself no matter what the consequences, and often they are unfavorable.

While Kafka did not give his major characters names, calling them K., for example, Beckett goes further and shifts the names of his characters in mid novel, mocking their identities by giving them at least two when they are unable to sustain even one. For Beckett, this method is of course a form of morbid humor (the M's of his characters' names are perhaps plays on the word morbid, or possibly on the French for death, *mort,* as one commentator has suggested).

Beckett conceives of man's downfall as a cosmic joke, and to disallow man even the use of a definite name (what everyone has from birth) is to mock his pretensions to any sort of equitable life.

Beckett's protagonists, as it were, pay their author back in kind by refusing to participate in life, as though his denying them a last name forces their negation of the world. For Beckett to achieve the disgust and revulsion that evidently are his goals, he must of course forsake a great deal, as would any novelist who limits his subject so severely. Man defines himself by meager wants and debased follies; to claim more for him is to substitute romanticism for reality. Beckett's rebel is the supreme realist: a dehumanized outcast seeking a dark corner in which society will let him chew, excrete, and sleep. In some ways, only Beckett offers a body of work that is consonant with the major tones of modern life, restricted though his material is to the sordid and the pitiful and the debased. He is great fun for those with little hope and much staying power.

For the reader who wants to be grim in a more traditional way, there is of course Ivy Compton-Burnett. Part of Miss Compton-Burnett's wit consists in the reproduction of her picture, that of a kindly old lady, on the back cover of each of her novels. One expects, as is the intention, a Grandma Moses, and finds instead a Medea or Clytemnestra. Ivy Compton-Burnett is funny because she is a master at blending opposites. By making startling revelations about people who seem the essence of respectability, she counterpoints several different kinds of reality to gain her comic effects. Take a Jane Austen character and add various ingredients derived from the Freudian unconscious, mix well with inadvertent incest, chance murder, fortuitous blackmail, and the reader is involved in Miss Compton-Burnett's peculiar invention.

The comedy of Evelyn Waugh, with its obvious debts to Firbank and Saki, is quite different, although neither he nor Miss Compton-Burnett has written the kind of high comedy which purges Folly, what Meredith defined as the substance of the Comic Spirit. What made Waugh's early successes possible was the fact that few readers questioned the assumptions on which his novels rest, taking for granted that the wit emanated from a rational and ordered mind skeptical of all nonsense. Perhaps because Waugh was so destructive, most readers accepted without dispute his similarity to his contemporaries: that he was a skeptic, a doubter, a mocker, a less verbose Huxley, a de-sentimentalized Forster. In fact, someone they could trust. Readers even consented to Waugh's questionable taste because his thrusts seemed to prick everyone and everything equally. Possibly because of this almost unqualified acceptance, the later *Brideshead Revisited,* with its religious fakery, and *Men at Arms* and *Officers and Gentlemen,* with their false patriotism and sentimentalized sense of duty, were such shocks.

One common characteristic of Waugh and several of his contemporaries is, as I have suggested, their inability to deepen and develop with time. When Elizabeth Bowen, for example, experiments in *The Heat of the Day,* she does little more than what Virginia Woolf had tried in *Mrs. Dalloway* fifteen years earlier. When Joyce Cary in *The Horse's Mouth* and elsewhere tampers with language, he barely scrapes the surface of what Joyce attempted with words. When Durrell talks about love in his Alexandria *Quartet,* he points toward but hardly reaches Lawrence's examination of love. When Graham Greene uses moral issues within a religious frame of reference, he is dealing with a subject that many nineteenth-century novelists wrote about extensively and with greater range.

A partial reason for this loss of adventure—aside from differences in individual talent—is that novelists now are so aware of techniques developed by their predecessors that they assimilate technical knowledge before their own material has sufficiently formed. The contemporary novelist is, curiously, an old man technically when he first begins to write. To be this knowledgeable while still an apprentice does have limitations; it tends to frustrate the trial and error experimentation that results in the major failure, the significant bad book, the first novel that misses full accomplishment while remaining important. The result has been fiction of considerable substance, but fiction nevertheless that is technically proficient without being daring, verbally incisive without being original, and full of ideas without being truly persuasive.

English and continental literature reached peaks in the first part of the century for a variety of reasons, not the least of which was that personal decisions—no matter how negative—still appeared to have substance. The world facing the contemporary novelist is of quite a different order. He looks out on ultimate chaos, on a world that is no longer seeking instruction, but destruction, a world possibly heading nowhere. It is difficult to create tragedy (or even high comedy) when all values are under question, for tragedy would appear to operate best in a relatively stable society.

With the partial loss of imaginative thrust occurs an analogous loss in style. Except perhaps for parts of Beckett's and Durrell's work, the contemporary novel is unique in that, although it does contain stylists, it offers not one writer in the grand style. The grand style entails the novelist's ability to surround his objects with words so that character and scene are permeated by language. Joyce in his way and Conrad in his are the two great prose stylists of the twentieth century, although their other merits and accomplishments are perhaps still debatable.

Lawrence Durrell has been hailed, and rightly, for attempting to write grandly. Yet even Durrell, despite his gifts, makes language seem adornment rather than essential. His literary tradition, like Conrad's in *Almayer's Folly* and Joyce's in *A Portrait,* is that of the late nineteenth century, but while the latter two came to develop their own styles, Durrell's remains somewhat otiose and languid. Durrell's prose is often close to the softness of Yeats' early poetry and the vague mushiness of much other *fin de siècle* poetry and prose, which reserved language chiefly for decoration. This lavish use of ornate language should not be confused with a grand style, which is distinctive despite its broadness and definitive despite its richness.

These comments should not blind the reader to the stylistic niceties of Elizabeth Bowen or Henry Green, even though Bowen and Green frequently gain their effects from what they exclude rather than from what they include. Beckett, whose background is continental, has attempted his own solution: to use language repetitively, evocatively, almost senselessly, until the word, as it were, isolates itself from meaning, and the reader is left with "pure" language. Since Beckett's purpose is to communicate through patterns of ideas, language becomes in his hands a different kind of medium from that of his contemporaries. The result has a peculiar impact, the force of an original mind that overpowers the reader on the novelist's own terms. With Beckett, verbal experimentation is not a conscious process, but the unique means through which he *must* present his material. He is of course arrogant enough to reject the reader who seeks easy entertainment. And yet in the passages that hit the mark, there is a world in each phrase, a universe in a paragraph. The grand style takes precisely these chances.

Language is not in itself a criterion of greatness—after all, when we read Tolstoy in English, we can recognize his genius although *his* language is not what we read. The same is true of any novelist's work when it survives translation. Nevertheless, language, whether in translation or not, indicates how seriously the writer wants to be taken. Language in the grand style—that is, language which embellishes, communicates, and strives for visionary effects—usually complements the content of a writer who is attempting more than the ordinary. It is safe to say that language indicates on what level he intends to appeal. If for Henry Green language is essentially a source of hilarious confusion and of romantic sentimentality, then this is the level at which Green aims. In a writer like C. P. Snow, the use of language indicates his aims clearly. Snow writes a lucid workable prose that rarely embarrasses us with its simplicity and, similarly, rarely astounds us with its cleverness. It is a prose that well suits a professional man's view of the world.

In the present generation of novelists, even those who can be called experimenters, there is little equation of "grand" language with innovations in the craft. Only two writers even attempt this, one a partial success, the other less sure. William Golding, who is best known in this country for *Lord of the Flies* (1954), combines the moral intensity of Snow, the verbal gifts of Henry Green and Lawrence Durrell, the narrative drive of Graham Greene, Beckett's ability to probe, and the technical skill of his major predecessors. Although Golding's novels thus far have demonstrated too much eccentricity for his gifts to be fully manifest, he heralds a more adventurous kind of novel, religious in a way, possibly moral, though at its best non-didactic.

Philip Toynbee, the son of the historian, has carried on the tradition of experiment in two of his novels, *Prothalamium* (1947), subtitled "A Cycle of the Holy Graal," and *The Garden to the Sea* (1954). The first of these novels is concerned with an innovation in the narrative sequence: the narrators, some eight in number, appear one by one, say their piece, and then disappear to make way for the next narrator. The material that each relates overlaps that which preceded and that which will follow. Some of the narrators are not present at certain scenes, and, accordingly, there is a gap in this part of the narrative. When all have had their say, the novel ends. Also, interspersed in the narratives are italicized passages which, the author reminds us, indicate what is overheard by that particular narrator, but said neither by him nor to him. The apparatus, consequently, is of great importance, for it forces an artificiality on the story process and obliges the reader to make several allowances for the novelist.

The experimental novel, however, must satisfy on some level other than that of the experiment itself. When *Ulysses* was still considered avant-garde, the careful reader, even if he missed the over-all significance, certainly perceived the verbal wit and the humor implied in incongruous juxtaposition of elements. There was something for the reader who almost totally rejected or miscomprehended the experiment. The same might be said for *Finnegans Wake*, although the qualifications here are admittedly somewhat different. But *Prothalamium*, with its ironic title of a song in celebration of a secular marriage, offers little humor, only a kind of verbal obliqueness in which words suggest things that are deliberately hidden from the reader.

In *The Garden to the Sea*, published seven years later, Toynbee attempted another experiment, this one more conventional: to dramatize, through separate narrators, fragmented parts of a single personality. The three sides of Adam, whose names suggest the man, are Noel, the voice of innocence; Tom, the voice of his fall; and Charley, the voice of his punishment. The three voices and Adam carry on a four-sided debate, with Charley (punishment) and Adam himself being stressed.

The theme from *Prothalamium*, with its emphasis on sin and redemption, on sensuality and punishment, is repeated in a form not dissimilar to that of the earlier novel. In Toynbee's hands, characters assume allegorical shape; and the method here—of allegorical figures representing different sides of man—has been a common device in dramatic poetry from Dante and Spenser to Goethe. In the novel, however, whose realism virtually relegated allegory to the dust heap, the use of allegory creates several problems, not the least of which is its failure to provide adequate characterization. Despite the derring-do of the technique, Adam is a bore, and his various voices are no less tedious.

One wishes that Toynbee had not published his novels until his technique had, so to speak, more chance to work with the material. The novels unfortunately seem all method, as often experiments in non-representational painting merely demonstrate something new without saying anything fresh. Since the two novels are inconclusive, they become their own worst argument for experimentation; nevertheless, the reader sympathetic to the genre must applaud a writer courageous enough to produce unpopular works —novels destined to be unpopular—because he believes in the potentialities of his craft.

Perhaps the chief argument against experimentation of this, or any, sort is that it tends to strip the writer of his full sense of life; for often the experiment paradoxically limits as it extends frontiers. Toynbee's novels appear to be specimens of this type of failure, in which certain rhythms of words and scenes are stressed at the expense of characterization and frequently of sense. There is always a thorny question for the critic to ask: is experimentation worthwhile when it often leads to ineffective work? To decry the new is certainly prevalent among popular critics who defend with exemplary energy what has worked well in the past. Like political reactionaries, they applaud what they recognize and reject what looks foreign. For the serious reader, however, the experimental novel signifies that something adventurous is being undertaken and that the art is healthy. All truly great novels are experimental in some way—whether in content or technique—and possibly the reason why many major contemporary novels disappoint is that the novelist has in the main disdained experiment. Retrenchment can also go too far.

As the experimental method has been shunned, so have the themes that might have enlarged the novel. The several wars of the last twenty years, for example, have not provided material for any major novels; one thinks only of Evelyn Waugh's two books on Guy Crouchback's adventures, Rex Warner's political allegories, Gerald Hanley's *Without Love,* Nigel Dennis's *A Sea Change,* P. H. Newby's *The Retreat*—all of them competent novels in some ways but none that stand out. There has also occurred a general retreat from the *Bildungsroman,* or long developmental novel, in which a young man serves his apprenticeship to life with its attendant failures and successes, to end up a wiser man. Parts of C. P. Snow's *Strangers and Brothers,* Anthony Powell's *Music of Time,* and Doris Lessing's *Children of Violence* are attempts at the *Bildungsroman,* but frequently the author loses his protagonist amidst social comment. Perhaps the only major contemporary *Bildungsroman* is Elizabeth Bowen's artistically successful *The Death of the Heart* (1939).

That novel aside, the *Bildungsroman* and the *Künstlerroman* (the development specifically of an artist) have declined because of their demands upon the author. The form requires long and involved plotting, also a hero, and, further, a society which believes in the possibility of heroes. In addition, the *Bildungsroman* is necessarily episodic—the structure of the novel follows a long development from childhood through success or failure, scene following scene in chronological order. In Conrad's hands, the shift is already apparent, a change in narrative from a complete progression that included birth, childhood, and adulthood to the presentation of certain crucial aspects in the moral development of the anti-hero or non-hero. Once the novelist has buried the hero amidst his commonplace contemporaries, then his birth is no longer miraculous, his childhood no longer significant, and his adulthood no longer challenging. What becomes interesting is the way in which the non-hero has to confront a situation that calls for heroism, or in which the anti-hero must summon up courage and reserves for a challenge he is inadequate to fulfill. Destroy the hero, as the contemporary novelist has done, and he destroys the episodic novel as well: the *Bildungsroman* and the *Künstlerroman* as major forms disappear.

The contemporary novelist evidently hopes to gain in sharpness of focus what his predecessors gained through bulk. As I indicated above, contemporary English novels—at least, most of the serious ones—are brief. If the novelist today wants to begin an extensive exploration, he must first construct the base from which he will operate. Most novelists facing a disintegrating world, however, become concerned solely with the base itself: they have little space to explore unknown territory. To salvage some order means the localization of the problem, an attempt to limit what is said. The novelist feels that since the world has lost its familiar identity, he can only cultivate his own literary garden, till the soil that is familiar, and leave the rest alone. Remove the assured and the relatively secure; remove a defined world which the writer can rebel against or defend; remove all props, and the novelist must pursue fragments of reality rather than the "whole." Paradoxically, we see, the very complication of outside pressure has forced the novelist to attempt simplification. Earlier, a relatively simpler world could be given the aspect of confusion. Now, the novelist tries to turn cosmic confusion into workable reality and to transform chaos into something comprehensible.

We must also recognize that the severe pressure of external events has resulted in a partial reaction against the art novel, which had its roots in Symbolism. C. P. Snow seems to be the logical leader of this quasi-defined movement. A former scientist, a civil administrator, a pragmatist, he disdains those who refuse to see the novel as solidly based in realistic fact. Thus, we note Snow's distortion of the significance of stream of consciousness, his attacks on experimentation, his suspicion of involved symbolism. Snow and those who agree with him (novelists as well as critics) argue that the whole movement attributed to Symbolism narrowed the novel, which can be recharged only by writers who face the "real" world. Yet Snow's own ideas, tending as they do toward the naturalistic, would, if realized, restrict the novel by reducing human motivation to its tangible elements and human actions to a chartable course. It is odd to find a scientist whose logic is Aristotelian becoming a Platonist in his distrust of the false poets who tell us "untruths." Snow's literary reactionaryism would raise barriers to imaginative fiction; for English life, taken straight without the "embroidery" Snow rejects, does not provide the depths and heights of behavior suitable for strictly realistic fiction. Snow unfortunately confuses the potentialities of the English novel with those, for example, of the Russian.

These remarks have frequently tended to illustrate what the contemporary English novel is not, and therefore may in part be overbalanced toward its negative aspects. To compare the fiction of one era with that of another is an inevitable consequence of criticism, but one that is valid only when the comparison, or contrast, brings forth values and does not destroy them. There will obviously be much that seems negative about the novels of *any* period when a great many of them are examined in detail; the comments below, nevertheless, should dispel any complacency that the contemporary English novel fails to generate its own kind of vitality.

A word on my selection of novelists: I discuss those writers whose major development occurred in the 1930's and later, that is, in the period after Joyce's *Ulysses* and the major novels of Lawrence. Except for the work of Beckett, which does provide some continuity, this time brought a turning point in the development of English fiction. Joyce of course was still very much alive and hard at work on *Finnegans Wake,* but his influence had ended with *Ulysses*. Huxley had already done his best work in the Twenties, Lawrence was recently dead, and Conrad, also dead, had not published a major book since *Victory* in 1915. By 1931, with *The Waves,* Virginia Woolf had written her most important novels, and E. M. Forster had not published any fiction since *A Passage to India* in 1924. By 1930, a new generation—our presently established one—was first beginning to be heard. In their hands, the novel was to mean something else.

II

Waiting for Beckett:
Quest and Re-Quest

EVEN THOUGH Samuel Beckett as a dramatist has frequently taken critical precedence over Beckett as a novelist, it is in his six novels* that his originality is demonstrated; the plays merely add a footnote to what the novels indicate with greater range and force. The plays themselves—*Waiting For Godot, Endgame, Krapp's Last Tape, Act Without Words,* for example—are fragments of the novels, episodes submerged in the larger context. The real Beckett—if one presumes to define him—is the novelist who almost arbitrarily broke off segments of his fiction and labeled them tragicomedies, monologues, mimes, et al.

Beckett's first two novels, *Murphy* (1938) and *Watt* (published in 1953, but written in 1942-44) were composed in English with definable English backgrounds, but the Irish-born novelist soon allied himself with a continental literary and philosophical point of view. In philosophy, he clearly rejected English rationalism and logic in favor of Descartes' division of mind and body; and in literature, he is closer to Proust, Céline, Sartre, Camus, and Ionesco, as well as to experimental writers like Robbe-Grillet and Nathalie Sarraute, than to the English novelists of the last hundred years. Only with Joyce and perhaps Dickens does he find sympa-

* *Murphy* (1938); *Watt* (1953); *Molloy* (1951); *Malone Dies* (1952); *The Unnamable* (1953); *Comment C'est* (1961)

thy, and then less for content than for certain devices and techniques which recur in their works.

Beckett is a Joyce gone completely sour, a Joyce who went underground after *Ulysses.* Had Stephen Dedalus failed at everything he tried and consequently become a bum, a tramp, or an aimless writer, he might have fitted into one of Beckett's novels, nearly all of whose protagonists are writers chronicling their own weary odysseys. Their aimless tales—the very point is their aimlessness—are egoistic ventures to note whatever keeps their past before them, for their present brings with it no pleasures. Even their past, however, is painful, an unrelieved string of misadventures and lost opportunities, of relationships forced upon them they never sought, of jobs and families and strangers bobbing up to torture them. In all instances, they become increasingly aware of the absurd difference between their small expectations and their even smaller fulfillment.

The use of the existential absurd becomes for Beckett, as much as it did for Camus, a metaphysical device to explore existence, and it takes many shapes. The "reality" of a Beckett novel is an exaggerated dream, a nightmare extended to cover past and future, a fluid manifestation of something seemingly preconscious. The world of Beckett's first novel, *Murphy,* has few of the touchstones we expect even in the symbolic novel. Compared with *Murphy,* the symbolic works of Conrad, Lawrence, and Joyce seem realistic projections of everyday problems. More the presentation of a philosophical problem than a novel in the ordinary sense, *Murphy* in some ways seems worked from the same material as *L'Étranger,* whose first version Camus conceived not long after Beckett's novel appeared.

Without forcing the parallel, the reader can see in both novels the attempt of the protagonist to remain innocent, to avoid the senseless contacts which the world expects of him. Murphy rocks himself in his chair, naked, bound (like a Greek hero being punished by the gods), but mentally free. No one can touch his mind: "And life in his mind gave him pleasure, such pleasure that pleasure was not the word." There is in both novels a Rousseauistic condemnation of the world: Meursault's refusal to weep at his mother's funeral is Murphy's refusal to work. In every situation, the protagonists must face the absurdity of existence in order to establish the tragic intensity of their own lives. Each lives differently from what is expected, and yet each expects not to be judged. Although there are no eternal truths, Murphy attempts to seek Truth in his rocker; naked and bound, he endeavors to leave behind a world of false appearances in a Buddha-like contemplation of reality. For Murphy, the real world is like Plato's cave of appearances, while his own "inner cave" is the substantial world.

A Beckett hero is always in conflict with objects around him, for only he himself has reality. Just as Descartes separated mind and body and then tried to re-integrate them, Beckett divorces people from objects and then attempts to find some relationship between them. The recent French novel typified by the work of Alain Robbe-Grillet, Michel Butor, and Nathalie Sarraute is, in one way, a footnote to Beckett's output of the last two decades. Robbe-Grillet has posited a world in which "Things are things, and man is only man"; that is, things remain unpenetrated, "hard dry objects" that are foreign to us.

A Beckett protagonist, be he Murphy, Watt, Molloy, or Malone, has long ago refused complicity with objects. Or else, objects have remained outside his attainment. In every instance, he is divided from the rest of the world, a stranger to its desires and needs. The dichotomy between his own mind and body finds an analogy in the outside world in the dichotomy between people and objects. Thus, Beckett's world operates in halves, and the dialectic of any given novel occurs when these halves conflict, when tension is created between mind and body, on one hand, and people and objects, on the other.

With this ground plan, it is no wonder that Beckett's characters lack clear identity. As they are themselves divided, they cannot identify what they are, and as the world itself is divided, they cannot be identified with anything outside themselves. Each novel, consequently, takes the form of a quest, chiefly the familiar quest for a self that was, ironically, never different from what the character presently is. It is of course in his emphasis on this symbolic motif, one in which the character seeks his lost self—equivalent to a lost paradise or hell—that Beckett allies himself with the major writers of the century. Despite the familiarity of the theme, however, Beckett's development is the unique product of an original mind.

In quest of an identity which is cosmic in its scope, a Beckett protagonist leaves the everyday world far behind. For Beckett, moreover, the quest is not melodramatic or tragic, but comic, the quest for a self that even the protagonist knows cannot be recovered. When one quests hoping to find something that constantly eludes him, the result is tragic for him; but when he seeks knowing that what escapes him now will continue to escape him, and he keeps seeking regardless of outcome, the result is often funny. Such a person has become a particular kind of fool, subject to practical jokes, cosmic ironies, paradoxical experiences; and none of these annoyances really matter. The seeker is merely playing out what he knows to be a game. So it is with Beckett's protagonists. They recognize that the divisions which have sundered them can never be healed and that they are expected (by whom?) to wait and play and expect. All of Beckett's characters wait, in their particular ways, for Godot, who can never arrive. For Godot would cure what ails them, and this solution is itself an impossibility in an absurd world.

In a world which neither punishes nor rewards, aspirations, hope, ambition, will itself are obviously meaningless. No one can attain anything—Murphy dies, the indirect result of obtaining a job. Molloy reaches his mother's room, but for what purpose? Moran searches for Molloy and becomes increasingly like his crippled quarry, his quest ending in a circle. Malone waits to die, decrepit and helpless. The Unnamable tries to find out what or who he is. Watt ends up in a madman's employ. And in a world in which attainment is impossible, so is tragedy. The growth and development necessary for tragedy are missing by design, for tragedy indicates coherent significance in the world. It suggests that goals, will, aspirations can work within a social framework which, potentially at least, is progressive, and this type of world is evidently absent in Beckett. So marginal as to be almost nonexistent, Beckett's characters nevertheless operate with an intense heat that makes a heroic action of hooking a chamber pot with a stick or finding a stubby pencil. Beckett's characters endure in their miniature world, but their endurance is without heroism. Endurance for Beckett, unlike Faulkner, has no heroic connotations. Rather because endurance is senseless, it is comic. For this reason, perhaps, Beckett has been accused of writing anti-novels, novels which deny life and find the denial itself funny.

The bum for Beckett is a metaphysical entity, a person so far outside "normal" society that his actions and behavior take place almost cosmically. By separating the character from objects around him and further by splitting the character into mind and body, Beckett is able to create a certain kind of fragmented reality. Inhabited by bums, tramps, misfits, and cripples, this world is a collage of surrealistic images pinned together less by narrative force than by states of individual feeling. Nuances of feeling have to resolve everything, and here Beckett suggests the central philosophical conflict that permeates all his work.

If states of feeling, or mind, or thought are the only ascertainable facts, then how does one account for the existence of things? If a thing is only what is apparent to the various senses, then no object really has substance or shape of its own; its form, obviously, will depend upon its appearance to the various senses at different times. One must, then, disbelieve almost entirely in things. In Cartesian thought, as in Beckett's, mind was more important than matter, the subjective more significant than the objective. The only way, according to Descartes, that one could make mind come to terms with bodies was through God. The argument ran that since God gives man a strong inclination to believe in bodies, if no bodies existed, then God would be deceitful; since, given the nature of God, this is impossible, then bodies exist.

What happens, however, if one removes God from the universe, as Beckett does? What relationship can there be between man and his possessions, between man and the external objects around him, if the connecting force, so to speak, is eliminated? The fact is that a kind of chaos results, the chaos of Beckett's novels in which the only order imposed is that placed there by the characters themselves who state the problem through their own writing. The fact is that Beckett replaces God by making the character into an author substitute who can then create his own world and himself draw the necessary connection between mind and body. Beckett's use of the accursed writer who assumes God-like functions is a familiar device from Baudelaire and Rimbaud. Beckett's writers—Molloy, Moran, Malone, the Unnamable—all create their own worlds, and their biggest problem is to resolve just this philosophical dilemma—the need to approach objects, to grasp objects, to make their peace with the world of objects. Often, their simplest (or most difficult) problem is to put their hands on the elementary things they need. Beckett undoubtedly minimized their needs—a stone, pencil, exercise book, stick, umbrella, bicycle—in order to reduce the relation between person and object to first principles, at which point the problem can be "solved" through comic rather than tragic means.

The emphasis on things serves another function as well, that of providing solid fixtures within the world of fact to afford relief from the meandering stream of the protagonists' consciousness. Joyce, for example, broke Bloom's verbal flow by carefully placing in the narrative numerous references to Dublin; so that Bloom was given substance, as well as mind, by his surroundings. Beckett works similarly. Without Dublin as background, he uses the familiar props of everyday life to convey a spatial dimension to his novels. The stress on objects, no matter how mean or paltry, precluded his characters from being refined out of factual existence into pure states of being. We have already seen that this awareness of spatial dimension as a counter to the characters' states of feeling has become the *raison d'être* of a "new wave" of French writers like Robbe-Grillet.

This emphasis on a spatial dimension by Beckett and the French writers suggests a curious turnabout on Proust's work, with its stress on the temporal dimension of memory. Beckett himself saw in Proust's novels, as early as 1931, the way in which art could decipher the mysteries of the universe, and he found in Proust's use of involuntary memory a temporal device for precisely such a stripping away of excrescences to get to essentials. In a letter to Antoine Bibesco, Proust had explained what he meant by involuntary memory, a theory that was to prove important to Beckett in two ways: both in its immediate influence upon him and as a way later of providing his reaction to temporal dimensions altogether.

Involuntary memory is concerned with that part of the mind which stores sensations of the past, as it were censored by voluntary memory, and which can be evoked by an odor or taste or a momentary feeling, what Proust later called privileged moments. Involuntary memory, like the psychoanalytic preconscious, contains a half-remembered, half-forgotten past which can be called upon at any moment of sudden revelation.

A voyage into involuntary memory is an attempt to amalgamate all time by penetrating below the surface into the depths that help define the "reality" of a human being. It is an anti-naturalistic device aimed at a psychoanalytic probe into character and personality, and it is precisely this that attracted the young Beckett. And although he later abandoned his interest in time as such, the method has become infused with his own work in a curious way. Deep within involuntary memory Beckett has discovered a lost paradise, indeed the only true paradise for both Beckett and Proust for the very reason that it is lost. Memory is of course the only way of uncovering it. So Proust worked in his seven volumes. For Beckett, however, the lost paradise can not even be regained in memory because, paradoxically, the irretrievability of the loss is what makes it paradise. To hope for more than this is to hope falsely, to deny what life really is. For Molloy, for example, paradise entails the memory of his mother which he seeks to regain by setting out on his impossible quest to find her; but were he to come upon her, the reality would deny the paradisiacal vision, and therefore the quest must be unsuccessful and self-defeating. Consequently, all quests in Beckett's novels, either in the pre-war *Watt* and *Murphy* or the post-war *Molloy, Malone Dies,* and *The Unnamable,* are foredoomed to failure. Once one's personal paradise has been lost—and in Beckett's world one may never even be aware of the loss—then this is the fact one lives with. If the reader can accept this attitude which is common to many of Beckett's protagonists, he can perceive some of the restrictions under which these characters live. These people have no illusions, for without a real paradise to hope for or dream of, illusions are illusory.

There is in Beckett, possibly as a direct result of his attitude toward Proust and everything Proust stands for, a hard realism which he tries to soften with comic devices from such diverse authors as Joyce, Sterne, and Swift. In the pre-war novels, which he wrote in English, the influence of English writers is more apparent, and the themes are less hopeless, somber though they are; but in the postwar novels, written in French, work which Beckett says is central to his entire outlook, the devices are less explicitly Joycean or Swiftian and closer to the grotesqueness of Camus and Sartre. In both periods, nevertheless, there is the Beckett speciality: a bum or tramp or outsider who is the Elizabethan fool reduced by disintegration to a shadow of his former self. Without any splendor, either intrinsic or that vicarious kind which might have rubbed off from his noble master, Beckett's outsider becomes the norm of a declining world, the universal fool. Now the bum is the master, simply because no other standard exists. Estragon and Vladimir waiting for the never-to-appear Godot, Moran on his strange quest to find Molloy and thus save part of himself, Murphy trying to avoid work and torturing himself more than work itself might, Watt attempting to see Mr. Knott whom he serves faithfully and dumbly, Malone endeavoring to live between Dish (food) and Pot (excrement), the Unnamable desiring silence but forced into an outpouring of words—all these are "dying gladiators," to repeat Horace Gregory's apt phrase, who are probing the limits of a meaningless world and coming to grief because of their very integrity.

Even though they are close to non-existence, "At times, indeed, almost ridiculous," they do not accept their roles as grotesque and pathetic beings. They astound us by their vitality and by their failure to crumble in situations that are self-destructive. Murphy's attempt to avoid work becomes a saga of human ingenuity and bravery. He defies all society in order to be himself, as much as Moran will forsake everything—his son, his dignity, his respectability, his warm home—in order to search for Molloy, whom he knows solely from the fact that the Molloy within all of us strikes a chord.

Fools though they may be, Beckett's characters achieve a dignity of their own; and because they wait for what they know will be nothing, they are comic characters in a tragic world. Reduced to Lear on the heath, a once noble man who is now far less capable than his Fool, they rage and rant against restrictions and in so doing ask the most important questions: in what tense should a person speak when his life is both going on and is over, and perhaps is neither? what does the flesh signify when experience has denied all forms of hope? what does one live for when both flesh and spirit give no pleasure and memory affords only pain? what do aspirations and goals mean to people for whom there is no purpose or connection to anything outside themselves? what happens when belief in both God and man has disappeared, when God is impossible and man is disgusting? what does one think of when life has become meaningless, and death is something one lacks energy to seek?

These are the questions that Beckett's gladiators ask, and none waits for a complete answer. The quality of their hopelessness surpasses that of any other characters in literature, with Céline's Ferdinand Bardamu and Swift's Gulliver perhaps expected. The two non-entities in *Endgame* who have survived their time and now seek life-and-death in ashcans are apt symbols of Beckett's world; to search further is to search for life, and Beckett's people are all death oriented. For them, pain and discomfort are a curious form of salvation in a world that tries to deceive them into being happy.

How, then, does Beckett make this view comic, for comic it is, although the comedy is qualified? Principally, his main device is his use of language that mocks, outrages, bores, clots, and exasperates, but language at all times in the hands of an expert. Secondarily, he uses parody, slapstick, the delayed joke, the juxtaposition of dissimilars, the paralleling of the familiar and unfamiliar—all aimed at creating a reality that is both fantastic and grotesquely true.

In *Murphy,* the titular character follows a language-clotted prospectus set up in a horoscope by Ramaswami Krishnaswami Narayanswami Suk for those Natives born under the sign of the Goat. The Native in question, here Murphy, if he follows Suk's prophecy is assured of success, and so Murphy checks with Suk at every turn in his fortune. Yet Murphy knows that his "prospects of employment were the same in both places, in all places" —he is the last man whom Suk can reach. Murphy is the asuccessful man, the death-oriented man. Suk's prophecies are for the go-getter, the man-of-the-world, the daring, adventurous sort who is willing to sacrifice and connive for advancement; and yet Suk is Murphy's God. The very terms, then, of Murphy's quest, caught as he is between Suk's prophecies for him and his own desire for rest and silence, are those of humor and outrage. Suk is of course a false prophet, one for a competitive world, but even so there is no one else for Murphy to believe in. However, although he arranges his ideas to suit Suk's, Murphy also recognizes the futility of any God whatsoever. For Murphy admits to himself that he is not of the big world, " 'I am of the little world.' " Why should he, he asks himself even while following Suk, cultivate "the occasions of fiasco, having once beheld the beatific idols of his cave?" And Beckett comments, in the words of Arnold Geulincx, a seventeenth-century Belgian Cartesian, *Ubi nihil vales, ibi nihil velis.* His epitaph on Murphy!

Suk, work, industry, cadging in the park—all these are inimical to Murphy's nature, and all are sources of comedy, for Murphy is only at home in his rocker, naked and contemplative, a Buddhist god contemplating nothingness. Retreating into the dark of his own cave-like existence, refined almost out of existence, Murphy pictures his mind "as a large hollow sphere, hermetically closed to the universe without. This was not an impoverishment, for it excluded nothing that it did not itself contain." A mind that desires ultimate rest and silence is forced into contact with a society that requests competition and work and ambition; and the result is comic. Murphy enters Magdalen Mental Mercyseat Hospital not as a patient but as a general helper, and finds the padded cells and his womb-like, tomb-like garret attractive. Successful with the patients, particularly with one who plays chess, delighted that the higher schizoids resist all treatment to make them "normal," and finding the padded cells a perfect retreat, Murphy enjoys inner peace by day in the asylum and repose at night in his garret. His withdrawal is virtually complete, and he dies a relatively happy man, cut off as he is from the world. Burned by his gas stove, he is later cremated and his ashes are scattered in a saloon, later to be swept up, indistinguishable from the butts, matches, vomit, and other refuse on the floor. Here is the end of

Murphy, and it is a triumphant one, for in death he is extinguished to the degree that he wished while rocking, Buddha-like, in his chair. His scattered ashes lost amid dirt and filth are symbolic of his way of life and of what he was: Suk's prophecies are defeated at every turn.

Watt, written four years after *Murphy,* consists of one series of parodies after another. Watt goes to work in the household of an unbalanced person, Mr. Knott. Just as Watt's name suggests a perpetual question (What?) with no chance of answer, so Knott's indicates a perpetual answer (No-t) with no chance of questions. But Watt never meets his employer, and so Knott cannot say No directly to Watt. Knott literally denies all sanity, negates all life. Daily life at Knott's house is so attenuated—the pace of a madman—that each activity takes on mythical qualities, for example, the mighty preparation of his meal, a conglomeration of all food and drink necessary for survival with no allowance whatever for taste or possible enjoyment.

Life in Knott's house proceeds at a snail's pace, and the servants go through their movements as though fated to do their job and then be doomed by the consequences. The impersonality allows for a comedy of errors: Watt tries but fails to meet Knott, and by the time of his dismissal (through intermediaries) has never confronted him. As in Kafka's *Castle,* the lack of confrontation is indicative of the absence of movement in the entire narrative, and the tragic humor of things that fail to take place becomes itself the substance of the novel. Beckett catches Watt's employment at a certain moment in time, and all moments appear the same, in stasis, *the* absolute moment. In this connection, Beckett ponders endlessly senseless questions to glean meanings from them and finds nothing except the moment itself: there are no meanings to Watt's quest (for what?).

It is a condition of Mr. Knott's employ that the servant in attendance on his food must find a dog to eat whatever Knott leaves. That dog must eat no more than what is left and therefore must not be fed in between meals, although nothing might be left for him; for he must have sufficient appetite to eat the entire meal if Knott is not hungry. This is, then, a problem fraught with several possibilities that Watt must work out; and he applies himself to it as if his own survival ultimately depended upon his supplying the dog. Watt works out in detail the relationships possible between Knott and dog, creating from nonsense an ingenious system of supply and demand, a virtual economic theory.

In a world of nothingness (of Knotts), Beckett suggests that the only meaningful problems are those of immediate existence and survival; and thought of this kind is fruitful because it depends on nothing but one's own ingenuity. To solve this type of problem—involving here dogs and food, elsewhere sucking stones, hats, shoes, pencils, and other insignificant items—is part of Watt's attempt to distinguish what is real from what is illusory. The dog and the food are real, but Knott is not. Close to Mallarmé in approaching nothingness as the essence of existence, Beckett uses Knott's house as precisely such a reflector of nullity. Knott's house is like Plato's cave or a hall of magical mirrors in which reflections move further and further from reality, so that ultimately one cannot differentiate reflection from original meaning. Beckett writes that "the meaning attributed was now the initial meaning that had been lost and then recovered, and now a meaning quite distinct from the initial meaning, and now a meaning evolved, after a delay of varying length, and with greater or less pains, from the initial absence of meaning." In prose that is both serious and a parody of seriousness, Beckett suggests that Watt's puzzle-like conundrums and solutions are attempts to fill in the void with meaning. Even naming things is difficult, for only the thing exists, not its name. "And Watt preferred on the whole having to do with things of which he did not know the name, though this too was painful to Watt, to having to do with things of which the known name, the proven name, was not the name, any more, for him."

All these devices are ways of creating some noise in the silence. And yet the noise itself leads to comedy. Watt arranges a huge apparatus of wasted human labor in order to provide a dog with the mess that Knott leaves in his dish. And the point is covered and re-covered in language that cuts back and forth, repeats, re-arranges, re-states, ever concerned with things that are ridiculous. In order not to waste substance that is valueless, Watt puts in working order machinery that multiplies infinitely the original wastage. As a symbolic view of the universe, this problem and its solution make Beckett's point.

Recurrence of names, words, situations, articles of clothing, pieces of furniture—recurrence in every possible way—is quite common in Beckett and helps provide substance for novels without narrative force. As the reader meets a long series of words repeated in various arrangements, he may ask exactly what purposes they serve, for often they are merely boring lines or whole pages to be skipped. The novel's forward movement stops as the various permutations and combinations are worked out until the entire arrangement is exhausted. Is this Beckett's private joke on the diligent reader who will stay with every word? Or is it that since Beckett's concern is not narrative, he has to gain substance differently, and one way is through language itself, a means of diverting the reader with words, both common and unfamiliar. It is equivalent to listening to syllables for themselves, once all desire for communication has been forsaken, similar to the effect Joyce gained from lists of words in *A Portrait* and *Ulysses*.

Beckett frequently uses words as an abstract painter utilizes lines—to signify no more than color and shape. Each element, whether line or word, stands for itself. Beckett may directly call attention to words and syntax, commenting on the effective use of a subjunctive mood or a passive voice. In still another way, words repeated and re-phrased force objects upon the reader. Later in *Watt,* the words tallboy, bed, window, and fire are re-arranged until the room, like Mr. Knott himself, becomes protean despite its meaninglessness. Words in solid repetition replace the camera eye; the author builds images by pounding them into the reader until the latter is forced to see in order to save himself. As a parody of naturalistic technique, this is Naturalism carried to its logical end.

By the time Beckett forsook English as his literary language and turned to French, his vision had shifted to even more grotesque images, no doubt influenced by the Second World War and its aftermath, but withal the general atmosphere of a "cosmic joke on man" still remains. In the trilogy beginning with *Molloy* (1951), there are evident changes, chiefly a deepening of viewpoint and a concern with tragic man, whereas, before, comic man poked through. No longer will there be the "happy ending" we saw in *Murphy,* in which the titular character disappears in the muck of a saloon floor and gains the anonymity he had always desired. Now, disappearance and anonymity, although still quite desirable, are beyond the attainment of characters who must fight blindly against life without even the chance of a hopeful death. Isolation, alienation, lack of identity—the latter intensified to an extent perhaps equaled only by Kafka's characters—are the common stuff of the trilogy.

Here, man is isolated not only from objects but from his own kind. He has no possible identification with nature as a substitute for his failings or as solace for self-doubt. Thus, Beckett's bums, tramps, and outcasts are beyond all hope of salvation, for they can survive only as what they are. Even the monologues they indulge in remind us that they can talk solely about themselves. As Beckett carries his Cartesian world to its fullest expression, there is complete doubt of the external world, with the characters' subjectivity a defense against their surroundings. Furthermore, there is little free will, the protagonists seeming like puppets of physical laws outside their control; and objects gain their aspect only from the way they are seen, for thought is clearly more important than external matter. The former we see transformed into a constantly running (dripping?) stream of consciousness, the outpourings of persons who must express themselves even though they, above all, desire silence.

Beckett's characters talk even when there is little to say. They are concerned with the might-have-been, with the other world which they do not inhabit. Beckett proposes: had they possessed teeth, they would have chewed; had they not been crippled, they might have walked; had they experienced sexual desire, they would have entered into the act with relish; had life been different, they might have felt love. Their entire lives are worked out in terms of the conditional tense, for conditions limit the possibilities of their reactions. Molloy even would have committed suicide had he not been afraid of the pain. And his entire quest is to establish connection with a mother whose whereabouts are problematical. ". . . I had been bent on settling this matter between my mother and me, but had never succeeded." Are we sure she exists? Molloy lives in a middle ground between the tortures of hell and the delights of heaven, with no chance of removal; like his fellow characters in Beckett's novels, he inhabits a purgatory where everything is doubted and memory itself is suffocating.

In purgatory, the problem is to gain or regain one's identity. For Molloy, identity will come only when he confronts his mother, whom he loves and hates. In the midst of his quest, he turns on her and affectionately recalls her memory in typical Beckettese: "Ah the old bitch, a nice dose she gave me, she and her lousy unconquerable genes." The two are joined together by the venereal disease they share, a common bond of illness and pain.

To establish his humanity and complete himself, Molloy must find his mother, precisely as Moran, in the second half of the novel, must find Molloy to complete himself. The novel becomes a circling and recircling of quests, of attempts to identity oneself through identification with another; an attempt, evidently, to set up some line of communication, however tentative and futile it might be. Moran himself plays with the idea of Molloy, recognizing that a Molloy—hungry, crippled, cold, helpless, questing for something we and he know he will never find—is part of everyone. Molloy is not a stranger to Moran: they are doubles. The person hunting for another is really searching for part of himself, and in finding him finds out what he is; the person hunted, likewise, must hunt and be hunted, and in turn. . . . Molloy's mother is his sexless crony, the son like the mother old and decrepit; and Moran, like Molloy, is crippled, crawling to his fate on legs that lack energy and force.

Not fortuitously, Beckett's characters are sexually vague: Molloy is virtually impotent, and Moran masturbates at every opportunity. Moran writes in his report: "I took advantage of being alone at last, with no other witness than God, to masturbate. My son must have had the same idea, he must have stopped on the way to masturbate. I hope he enjoyed it more than I did." And Molloy, taken in by a woman whose dog he has accidentally killed, meditates: "Don't be tormenting yourself, Molloy, man or woman, what does it matter?"

Molloy and Moran can do without love, although they search for that too; Molloy finds his senseless kind, while Moran has barely enough energy to masturbate. Both have heard about sexual feeling, and Molloy before dying would like to experience it. The search for love becomes a parody of love. With an old, arid and flat crone, no better than a goat, Molloy discovers the great passion which all the world seeks.

The break in the center of the novel, when the narrative is diverted from Molloy seeking his mother to Moran and his son seeking Molloy, is basically sound both philosophically and psychologically. Together, the four—really three, as Molloy and Moran are halves of one person—form an attenuated family of three generations, from grandmother through son and grandson. Somewhat like a Henry Moore family unit with the divisive hole in the center, Beckett's group has difficulty in connecting one to the other. Molloy is in a way Moran's son's stepfather, and Moran is perhaps the stepson of Molloy's mother, who is in turn the stepgrandmother of Moran's son, and so on through a typical Beckett ploy.

And who is Moran and what does he know of Molloy? Moran identifies himself while describing the Molloy he has never seen:

He had very little room. His time too was limited. He hastened incessantly on, as if in despair, towards extremely close objectives. Now, a prisoner, he hurled himself at I know not what narrow confines, and now, hunted, he sought refuge near the centre.

He panted. He had only to rise up within me for me to be filled with panting.

Even in open country he seemed to be crashing through jungle. He did not so much walk as charge. In spite of this he advanced but slowly. He swayed, to and fro, like a bear. (p. 154)

Moran searches for this image of Molloy, as Ahab after the white whale, not for himself, but on "behalf of a cause which, while having need of us to be accomplished, was in its essence anonymous, and would subsist, haunting the minds of men when its miserable artisans should be no more." (p. 157)

As Moran searches, it occurs to him that he is looking for more than one Molloy, perhaps for three or four: the one who lives within himself; next, his caricature of Molloy; further, Gaber's (the messenger's) version of Molloy; and then the real man of flesh and blood. To these might have been added other versions, including that of Molloy's mother, if she exists, and that of Moran's son, if he knew what he was looking for. For if Molloy is part of Moran, then the latter's son, by helping to find Molloy, will also be completing a part of himself. Through Molloy's finding of his mother—apparently an impossible goal—Moran's son indirectly will find another part of himself, and so on. The circling is of course part of the scheme, for Moran himself, unable to find Molloy, circles back to his house at the end of the novel; and the book which began "It is midnight. The rain is beating on the windows." ends with "It was not midnight. It was not raining." By negating the original statement, the narrative is completed.

There is obviously no final answer, as Beckett indicates when he turns to a refinement of the *Molloy* material in *Malone Dies* and *The Unnamable,* written in the late 1940's and published in 1952 and 1953 respectively. There are, however, several avenues of speculation. Beckett's intent is possibly to argue the cyclical quality of human experience, much as the Joyce of *Finnegans Wake,* following Vico's theories. In the cycle, the individual is reduced, rejected, almost redundant; for what is one human life against the vast recurring episodes of historical epochs? For Beckett, to construct such a cycle of human experience is tantamount to destroying character, to eliminating heroes, to cutting off differences in order to show the similarities among men. While most of his English contemporaries have been interested in revealing differences, Beckett has demonstrated likenesses: thus the searches, both inner and outer. When men cut away all external appurtenances, Beckett seems to suggest, what remains is the bum, the tramp, the outcast. The common denominator is a quest for survival, and that all men share. In the cycle, man's goals lose meaning; what are personal attainments? what is a hero? what is character itself? what is society, with its restrictions and admonitions? What does matter is man's ability under the worst possible conditions to say, "I exist, and I survive in my own way." All of Beckett's protagonists make this statement, and their ability to recognize only this aspect of life makes meaningless the rules of the ordinary narrative. Consequently, narrative, plot, story, realistic structure disappear in Beckett's novels as rapidly as does the desire for goals and attainments in his characters.

Malone Dies, as well as its successor, lacks the relative clarity of *Molloy;* both Malone and the Unnamable of that novel have gradually refined themselves, so that time and place, and even name, are confused with the chaos of their desires and frustrations. Enclosed in a home for the helpless, Malone has returned to a womb-like "paradise" that is in several ways similar to hell. Diminished in his wants to those of a baby—he lives between eating dish and excreting pot—he is a conduit between two holes, food intake and waste outlet. He has come there to die, his only activity being to write about himself with a pencil and exercisebook which constantly elude him.

To create some order from chaos, Malone must write, and his story is of man, Sapo, and of son of man, Macmann. Just as Molloy wrote of his quest and Moran of his—both reports about man —so now Malone; and then later, the Unnamable tries to give shape to confusion by telling stories about Mahood (Manhood?). All three writers try to preserve images in something more substantial than memory, and all use writing (art) as a way of making the moment immortal. In his long essay on Proust, Beckett recognized this traditional use of art; and here we see him attempting to retain *the* moment by creating tensions among four elements: the writer himself as a person, the story being written, the ability of the writer to write, and the larger story which encloses the writer from the author's point of view.

Malone writes about Sapo, the species itself, a story of universal significance. Sapo goes out into the world and meets the Lamberts; Lambert is a pig-sticker, the practitioner of an ancient and dying craft. Then Sapo fades from the story, and Malone appears, as if it were his story; and what difference, anyway? Can one differentiate? and at this stage, what does one differentiate between? Malone is concerned only with hooking things he needs—his exercise book, his pencil, his dish and pot when he feels hungry or becomes aware of an urgent spasm.

Circling around Malone and indistinguishable from him are the Murphys, the Merciers, Molloys, Morans, and Malones. This latter use of Malone indicates that perhaps he is not real, or else exists only outside himself, suggesting further that his presence as a writer is non-substantial, merely a sport of the author's. Does Malone even exist? If so, what is *his* story?

In this trilogy after the horrors of the war years, Beckett has concerned himself with questioning the validity of reality itself. In *Murphy* and *Watt,* as we have seen, he tried to reach some rapport with real objects, although they remained for the most part outside man's control. In the postwar trilogy, Beckett no longer separates men and objects, the subjective and the objective; he now wonders whether there is even such a thing as existence and asks what is inside and what is outside. This view entails evidently a traditional philosophical gambit, but rarely has it become the stuff of the novel to this extent. True, Joyce in *Finnegans Wake* merged subject with object, Earwicker with his surroundings, but the act of merging indicates that the author believes in the things he is merging. Malone instead asks: "How many have I killed, hitting them on the head or setting fire to them? Offhand I can only think of four, all unknowns, I never knew anyone." (p. 63) One of those he has killed, we recognize, may have been himself, and this is a dead man's diary, the story of a hypothetical Malone writing about a Malone who is dead.

Malone ends as he began, his first line being, "I shall soon be quite dead at last in spite of all," and his last, ". . . I mean / never there he will never / never anything / there / any more. . . ." Malone fades and whispers his way out of existence, whimpering, declining into nothingness. Did he ever exist?

The Unnamable begins with "Where now? Who now? When now?" all the temporal and spatial questions that man asks about himself to gain self-identification; and the beginning is typical of the whole. The Unnamable is unable to find his bearings, and his entire monologue is directed toward giving himself a name, place, time. He says: ". . . I'd demand no more of me than to know that what I hear is not the innocent and necessary sound of dumb things constrained to endure, but the terror-stricken babble of the condemned to silence." (p. 94) Babble and silence form the twin nodes of his behavior; he babbles compulsively while he desires silence, the one combining with the other. He must babble, for only through language can he establish that he exists at all; to stop babbling is to destroy himself. And yet he recognizes that the babble itself leads to nothing. "In the meantime no sense in bickering about pronouns and other parts of blather. The subject doesn't matter, there is none." (p. 102) Here, there is a meeting of the grammatical point with the theme. In another place, his concerns remain the same: ". . . tell me what I feel and I'll tell you who I am." (p. 134) It is not that simple, however. For he will not understand what people are saying when they tell him about himself. His identity must remain disguised, he must live solely on and with words. ". . . no need of a mouth, the words are everywhere, inside me, outside me, well well, a minute ago I had no thickness, I hear them, no need to hear them, no need of a head, impossible to stop them, impossible to stop, I'm in words, made of words, others' words, what others, the place too. . . ." (p. 139) Disembodied words identify the Unnamable, but, ironically, there is no word for his name.

When the Unnamable states that ". . . where I am, I don't know, I'll never know, in the silence you don't know, you must go on, I can't go on, I'll go on," there is an image of a blind man without a name heading into the world in a direction he does not know, a world of whose existence he is not even sure. Meursault, in comparison, has values, comprehension (however baffled and enigmatical), and beliefs—he knows where he is heading: toward any experience that will make his senses tingle.

For a Beckett character, there is no such sense of even minor triumph; there is no awareness that an abstraction like triumph exists. Abstractions denote a world in which heroism is possible, and heroism has been washed away by successive generations of Malones, Murphys, Merciers, Watts, and Unnamables. They and Sapo, Macmann, and others like them are all that remain; and for them to believe in abstractions would mean they believe in their own substantiality, in as much as we can measure an abstraction only against something that is real. Once again, Beckett asks, What is real? what is not?

The Unnamable goes on without integrity (what is it?), without belief (in what?), without identification (what is his name? where is he?), without knowledge of what his guilt is, without a desire for life, without any of the props on which man usually supports himself. He survives and will continue to survive simply because his body continues to function. In a universe without purpose, and without even a name, there is no salvation for there is no sin; and even if there were sin, there would be no salvation. As an expression of postwar hopelessness, indeed of cosmic despair, Beckett's trilogy, better than any other work of our time, Céline's perhaps excepted, catches the nihilism and pessimism of man without belief in either God or himself. His characters mean well, and unlike Céline's, they do not hate; but their fate is even worse. For Céline's Bardamu at least gains his identification through what he opposes, but this simple pleasure is denied Beckett's Malone and Molloy. When they hate, their vehemence can be turned against only themselves; and their struggle to survive in the destructive element of non-life is their only means of identification, hopeless though it is and helpless though they are. The momentary and almost illusory gleam of hope that Camus sees in Sisyphus's absurd labor, Beckett transforms into man's desperate quest for answers that will forever be denied to him.

III

Lawrence Durrell:
Physical and Metaphysical Love

S U R E L Y M O R E T H A N any of his younger contemporaries, Lawrence Durrell has returned to the literary conceptions of major novelists like Conrad, Joyce, and Lawrence in England and Gide and Proust in France. Akin to them in their dissatisfaction with existing forms, he has himself tried to develop new techniques of fiction, although, obviously, experimentation is not always equivalent to excellence. Nevertheless, in the Alexandria *Quartet*,* Durrell has written an ambitious and exciting sequence of novels which immediately bears superficial comparison with Joyce's *Ulysses*.

Like Joyce's Dublin, Durrell's Alexandria defines the actions of the characters and in major part makes them what they are. The nationalism of the Dubliner is transformed into the sensuality of the Alexandrian; the narrowness of the Irishman into the flexibility, the sinister softness of the Egyptian. In both novels, the sense of place dominates. Durrell has himself commented (in the New York *Times* Book Review of June 12, 1960) that the artist must attend "to what the land is saying," conform "to the hidden magnetic fields that the landscape is trying to communicate to the personality." In another passage in the same article, he wrote, perhaps with D. H. Lawrence's remarks about the American novel

* *Justine* (1957); *Balthazar* (1958); *Mountolive* (1959); *Clea* (1960)

in mind, "I have evolved a private notion about the importance of landscape, and I willingly admit to seeing characters almost as functions of a landscape. . . . My books are always about living in places, not just rushing through them."

Working along with place in the novels,* Durrell points out, is a time sequence which he calls in a note to *Balthazar* "a soup-mix recipe of a continuum." Time, he comments, is stayed, and the four novels are not connected sequentially, but as siblings. That is, they overlap and interweave in a spatial relationship, with only the fourth novel representing clock time and acting as a true sequel to the first three. Unlike Proust and Joyce in this respect, Durrell is not concerned with memory (Bergson's duration of time), which is psychological and not clock time. Durrell is trying to capture a space-time continuum—he remarks that he turned to science to find the unities that the novel does not offer. Thus, each succeeding novel, picking up the narrative from the point of view of a different character while fixing the other characters, will cover approximately the same time periods as the preceding one. Only *Clea* will carry time forward.

Durrell notes further that the subject-object relationship is of prime importance in any novel in which space and time are significant. The point is simply that Darley, the narrator of the first two volumes, *Justine* and *Balthazar,* assumes importance as a character in *Mountolive* and *Clea,* moving, as Durrell puts it, from subject status to object status.

What does this theorizing of subject and object mean? What importance does Durrell place on this "soup-mix recipe" in which three parts of space and one of time add up to a unified novel? Possibly, Durrell's object is to approximate the kind of novel in which the very writing becomes itself the substance of the narrative. Nearly everyone in the *Quartet* is a writer: Darley himself; Pursewarden, the novelist whose remarks are quoted as a running

---

* Francis King, a young writer of considerable talent, uses Greece as Durrell uses Alexandria. In *The Man on the Rock* (1957) and *The Dark Glasses* (1954), King's *mise en scène* determines to a large extent how his characters will act; Greece in one, Corfu in the other, defines their sensuality, their moral breakdown, their gradual dissolution. Spiro, in the later novel, is in several ways a male Justine, fascinating but deadly, a satanic force which attracts and then destroys.

commentary on the story that Darley is narrating; Jacob Arnauti, Justine's first husband, who wrote *Moeurs,* in which Justine herself is possibly a character. There are, in addition, diaries (Justine's, Nessim's), memoirs, letters, et al.

We see that like Gide in *The Counterfeiters,* Durrell in the *Quartet* is often concerned with the purely technical problem of writing a novel, and the author's emphasis on space-time and subject-object is simply one way of making the novel protean and ever-developing as the reader views it from different aspects. Durrell cites his influence from science, and a free use of Einsteinean physics is obviously behind the space-time continuum. In this respect, Einstein's theory of relativity, applied loosely to literature and particularly to the novel, made it difficult for the author to assume fixed points of reference. Since objects changed in their physical appearance, depending on who looked at them, the novelist could no longer assume that things appeared as they did. The relativity of appearances assumed major proportions, for all things (including love) hitherto seen as fixed and immobile were now observed in relation to other things; and the novelist trying to work this idea into the framework of his novel had to keep the story moving, letting the various characters tell it in contrasting ways. Thus, Joyce in *Ulysses,* Gide in *The Counterfeiters,* Conrad in *Nostromo,* Virginia Woolf in *The Waves* viewed a world of fluid relationships, and Durrell is clearly in this company.

The epigraph to *Justine* from Freud, to the effect that every sexual relationship involves four people, is not merely a sensational misinterpretation of the original—Durrell works the idea into the texture of space-time considerations. For if Einstein upset notions of a stable physical world, Freud obviously upset those of a stable internal world; all relationships, and none more so than the nature of the sexual act, are ever-changing. To capture a sense of this change without working over the past, as Proust and Bergson did, was apparently Durrell's aim in the *Quartet.* In brief, to create a dialectic between physical and metaphysical love.

This point of view suggests the need for new techniques, and the space-time continuum is Durrell's attempt to approximate the complexity of love as it grows and diminishes, with couples forming and reforming, so that an almost endless number of combinations is possible, many occurring simultaneously. Only the affair between Darley and Clea is moved ahead in time, but that between Darley and Justine goes on concurrently with those of Justine and Nessim and Justine and Pursewarden, while Nessim and Melissa as well as Pursewarden and his sister, Liza, are also paralleling the others. The so-called workpoints that Durrell cites at the end of *Balthazar* and *Clea* indicate that the relationships can continue into infinity, each one setting up the terms for a future or parallel relationship, so that every meeting will suggest still another one.

In *Balthazar,* which contains Balthazar's Interlinear, in itself a manual of novel technique, there appear the titular character's comments:

". . . if you [Darley] wished somehow to incorporate all I am telling you into your own Justine manuscript now, you would find yourself with a curious sort of book—the story would be told, so to speak, in layers. Unwittingly I may have supplied you with a form, something out of the way! Not unlike Pursewarden's idea of a series of novels with 'sliding panels' as he called them. Or else, perhaps, like some medieval palimpsest where different sorts of truth are thrown down one upon the other, the one obliterating or perhaps supplementing another." (p. 183)

Durrell's aim, like Balthazar's, is to achieve a fugue-like simultaneity, so that at each moment of the novel all of Alexandria is in movement, ever-changing and developing. In an analogy from music, the first three novels are polyphonically developed themes in a huge symphony in which the fourth novel acts as a lengthy recapitulation. The writer, consequently, can interweave his themes and play off, so to speak, one sound against the other. In an interview in the *Paris Review,* Durrell admitted that the publication of the novels in sequence instead of simultaneously defeated the purpose of the work, but he needed money!

"Well this novel is a four-dimensional dance, a relativity poem. Of course, ideally all four volumes should be read simultaneously, as I say in my note at the end: but as we lack four-dimensional spectacles the reader will have to do it imaginatively, adding the part of time to the other three, and holding the whole lot in his skull."

This attempt to create layers of reality which can be absorbed simultaneously is, as Durrell admits, not original, although the creation of this world through several "simultaneous novels" is new. Eliot in "The Love Song of J. Alfred Prufrock" was attempting simultaneity of images and scenes in 1909, and Conrad in *Nostromo* in 1904. Later, in the work of Joyce, Dos Passos, and Virginia Woolf, the device becomes commonplace. Among Durrell's contemporaries, C. P. Snow—who, as a scientist, really knows about relativity—is trying something similar, with, however, less brilliance and *éclat*. Using a more or less fixed cast of characters throughout his novels—allowing for deaths and the appearance of younger people—Snow overlaps situations and fits in relationships that have occurred previously only in shadowy form. The result often is simultaneity of action within different novels. Analogous to this is Anthony Powell's series, *The Music of Time,* whose title suggests the method.

Snow's latest novel, *The Affair,* indicates that he may have reached the same point that Durrell did with his sequence, for Snow has carried the time element forward past the point of the previous latest novel, exactly as Durrell carried *Clea* forward in time. Thus, *The Affair* jumps five years beyond *Homecomings,* which covers the period from 1938-1948; the overlapping which has characterized much of the series appears to have ended, at least temporarily. Similarly, Durrell's workpoints at the end of *Clea* would move the sequence forward in time, except for the one that reads: "Hamid's story of Darley and Melissa." The latter, however, would simply be another aspect of a relationship that we already see in detail through Darley's eyes and would not significantly open up further aspects of the narrative. But even though Snow and Durrell have reached about the same point in their sequences, here the comparison ends, for two more dissimilar writers could not have undertaken a somewhat similar literary odyssey.

Durrell's explicit theme is an examination of modern love in its various aspects, a theme that in itself generates curiosity when it derives from an Englishman. Clearly following D. H. Lawrence in his attempt to "free" the English novel, Durrell suggests that sexual love—almost the only kind that exists for him—is a form of knowledge, literally as well as etymologically. " 'He knew her,' as the Bible says!" Clea then adds that sex " 'is the joint or coupling which unites the male and female ends of knowledge merely—a cloud of unknowing! When a culture goes bad in its sex all knowledge is impeded.' " The sexual demand, she seems to suggest as Durrell's spokesman, is also the cultural demand; and the spirit of place, when it operates effectively, will in itself force a certain kind of sexuality, a particular kind of love.

Durrell will not divorce sex from love, and when his couples unite, they do so sexually, demonstrating that the relationship, at least then, is physically right. Alexandria provides the sensual background: the sense of place allows a naturalness of sexual expression that borders on the promiscuous, and at the same time it suggests a healthy freedom from puritanical repression. Consequently, Durrell both follows Lawrence's quest for sexual freedom and rejects Lawrence's horror of promiscuity. Often, what Durrell calls love is sexual passion, bodily expedience, a need for physical relief, a physiological moment when intercourse is possible—but rarely does love express the deepest feelings of which an individual is capable. His couples pair off too easily for real love to be at the root of their desire. Love, as Lawrence realized, affected the lover and caused changes in personality that stemmed directly from his feelings. A person in love was one possessed. Love, accordingly, allowed for little else and thwarted other activity. For Durrell, however, the feeling of love partakes too readily of the sensuality of Alexandria, and therefore without real love the novels lack adequate tension.

In the serious novel, love should of course create conflicts, whether they be conflicts within one's own feelings or with society. It is evident, from the dramatic effectiveness of the love scenes in his better novels, that Lawrence realized this. In the easy freedom of *his* lovers in their sexual relationships, however, Durrell is surely closer to Henry Miller than to Lawrence. Miller, perhaps even more than Lawrence, helped free the literary atmosphere, and Durrell's *Black Book* (1938), a shadowy source for the *Quartet,* shows Miller's influence. For both writers, Durrell and Miller, the sexual relationship is spontaneous, neither the cause of tensions nor the direct product of neurosis. Love frees rather than imprisons the individual. Love and sex are equated indivisibly, and the lover gives of himself as freely as he wishes to receive. In Miller's view, one holds nothing back, has no regrets, and asks no more than one is willing to offer. A novel based on such a philosophy can be robust, humorous, and sympathetic, but it cannot be serious, tragic, or even dramatic.

Durrell at his best fluctuates between Miller's and Lawrence's views. Since the publication of *The Tropic of Cancer* in the thirties, the world's problems have multiplied, as Durrell realizes, and this attitude must carry over into the love relationship as well. The freedom for which Miller agitated is now more complicated, especially after Lawrence himself imposed a sense of responsibility; accordingly, Durrell focuses his attention somewhere in between. He offers not so much a sense of responsibility in the relationship as a shearing away of the demand for happiness, so that the lover, even while loving, recognizes that he is at the mercy of an uncontrollable doom. Durrell, accordingly, seems more interested in the psychology of love than Miller, and here he once again approaches Lawrence's views. For Durrell, love can be spontaneous—between Darley and the sick dancer, Melissa, for example; but it can also be tortuous—between Nessim and Justine, Darley and Justine, Pursewarden and Justine, Pursewarden and his sister, Liza. The very ease with which these characters indulge in physical love bespeaks a certain sadness—that love has little significance when sensuality overwhelms.

Always in the background of these major affairs are the even more tortured and grotesque minor ones, involving the dissolute Capodistria, the sensual Amaril and Pombal, and various homosexuals and bisexuals. The result is a mosaic of happy and unhappy affairs, ever-expanding and contracting like the novel form itself. No one relationship ever stands still, for doubling affairs (while Justine is married to Nessim, she uses Darley to get closer to Pursewarden, whom, according to Balthazar, she really "loves"), paralleling situations, and involutions in time all keep the love affairs protean. If one compares the love element to a chameleon, he can see how the affairs are constantly assuming new colors, new formations, new positions to suit the moment. Never remaining fixed, each affair blends into its background and becomes virtually indistinguishable from it.

A long section from Pursewarden's Notebook which fills the center of *Clea* indicates the method operating in the love affairs and underscores the form of the *Quartet:*

No, seriously, if you wished to be—I do not say original but merely contemporary—you might try a four-card trick in the form of a novel; passing a common axis through four stories, say, and dedicating each to one of the four winds of heaven. A continuum, forsooth, embodying not a *temps retrouvé* but a *temps delivré.* The curvature of space itself would give you stereoscopic narrative, while human personality seen across a continuum would perhaps become prismatic? Who can say? I throw the idea out. I can imagine a form which, if satisfied, might raise in human terms the problems of causality or indeterminancy. . . . But tackled in this way you would not, like most of your contemporaries, be drowsily cutting along a dotted line. (pp. 135-6)

Like the earlier twentieth-century novelists, Durrell sees the novel in terms of form, and what he says here, in Pursewarden's words, is close to what Joyce practiced in *Ulysses;* for by sifting ever-changing material through his three main characters, Joyce tried to achieve the prismatic effect of the continuum which concerns Durrell. In the *Paris Review* interview cited above, Durrell remarks his obsession with form, with shaping and re-shaping the novel, admitting that his interest may be an indication of a second-rate talent—an inability, he suggests, to meet his material straightforwardly. Durrell perhaps had in mind *Mountolive,* the third movement of the *Quartet* and clearly the weakest of the four. There, except for the simple flashback, the involved technique has been more or less abandoned; the narrative is in the third person, and the material comes shaped as an orthodox novel. Not surprisingly then, this is the least effective of the novels, the one least able to stand by itself.

Before examining the ideas which float in and out of this ambitious undertaking, one wonders what in Durrell's literary career led to a project which, while less persevering than Snow's *Strangers and Brothers,* does become the first attempt in a generation at a long, philosophical novel. In *The Black Book,* which preceded the *Quartet* by twenty years, the reader finds a very young book (Durrell was in his twenties) which is full of Henry Miller's verbal fluidity, Joyce's stream of consciousness, Huxley's cruelty and sarcasm, Norman Douglas's wit. More a stream of reminiscences, jokes, and parodies than a novel, *The Black Book* withal has within it the concern with form and expression that were to appear so strongly in the later work. Nevertheless, for the next twenty years, Durrell, while publishing more novels and much poetry and travel literature, did not return to the style of *The Black Book.* As he mentions, however, the *Quartet* was germinating for fifteen years, and the result is often close to what was first suggested in that early novel, whose patches of humorous obscenity seem directly out of Henry Miller's work.

The reader faced by the ambitious size of Durrell's project is foolish to quibble over the discrepancies, irrelevancies, and melodramatic statements found throughout the *Quartet.* All the excesses and faults—most of which concern his inadequate development of character—are, finally, secondary matters once one accepts what Durrell is doing. In a work that attempts as much as the *Quartet* does, one should ask only big questions: where does the work fit as literature? does the form suggest new terms which will affect the novel in the future? does Durrell, as he indicates, set up a "crisis in the form"? Finally, is all the experimenting worth the substance that results? The questions themselves establish as significant the work under scrutiny. English novels of the last thirty years, often exciting, often surprising, often major, have rarely afforded this kind of query, not, in fact, since *Ulysses* or some of Conrad's and Lawrence's work. In brief, one asks if Durrell has created a major work for his generation, or merely a pretentious melodrama riddled with pompous techniques.

Durrell's presentation of character suggests the kind of novel he wished to write and reveals both his strong and weak points. As he himself recognized, his characters lose stature by being placed against a background which seems to determine what and who they are. The spirit of place is so strong that Nessim, Justine, Narouz, Leila, and others have lost all moral purpose, demonstrating what Lionel Trilling has called their "peculiar negative relation to the will," or what Durrell himself has designated as their tendency "to be dummies." He claimed that he was trying to convey "stereoscopic narrative with stereophonic personality," trying to light up characters and action "from several different angles." Seen this way, the characters are partially explained, but they still lack the inner urgency that would, in a realistic setting, give them tragic stature.

Durrell's characters move in Alexandria as though immersed in an atmosphere forever unknowable to them. As an adherent to the ideas of Georg Groddeck, perhaps Durrell is equating Alexandria to Groddeck's "It": that is, the "It" as a container of all those forces which influence man and make him the mysterious creature he is. The container itself, the "It," can never be analyzed; it must remain, as Durrell remarks, "a forever unknowable entity, whose shadows and functions we are." Durrell's acceptance of the mysterious "It" and his recreation of this force in the shape of Alexandria also are allied to his interest in the occult, manifest in the *Quartet* in the form of spells, predictions fulfilled, enigmatical pronouncements, religious ceremonies and rites. Durrell's use of the "It" furthermore allows him to break out of the restrictions implicit in Freud's concept of the Ego, although at the same time it keeps his characters amorphous and undefinable.

The problem Durrell had to face, and which the reader must respond to, is this: if will-less characters are arranged in various tableaux against a sensual background which determines their action, then how can the author describe them in tones often suitable to tragedy? For characters without will, without the desire or need to impose themselves on their surroundings, are figures curiously lacking in any tragic sense. And it seems that the characters in the *Quartet* must be taken tragically, or else the work will collapse into a kind of poetic or showy phantasmagoria.

In Nessim, perhaps more than in any of the other characters, the lack of inner and outer response is apparent. The inner man in Nessim seems dead, or at least relaxed to the point of dormancy. And yet he is a successful public figure, we are told, an antigovernment conspirator in the Copt underground and a man who wants to subdue the unfathomable Justine. In brief, he is to be a protagonist of more than average size, a doer and a lover. Yet Nessim curiously lacks purpose—he appears tired even before Durrell puts him to work. He chiefly shows emotion by racing his huge car on the sand dunes and whipping up furious bursts of sand, actions which both cloud his intentions and express his emotions. He responds to Justine's infidelities with taut lips, allowing her freedom if he thinks it will enable him to hold her. Nessim is both noble and inexplicable—what Durrell would perhaps have us believe is a typical Copt, proud, a victim of his passions, an Egyptian version of Mountolive.

Nevertheless, either by design or chance, Nessim is singularly colorless. Almost the only time he engages Justine and the reader occurs when he talks of the Copt conspiracy, and then he seems involved in something that touches him. Before that, and even after, he remains smoldering, watchful, inactive. This affliction, however, is not confined to Nessim; it seems to spread out and engulf Justine as well, despite her energetic flitting from one affair to another. She enters into sexual activity with a peculiar lack of desire, as though she has to be satisfied, and if she can be entertained also—Pursewarden does entertain her—then so much the better. For Nessim bores her, as he should; and she should also bore Nessim, for except for an occasional intuitive remark, she is lacking in all but superficial physical attraction. Darley finds her haunting, as does Nessim—Pursewarden sees her clearly as a physically attractive bore—but the reader is left less with her over-all seductive powers than with her availability as a bed warmer.

As an energetic counter to Nessim, Pursewarden is to dominate the mind of the novel as much as Nessim (without apparently being very active), behind the scenes, is to dominate the action. Pursewarden's remarks become a running critique of Alexandrian life, for besides the major sections devoted to his presence and his Notebook, there are his epigrammatic sayings scattered throughout the *Quartet*. Pursewarden is clearly always with us, whether living or dead, whether physically present or not. Pursewarden, then, must be made to appear significant, and his presence must bring awe to the reader as it does to the people who know him. Yet, he seems less than the towering genius Durrell would have him to be, and his apothegms are often trivialities made to appear clever through verbal inversion. Durrell, early in *Balthazar* (p. 23) writes, through Darley: "And Pursewarden on another occasion, but not less memorably [said]: 'If things were always what they seemed, how impoverished would be the imagination of man!' " This remark, little more than a pompous cliché, comes after Balthazar's own comment, " 'Truth is what most contradicts itself in time.' "

One by one, the major characters in some way fail to satisfy: Darley himself is often what Pursewarden says he is: "a brother ass," one who falls in and out of affairs and seems unmasculine despite his success with Melissa, Justine, and Clea. He himself writes somewhere that his appeal is his detachment, his almost negative quality. His very lack of apparent desire for anything relaxes his partner and constitutes his attraction. Pursewarden does read Darley correctly—" 'But Brother Ass [both affectionately and disparagingly], there is a whole dimension lacking to what you say. How is it possible for one to convey this in Oxford English?' " (*Clea,* p. 125) Darley, perhaps, is the least willed of all. He falls into temporary affairs and then leaves Alexandria with the child of Nessim and Melissa, his own mistress. His real self—what is Darley actually like?—never seems to be engaged. Is he no more than Isherwood's camera?

Justine herself, the great temptress, the object of desire in all males, is often little more than a vampire, whose attraction is not that of a female but of an evil spirit who will torture the male and then nullify him. She becomes, on several occasions, one of Aubrey Beardsley's lean, blood-sucking women, clearly a carry-over from *fin de siècle* literature and art. Her inability to give of herself is itself a mark of her will-lessness. She too is trapped by forces she cannot control. A real child of Alexandria despite her "foreignness" in the city, she is caught by the spirit of place and dances to its demands. While able to convey some of Justine's grotesqueness and obsessiveness, Durrell is unable to make her attractive enough so that the reader can feel her magnetic pull. Rather than seductive, she seems dry, squeezed of spirit.

Clea, whose varying moods supply the substance of the fourth volume, is a more fleshed Justine, perhaps more attractive in certain ways, but nevertheless as doggedly self-centered. Unfortunately, when Durrell tries to give characters will, he makes them selfish and solipsistic. Clea is Durrell's attempt to create a woman who is neither will-less like Melissa nor obsessed like Justine. Not unlike the others, however, Clea is a child of Alexandria. Through her painting, she tries to find a way of expressing her kind of reality, possibly one that would cut her ties with the city. Her slough of despond, like Darley's, coincides with her inability to create, and paradoxically she rediscovers her talent only after she has lost her hand in an accident. Under the tension of perhaps losing all, she finds herself; and at the end, again like Darley, she is once more sure of herself. The cycle has recurred: Darley is ready to write anew, and the *Quartet* can go on indefinitely into another series of novels which Darley will write and in which he will be a peripheral narrator. Clea is ready to paint. . . .

In Clea's characterization, nevertheless, there is much that is hackneyed. She runs to Pursewarden with the plea that he take her, for as a virgin she is unable to create, and a sexual relationship, she hopes, will make her creativity flow. She is given to emotional tales. She tells of Liza when shown Pursewarden's death mask: she "held it to her breast for a moment as if to suckle it, with an expression of intense pain, her blind eyes seeming to grow larger and larger until they overflowed the whole face, and turned it into a cave of interrogation." (*Clea*, p. 115) She is absurdly sentimental: when Semira appears finally with a nose, joined in marriage to Amaril, Clea weepingly says to Darley: " 'Do you mind if I get a little tipsy tonight to celebrate her successful nose? I think we can drink to their future without reserve for they will never leave each other; they are drunk with the knightly love one reads about in the Arthurian legends—knight and rescued lady.' " (p. 93)

Two qualities Clea shares with the other characters are a failure to feel responsibility and an allegiance to her own sensations. Perhaps the influence of the city precludes responsibility, structured as it is on the individual needs and desires of its citizens. Perhaps, also, this lack of personal responsibility is attached to her will-lessness—she will drift wherever her sensations lead her. Nevertheless, this lack of tension between a moral self and her desire for fulfillment gives her a curiously childish manner. Clea is immature when she tells of her affair with someone (Amaril) she had admired, a chance affair that seemed to revivify her. During the course of the affair, she becomes pregnant, unknown to her lover, and, to preserve his independence, " 'I knew I should have to destroy the child. I bitterly regretted it. . . . Apart from that I had nothing to regret. I had been immeasurably grown-up by the experience. I was full of gratitude, and still am.' " It is difficult to take Clea's feelings seriously after this episode. Any action appears suitable if it advances her notion of maturity, if it has some effect upon her. Her ease in resolving all such feelings conveys the outlook of a selfish and expedient adolescent. Egocentric, vain, puffed by self-importance, she lives without wisdom.

Like Clea, all the main characters lack a sense of guilt, the reason probably being that the Alexandria which has overwhelmed them takes no account of guilt. Guilt has been transformed into sensationalism, and is of course preferable in that new shape. If the sensation pleases, then the act or thought involved is valid. The characters' lack of will does not entail a withdrawal from sensationalism but from guilt: they refuse to be bothered by moral considerations. I do not of course refer to those considerations which concern sexual morality, but to those which give each person a sense that his happiness is restricted by certain bounds, and that by transgressing these bounds he at least changes. Durrell's Alexandrians do not have this inner censor, and therefore seem immature. They make melodramatic gestures, seek sensory pleasures, but have little realization of what they really are. They play-act at roles which they have assumed, rarely recognizing that the role and their self have become interchangeable and that they have lost their identity. Perhaps this play-acting is the sole point of their existence.

What happens to Pursewarden is a case in point. Durrell leads us to believe that Pursewarden commits suicide when he finds that Nessim is involved in the conspiracy despite everything Pursewarden believes about him. Thus, the great writer has killed himself as an act of honor: to tell Mountolive about Nessim would be a breach of friendship with the Egyptian; yet not to tell Mount-olive would mean a breach of his position as an intelligence officer. The suicide is a way, then, of preserving his honor, and Purse-warden, we are led to believe, is truly an honorable man. This, however, is not the situation at all. He has killed himself because a letter from his sister, Liza, informs him that their incestuous re-lationship can no longer continue, for she has met the man of her dreams, Mountolive himself. This new turn Pursewarden cannot face, and he commits suicide, ostensibly as a "marriage gift" to Liza. Nevertheless, disappointment in love, not a sense of honor, dictates the terms of his death. Had Pursewarden had to choose between Nessim and Mountolive, then Durrell would have faced directly a sensitive moral situation. Instead, he saves himself from straightforward treatment by introducing a *deus ex machina,* an ironic twist that nullifies Pursewarden and his brilliant sayings.

In the creation of the lesser and secondary characters, this evasion of moral issues is not important, for the peripheral char-acters provide little more than color and tone. Durrell—in this sense like Dickens—is often more successful with his minor fig-ures than with his major characters. Particularly excellent are his males on the make for women or for other men. Pombal, who finally finds his true love—and then sees her outrageously killed —is an excellent portrait of a rake brought low by the love of a good woman; and Scobie, who gets a thrill from dressing in women's clothes to entice visiting sailors, is superb as the police chief finally sanctified as El Scob. Balthazar, however, is shadowy, sometimes sinister, containing facets of the other characters, more a cross-sectional character than a distinct personality. The same is true of Dr. Amaril, the man who falls in love with a pair of hands at a carnival and then traces them to their owner—only to find that she has no nose. However, he loves her anyway, and contructs one for her. Such is the nature of affection!

Narouz, Nessim's feral younger brother who combines savagery with affection, is Durrell's attempt to capture the non-city type, the Egyptian who chooses to stay close to the soil. There are forces operating in Narouz which make him attractive as a char-acter, particularly his powers of destruction (symbolized by his huge bull whip) which conflict with a childish tenderness, a desire to love and be loved. For Narouz, the bull whip symbolizes the strength which he wishes to have and which is denied him because of his disfiguring split palate. The whip, further, is for him a way of imposing himself on the world, and its cruelty is an expression of his desire to destroy those who will reject him. The whip becomes his power, his sexuality, his sadism, and it contrasts sharply with the weapons that the more sophisticated Nessim employs. Narouz, nevertheless, provides an example of a baffled will which action in the Coptic conspiracy fulfills. A rebel, a revolutionary, a displaced person within his own family, Narouz has qualities which differentiate him from his brother and from the other characters in the novel. In his inability to come to terms with a life that has forced him underground, he grapples with inner powers denied to Nessim.

Clearly, if we judge Durrell's *Quartet* solely by its characters *as realistic figures,* we will find it wanting. His people add little to what we already know, and he loses dramatic conflict and tragic potentiality by virtue of their lack of will. Perhaps something even less than tragedy is precluded, as Durrell recognized in the *Paris Review* interview when he said that his "interest in form might be—I'm talking seriously now, not modestly—an indication of a second-rate talent." For several reasons, Durrell is not minor, although he lacks the scope and dramatic quality to make him absolutely first rate; but the measure of his success must be found in his very manipulation of material that on its face does seem unpromising.

To return to his area of strength, we must return to his sense of place, for his characters play out their roles against the everpresent background of Alexandria. They both gain their individuality and endure their will-less lives as a result of their powerful identification with the city. Durrell has indeed created a world which people inhabit, although they pursue stylized, not realistic, lives, as if in an Eastern fairy tale.

Durrell's *Quartet,* we quickly recognize, is virtually the direct opposite of the realistic novel. While it is true that both Snow and Durrell are attempting something similar in their sequential works, the two writers suggest two separate halves of the English novel of the last twenty years. Durrell is heir to the "arty" tradition, with its emphasis upon style and form; Snow is a product of the "solid" tradition, with the absence of form a conscious attempt to bring the novel back to real people and their social setting. Snow's characters are realistic or they are nothing—they have little other life except that which exists directly in the novels. The quality of their imagination rarely bothers them or us, and their everyday acts in a real world constitute the bulk of Snow's concern for them. Durrell's people seem to have very little everyday life, or when they do, they carry on as people for whom work does not really matter, unless it is creative work. His world is one of writers and painters, people who themselves are interested in style and technique, people for whom their work in the arts is an expression of their lives. Perhaps that is the only thing that can sustain them in Alexandria.

For Snow, individual expression, particularly that of scientists and their work, is never isolated—it is always against a social setting; and therefore the scientist, as well as the administrator and statesman, has to be socially responsible, has to respond to others within a moral frame of reference. In Durrell's Alexandria, work does not seriously intrude upon the inner lives of the characters; for most, work is secondary or at least something that can be put aside. Durrell is as obviously interested, then, in the inner man, as Snow is in the outer, social man. Therefore, if we judge the characters of each by the same measure, we will condemn Durrell's for lacking moral realism and Snow's for lacking imaginative selves.

In Snow's work, the will is everything: his main character, Lewis Eliot, has virtually willed himself to his position of eminence, a government post in the latest novel, *The Affair*. In Durrell's work, there is little eminence, just as there is little will. There simply is no one around to measure eminence; since the individual is removed from the social world, his behavior and his desire for sensations are both aimed at self-gratification. Undoubtedly, each author is rebelling against everything the other and his tradition stand for. Using American writers as touchstones, Philip Rahv has distinguished between the Palefaces (James, Hawthorne, Melville) and the Redskins (Twain, Dreiser, Wolfe), and while the English novelists cannot be placed specifically within these categories, a similar point, with suitable qualifications, might be made about them.

Durrell's pigmentation is obviously close to that of a Paleskin, although to call Snow a Redskin is not only to mix a color metaphor but also to confuse an issue. The major English novelists, at least in this century, have straddled both worlds; Conrad, for example, experimented with the "arty" novel, as did his Paleface contemporaries, but at the same time he was concerned with a world that involved Redskins—action, storms, heroic figures. He, as it were, discolored the Redskin world (Haggard) by treating it with Paleface delicacy (Flaubert, James). Durrell is clearly within this tradition; while Snow, lacking the robustness of the Redskins and the need to experiment of the Paleskins, has qualified the aims of both to write the new novel of gentility, in which traditional values once more predominate.

All this is by way of trying to place Durrell's elusive accomplishments. It would be a mistake, as I have suggested, to stress realistic representation of character in novels as stylized as these. Durrell's aim is the creation of an adventure-filled world, a fairy tale world in which the id is freed of its censor. In attempting to present the life of Alexandria, Durrell is concerned with creating a myth of the city and its inhabitants without giving the latter the particulars of motivation that the realistic novel demands. Perhaps Durrell means by a "crisis in the form" of the novel no more than a return to romance and adventure at the expense of character. Not fortuitously, Durrell is at his weakest when he speaks directly; *Mountolive* is surely the weakest of the *Quartet,* and that novel is narrated by a third-person observer. Not only the technique has been simplified, but the main character himself contains few complications. Mountolive is complacent, believes in the mystique of the British Empire, and pursues his affairs with a sharp sense of self-control—he has little left over for imagination. Prosaic, expedient to a degree, a figure operating in the large social world, Mountolive is a successful diplomat, and that, as Pursewarden recognizes, precludes the man from becoming fully human.

The other three novels do not attempt realism of this sort, and therefore the characters, although often unpersuasive, are nevertheless of greater interest than Mountolive. As soon as Durrell can move from the official world into the underworld of Alexandrian life, he immerses his characters in an ambience that fits them. As soon as he emerges directly into the upper world and talks of it without irony or parody, then he becomes mechanical. For if we perceive that the four novels are, in part, exercises on how the novel should be written, to expect a realistic response is to read the *Quartet* incorrectly. Durrell has returned to that "arty" method in which the writer creating his work is concerned with how to form just such a work, and so on through all the Chinese boxes. Durrell's characters, consequently, almost all write, paint, even photograph, and the world they construct through their art or pseudo-art is the ever-changing one that Durrell, *their* creator, is trying to convey. The nature of change, the inner structure of a city, the impotence of human desire, the frustration of attempts at happiness, the reduction of adults to will-less children—these are the characteristic motifs of the *Quartet*.

Without realistic characters, the *Quartet* contains little so-called "thought," for the intellectual level of such a novel is a composite of all the twists and turns of the narrative. The residue of thought in a stylized novel is always less, we realize, than what the novel actually means. Thought itself is denigrated, made secondary to feeling, emotion, and "blood consciousness." "Joy unconfined" is evidently for Durrell the epitome of man's quest for salvation, and the joy in mind is of course secular in nature. Like Lawrence and a long line of English romantics, Durrell is trying to replace traditional religious views with a secular philosophy, and in Alexandria, despite its horrors and grotesques, he finds a modus vivendi for modern man. ". . . that there is hope for man, scope for man [says Pursewarden], within the boundaries of a simple law; and I seem to see mankind as gradually appropriating to itself the necessary information through mere attention, *not reason,* which may one day enable it to live within the terms of such an idea— the true meaning of 'joy unconfined.' " (p. 239, *Balthazar*) Then Pursewarden, as though this much ratiocination were already excessive, turns away embarrassed from trying to put into words what is only a vague feeling.

The true salvation for those who can, is to create. Pursewarden in the same section of *Balthazar* remarks the difference between his art and his life: "Now in my life I am somewhat irresolute and shabby, but in my art I am free to be what I most desire to seem—someone who might bring resolution and harmony into the dying lives around me." The act of creativity is no more, however, than bringing out the best part of oneself. The thinking self is the restricted part, the unthinking and feeling self the only expanding part. Durrell's emphasis on sexual passion and its identification with love—"sexual love *is* knowledge"—is an effort to attain freedom for the individual. The mere choice of Alexandria (Yeats' Byzantium) as *the* place indicates Durrell's desire to remove himself from a mechanical world to a world in which easy sensuality allows man to flower or become corrupted, in either instance freed from the demands of civilization and industrialization.

Mountolive, of course, brings the mechanical world to Egypt in his mission, and perhaps for this reason he is a counter to the other characters. He can never be assimilated into the bloodstream of the city—it will always be foreign to him, and he will always be foreign to it. In his Notebook that comes at the center of *Balthazar,* Pursewarden answers, as it were, Mountolive's assumptions about the world and the way it runs: "We artists are not interested in policies but in values—this is our field of battle! If once we would loosen up, relax the terrible grip of the so-called Kingdom of Heaven which has made the earth such a bloodsoaked place, we might rediscover in sex the key to a metaphysical search which is our *raison d'être* here below!" Mountolive, who accepts the British Empire, obviously cannot concur in this view; he and Pursewarden, despite their comradeship at the Embassy, are opposites as persons and opposites in their views. Between them, they could divide the world, but it is clear that Durrell's sympathies—indeed, the sympathies of nearly all the characters in the *Quartet*—are with Pursewarden.

Durrell, then, is solidly within an English tradition first suggested by Fielding and later stressed by Dickens which sees in the flowering of emotions a way of building a secular metaphysics; and which, conversely, sees in reason the villain who will stifle and smother all life. *Ulysses* as well as Lawrence's major novels, especially *The Rainbow* and *Women in Love,* brought the tradition to a climax; and among Durrell's contemporaries, it appears in one form or another in the work of Joyce Cary, Elizabeth Bowen, and Henry Green. It is, not unusually, a characteristic of the combined Redskin-Paleface attitude.

Durrell's acceptance of something akin to "blood consciousness" is not, however, as dogmatically stated as in Lawrence's own work. Durrell does not preach and exhort so much as present his views in fragments which later are to be reworked into artistic creations. Accordingly, we have, as we have seen, a surfeit of notebooks, memoirs, diaries, and books—all presenting points of view about man and the world he lives in, but all of them diverse. The sum total of these writings is really the substance of the *Quartet*. In writing about creators who themselves, so to speak, create the novels, Durrell is less "anti-intellectual" on the surface than Lawrence. In both art and sex, he seeks salvation; the assumption is that the man without artistic interests can still engage in sex, and while both are preferable to either alone, either is sufficient to free the embattled spirit.

The object is, ultimately, for man to become greater in his own spirit than even in his art. Balthazar had once asked Pursewarden what the object of writing is, and the answer came: " 'The object of writing is to grow a personality which in the end enables man to transcend art.' " Characteristically, the message, one of Pursewarden's (and Henry Miller's) best, was scribbled on the back of an envelope, something that he carelessly might discard. Yet, the core of all his belief is here, a point that Durrell repeats in several ways throughout the novel. Darley and Clea, for example, can create only when they have gained rapport with their selves and with the world: once in this kind of communion, they are artists again, and the art itself is merely an expression of their newly-won stability. Pursewarden's message to Balthazar is concerned, finally, with how man should *live*. And Durrell himself, throughout the *Quartet,* is concerned with ways of living, although, as I have indicated, these ideas do not appear directly.

In more general terms, the Alexandria *Quartet* shows that the novel as a quasi-experimental form does not have to be in decline or even weak. The verbal exuberance that accompanies the intricacies of form demonstrates that language, like the material it conveys, can be protean and many-colored. Around Durrell there exist several extremely competent novelists—Snow, Greene, Elizabeth Bowen, Henry Green—but none of them has been daring in terms of the novel genre itself. Henry Green's novelties are mostly with language, not form, and the others are generally unadventurous in their use of technique. If one reads Durrell on the level of total accomplishment, the Alexandria *Quartet* will return him to the days when the novel was large, experimental, and daring enough to break outside a relatively small world. Durrell conveys to us the adventure of the novel, gives us the expectancy we should feel when we pick up a work of fiction. He transports us to a world he has created, and without making us feel guilty, innocent, edified, or even virtuous, he fills in his stylized world with people who experience various shades of emotion, who suffer pain and anguish and joy; and this he does without snobbish anti-intellectualism, although, ultimately, his point is that "attention" not reason will save. The novel is indeed healthy when there remains such an answer to realism. Even if character is often sacrificed to romance, one is grateful for fiction that comes in the grand style.

IV

The Politics of Conscience:
The Novels of C. P. Snow

WITH THE PUBLICATION of *The Conscience of the Rich* in 1958 and *The Affair* in 1960, C. P. Snow is clearly emerging as a firm literary figure. Both novels are part of *Strangers and Brothers*,* the continuing series on which the scientist and civil administrator turned novelist has been working since 1940. Through his narrator, Lewis Eliot—who functions somewhat similarly to Marcel in Proust's great novel—Snow has set out to examine the moral conscience of England in the years following World War One. No iconoclast or protestant, Snow is primarily concerned with the inner workings of traditional institutions and the ways that these elements of society are perpetuated; thus, his interest in lawyers, scientists, academicians, and administrators: all the groups who have assumed power in the twentieth century and make the decisions necessary for civilized life.

 ˙Snow's characters, as we meet them in *Strangers and Brothers,* are usually involved in a test or conflict when personal ambition and social conscience are at stake. Anxious to catch the conscience of an individual when subjected to everyday temptations,

* *Strangers and Brothers* (1940), years covered—1925-1933; *The Light and the Dark* (1947), 1935-1943; *Time of Hope* (1950), 1914-1933; *The Masters* (1951), 1937; *The New Men* (1954), 1939-1946; *Homecoming(s)* (1956), 1938-1948; *The Conscience of the Rich* (1958), 1927-1936; *The Affair* (1960), 1953-1954

as well as to the large temptations that make or break careers, Snow is understanding about those who are unable to resist quick rewards, and unsentimental about those who retain their principles despite the promise of personal gain. In short, Snow is that phenomenon among twentieth-century novelists: a serious moralist concerned with integrity, duty, principles, and ideals.

The fiction that Snow writes is akin, in technique and manner, to the average Victorian novel of Thackeray, George Eliot, or John Galsworthy, although it is less complicated in narrative structure and character development than the work of the former two and more closely reasoned than that of the latter. Snow eschews the impressionism and symbolism of Joyce, Virginia Woolf, Lawrence, and Conrad, and in so doing returns the novel to a direct representation of moral, social and political issues. His novelistic world is not distorted or exaggerated: his work rests not on artistic re-creation but on faithful reproduction, careful arrangement, and common-sensical development of character and situation.

Specifically, Snow asks, what is man like in the twentieth century? how does a good man live in a world of temptations? how can ambition be reconciled with conscience? what is daily life like in an age in which all things are uncertain except one's feelings? If, by some not impossible chance, the world were suddenly to be destroyed and only Snow's novels recovered by a future generation, the historian of that day would have a fairly good idea of what a responsible twentieth-century man was like merely by following the author through the vast labyrinths of a bureaucratic society where the individual, without visible guidance, must himself find his way or be lost. In his intense realism of conception and execution, Snow believes that man must constantly come to terms with himself in every act, and that the conscious individual is responsible only to himself for whatever course he does take. In brief, he has the faith of a moral agnostic.

Consequently, in what is perhaps the best volume in the series, *The Conscience of the Rich* (1958), Charles March—a long-time friend of Eliot's—with full awareness of what he is doing cuts himself off from his family circle by choice of profession and wife. The consequences of his act, he knows, will be his disinheritance from family, fortune, and religion. Yet his choice is not heroic, certainly not comparable to Stephen Dedalus's to fly from Ireland. March decides, rather simply, that he is unfit for law and more suitable for medicine, at the same time standing behind his wife when he finds she is a communist out to ruin the name and reputation of his rich uncle, Sir Philip. He is no idealist, no Don tilting at windmills; instead, he recognizes that life forces choices—often almost invisible to the outsider—which in themselves mock pretentiousness. The fact that a person can recognize the choices involved is, to Snow, an indication of his maturity. Often, the decision itself is secondary to the realization that it is there and must be acted upon. Accordingly, the burden of decision is the sole heroism that man is ever called upon to bear. By choosing his wife and his career as general practitioner, March chooses the way of manhood, although had he decided in favor of his father, family, name, and religion instead, Snow suggests, he would by no means have been hypocritical or reprehensible.

The entire series of *Strangers and Brothers* is concerned with the conflicts that moral issues impose on basically decent people. Lewis Eliot, Snow's narrator, is himself of moderate abilities, more renowned for his solidity and good judgment than for his talents, which are not exceptional. Eliot is clearly a man of our times: ambitious, but aware of conscience; anxious to gain comfort and power, but cognizant that advancement means moral struggle and compromise with ideals; desirous of recognition, but afraid to lose dignity in achieving it.

From his beginnings as a poor schoolboy with dreams of a better future, Eliot has been aware of what happens to the individual when he loses his sense of judgment; to avoid chaos, he learns, one must be moderate and flexible. Even though personal interest will count for a great deal with Eliot—Snow emphasizes his ambition in *Time of Hope* (1950) when he takes a long chance on winning a law scholarship—his decisions are rarely indecently personal. He recognizes that in a world in which personal interest *is* necessary the only test of a "good" person is how far he responds to the demands of decency and responsibility, how committed he is to values that go beyond ego and will.

Throughout all the volumes of *Strangers and Brothers*, whether they are concerned with Eliot's public life as lawyer, academician, and civil administrator or his private life with the schizoid Sheila Knight, conscience becomes the guiding force, at times almost an obsession. This word, evoking as it does a sense of provincial Victorian morality and smug religiosity, is used here as the sole basis for a secular society. Snow, however, drops the moralistic and didactic connotations of the word, and, as a twentieth-century novelist, equates it with responsibility, the area within which each individual who has the power of choice must make decisions. Thus, George Passant, Eliot's friend—whose superabundant id runs like a counter theme to Eliot's calm judgment—is always an incomplete man despite the nobility of his ideals; for he, in the long run, lacks conscience, and he is punished by losing an administrative post for which he is perhaps over-equipped.

Passant, unlike Eliot, becomes for Snow a man whose insufficient sense of responsibility mocks his ideals, one who fritters away in inconsequential acts a truly remarkable talent. The world is divided, Snow suggests, between the Passants and the Eliots; the one voracious in his intellectual appetites, but weak in judgment; the latter less capable, less talented, but able to muster control when needed. In the modern world, it is evidently the semi-talented who lead. In *Homecoming(s)* (1956), Eliot recognizes that the George Passants are too brilliant and undependable to find easy niches, while the good second-rate man can rise almost to the top. Similarly, in *The New Men* (1954), Luke, the brilliant scientist, is almost too bright for those he has to lead, and it is Eliot's brother, Martin, who could supersede him, mediocre as Martin is. A man like Hector Rose, who as a top administrator manipulates people, is sure, with his moral certainties and conforming imagination, that he knows who will rule the world. He turns down the Passants so that his own position will not be threatened, for the genius can make rules of his own; for genius Rose offers judgment, for original thinking, the comfort of safe conformity. In the growing bureaucracy, the administrator, as Max Weber has firmly persuaded us, makes the important decisions and wields the significant power. Moreover, Eliot recognizes that Rose *is* probably right—he does favor the percentages; but what a human waste results from enforced conformity!

One of the real issues in our century, Snow indicates, is how to utilize the talents of a man for the benefit of the country and for his own benefit. *Homecoming(s)*, *The New Men*, *The Masters* (1951), as well as parts of the other novels, show Eliot as he at various times must pass upon a man's worth. The only way to deal with people, he recognizes, is to assume their fallibility—and then try to work with them. In *The Masters,* he supports Jago for master *because* Jago is human enough to recognize his limitations, and his opponent is not. If, like the nineteenth-century liberal, we suppose the perfectibility of the world and of people, then we are basing hopes on an unattainable ideal which by its very deceptive nature is dangerous. If one presupposes frailty and imperfection, then one knows where to compromise. Thus, Lewis Eliot works with what is available, and what he succeeds in obtaining is always less than what is desirable, but always more than he would have gained by bull-like methods.

Such a way of life is not a *moral* compromise, but the compromise between what one wants and what one can hope to obtain in an imperfect world. To recognize that one must keep his moral person intact and yet be a realist is to be mature in Snow's world. In a society in which the traditional hero and villain no longer have meaning, the man of moral stature who works with the material at hand is the real hero. Society, Snow indicates, depends on the kind of person represented by Eliot: dedicated to some extent, but responsible and flexible enough to change when he sees that in flexibility lies the road to social and political survival.

Evidently, with this kind of hero and this kind of subject matter, Snow cannot be brilliant, eccentric, or even strikingly original. His hero seems already middle-aged in youth, and the novelist himself argues that life works its way out in compromises. From either hero or novelist, little of sensational value can result. There are few severe dramatic turns in the narrative, few visions or conversions in the main characters, little violence of action or emotion; the ripples on the surface of life are small indeed. Eliot never sparkles, is hardly romantic, seems more imposed upon than imposing. He is, in several ways, a staunch Victorian, only one with a more realistic sense of social fact and greater moral flexibility than most. He derives, in part, from Mr. Knightley of Jane Austen's *Emma;* he is, as well, a more complex Dobbin (*Vanity Fair*); and among twentieth-century characters, he recalls Conrad's Marlow, although Eliot is more intelligent and less restricted by a rigid world of honor, integrity, and loyalty.

Nevertheless, no matter how one chooses to look at Eliot, he is not a romantic character. His shabby beginnings—perhaps like Snow's own—impose a sense of reality from the start, and his calling as a lawyer keeps him close to facts, not to flights of imagination. He is, as his acquaintances often tell him, weighty, even prosaic, and very safe; people confide in him, ask his opinion, honor his judgment. Yet he has charm of a sort: as an intelligent man in a world of unintentional nonsense, he is almost an anomaly, as Snow himself is as a novelist. Both the creator and the created are plain men. As Lionel Trilling has written, he could imagine Snow's having asked himself what qualifications he had to be a novelist, only to answer depreciatingly:

> No strange or violent or beautifully intense vision of life. No new notions of the moral life—on the contrary, a set of rather old-fashioned notions chiefly about loyalty and generosity. The best he could muster under the moral head was a belief that it was quite hard to live up to even these simple notions. "It is not much to make novels with," Mr. Snow thought.

Smilarly, Lewis Eliot's talents are modest, his ambitions within reason, and his successes not out of proportion to his intentions. He does his work quietly, without fuss. His virtues are those of calm and rather colorless efficiency, and he is obviously insufficient to carry the weight of eight fairly long novels. Therefore, around him, Snow has created several recurring characters, of whom only George Passant has so far been mentioned. Another is Charles March, Eliot's rich friend who begins in law and ends in medicine; a third is Roy Calvert, the center of *The Light and the Dark* (1947), whose brilliant scholarship is vitiated by his headlong plunges into depression amidst periodic hysteria. As these are Snow's weightiest characters, so the most interesting of the novels are *The Masters,* his best known, and *The Conscience of the Rich,* his penultimate; also of consequence is the aforementioned *The Light and the Dark,* which covers the same time period as *The Masters,* while emphasizing different aspects of Calvert's and Eliot's relationship to the Cambridge college where they are Fellows. The three novels, with Calvert and Eliot within the first two, and Charles March the center of the third, form a trilogy concerned with the struggle for power, whether it be the tangible power of leadership in a political world, or the power politics of Cambridge Fellows, or the power struggle of individuals to realize their own potential. In his stress upon various aspects of power, Snow, almost alone among his contemporaries, is concerned with the thrust of the individual will as it seeks its justification.

The Light and the Dark is, in one way, a preparation for *The Masters,* overlapping the latter in time and containing, although only in summary, the struggle of wills at a Cambridge college. The light and the dark of the title refer to the conflicting moods of Roy Calvert, a brilliant scholar in Near Eastern languages, first introduced as an adolescent in *Strangers and Brothers* (1940), remaining peripheral in *The Masters,* and mentioned in passing in *Homecoming(s).*

The son of a rich industrialist, and favored by a graceful manner and appearance, Calvert is a young man of great ability, bringing to bear upon scholarship the intensity that Eliot lacks; yet the boy has impulses which draw him toward self-destruction. In his varying moods, from melancholy to manic, Roy reveals a variety and range of emotions never disclosed by Eliot, who moves in a "sane" world that is too small to contain Roy. While the young scholar lives through other people, and is given substance through interchange with them, he rarely finds them sufficient and frequently uses them as props for his ego. Accordingly, the novel is itself less a plotted narrative than a series of episodes in which Calvert can reveal himself; and what he reveals is perhaps of greater interest than that afforded by any other Snow character, with the possible exception of Charles March in *The Conscience of the Rich.*

The dramatic conflict of the novel centers, for the most part, around Roy's election as a Fellow to a Cambridge college, the precursor in its way of the election of a master in *The Masters.* Roy is undeniably brilliant, but his personal life leaves something to be desired, and his enemies, themselves less talented than he, are fearful of the scandal connected with his philandering; the repute his abilities will give the college concerns them less. His work in reconstructing an obscure language hitherto undecipherable has secured his place as a scholar of renown. But Roy's life does not find complete fulfillment in his studies; he is unable to come to terms with himself, and often the philology is merely an escape for his energies. Frequently finding his work unsatisfactory, he seeks refuge in his feelings and finds them also wanting. Accordingly, since he cannot believe in himself, he seeks for something external. What he wants is particularly the authority of God, and is willing to accept any kind of dogma and practice if only he can believe in a supreme authority. But he is unable to summon the final faith which would make God real to him, and once again he is thrown back upon himself, where he recognizes his insufficiency.

In his mixture of depression and elation, Roy assumes the mantle of a tragic-comic clown, striking at hypocrisy and crassness wherever he finds it, yet at the same time mocking his own anxieties. Inflexibly honest, yet terribly immature, Roy causes terror to those who recognize his moods. He attacks, indiscreetly, the pretentiousness of Sir Oulston Lyall, a Near East expert, and by so doing almost brings down upon himself the entire scholarly world; what he does is admirable, but the way he does it is improper—he attacks Sir Lyall with insufficient evidence before a gathering of his peers, despite the fact that the old scholar has generously supported Roy's application for a fellowship. Thus Roy comes close to the reactions of several of Snow's major characters, including Eliot himself, George Passant, and Charles March: he is torn between honesty and gratitude, between what involves personal integrity and what is considered sporting, between the claims of his own nature and the demands of a social conscience.

In another way, Roy's inability to have faith in God is obviously his inability to have faith in himself, for in lieu of God he throws himself into the German revolution of the 1930's in order to identify with power and authority. In the Germans under Hitler, Roy finds the kind of power that appeals to his weaker side and completes him, although he entirely rejects anti-Semitism and

even helps several Jews to escape persecution. The sheer dramatic force of the movement entices him, and he loses his ability to
distinguish between power for good ends and power in itself. Roy
here is close, in one way, to the disgruntled German intellectuals
who supported the fascist movement because it satisfied them
emotionally, at the same time denying their intellect in doing so.*
Eliot disagrees violently with Roy and argues the facts of German
expansionism; yet he understands to some extent what his friend
is going through, how all his academic attainments are insufficient
to fill a certain void. Eliot himself had felt such a void, and in
marrying the schizoid Sheila Knight had tried to effect a relationship with a woman who, he suspected strongly, could not be
reached at all. Within men, Eliot believes, there are forces operating which are inexplicable, self-destructive, and powerful enough
to overturn well-balanced minds. Snow writes:

> I [Eliot] believed that some parts of our endowment are too heavy
> to shift. The essence of our nature lay within us, untouchable by our
> own bonds or any other's, by any chance of things or persons, from
> the cradle to the grave. But what it drove us to in action, the actual
> events of our lives—those were affected by a million things, by sheer
> chance, by the interaction of others, by the choice of our own will.
> (*The Light and the Dark*, pp. 367-68)

Roy's desire to seek death as the only possible solution to his
periods of depression leads to his enlistment in the air force, where
he feels sure he will die. Yet once he starts his series of raids over
Germany, he becomes afraid. Now married, with a child, he
wants to play with death as an abstraction, as a possible escape
from the dark periods which he dreads, but death as something
tangible he rejects. Fearing death and also fearing one side of life,
Roy becomes a haunted individual living in a kind of no man's
land devoid of satisfaction. He does die, but his problem remains
—there are uncontrollable forces which man is rarely able to conquer or even sustain, and these, irrespective of his talents, will
destroy him or so weaken his will that he becomes ineffective.

---

* In addition, of course, Roy is trying to exorcise demons which have pursued him in every aspect of his life.

Similar forces recur in much the same setting in *The Masters,* which is Snow's fullest treatment of the power struggle within men. Although the focal point is ostensibly the election of a new master to replace the present one who is dying of cancer, the college is, in fact, a miniature society, and the problem becomes how to use the power that is attached to this society. Power, in brief, will be the key to the novel. What is power? How do honest men use it and misuse it? How does it change honest men? How are decency and integrity compromised by power? How does power bring out the worst and best in men? Finally, Snow asks, how can power be used to gain progress when power itself, in a college world, is more individual than communal?

In *The Masters,* Lewis Eliot has left off attempting to establish a law practice for himself and has entered academic law, on the basis of which he becomes a Fellow at a Cambridge college, now much matured from the young pusher we met in *Time of Hope.* He retains his outside interests as consultant to a London firm, but his failing energies make it difficult for him to pursue a full law career; he recognizes that he would not be first rate, and, in addition, that the presence of his schizoid wife would make social relationships impossible. Also, he is not equipped emotionally and mentally for the long pull; rather than try private practice, Eliot takes refuge in academic life, where he finds, to his sorrow, that the tensions and conflicts are not dissimilar to those he wished to avoid in public life.

Eliot, nevertheless, is the focus of rationality, the one man who can be relied upon for unselfish judgment. In the minds of the other Fellows participating in the election, the desire for power, whether it be that of giving or receiving, dominates. Brown, the conciliator, wants the sort of power that makes other men dependent on him; he will put them into jobs that he has designed to suit their talents. Chrystal wants recognition, the deanship for example, and to be known as a man of power, although he would be satisfied shaping the power. He desires, as Snow says, to see and feel his own strength. Jago—the candidate of Eliot's faction—wants to be first so as to enjoy the trappings, the titles, the ornaments of power. He is excited by the prospect of the big house the master obtains, by the entrance of his name into the history of the college, by the prestige attached to the office, by being addressed as master. Further, as an ambitious man, he believes that there are things only he can do for the college: therefore, he ties his own ambitions to the college's progress and development. In his messianic role, he becomes, as it were, a faulty and weak man with a mission. With power, he would blossom, he believes, although in actuality he might descend into meanness and contempt for others with less prestige. He is not a humble man, but is prodigal in his extravagance.

The limit of power here is the limit of decency. These men are little more than politicians, Snow points out, in the way they conduct themselves and in their quest for personal satisfaction. Involved in secret alliances, after-hour cabals, conspiratorial voting sessions, intrigues toward candidates—all the rituals more closely attached to the selection of a king than a master—they work barely within the restrictions they consider proper. They try to be scrupulous and just, especially when near the young, although they know better than anyone else how private ambition compromises public honesty. Their ruthlessness is something they find difficult to equate with their academic idealism, for more often than not they let personal interest dictate where reason should rule. Snow compares their tensions to war hysteria.

Paralleling the drive for official power by the Fellows is the attitude of Sir Horace, a wealthy benefactor of the college, who relishes the power of giving or withholding money as he sees fit. He recognizes that his is power to use, and he is careful to squeeze the full worth from his position. Like Chrystal, he cherishes power just for the feel of it. Strikingly, all the Fellows accept the fact that Sir Horace is an important man simply because his money can do much for them: they worship his kind of power as much as they do their own. They are hard-headed enough to recognize that they are dependent on Sir Horace, and that his world makes theirs possible.

In the meeting between the Fellows and Sir Horace, one finds all the cross-currents of life in the larger world. The sense of *noblesse oblige* which each practices is a recognition that the two are interdependent in their ultimate welfare. The Fellows can guarantee that his cousin will pass his examinations, and they can grant Sir Horace intellectual respectability for a price. Through them, he can enter history. He, on the other hand, makes it possible for them to put up new buildings, to expand their facilities, but, most of all, to feel contact with the outside world. His money will give them a sense of power that transcends the confines of the college. In the meeting of the academic and business worlds, we have a union, Snow suggests, between two of the major forces in contemporary society: each admires the other, although both remain suspicious, the academicians of the ideals of the business world and the businessmen of the unreality of the academicians. Nevertheless, their differences, in the end, are fewer than their similarities; they both, in certain ways, want the same things: power, recognition, the ability to give. Both have the need to expand.

As the time for the election approaches, the will to power demeans all concerned, except Eliot, whose choice never wavers and whose course is one of decency and reason. To gain public power, Snow indicates, one must lose dignity, for in acquiring power there is the loss of the better part of man, particularly the loss of balance. Jago, for example, becomes increasingly anxious as he fluctuates between success and failure, as he sees the mastership first slipping from him and then returning within his grasp. The maneuvers behind his back seem like an undermining of his position, and he resents intrigue even from his own side. He wants to think that the mastership will become his as a result only of his own achievements, and that he alone has the power to assume the title. By dividing the power with others, he feels himself divided, as if losing part of the honor by having to grant that others have helped him.

Precisely because Jago is insecure and frail, so aware of his fallibility, Eliot favors him over Crawford, the successful scientist, who remains to the end sure of himself and his own powers. Eliot reasons that *because* Jago is unsure, he will recognize frailty in others, and once the mastership is his, he will take into account human failings. Power has less chance of destroying him because he will continue to perceive human limitations. Crawford, however, will not question himself or others, and, lacking Jago's flexibility, may use power with the unquestioned assurance that he is doing right.

Perhaps more than any of the other Fellows, Eliot is aware of the flaws of basically decent men and how easily they confuse personal ambition with social conscience. As one who endeavors to be objective—he admits to a dislike for Jago at the beginning of the novel—he tries to probe the area where compromise will yield the most; we remember that he is a trained lawyer. In Crawford, he fears the use of pure power by a man who has never had any doubts about his superiority and perfection; in Jago, he finds a man beset by personal fears and doubts, actually the lesser man on the record. Yet Jago, by virtue of his very doubts, will examine his conscience with more exactitude before taking a course of action. Crawford, the man without a dent in his self-confidence, may be the potential dictator as well as possibly the better master. Probing the two men—and Eliot has nothing against Crawford, who honorably remains above the politicking—Eliot chooses the lesser man as providing the smaller degree of danger to the community at large.

Crawford finally wins the mastership when Chrystal, who wants to be known as a man of power, shifts his vote from Jago to his opponent. Amid all the strands of compromise, Chrystal decides that he has been on Crawford's side for months. Chrystal is, in fact, moved by vacillations he does not even understand, and while having aligned himself with one party, he begins to feel things he does not recognize, until he makes his final decision to support Crawford. Men who seem to know their own minds best, Snow suggests, often are beset by doubts and fears below the surface which dictate their final decisions. The drive for power in Chrystal makes him, finally, identify with strength; he needs to be triumphant, regardless of how he compromises himself.

The master having been chosen, the college seems to return to normal, the Fellows putting aside their differences to work together under the new master. Yet the struggle does not end that easily, for each man has had to look at himself in a new and hitherto undiscovered way. They have all been touched on their most sensitive points. Only Eliot remains unchanged by circumstances, for he knew exactly what he was doing, his actions being free of personal interest. Only he retained his reason throughout, and this because he was unaffected by the emotional cross-currents. Chrystal, for example, learns something he never knew before; Brown recognizes that even his mature awareness of conciliation cannot take everything into account; Jago must face all his fears and insecurities. Nothing is exactly the same, although the surface will continue smooth. Consciences have been touched, weak spots revealed, wounds uncovered. Yet the Fellows will once again show allegiance to the college, all the time coming to terms with themselves; until a new master must be chosen.

In *The Conscience of the Rich,* published seven years after *The Masters,* there is also struggle for power, this one involving the religious and political world, as well as social and personal relationships. As the novel begins, Eliot has finished his law examinations and passed well enough to win a scholarship and be articled to Herbert Getliffe, a London lawyer. His friend, Charles March, has also passed high, but not high enough for a scholarship, which he does not need or want. More talented than Eliot, he is, by virtue of his background, less motivated by financial insecurity and personal drive. His family, the well-known Marches, is part of the rich and settled upper-class Anglo-Jewish world that is comfortably and complacently sitting out the trouble between England and Germany prior to the Second World War. The Marches are not very religious Jews in their practice, but certain conventions have become important for them. Huge Friday night dinners, with fifty or sixty guests, form the basis of family solidarity; at these gatherings, which the older generation insists upon, the family is consolidated through forced attendance, although the younger people already look upon the dinners as unamusing anachronisms. There, a review of news and gossip prevents any eccentricity from escaping the ears of all, and the family unit becomes a way of exerting social pressure on the potential deviator. As a miniature world, the family prevents Charles March and his sister Katherine from forgetting their Jewishness, returns them to it, at least once a week.

The leading influence in this particular segment of the March family is Leonard, Charles's father, whose conventional tastes and aims have fixed him in a pre-industrial dream world, unable as he is to come to terms with changing times. His children, of course, are very much of this century, and the conflict between them and the elder March is, in one way, the conflict of one century's institutions with the ideas of another; in a second way, the conflict of Jewish conventions with the non-Jewish attitudes of the nearly assimilated children. The problem, then, becomes one of compromise: how far will the children compromise to keep Leonard satisfied? how far will he move to placate them?

On Leonard's part, there is always the nagging fear that he has failed to realize what talents he might have had, and that his life, full of crochets and old-fashioned opinions, is basically meaningless; therefore, the worth he places on tradition, on external forms, on the self-righteous opinion of the family group, on his Jewishness to set him and the family off from the rest of society. His religion is certainly not that which involves the God of Moses or the Covenant of the Ark; it is, almost solely, a means of social snobbery. Like Cain, the Marches are marked, and consequently they have good reason, they feel, for retreating into isolation, while maintaining their good living, fine houses, and other signs of material distinction. In many ways, their Jewishness becomes merely an excuse for exclusiveness, a cover for personal deficiencies.

Nagged by the fear that his own life has been a failure, Leonard lives through his children, turning in hope particularly to his son, Charles. All his rejected dreams center on Charles, and his attachment becomes obsessed with his desire to maintain the family honor. The need for outward success becomes obvious. But Charles, while fond of his father and careful of his feelings, is anxious to break out of the family mold and acts counter to his father's wishes. As a lawyer, he is within a world acceptable to Leonard, but as a doctor earning his own way, he is reprehensible, even slightly ridiculous. Charles's desire to be a doctor—to feel useful by being responsible—indicates to Leonard the breaking up of the family unit, for no March with any regard for the family would turn to medicine, especially to being a general practitioner.

Accordingly, the tensions appear in several ways: in personal terms, Charles's sense of personal responsibility versus his father's sense of family honor; in religious terms, the son's conflict with Leonard's Jewishness (*including* its warmth), plus the Jewishness of the Marches versus a non-Jewish world; in social terms, family and tradition versus the coming disintegration of the family unit, as well as the ghetto attitude (however gilded) of Leonard versus the cosmopolitanism of Charles and his sister; in political terms, the radicals (the younger people) versus the conservatives (Leonard, Sir Philip March), and within the former, the communists (Charles's wife, Ann Simon) in conflict with the non-communist left (Charles, Lewis Eliot); and all this against the background of evergrowing political conflict between England and Germany in the 1930's.

By denying his Judaism—and becoming a doctor is an outward symbol of this negation—Charles feels that he has found one of the ways to counteract his family and gain independence. His religion, tied as it is to tradition and continuity, binds him to a course of action with which he cannot personally identify. He feels he will be fixed, unalive, and inactive as long as he remains part of Leonard's world. To be a doctor, however, is to differ from the family pattern, and Charles naturally equates his change of profession with his disdain for the forms of Judaism retained by his father. By overthrowing his law career, in which he could be very successful if he wished, he partially nullifies the traces of the past and particularly the traces of his father's very strong control over him.

His marriage to Ann Simon, similarly, isolates him politically from his traditionally conservative family. While he does not share Ann's political views, he stands behind her by refusing to make her head off a communist report that will ruin Sir Philip, Leonard's older brother. This decision becomes his moral battleground, paralleling in its way his choice of profession. His moral struggle here is merely a continuation of his struggle against the past; the conscience of the rich is working on him to make him individually responsible. To remain a March in the sense that Leonard desires is to remain safe and protected at every turn of fortune, isolated from life by family wealth, position, and name. Charles recognizes that to be safe is to deny life, and his conscience refuses to allow him to avoid dangers, the first of which is to throw off the family burden, although he is more than willing to retain the love implicit in his father's relation to him. The crisis over Ann, who must herself, uninfluenced by Charles, decide what to do about the information that will destroy Sir Philip's reputation,

becomes the crisis of Charles's own life: here he can achieve manhood through self-identity or remain all his life under Leonard's
control.

Within this struggle for power, Snow is interested in catching
essentially unheroic characters at their moments of decision and
watching how they react. Each act, he recognizes, is moral only
when it grows from the whole person; an immoral act, he suggests, will not come from a fully conscious person, for the conflict
itself confers nobility. Thus, Snow is concerned with mature and
wise people who are aware of duty and discipline, who realize,
like Eliot, that much of life is necessary compromise between
desire and fulfillment. The individual, in these terms, is clearly not
a traditional hero—on the contrary, the humble everyday acts of
living are the sole terms of one's heroism, which is within the
reach of *any* moral character. With the hero in Victorian and
modern fiction having declined from his traditional position, Snow
shows that the only kind of hero left is the person who assumes
responsibility and makes personal choices, in themselves part of
his struggle to gain self-identity.

Snow has attempted in his modest way to bring fiction back to a
concern with commonplace human matters without making the
novel either journalistic, naturalistic, or prophetic. Accordingly,
his characters, also modest in aim and conception, are of mixed
qualities, neither totally attractive nor completely forbidding.
Charles is often spiteful and scornful, yet loyal and dependable;
Eliot himself, merely a sounding board in this novel, makes an art
of compromise when compromise is viable and principle is not;
Leonard March is idiosyncratic, yet upright, and his eccentricities
never make him a caricature—he is of a time and place, and he
fits. If he has cut himself off from the present—his deafness is a
physical indication of this—it is because he recognizes that the
present is corrosive, and he refuses to let reality interfere with what
his inner ear tells him is true. He has been unable to grow with
age, and wisdom is clearly not his. Blinded by his own failure,
rather than by ignorance, he will not see what he chooses not to
see, and he loses his son because of this. Although he retains
dignity, he must, as Charles realizes, be superseded.

Essentially, *The Conscience of the Rich* is a novel about individuals; however, it is also a history of England in the 1930's when the Charles Marches could still make their own decisions. Charles's discomfort with his Judaism, for example, is the difficulty of a whole generation trying to discover its own conscience. In changing times, the old alignments, he finds, no longer make the same sense. Charles's decision to come to terms with himself, then, is the decision that the entire age must make. Snow's real talent lies in his ability to demonstrate cogently that the response must come from within, that it must be a moral response, and that it must retain a note of social responsibility while fulfilling the individual. As Lewis Eliot in the earlier volumes had turned inward and in his own moral conscience found a modus vivendi that would serve him uniquely, so too Charles March must make peace with his conscience, regardless of the demands that others will make upon him. Only then, can he, unlike his father, realize himself.

After *The Conscience of the Rich, The Affair,* which returns to the Cambridge of *The Masters,* seems anti-climactic, although it is exciting as a suspense story replete with mysterious intrigues and a courtroom scene. Snow's novel—whose title, incidentally, derives from the Dreyfus case—superficially recalls James Gould Cozzens' somewhat pompous *By Love Possessed,* which mixed basically unsympathetic characters with legal highjinks to stir up interest that is really less than meets the eye. Cozzens' purpose, however, was to show how morally shaky the people are who hold positions of trust, while Snow's is to demonstrate that justice —at least in England—eventually triumphs despite the moral shakiness of the individuals who make the decisions. Snow is here concerned with clearing the name of one of the college Fellows, Howard, of scientific fraud. Most of the important characters from *The Masters* are still alive, and they display their talents in much the same way they did in the earlier novel.

This novel, more than any other of Snow's, takes the form of a mystery-suspense work, with the actual outcome of the college trial held until the virtual end. Snow makes Howard—the man accused of perpetrating a fraud in order to gain academic prestige—into an intense, unlikable young man, a sneering, dominating, complacent Marxist who jeers at the very institutions and people trying to help him. By making the object of injustice himself unpalatable, Snow isolates the act itself and weighs the scales heavily against those who want justice. He stresses that human feelings are not at stake—clearly all feeling runs against Howard—but simply the institution of equity for all. Even Eliot, who so often in the past has been willing to accept abstract principles rather than the man, is taken aback by Howard and is wary of helping him, although he is finally drawn into the case.

Snow emphasizes that Skeffington, a rigid conservative who is the very opposite of Howard, despises the latter and everything he stands for, but he must see justice done, no matter whom he hurts. Perhaps the very weakness of the novel lies here: that people like Skeffington are not concerned with human relationships but with the abstraction that justice is at the core of the English people, and it must be effected. One of the fine qualities of *The Masters* was Snow's ability to embody the abstractions of different ideals and ideas in the form of recognizable people who fought out their petty ambitions in a daily give and take. No matter who they were, they reacted to each other as human beings, and Snow saw their flaws not in terms of abstract principles but of real people caught between what they wanted and what they saw they could have. The same kind of give and take was dramatized in *The Conscience of the Rich,* wherein Snow did not forsake principles, morality, justice, and those other abstractions which form the spine of *Strangers and Brothers,* but managed to flesh them out. In *The Affair,* the flesh has melted away, and often only the bony abstraction remains. This novel, consequently, seems akin to the earlier novels when Snow's hand was less sure and often more committed to abstract ideas than to people themselves.

Most of the characters have little meaning except as carry-overs from *The Masters* or as participants in a drama in which they themselves have no personal interest. Skeffington, for instance, the man who pursues the case with single-minded energy, is a relic of British justice, a man who inexplicably fights for what he knows to be correct even though he despises the object of his struggle. Eliot himself is drawn in against his will; Francis Getliffe does not wish to be bothered; Arthur Brown is afraid of the upset, and so on. They all react to the abstraction of justice, not to men themselves. In Snow's previous novels, the reaction was to both, and the conflict was between specific individuals and the principle involved. Here the man is so personally disagreeable that there is no question of like or dislike—no one could feel favorable toward him, and, consequently there is little conflict. The characters find they must support justice despite themselves, and while justice is always admirable, it cannot be isolated without the novel becoming an exercise in English equity.

Readable and suspenseful though it is, *The Affair,* accordingly, has about it the odor of the exercise. Perhaps Crawford's complacent comment at the end of the book indicates what is wrong: " 'I think I remember saying that in my experience sensible men usually reach sensible conclusions.' " It was precisely this point that remained in doubt in the more recent novels: sensible men were perhaps not quite so sensible when their personal needs were involved; their decisions were not so just as they might have been had they not been expedient men. In those novels, Snow questioned the very bases on which men judged each other and showed that motives were more complex than any disinterested belief in justice, equity, or reason. Good men could be hurt by institutions, though these institutions were necessary to protect the larger rights of individuals. There was, accordingly, almost constant paradox: the institution could not be allowed to deteriorate, although institutions themselves can be evil. There was an acute awareness of the duality of man in a secular world, a mature acceptance of his allegiance to himself and things external.

Here, however, the man is no longer in question; he is merely a disembodied cause, someone to be saved and then discarded, as he is at the end of the novel. Snow is demonstrating a thesis: that a Marxist, even when opposed by everyone, must be afforded his rights in a democratic society. His rights, in fact, must perhaps be more carefully watched because he makes demands on men— even more than a conformist would—that test their sense of justice. An outsider, according to this reasoning, must be afforded special treatment. As a political and social doctrine this is just, Snow would of course argue, but embodied solely to illustrate this point in a novel, such material is weak.

The Affair, to digress for a moment, received as good a press as it did because several critics had discovered *Strangers and Brothers* and found Snow to be an extremely intelligent practitioner in the novel. Seen against the background of the whole series, however, *The Affair* does not have the complex qualities of *The Conscience of the Rich, The Light and the Dark,* or *The Masters.* More abstract than any of the others, it depends almost solely on that sure-fire device, a courtroom scene in which the case first appears lost, only to be won back in the final minutes by new information that casts doubt in the mind of the jury.

The strengths and failings of *The Affair,* paradoxically, have their origin in Snow's explicit aim, which is to show how reason, particularly scientific reason, functions in the lives of men. Reason, as Snow amply demonstrates, serves many masters and can be manipulated for many purposes. Even men of science, for whom reason should be a god, cannot judge equitably when their own needs and prejudices are at stake. Nor can reason be defined with absolute precision; the reason of the laboratory is not the reason of the world, and it is the task of men like Lewis Eliot to bridge the gap between the scientific and the humanistic communities: strangers must somehow become brothers. In *The Two Cultures and the Scientific Revolution,* a recent essay on the same problem, Snow merely repeats in socio-political terms his lifelong effort to connect the two cultures.

The Affair nevertheless demonstrates that reason, while it can be brought to the service of justice, does not in itself provide fiction of any depth or persuasiveness. The book suffers from an excess of reason; the characters know exactly why they support and attack Howard; Eliot analyzes his motives in the minutest details, and knows just where he went right and wrong. There are few of the imponderables which, previously, made both Roy Calvert and George Passant interesting—in the former a depression and death drift that reduced his powers, in the latter an exuberant brilliance and sensuality that made lesser men reject him.

The point of view expressed here, then, narrows the range of the series. *The Conscience of the Rich* showed a broadening of Snow's powers as a novelist, for the people there reacted not to abstract justice, but to conflicts within themselves. Snow's novels tend to be weakest when people confront something outside of themselves, strongest when they must come to terms with the tortured man within. *The Masters* is a powerful novel, albeit minor in scope, because each character has to measure himself not against issues, but against what he is in relation to the issue. Whenever Snow shows characters who have lost this sense of self-conflict, whenever he presents characters who retain only their social functions, then he tends to present cardboard figures.

Consequently, *The Affair,* number eight in the series of eleven novels which will comprise *Strangers and Brothers,* adds little to the whole. The moral decisions that must be made have been formed in one way or another in the earlier novels: decisions made by George Passant and Charles March, for instance. The limitations of Snow's kind of positivism become apparent. All behavior, provided it is rooted in sanity, can be explained, and ultimately forgiven. All motives are relative to the holder. This view assumes that we can *know* why a person acts in a particular way, that there is such a thing as clarity in the difficult area of motivation and intention. Such an attitude is similar to that of those naturalists who assume that behavior is composed of a stimulus and a corresponding effect, that a given environment generates a given behavior.

Snow is obviously closer to such naturalists than to any other group, but in his best work, as in the best work of Zola, Bennett, and Galsworthy, he moves away from theory and lets the human being determine his own course. Thus, we have a Charles March who must cut himself off from his ostensible roots in order to gain stability of a sort. Reason here must constantly come to terms with irrational elements within the character—in working out this conflict, Snow wrote what is perhaps his richest novel. In *The Affair,* he provides us with a display of naked reason, and as a result writes one of the weakest books of the series.

With Snow's work, certain tendencies in the English novel from Jane Austen to the present have come full circle. Although lacking Jane Austen's irony as a comic freeing force and as a means of returning her characters to a social norm, Snow uses man's social conscience as a way of avoiding chaos. Moreover, in his concern with man's moral nature, in his use of a straightfoward narrative technique, and in his understanding and forgiveness of temporary deviations from "correct" behavior, he is indeed close to the mature Jane Austen of *Emma* and *Persuasion,* as well as to several other of the major nineteenth-century novelists. In still another way, Snow has returned to the moderation and proportion of the Greek dramatists, finding in their attitudes the wisdom necessary to preserve a balanced society in which personal interest is both present and necessary. Snow recognizes that personal ambition, if unfettered, can destroy decent life, and that with civilized people the only test of a "good" man is how far he responds to the demands of decency. The power of conscience becomes, under these conditions, a social necessity.

V

Graham Greene's Demonical Heroes

IT HAS BECOME a commonplace of literary criticism that the hero in major western fiction has more or less vanished, or, at least, become bourgeois, diminished in stature, somewhat trite in his demands upon life. Often, the hero is characterized as an anti-hero, a figure like the tragic-comic Bloom of *Ulysses,* the self-destructive Jim of Conrad's novel or K. of Kafka's, or the fumbling "angry young man" of Kingsley Amis or John Wain. The background for the anti-hero is of course closely connected to changes in the literary as well as political, religious, and social character of the western world and, therefore, precedes by many years the work of the twentieth-century authors in whom the phenomenon is most apparent. One finds such changes, for example, beginning in France during the reaction against romanticism on the part of the realists, Stendhal, Flaubert, Maupassant, and (later) Zola, a reaction which brought with it inevitable disdain for the romantic hero with his simple purity, natural goodness of heart and action, and basically Christian morality, a hero who was an aristocratic Christian knight in modern dress. The realist-naturalist novelists, interested as they often were in the seamier aspects of life, could not help but reject the superficial façade of gentility with which a romantic writer surrounded his protagonist. Then, precisely as these nineteenth-century realists probed from the outside to destroy most heroic notions, so, later, twentieth-century writers were to probe from within with much the same effect. Thus, in France, Proust, Gide, Céline, Camus, Sartre, and several others have followed where Stendhal and Flaubert began.

In England, the anti-heroic type is found—curiously, one is tempted to say—within the works of Dickens, who, despite his "soft" young men and women, often qualified their romantic success with a sense of corrupt failure. We have only to compare Pip in *Great Expectations* with the typical heroes of the then very popular and now forgotten romantic novels which appeared in such great numbers in the second half of the century. Or else, compare the much chastened heroes of Thackeray and Meredith or the heroines of George Eliot with their romantic contemporaries, and then we see where the tradition begins to gain force. In Meredith, for instance, the idea generated its own kind of novel in which the ego of the central character proves self-destructive, for the "hero" (now necessarily placed within inverted commas) can no longer get back into the society which he wants to enter, and now, broken or dead, he is almost completely ineffectual. One thinks of Richard Feverel, Sir Willoughby Patterne, Nevil Beauchamp. Then, a few decades later, with the turn of the twentieth century and the introduction of psychological phenomenon into English fiction, novelists like Conrad, Joyce, and Forster helped put the hero into an early grave. Conrad, with his self-destructive protagonists, persecuted his heroes while he probed their central corruption. Joyce created an egoistic Stephen Dedalus, whose self-centeredness precluded his being anyone's hero but his own. And Forster poked at the corners of the human character, unearthing all kinds of contradictions, odds and ends of behavior which showed with finality that the romantic hero had perished as a serious literary creation. Further, D. H. Lawrence and Virginia Woolf, despite their large differences, here agreed that character must be created anew and that all the old figures, including the superficially charming romantic hero, must be superseded by an inner vision. And this vision is more or less the one that has predominated in the significant English novels of this century. Tragedy is now that of the "fallen democrat," the "struggling bourgeois," the "awkward outsider," all of whom, in the absence of a believable God, try to believe in themselves.

In attempting to recover the "hero" for a democratic age, Graham Greene has taken the "fallen democrat" peculiar to our time and tried to raise him through suffering and pain to more heroic stature.* Having assumed that the romantic hero is surely dead, Greene still believes that man can be heroic, although in his terms heroism takes on a different hue from that in previous times. Greene has reached back beyond the superficial romantic hero of the nineteenth century to the Greek concept of tragedy, at the same time remembering that Greek tragedy in itself must be modified to suit a basically irreligious, democratic age. Greene feels he must allow for the "fall" that is central to Aristotle's view of the tragic hero; but here that "fall" is man's demonical descent from grace, and his attempt to embrace faith in a seemingly godless universe is the measure of his heroism.

For Greene, the essential human tragedy, implicit in the gap between what man wants and what, because of personal limitations, he is able to attain, is ironic. The latter, his capacity, mocks the former, his desire. Caught between the two, man must evidently fail unless he has a vision of something beyond himself. For him to concentrate solely on his own limitations is to demonstrate indifference to anything that might be greater. In brief, the self-satisfied or indifferent individual precludes his own tragic role, for he places himself beyond the reach of a powerful force, a force, incidentally, that may lead to severe unhappiness as well as to limited happiness. However, if he recognizes an outside transcendental force, the individual is caught by a phenomenon more powerful than himself, and he reacts; he feels inadequate; he becomes a potentially tragic hero.

---

* *The Man Within* (1929); *The Name of Action* (1930); *Rumour at Nightfall* (1931); *Stamboul Train* (1932); *It's a Battlefield* (1934); *England Made Me* (1935); *A Gun for Sale* (1936); *Brighton Rock* (1938); *The Confidential Agent* (1939); *The Power and the Glory* (1940); *The Ministry of Fear* (1943); *The Heart of the Matter* (1948); *The Third Man* (1950); *The Fallen Idol* (1950); *The End of the Affair* (1951); *Loser Takes All* (1955); *The Quiet American* (1956); *Our Man in Havana* (1958); *A Burnt-Out Case* (1961)

Greene has recast the Greek hero, accordingly, to suit a Christian framework, at the same time qualifying the term "hero" itself. The Greene hero, in this way like that of the Greek dramatists, is religious; that is, he operates according to the religious beliefs of his times and gains much of his force and substance, both negative and positive, from surrounding religious ideas. In our day, however, the religious framework within which the Greek dramatist worked is non-existent or, at best, marginal; so that the novelist must "create" both the surroundings and the hero. Thus, while the Greek tragedian could take the religious values of his age for granted and write confidently within them, Greene has had to make these values themselves seem plausible to an audience accustomed to a more secular life and literature. His purpose, evidently, is to recover tragedy in a democratic world, to re-create the Christian "hero," and to make credible the religious world which the Greek dramatist accepted as fact. Greene's mission in his major novels, then, is to write Greek tragedy without forsaking a Christian God.

Because Greene believes that from impurity will come purity, from demonism saintliness, from unbelief belief, from vice virtue, his "heroes" often seem closer to demons than to saints. Nearly every serious Greene protagonist, despite external expedience and even personal degradation, has a vision of saintliness, while his inner conflict, often not apparent to him, results from his inability to live up to his ideal. In these terms Greene places the tension between pride and moderation, analogous to the conflict of the Greek tragic hero. Like Oedipus, whose pride has overwhelmed his sense of reasonableness, Scobie (*The Heart of the Matter,* 1948), Pinkie (*Brighton Rock,* 1938), and the whisky priest (*The Power and the Glory,* 1940), for example, all recognize how far short they have fallen of the ideal, how mortal they really are. In *The Confidential Agent* (1939), one of his entertainments, Greene retells the *Song of Roland* to illustrate explicitly this theme of false heroism and pride which deceive men into thinking themselves gods.

The Berne MS of the *Song of Roland,* discovered and annotated by Agent D., a disillusioned "hero" himself, destroys the romantic heroic picture of Roland and puts in his stead an Oliver who is realistic and who is the real "hero" simply because he avoids heroics of an obvious sort. As D. points out:

> "That's the importance of the Berne MS. It re-establishes Oliver. It makes the story tragedy, not just heroics. Because in the Oxford version Oliver is reconciled, he gives Roland his death-blow by accident, his eyes blinded by wounds. The story, you see, has been tidied up to suit. . . . But in the Berne version, he strikes his friend down with full knowledge—because of what he has done to his men: all the wasted lives. He dies hating the man he loves—the big boasting courageous fool who was more concerned with his own glory than with the victory of his faith. But you can see how that version didn't appeal—in the castles—at the banquets, among the dogs and reeds and beakers; the jongleurs had to adapt it to meet the tastes of the medieval nobles, who were quite capable of being Rolands in a small way—it only needs conceit and a strong arm—but couldn't understand what Oliver was at." (Pp. 59-60)

By downgrading heroic roles in general and unthinking heroes in particular, Greene, like the author of the Berne MS, leaves room for the humility that is clearly part of a tragic vision. Roland, the so-called hero of the Oxford MS, believing that he and only he can conquer, thinks he is God, while Oliver, the "real hero" of the Berne MS, knows that he isn't. Thus Roland, like Oedipus in his tragedy, plays God and becomes a proud fool, while Oliver, allowing God's intervention, retains the strength of the humble. This is almost a "parable" of Greene's claim that only through humbling oneself before "God" can one become truly heroic. If one disbelieves in his own perfectibility—the "false hero" of course believes in just this—he then allows for the ingress of sin that makes him need God. The imperfect man, the one closest to the devil, is, for Greene, precisely the one who is in need of God, and although Agent D., in *The Confidential Agent,* is agnostic, he is surely close to God in his humble sense of failure.

We see, then, in nearly all of Greene's work that what is true of Agent D. also holds for Scobie, the whisky priest, Bendrix (*The End of the Affair,* 1957), Minty (*England Made Me,* 1935), Francis Andrews (*The Man Within,* 1929), Querry (*A Burnt-Out Case,* 1961), even Pinkie. The failure, the devilish man, the seeming anti-hero is somehow, unconsciously, approaching God; for in failure, not success, we fathom our sins and recognize our faults. We see again that Oliver and not Roland is the real "hero." Greene's belief that the failure is nearer God than the success is of course close to the Greek idea of hubris: in this view, the successful, boasting man, full of overweening pride, challenges the order of the universe by considering himself greater than the gods, and at this point, when he attempts to expand from man-size to god-size, at the very apex of pride and vanity, he is struck down. Thus, also within the Christian world, God operates, although He retains sympathy and pity for the failure, for the one struck down. In fact, He reserves his strength and force, Greene often seems to be saying, almost exclusively for the ones who approach the devil. The lovers of God do not necessarily find Him through their belief. He is more likely to be discovered by the tortured deniers. Thus, those who hate may be closer to God than those who love; those who deny closer than those who believe; those who despair closer than those who are elated; those who kill closer than those who save or try to save; those who commit suicide closer than those who fear to; those who ponder despair closer than those who accept dogma. In every instance, Greene feels that God seeks out the ones who would deny Him, for they are probing the very roots of His existence, and with this, God can sympathize. God is, in Greene's terms, reborn only in those who question Him, and dies within those who acquiesce unquestioningly to His supremacy.

Accordingly, the major contrast in several of Greene's novels occurs between the conventional believers, who live according to the Church's dictates, and the conventional unbelievers, who flout belief of any sort. And yet, as we see, Greene avoids the easy solution that the believer will be saved and the unbeliever damned; in fact, he turns the stereotyped formula inside out. His unbelievers wallow in a kind of dumb despair that would seem to preclude their salvation. Obsessed as they are with their transgressions, they often fail to recognize that they are not gods and that God has powers which they cannot understand. Nevertheless, in this scheme, Scobie, who has sinned mortally by taking communion without prior absolution and who commits suicide—the final and unredemptive act of despair—can be saved by God's grace if

He should so wish; nothing Scobie has done precludes the possibility.

Scobie of *The Heart of the Matter,* as well as the whisky priest of *The Power and the Glory,* is undergoing that kind of re-evaluation of self in which he becomes a focus of failure, and failure itself and love of failure become, as it were, a way of life. Unsuccessful in his career, not in love with his wife who cannot share his interests or even come close to understanding him, lacking money, respect, and often dignity, dissatisfied with his religion (he is a convert), Scobie, now isolated and alone, is approaching that state of acedia which places him outside the ken of other men and which even denies the efficacy of God's grace. Still faithful to his ideal of honesty and integrity, Scobie gives up hope. The only thing that can bring him back momentarily to a community of men is his affair with Helen, who, having lost her husband in a shipwreck and drifted in the open sea for forty days while waiting to be saved, comes to him as a piece of flotsam. She is, like Scobie, a derelict, and only with her can he find some kind of love—he can, in his condition, turn only to another failure. Through love for a failure (as God will perhaps love him), Scobie has a temporary desire for life, although this too passes when his wife, the symbol of all his past deficiencies, returns to him.

Like a Greek protagonist, Scobie is fixed within his character, unable to resist what he is and what he is becoming. Once again analogous to the Greek dramatist, Greene finds nothing easy in life, nothing flexible or soft; for as man has put himself into his situation, so only man, with the possible aid of belief if it is forthcoming, can extract himself. Although "miracles" do occur in a Greene novel, they never "save" a character; only suffering, inner conflict, soul-searching tension, recognition of self—all the qualities a Dostoyevskian hero must acquire, and here, as elsewhere, we see the great influence the Russian writer had on Greene— can help a Greene character by making him dissatisfied with the devil.

Greene has, as it were, revised the Christian novel: if the prototype of the Christian quest is Bunyan's *Pilgrim's Progress*— the quest of the good man for virtue, for the Heavenly City of God—then Greene has indeed changed the procedure. In

Greene's work, the quest is undertaken by a sinner who stumbles along the way to the Heavenly City, almost forsaking God and embracing the devil in his crude inability to fulfill what God requires. Greene is concerned, in a way, with how the Christian underground and marginal man can be saved, how the poor in spirit, the weak in will, the proud in soul can be saved; the rest, he suggests, can take care of themselves.

God's force here, as the power of fate in Greek tragedy, is directed toward those who think they are least subject to it or deserve it. In earthly failure, God sees potential salvation; in vain success, He sees weakness; in satanical pride, He sees the capacity for humility; in indecision and denial, He sees the possibility of faith. Only indifference, Greene claims, can destroy God. In several ways, then, Greene has turned tradition upside down: rather than accepting his belief, he examines his unbelief and measures its strength. And while the actual "leap" into faith that his protagonists take may not be fully persuasive to the lay reader, nevertheless the conflicts themselves are often cogent, given the nature of a Greene character. Greene asks, among other things: what can God mean to a man who rejects Him? to one who traffics with the devil? Further, what does God mean in a world that seems compounded of evil? Who will prove stronger in the battle for man's will, God or the devil, even though God may bring more pain than the latter? Greene suggests, paradoxically, that in reaching out for the devil, one may well find God intervening; and conversely, in reaching for God, one may indeed find the devil. While the Church may demand conformity of behavior and belief according to fixed dogmas, God, like the devil, operates inexplicably, apart, if necessary, from the Church's body of dogma. In his concern with evil and the demonical hero, we see that Greene is closer to Dostoyevsky and Mauriac than to any Anglo-American tradition of the religious novel.

The whisky priest of *The Power and the Glory* is the last priest in the state, his fellow priests having been outlawed—killed off or forced to marry in a purge by a local dictator. He can try to escape or he can live a normal married life that mocks his former vocation. He can save his soul or his body. The whisky priest reluctantly stays, but he is constantly reminded of the fact that he is not worthy of the role cut out for him: to be, in effect, a martyr. If Christ is his ideal, he sadly fails to live up to this high conception, for he drinks to excess, has fathered a child, and is not even sure he can practice his profession when fear overtakes him; in brief, he is, according to Greene, a devil ready for sainthood. Full of self pride, the whisky priest, like a Greek hero, is partially ennobled through suffering, doubt, and self-realization. At every point, the priest is made aware of the depths to which he has fallen, aware that the devil has indeed entered his body and exorcised his God. In denying God, the priest comes close to Him, analogous to the Greek protagonist who comes closest to the powers of fate exactly while flaunting his pride. The very terms of denial contain the seeds of attachment; denial belies indifference, is, indeed, the first step toward acceptance.

Similarly, *Brighton Rock,* whose background seems more suitable for Dante's infernal sufferers or Milton's proud demons than for inhabitants of contemporary England, is full of demonic characters, with Pinkie as a juvenile Satan and his followers as fallen angels. Pinkie himself, a pathological killer, is first cousin to the superman who thinks he can conquer everything in his way. Pinkie's vision is to be an Alexander of crime, to be a man-god; and, like Dostoyevsky's Raskolnikov, he conceives of himself as possessing powers which make him superior to those around him. "No more human contacts," he dreams, "other people's emotions washing at the brain—he would be free again: nothing to think about but himself." The only thing that matters in a world that went to pieces the day he saw his grunting parents tossing on their bed is self-satisfaction, self-appeasement: since they abandoned him to indulge their lonely passion, he will, in turn, abandon everyone else. Like the child he really is, he must gratify himself; and he must not be crossed, for he will kill to protect his interests. The chief difference between Pinkie and the "romantic" figures, like Raskolnikov and Julien Sorel, who preceded him, comes from Greene's recognition that the humility, the obedience, the sense of good and evil implicit in a former age, values threaded right into the social fabric, can no longer be taken for granted. Now, anything goes, and in such a society, the Pinkies will exist in ever greater numbers—they will become the norm, not the anomaly.

Even a sense of mortal sin cannot make Pinkie humble, and this force, Greene suggests, is the strongest that can be exerted upon him. Put another way: Pinkie is so far outside normality and so bizarre in his demands upon life that he functions beyond all laws of God and man, and even the law of God, so much stronger in effect upon Pinkie than that of man, is still inconclusive. The Pinkies are to that degree outside the control of human society. This is, according to Greene, a measure of the difficulty. If we wish to control them, we must leave it to God's law, which, while it may seem ineffective, is still the only force strong enough to penetrate someone like the satanical Pinkie.*

Raskolnikov, for example, could be reached through love of God, through love of a good woman, and through love of mother country (one way of saying family), but these values predicate a society that can affect a person; the values are still implicit in the society, still latent in the individual. But remove all these values, as Greene does, and the barriers fall. Such is the condition or atmosphere in which we meet Pinkie, or Scobie, Bendrix, Agent D., the whisky priest, James Raven (*This Gun for Hire,* 1936), Grünlich (*Stamboul Train,* 1932), Francis Andrews, Harry Lime (*The Third Man,* 1950), and several others: who is responsible? who can place strictures? who can judge? is Pinkie guilty?

Any substantial conclusions are apparently outside the area allowed to man; only God can answer by extending His mercy and salvation, Greene says, to those He feels worthy of it, and He may well extend grace to those who seem to deserve it least. As the priest tells Rose: " 'You can't conceive, my child, nor can I or anyone—the . . . appalling . . . strangeness of the mercy of God.' " When Rose mentions that Pinkie was a Catholic and knew

---

* In a novel that combines Greene's paradoxical belief with Conrad's nihilism, Gerald Hanley (in *Without Love,* 1957) writes that it is better to fight God and to sin in doing so than to feel nothing, "for the love of God is alive in that resentment of the struggler and we do not know the size of the hunger in the secret heart." Hanley's Mike Brennan is a Pinkie grown up, the "adolescent" of our times who will destroy and be destroyed because life offers him no other alternatives.

that he was doing wrong, that is, explicitly damning himself, the priest answers: " *'Corruptio optimi est pessima.'* " Then he continues: " 'I mean—a Catholic is more capable of evil than anyone. I think perhaps—because we believe in him—we are more in touch with the devil than other people. But we must hope,' he said mechanically, 'hope and pray.' " He claims that Pinkie's love, no matter what kind it was and no matter how filled with shreds of hatred and revulsion, is an indication of some goodness. Love is necessary; and who can tell what it means, no matter what the intention? Sometimes, one expresses love, as the wicked Frenchman (Charles Peguy) in the priest's little story, by seeking damnation in order to express sympathy with all the damned. This, too, is a kind of salvation in God's eyes. Unlike Milton who was anxious to explain the ways of God to man, Greene is eager to demonstrate that the ways of God must remain inexplicable.

Greene has staked everything on his "demonic hero," who, by turning all accepted values upside down, has come to understand God through knowledge of the devil. These heroes operate within a decay-saturated world, a world as much corrupted as that of Conrad's novels; yet unlike the heroes of the latter, they do not turn inward so much as upward or downward. In their attempt to transcend themselves through a knowledge of both God and the devil, they try to regain some sense of balance in a corrupted universe. In short, they seek God in what appears to be a devil-controlled universe. This is, in a way, their heroism. Yet throughout their martyrdom, they are fully aware of the puniness of their selves, aware of the baseness of their desires in contrast with the transcendency of their hopes. To "leap" the gap between the pride which damns and the humility which saves, they must suffer the pains of conscience; and in their suffering, they come to terms with their individual salvation.

As an attempt to regain a tragic view of the universe through the use of this kind of hero, Greene's novels have their limitations as well as their virtues. Greene believes strongly that, as he wrote, ". . . doubt and denial must be given their chance of self-expression. . . ." Yet the "leap" his characters make from earth to heaven is rarely effective, except, perhaps, in *The Power and the Glory,* and there the whisky priest *begins* as a man of God.

The transcendental apparatus is often in excess of what the figure can bear, for Greene's characters frequently cannot rise to the vision he has of their potential greatness. Unlike the Greek dramatist, Greene cannot draw upon an entire culture. The ideas he is anxious to develop are rarely alive within either the characters or those surrounding them. Therefore, everything becomes contrived: he must present a hero capable of commitment, surround him with the conditions which will make commitment possible, and provide temptations and counters; finally, he must make the reader believe in the "leap" that the hero will make to insure his salvation. And Greene must do all this without the aids that the Greek writer could take for granted. Nothing can be assumed.

Furthermore, we as readers are conditioned, more or less, to a literature in which these "leaps" are rarely taken, and to a life in which the "leap" itself is suspected of being factitious. We accept easily enough, for instance, Kafka's traps for his frustrated heroes, Conrad's crushing of his finest protagonists, Joyce's reduction of his characters to lower-middle class Dubliners, Lawrence's obsessive deification of gamekeepers, Hemingway's emphasis on hunters and bullfighters, matters now implicit in our literary culture; however, when Greene tries to go beyond to create an aristocracy of the spirit, we feel that tragedy now becomes subservient to religion. Yet, it is the serious reader of Kafka, Joyce, Conrad, and Lawrence whom Greene wants to engage, the very reader who will most damagingly question either his assumptions or his results, or more likely both.

If Greene had meant his several "quests for God" as contemporary symbols rather than as real acts of belief, then perhaps the difficulty would be partially removed. Our literary heritage being what it is, it is difficult indeed to accept a tragic vision as long as there is a "religious out." In just this area, Greene perhaps fails to convince. Although the spiritual struggles of his characters are remarkably effective, and although their tensions are similar to those of the greatest characters in literature—yet the "leap" that each takes, by its very nature, reduces the tragic content. The Greek hero had no redress once he had fallen: salvation was nowhere apparent. When salvation appears, tragedy becomes romance, and the rules change; though, obviously, Greene is concerned with the tragic and not the romantic. The fact that his characters obtain actual rewards or that reward is implicit in their existence diminishes tragic power, makes the author seem a meddling intruder. A more secular author like Conrad, for example, has Axel Heyst (*Victory*) recognize his guilt for having abandoned mankind in order to pursue solitude; but while he realizes his destructive attitude, this realization is not enough to save him. His sacrificial death is necessary.

In Greene's world, few are past saving. Even Pinkie, who has reached so far into the lower depths, can be saved because he did love at one time. The Christian attitude explicitly applied to the novel dilutes the tragic vision. Perhaps tragedy in its real sense can exist only in a world stripped of the Christian amenities, one in which heaven, paradise, and salvation are pleasant but meaningless terms; for the tragic man's fate, as Hardy well knew, is determined by his character. Give men even the limited "escape" that Greene permits his characters, and they forsake their tragic roles; no matter how severe their crime, they can still "leap" from their situation.

Greene's use of the "demonical hero" who can attain salvation through God's almost arbitrary use of grace, raises several interesting questions both to the religious and secular reader: what is the use of legal boundaries placed upon man if they are merely temporary and finally meaningless, if God may choose to ignore them in His judgment? is not someone like Ida (in *Brighton Rock*), a non-believer, preferable to someone like Pinkie, a warped believer, even though God may eventually choose to save Pinkie and damn Ida? if the kingdom of God is preferable to the kingdom of Man, is it not true that anything really does go, and that man's conduct, even when it is righteous, is then of little worth? if forgiveness, as Greene indicates, is forthcoming according to God's wishes, which no one may hope to understand, what is to prevent chaos, the frenzy of those who wait for God's judgment and flout Man's law? Is Greene perhaps more interested in saints than in people?

By indicating that God can save where's Man's devices fail, does not Greene claim the very kind of "inside" knowledge of God that he states it is impossible to have? Is there not implicit an underlying arrogance in his message, a lack of humility, especially in his claim that the Catholic more than anyone else is closer to the devil? Further, why should pain lead necessarily to belief?

And yet Greene has probably come closest of all "religious" novelists in English to retaining the terms of tragedy without forsaking a Christian framework. By working with sordidness, a commonplace in major twentieth-century fiction, Greene attempts to make his demonical heroes play the game of his secular contemporaries. Yet the very nature of the enterprise is partially self-defeating, even after one grants his great success in creating drama, tension, suspense, excitement, and intellectual sport. But this is not tragedy. In Greek tragedy the realization of one's wrongdoing was the crisis of one's life. The fall allowed no ascension. In Greene's world, the "fall" still permits redemption; in the universe there are rewards of which man may partake. If something can save the hero, whether he is demonical or not, he is not truly tragic.

In 1938, Greene traveled widely in Mexico and in the following year published *The Lawless Roads,* an account of his Mexican sojourn. In chapters five and six of that book, there occur several paragraphs about a drunken priest who held out against the police for ten years in Tabasco, a small province in the south of Mexico where the clergy had been proscribed. Greene describes him: "He was a little lost, poor man, a kind of Padre Rey [a married priest]; but who can judge what terror and hardship and isolation may have excused him in the eyes of God?" From the unequivocal, intense religious belief that Greene shows in *The Lawless Roads* comes the paradoxical faith of the priest; the author turns particularities of autobiography into a universalized fiction. While *The Lawless Roads* provides some of the facts and attitudes for the novel, the work of fiction demonstrates an imaginative breadth nowhere found in the travel book.

The Power and the Glory (first published as *The Labyrinthine Ways*) is concerned with the (by now common) theme of isolation. Greene's priest is, here, similar to Conrad's Jim; the chief difference is of course that the priest is actually being chased while Jim imagines Furies that exist only in his own consciousness.

But whether the Furies are inside or outside makes little significant difference, for the important element is the character's reaction to them. Step by step, the priest moves away from his former life; all familiar objects—clothes, materials for the mass, slips of paper from the past, even memories themselves—drop away, and like Jim he is stripped to his fears and weaknesses. What identity does a man have when he is deprived of everything he holds essential? Further, what identity does a priest have when he feels that even God's grace has forsaken him, and he is left floating in a spiritual purgatory, neither saved nor damned, simply uncertain of himself and of his relation to God? And, finally, what kinship can such a priest have with his worshipers when he feels he has failed them as much as he has failed himself and his God?

Greene's novel of the whisky priest pursues a theme similar to that of his other major novels and many of his entertainments, although its intensity here marks this as perhaps his finest book. Like Scobie, the priest is closest to God when sinning. To understand deity, Greene suggests, one must, like Job, always be tempted; the orthodox believer deprived of God's indulgence remains on the periphery of true faith. The true believer reaches out for the devil and instead finds God. Despite the commission of a mortal sin, he may find that God forgives him. Apparently more interested in evil than in good, Greene presents individuals, like Dostoyevsky's Ivan or some of Mauriac's "heroes," whose spirits become battlegrounds between the forces of God and the devil. Greene suggests the Manichean heresy: good and evil fight over man continually, and we are never sure who wins, for the ways of God, by their very nature, are inscrutable.

Greene's God is an enigmatical being who extends grace in ways that man can never understand, and when the priest offers this as his faith, the lieutenant justifiably thinks the priest is deceiving him. As one of the several parallels and opposites to the priest, the lieutenant exemplifies the political world, the commissar who has little use for the yogi. The battle between the priest and the lieutenant is a battle for the minds of men, as much as God and the devil battle for the mind of Ivan Karamazov. The lieutenant offers a new kind of church, one stripped of faith, superstition, and hope, one based solely on the material needs of the people. This is a church of the world, and the lieutenant is its ascetic priest.

In his asceticism, the lieutenant (unnamed, as the priest is unnamed) apes what he thinks should be the virtues of those he opposes. He simply transfers the values of the clerical orders to his own: no indulgence in sensory pleasure, no swerving from the path of righteousness, no guilt about the commission of a bad act in order to insure a future good, no qualms about effacing self in favor of the public welfare. In his doctrinaire political and economic beliefs, he challenges the church on its own grounds: the means justify the ends, and the battle is to the death. The lieutenant, in his priestly role, accepts everything the church stands for except the altar.

The priest, on the other hand, accepts little else but the altar. Greene leads us to believe that he was never a very devout priest, for he suffered from pride in the days when he was honored with good dinners and fine wines. He grew fat, and he expected obeisance as his right. He aligned himself with traditional power against the peasant. The lieutenant, however, will kill in order to help the peasants, often against themselves; and he is willing to shoot hostages if necessary in order to discover the hiding place of the last priest in the province. The lieutenant, thus, finds himself injuring those he has sworn to help; while the priest finds himself injuring the God he has sworn to love.

As a man of the people, the lieutenant is willing to die to effect his ideas—justice and equality for the peasants. As a man of God, the priest is afraid for his life and unsure about being a martyr to the church. Years of isolation have worn him down, so that he is unable and unwilling to call upon reserves. Consequently, the roles of the two men have been reversed. The lieutenant will sacrifice himself for his ideal—to free his people, despite themselves, from superstitions and the oppression of the church; the priest is also aware of an ideal but is unable to sacrifice himself for it. The lieutenant, the devil's agent, is strong in his desire to destroy God's image on earth, and the priest, God's representative, is weak in defending God's image. The priest constantly warns his admirers as well as the lieutenant not to judge the church and God by his own example, for he is a bad priest, but nevertheless, he suggests, the best the province has at the moment—in fact, the only one.

Yet God endures in the hearts of the people despite the militant activity against Him, and this persistence of course "proves" Greene's point. For just as God endures in the people's hearts, sullied though He may be by the visible church, so does He endure in the priest's heart, defiled though He may be there. Both the priest and the lieutenant are striving for sainthood, paradoxically, without either asceticism for the priest or humanitarianism for the lieutenant. But only the priest—because he is inevitably humbled by God—realizes how difficult it is to be a saint. The lieutenant, in his do-good arrogance, can never recognize this point. Thus, fundamentally, they must be different.

The lieutenant's world is predicated on the assumption that good men will always be forthcoming to perpetuate his ideal; but the priest suggests that there is no guarantee, for only belief can insure the humility that might prevent the persecution of the people in the name of enlightenment. This is the same point Conrad made in *Nostromo*—a novel, incidentally, that hangs heavily over *The Power and the Glory*: what will happen after Charles Gould's death when a man less dedicated to the silver mine takes over in the name of self-interest? What protections are there, then? There is, obviously, no possible answer. The priest says to the lieutenant: " 'It's no good your working for your end unless you're a good man yourself. And there won't always be good men in your party. Then you'll have all the old starvation, beating, getting rich anyhow.' "

When the lieutenant asks the priest's motives in staying when everyone else left, the latter replies using the same kind of paradox with which Jesus answered his questioners. The priest admits his deadly pride, and says that like the angels he fell because he conceived of himself as godlike. And he argues, well-schooled, it seems, in Greene's peculiar theology, that precisely because it was dangerous and difficult, he remained out of pride, and not to further God's interest. He denies following God's wishes and trying to become a martyr and saint. Greene reminds us that one does not necessarily serve God by accepting danger in His name, for God's grace can operate incomprehensibly. Perhaps, then, only the weak, the criminal, the evil, the proud are saved; damnation awaits the pious, the humble, and the devout.

Had Greene left the priest at this point, involved in his indecisions, then the novel would have been compelling. As long as the priest and the lieutenant oppose each other, all the ironies and paradoxes of their conflict are dramatically forceful. Once the priest convinces the lieutenant of his sincerity and the fickleness of God's ways, the novel declines into a tract, and the character of the lieutenant loses sharpness. There is much ineffective sentiment in the priest's recognition of the lieutenant as a good fellow and in the lieutenant's realization that the priest is also interested in the peasants. The two cross each other's paths as brothers, Greene indicates here, one looking after the spirit, the other after the body; and sadly, one must die—Cain must kill Abel. At this point the novel becomes effusive, and the final section devoted to the saving of Luis, who had first shown loyalty to the lieutenant and then to the priest, is as false as the priest's former agony was real. Only the character in conflict without any chance of salvation can provide the tragic tone that this novel requires, unless it is to sink into bathos and melodrama. Greene evidently became seduced by doctrine, and, unwilling to desert his paradox, marred with specious arguments the dramatic tension of the earlier parts of the novel. For the priest held in suspension is a believable character; as soon as he finds God by finding himself, however, he is less effective dramatically than spiritually. With the priest's ultimate salvation, which only a believer can accept, the novel becomes meaningless as a work of art.

In many ways, nevertheless, despite its flaws, *The Power and the Glory* is a political-religious novel in the manner of *The Brothers Karamazov* and *The Magic Mountain*. The surface detail, as in every political novel, masks the interplay of antinomies: the political versus the religious, the dictator versus the saint. Greene twists the opposition from its usual course by making a whisky priest with an illegitimate child God's representative on earth; and even more than merely representative, the sole representative in the entire state, God's last man to struggle against His earthly enemies. This is indeed a frail Jesus among the sinners, a debilitated Jesus who must do God's bidding when he is unsure of what he bids for, an anguished Jesus who is as much magnetized by the world he opposes as by God's will. The use of the whisky priest to represent the best that faith has to offer conveys both the strengths and weaknesses of the novel. Perhaps only in Scobie of *The Heart of the Matter* was Greene able to present a weak man with so much of a burden, the burden of sin and grace and heaven and hell. The problem, however, is more fierce with the priest than even with Scobie: for Greene is asking how a man dedicated to God must live in the world under circumstances in which God's aid is tenuous.

Like most powerful novels of the individual and the surroundings he lives in, *The Power and the Glory* is loosely existential, in much the same way as the work of Mauriac and Dostoyevsky. In all three, their Christian existentialism does not preclude a secular view from becoming attractive, and the existential quality of their novels often takes the character of a tension between those opposing values. In brief, how does one live, priest or not, when faith tells one thing while experience tells another? how does one live when heart and mind are split, and neither can follow the other? finally, how can one live when vacillation and weakness are more apparent than the strength one needs to survive? Scobie and the whisky priest both recognize that the only way to achieve salvation is by attaining martyrdom or sainthood, or both. Scobie tries to reach his through suicide, an unforgivable sin, and the priest through offering Catholic blessings to a dying American gangster, who refuses them.

It is a further part of Greene's irony that his priest should risk everything over an American criminal who is dying in the province and needs absolution (for what?). There is of course only a small difference between them, and when the priest offers conditional absolution to the criminal, he proffers what he hopes God will offer him: at least conditional absolution. Greene writes: "At the best, it was only one criminal trying to aid the escape of another— whichever way you looked, there wasn't much merit in either of them." Like Jim's relationship with Gentleman Brown in the Patusan section of *Lord Jim,* the connection between the murderous American and the Mexican priest disallows righteousness on the part of a man with a past. Like Jim, the priest recognizes that his past frailty disarms him, and that he can offer only the minimum of what God allows. To confess people, to offer them moral solace, even to give absolution—all these are mockeries when given by a bad priest. The criminal who is hounded by the authorities is a vague existential parallel to the priest who is also hounded by the authorities. It is not fortuitous that Greene has the priest captured while he is trying to save the one man who would seem farthest from God's salvation. The priest boasts that as long as there is a single man damned in the state, then he too will be damned. To save the man least able to save himself is a mark of his devotion, and for him to save a fellow criminal is a mark of God's irony in a universe that remains inscrutable.

As the priest moves further from his original identity, as he tries, with increasing difficulty, to reconcile the pride that damns with the humility that saves, as he almost literally is chased by the "hound of heaven and earth," he gradually finds out what he is. This element of knowing oneself, which usually comes from within a Greene character under the stress of severe external events, takes the form of repentance that God requires, and is similar in its way to the recognition that the Greek dramatist required. The chase or something akin to it forces an inner response previously ignored by the character. Only under stress does the priest recognize what a proud and vain man he was in the past when he courted good meals, comfortable quarters, and slaked his own thirst rather than that of lost souls. Only under stress does he see how far short of God's perfection he has fallen. And only under stress does he feel for mankind the kind of pity that is allied to charity. The violence of many of Greene's novels is perhaps predicated on this belief: that only violence or stress or chaotic conditions can upset a man's complacency and create out of his former indifference the kind of belief necessary for his salvation.

As I mentioned above, this attitude is not dissimilar to a tragic one; indeed it would be compellingly tragic if not for ultimate salvation which eases over the crises of real tragedy. The stress of the chase here is the stress of a disclosure in a Greek play; and after this recognition of what he is, the character steps out a new person, stripped of indifference and complacency. This new person is usually completely crushed, but we are led to believe that he is preferable to the former being who lived by illusions. The "resurrected" man, while virtually destroyed, must gather the shreds of his now unfamiliar life and try to survive through self-knowledge; he can no longer disguise what he is and gain strength by virtue of his disguise. He must live with the truth about himself even if it destroys him. The Greek dramatist stopped at this point, and the tragic element was obvious. Greene goes one step further and offers God's salvation to the man resurrected by his recognition of what he is.

At this point, the secular reader is troubled as the novels lose cogency as literature. The force of narrative and character, even for the secular reader, was obvious. The intimation, however, that a miracle has perhaps occurred, that a damned man may be saved, and that God's grace can operate in ways unknown to man and therefore must remain inexplicable are perhaps the necessities of faith but barely the stuff of novels filled with dramatic irony. Devotional, religious, godly, all these things a novel concerned with salvation may be, but when they predominate to the exclusion of all else, then they enfeeble the drama. In attempting to reconcile Christian romanticism with the starkness of Greek tragedy, Greene has tried to write cosmic novels in which the author asks many of the significant questions. That Greene has attempted so much and achieved the power of nearly first-rate novels is not to be denied; but to claim more for them is to read in the religious hopes of the reader.

One only raises these disclaimers because Greene does try to provide some final solution, tenuous and diluted as he recognizes it must be in the modern world. The priest answers the lieutenant that it is not advisable to give the poor man power, because then he stands less chance of gaining heaven. "It's better to let him die in dirt and wake in heaven—so long as we don't push his face in the dirt." Greene offers the traditional paradox of religious humanitarianism—help people who need it but not too much, for they may lose their souls with prosperity: an answer that is obviously insufficient to the secular reader and to the lieutenant whose own brand of expedience is insufficient as well. The novel's entire force is vitiated by the priest's verbalization of his ideas, for how trite they are in juxtaposition to his personal agonies. This is a novel about just that feeling—agony—and when it becomes explanatory, discursive, argumentative, it loses its meaning, which is simply that men find it difficult not only to live up to their ideals but to have ideals at all.

VI

The World of Elizabeth Bowen

EVEN THE POSSIBILITY of being a hero or committing heroic acts is far removed from Elizabeth Bowen's world. Like Graham Greene, she is interested in good and evil, but her statement is more muted. The difference between the two authors would seem, in brief, to be that between a man's vision of the world—brutal, heroic in scope, broad in implication—and a woman's—more immediately personal and closer to the facts of daily reality. Life which for Greene because of Christianity is heroic is for Miss Bowen trivial and frustrating.

Nevertheless, they are both concerned with good and evil, although sermon is much closer to Greene, as it is to Joyce Cary and C. P. Snow, than to Miss Bowen. Still, not unlike her most apparent literary predecessor, Jane Austen, she weighs her morality carefully and concocts a curious kind of moral universe; but unlike Jane Austen, Miss Bowen's good people are not always rewarded nor are the bad ridiculed. Often, the good are rebuffed and humiliated, are shown that their sympathies and values are meaningless in a mechanical universe. The innocent and the good suffer for the crass casuality of the guilty and the evil, but even to use these terms is to suggest contrasts stronger than those Miss Bowen provides.

One of the obvious qualities of her heroines is their frailness, their ability to bend. When we think of them physically, we think of somewhat angular, finely-made young women and teen-agers; girls who do not carry too much flesh, although often they have good figures; girls who still retain something of the cradle and the child's room and the pains of adolescence. Frequently, they are adolescents. Their ability to bend themselves into protean positions, then, is almost physical. We think of them as we do of curves, especially concave lines—this is especially true of Portia of *The Death of the Heart*—and exactly as they are flexible physically, so emotionally and psychologically they try to fit themselves into and around other people.

With heroines of this sort, an author will be more concerned with fusing characters than with differentiating sharply between them. Even the author's sense of good and evil will tend to merge them one with the other; the conflict will become resolved less in clear colors than in various shades of darks-and-whites, in muted grays.

This, essentially, is what we find in Elizabeth Bowen's novels: a sense of good and evil blunted by the fact that the two qualities are really aspects of the same thing. We find, also, that the innocent, good person is very often the cause of the evil and guilt that is manifest in his antagonist. Frequently, the good person is drawn to the evil one, for good and evil in this scheme lie within the framework of what are considered "normal" human relationships; and humiliation becomes the sole vehicle of evil action.

This view of human nature places Miss Bowen much closer to the feminine tradition in English literature than it does to the masculine. Like her early nineteenth-century predecessor, she believes in clarity of detail, precision of phrase, and irony of expression, in exploiting the humorous while eliminating the sentimental, in destroying the hypocritical and the vain, in maintaining the traditions of the past against the incursions of the present. Yet she cannot be certain of what is right, as was Jane Austen, and when her doubts do appear, she finds herself close to the assumptions of the twentieth-century novelist: unsure of what success entails, doubtful of what love is, afraid that romance can be easily maimed or destroyed, aware that relationships hang precariously on unknown threads whose clues are mysterious. In brief, she finds herself in the world of Virginia Woolf and Katherine Mansfield.

Nevertheless, Elizabeth Bowen's novels are more a measure of the past than of the present, more a mirror of a still sharply-remembered childhood than of a problematical and uncertain adulthood. What she focuses upon in her most brilliant novel, *The Death of the Heart,* she has repeated in her major fiction before and after: the loneliness of the teen-ager; the isolation of the child amid adults who seem to lack feeling, hope, or illusions (one thinks of James's *What Maisie Knew*); the need to reach out and find love, even while one realizes that he cannot successfully "connect," to use E. M. Forster's sense of the word; the impossibility of depending upon anyone except oneself, the necessity of cultivating one's own resources. Obviously, Miss Bowen is an intensely feminine novelist, showing allegiance to authors as different as Fanny Burney, Jane Austen, George Eliot, Virginia Woolf, and Katherine Mansfield, with more than passing reference to Henry James, perhaps the most feline of male writers. Since, therefore, she is concerned with the intangibles of the human personality, she is often inadequately described as a novelist of sensibility.

In *Notes on Writing a Novel,* Miss Bowen defined the object of a novel as the "non-poetic statement of a poetic truth," further qualifying that the "essence of a poetic truth is that no statement of it can be final." By poetic truth, she undoubtedly means those elements within as well as outside people which remain undefinable except in the kind of approximation which language allows the novelist. Thus, in talking about love, human relationships, and "connections" between people, she tries to indicate emotions that lie beneath language; the poetic truth of these feelings must, however, be caught by "non-poetic statements." These are the limitations within which every novelist must work. At her most successful, Miss Bowen has created women who represent the filminess of existence, who convey the daily pains involved in the act of living under conditions which stifle what one really feels. In one way, all of Miss Bowen's novels are concerned with "the death of the heart," which is for her the chief "poetic truth."

Like many of her contemporaries, Miss Bowen is not attempting the big novel; as she remarked in her Preface to her collection of "war stories," *Ivy Gripped the Steps and Other Stories* (1946), she is delineating particulars, to the almost total exclusion of the generalized statement necessary for the all-inclusive novel:

> Painters have painted, and photographers who were artists have photographed, the tottering lacelike architecture of ruins, dark mass-movements of people, and the untimely brilliance of flaming skies. I cannot paint or photograph like this—I have isolated, I have made for the particular, spot-lighting faces or cutting out gestures that are not even the faces or gestures of great sufferers. This is how I am, how I feel, whether in war or peace time, and only as I am and feel can I write.

By centering many of her novels around the sensibility of a young girl or woman, Miss Bowen, by this very means, reduces the world of experience with which she will be concerned; for to maintain realism, she must sift through the girl's mind only those aspects of reality which can be received and acted upon. Furthermore, by keeping this young girl at the center of the novel, the novelist has forsaken any possibility of enlarging the scope of vision through more demanding personalities. This method is of course a conscious way of restricting one's canvas, as her remarks above indicate, a limited canvas which can by its very restriction provide an intensity that a more diffuse technique might disallow. There are, then, virtues in Miss Bowen's manner of approach, although, as I indicated earlier, she will not try for the big themes, the large movements, the major rhythms that the novel until the last two or three decades has demanded.

Moreover, before cataloguing the virtues of her method, we should point out in precisely what areas it fails. This type of novel has to eliminate all large social questions; it can never be socially realistic, either in Dreiser's or Joyce's sense, for that type of novel requires the breadth of a panoramic vision. Joyce Cary, with too little panoramic skill, tried to attain just this breadth in his political trilogy, but failed for the simple reason that his skills lay closer to those of a writer like Miss Bowen than, for example, Mann, Dostoyevsky, or the Conrad of *Nostromo*. Thus, the large issues of the day, whether treated directly as in the sociological novel, or indirectly as in the psychological novel which generalizes on the sociologist's particulars, will not be represented in Miss Bowen's canon. Her novels with their classicism of form and their attempt at exclusion will return, instead, to the relatively uncomplicated structures of a hundred and fifty years before.

This is not to say that character cannot be superbly created within Miss Bowen's terms; it is merely to claim that character as such will be quite different from what we find in Lawrence, Joyce, Conrad, Virginia Woolf, and E. M. Forster. Only Graham Greene and Samuel Beckett, among major writers of the forties and fifties, have stayed within the traditions of the psychological creations of their predecessors. Miss Bowen, like Henry Green and Joyce Cary, to mention only two contemporaries, frequently has chosen to give her characters airiness instead of depth, insecurity instead of subversive thoughts, awkwardness instead of cosmic maladjustment, isolation in family terms instead of eternal loneliness. Consequently, her young girls begin to recur monotonously, their afflictions frequently unchanged, their development fixed, their powers of reaction limited.

From her first novel, *The Hotel* (1927) through *A World of Love* (1955), some seven novels* and several volumes of short stories and miscellaneous works later, Miss Bowen has caught the relatively unappetizing lives of her characters as they try to make sense of an existence which is neither calamitous nor evil, at times merely boring. Like the Henry Green of *Party Going,* Miss Bowen in her early novels has caught (another Green title) postwar "dissolutes" who do not have the energy or forthrightness even to dissipate on a large scale. Their agonies are minor, their worries marginal, their gossip tedious. The world of *The Hotel* is full of such chitchat; the lives of its inhabitants are summed up in one Victor Ammering, who, with a splendid war record, a public school and university background, is unable to obtain a job, and now at thirty hangs around waiting for something to happen to him. Give him wit, and he would be a typical

---

* *The Hotel* (1927); *The Last September* (1929); *Friends and Relations* (1931); *To the North* (1932); *The House in Paris* (1936); *The Death of the Heart* (1939); *The Heat of the Day* (1949); *A World of Love* (1955)

young man from an Aldous Huxley novel of the twenties; for example, with more ego and a desire to write poetry, he would be Denis of *Crome Yellow* (1921); with inventive ability and a beard, he would be Gumbril Junior of *Antic Hay* (1923).

The hotel itself becomes background for post-war uselessness, an ennui that reduces everything to loveless romances, gossip, and meaningless meals; a kind of unmagical mountain in its isolation from a healthier reality (which we never see), the hotel is an epitome of the world.

Into this world of frustration, lost hopes, awkward and marginal people, Miss Bowen thrusts Sydney Warren, her own version of Jane Austen's Elizabeth Bennet, dissatisfied, intelligent, bored, disappointed, and marriageable. Despite her intelligence, she is desperate in her loneliness and in her marginal position in the hotel world; an older model of Portia (*The Death of the Heart,* 1939), Lois (*The Last September,* 1929), Theodora (*Friends and Relations,* 1931), Pauline (*To the North,* 1932), Jane (*A World of Love,* 1955), and a contemporary of Karen Michaelis (*The House in Paris,* 1936), she waits out her lonely existence without much hope. In grasping at anything and anyone, she accepts an offer of marriage from an unworldly clergyman twice her age, naïve, occasionally hysterical, a clown rather than a man to be taken seriously, a protector in the most dubious sense. In a Jane Austen novel, he is of course the man the heroine with good sense must reject, as Elizabeth Bennet rejects Collins, a man accepted only by a desperate minor character using him to avoid spinsterhood. That Sydney considers him seriously indicates her inability to cope with life. Like Huxley's and Fitzgerald's young men, she is a postwar waif, innocent and immature despite her sad wittiness.

Few of Miss Bowen's succeeding heroines are as aware of the world as Sydney Warren; most are aware only of themselves. Typical is the young girl, Lois, of *The Last September,* a slight lyrical novel that some English critics inexplicably rank among Miss Bowen's best, even ahead of *The Death of the Heart* and *The Heat of the Day.* Lois moves silently among the Anglo-Irish establishment that lives precariously amid violence during the occupation of Ireland prior to the Treaty of 1922. Symbolic to a degree of the curious and frustrating situation is the temporary attachment that Lois forms to a young English officer; a somewhat callow version of Sydney Warren, Lois is caught in the general uneasiness that surrounds the conflict. All emotions are below the surface, so far below, indeed, that one often doubts their existence. As Miss Bowen later realized, when her powers deepened (they rarely broadened), the throb from below must at least be suggested by surface detail, although not until *The House in Paris* was she able to dramatize the surge and pull of powerful feelings which rarely rise to the surface.

In *Friends and Relations* (1931), which followed as Miss Bowen's third novel in three years, the superficialities of social comedy predominate; the world and characters of the later novels are still in embryo. Nevertheless, in the conflict between the generations, she was foreshadowing what was to appear in her major work; as yet, however, the dramatization and presentation of the problem which come from the artist's full commitment to his material are lacking.

The world of incomplete relationships which *Friends and Relations* demonstrates is deepened and given tragic trappings in *To the North,* which appeared the following year. Here, as in her earlier novels, Miss Bowen connects people in meaningful relationships only to separate them before these relationships can mature. Nearly all attempts at understanding, love, and emotional attachment lead either to misunderstanding, or to alternating love and hate, or to frustration of emotional needs. Even after a character recognizes that he must give himself, he cannot find anyone who will accept him. Since the demands made usually differ from what is offered, the giver and taker lack rapport; their lack of connection becomes, in her major novels, a symbolic misunderstanding that separates Miss Bowen's world from Jane Austen's and relates her themes to those of the twentieth century.

In *To the North,* we have what seems to be a comedy of manners in the style of Evelyn Waugh, except that Miss Bowen lacks the sense of parody that goes with this kind of comedy. What Miss Bowen is really concerned with is the impact that an ambitious, ruthless barrister, Markie Linkwater, has on two young women, Emmeline Summers and Cecilia Summers. Mysteriously possessed, Markie is alternately ambiguous and lucid, desperate and childish, witty and demanding. He is a disturbing male force, one who creates situations and sets up conditions that cannot be met by Emmeline in a normal manner; she gives more than he wishes to receive, or gives what he doesn't need.

With Markie, Miss Bowen has a new kind of character, really the first of her unsuccessful male characters who go beyond the role of lover. Markie foreruns Max of *The House in Paris* and Robert Kelway and Harrison of *The Heat of the Day*. These characters remain partially unsuccessful, for their apparent impenetrability is an indication that the author is willing to settle for mystery when she cannot clarify. Markie, like Max and Robert, is the kind of character with whom she is relatively helpless; a male of inexplicable motivations and intentions, he remains beyond the pale of what society sustains.

Evidently, Emmeline, Markie's mistress, is also caught by a frenzy of emotions which she, too, does not understand, for rather than lose Markie she kills both of them in a car accident. This bright and sparkling beautiful woman who runs a travel bureau, who is willfully emancipated and moves as she wishes among the successful and the attractive, is compulsive, self-destructive, obsessed, desperate, characteristics which appear to operate almost independently of the social creature called Emmeline Summers. Yet, as Miss Bowen develops her novel, Emmeline never quite lives up to the feelings expected of her or what the situation demands.

Her sister-in-law, the widowed and beautiful Cecilia, on the other hand, has met and rejected Markie; her meat is not such a ruthless young man but the socially acceptable although slightly eccentric Julian Towers, a man lacking both the destructive drives and peculiar energies of Markie. This kind of affair, the one between Cecilia and Julian, is suitable only for comedy, as Miss Bowen must have realized; for in her next novel, *The House in Paris* (1936), she continues the subversive love affair, as it were, of Markie and Emmeline and writes her first tragedy. Here, in this her own favorite novel, Markie is translated loosely into Max Ebhart, ambitious, ruthless in personal relationships, curiously charming, intense in his European-Jewish manner, and obsessed by thoughts and motives he is evidently unable to control. Despite the possibilities of a brilliant future, Max commits suicide when, apparently hypnotized by Mme Fisher, he breaks off his engagement to Naomi Fisher to marry Karen Michaelis. In Max, Miss Bowen has one of her potentially most interesting characters, a man whose motivation lies deep beneath the smooth surface of his social behavior.

In this novel, which is, incidentally, a *tour de force* of technical improvisation, all the strengths and weaknesses of Miss Bowen's methods are manifest. *The House in Paris* is such a powerful work because it forced a commitment of Miss Bowen's powers that no previous novel had elicited. Until this novel, she had, as it were, drifted with her talents, writing superficial comedy or depicting young romantic lovers, failing to sustain people in their most desperate moments. If anything, the situation in *The House in Paris* is desperate, and made more so by the curious children who pass through the house and provide an indirect comment upon the antics and faults of the adults. The children are like flotsam and jetsam that have floated up from the social wreck. Surely, Leopold, that precocious offspring of Max and Karen, an unlooked for and unwanted phenomenon that is forming in Karen's womb as Max kills himself, is a constant reminder of how the adults of the world orphan their children. Miss Bowen has herself remarked that Leopold is her favorite character because of his grittiness in standing up to an adult world that has engulfed him in its careless evil.

Leopold, along with Henrietta, the other child temporarily in the house in Paris, is vulnerable and terribly alone despite his confident exterior. Although both children present surfaces quite different from the fearful, lonely, and wounded individuals that they are, each is vulnerable to everything. Leopold's position is terrifying. As a child frozen within himself and isolated in a house that rings with sad memories, all of which bear upon him, Leopold is truly parentless, unwanted. Like Portia of *The Death of the Heart* (1939), Leopold came along as an accident, something that upset all plans and defied solution. What was almost casual becomes an explosion, and Leopold, precocious and absurd, is shunted around. Yet, what increases the terror of the situation is that everyone *means* well for Leopold; but no one can reach him.

As a nasty reminder of a passion that went wrong, as an unnecessary adjunct to a brief flareup that defied convention and morality, Leopold is all defenses, all awareness, all consciousness. With his Jewish blood (from Max), he seems more sensitive, more outside than the others. On him, as they all feel, the sins of the parents have been visited; and yet Miss Bowen does not sentimentalize Leopold. As precocious as Henry James's Maisie, another child surrounded by expedient adults, Leopold is not easy to take, what with his guarded manner, his adult sense of evil, and the roving immaturity that keeps poking through to make him miserable.

The house in Paris becomes, then, a place of hate, thwarted love, frustrated emotions in which man's feelings never find satisfaction. All relationships that fill the house—the house, ironically, before Max's suicide, is an expensive finishing school—are tortuous and unhappy, incomplete, blocked before they can mean anything. Inhabiting the house are Naomi, who finds her entire world nullified, and her mother, who must destroy everything that crosses her path. The two women are similar in their differences: Naomi attempts to do good at the expense of herself, and her mother to do evil, also at the expense of herself. Both sustain themselves with unhappiness; both negate life at its simplest, and both are willing to perish if they can remain within character.

All the persons in the novel, then, operate at a pitch close to hysteria. The entire narrative works toward the big scene when Karen, having stolen Max from her friend Naomi and then having pushed the child of that affair upon the martyr of the house in Paris, will return to face Naomi and claim Leopold. In the first part of the novel, the reader's present, Leopold arrives at the house and we are led to believe that his mother is coming for him; in the second part, through a long flashback we discover how he comes to be there; in the third, Miss Bowen returns to the reader's present in the house in Paris and we see Ray Forrestier, now Karen's husband, come instead of her. The potentially big scene is avoided: Naomi and Karen do not confront each other.

Despite Miss Bowen's avoidance of the emotional potential,

nevertheless, underlying the novel there is a kind of sadness that seems fresh and new. To define the quality of sadness is one of Miss Bowen's motifs in all her work, but too often the quality becomes lost in trivial characters. In this novel, sadness becomes a way of life, for Karen and Naomi in the older generation, for Leopold in the younger. The quality of sadness is best defined by one's degree of isolation, a fact that Miss Bowen indeed demonstrates as well in her non-fiction. In *Bowen's Court* (1942), her long history of her ancestral family home in County Cork, she writes of her own childhood, her father gone because of temporary mental illness, her mother dying:

When, leaving the steps, I returned to the library, I could see from its look that my mother would not come back. Indomitable loneliness once more reigned; the weather reflected itself in the glass bookcases of what appeared to be a finally empty room. My grandfather Robert's billiard table now blocked the library: I got out the faded billiard balls and pelted them rapidly up and down. (p. 315)

The lonely child in the large, empty County Cork home, with its vast memories of the past extending back hundreds of years, becomes, in one way, the lonely Leopold in the large house in Paris, tended by the martyred Naomi Fisher, with Mme. Fisher, a kind of revenging evil spirit, dying upstairs. In this situation, a lonely child is absurd, for often the problem is not how to love him or how to make him love, but simply what to do with him.

Miss Bowen is concerned with the intensity of personal isolation against familiar backgrounds, like the loneliness everyone feels in the house in Paris or what Karen feels when she meets Max on the French or English coast:

There are degrees in being alone with someone. It was not till they had driven down to Sandgate hill—not till they were, even, clear of Sandgate itself, on that flat stretch of road above the beach, passing cream-coloured houses with gardens of tamarisks—that she saw what made them completely alone for the first time: there being no sun. . . . Till today, they had not, when alone, ever been two; always either three or one. Now, what they did was cut off from any other things, their silence related to them only. (p. 149)

Unlike Conrad, for example, whose characters leak out their lonely lives in cosmic isolation, against the background of strange islands and merciless sea and sky, Miss Bowen puts her characters into relatively familiar surroundings, particularly those filled with sad memories, and then carves in bas-relief the isolated individual. Her method is, of course, more restricted and low-pitched, but at the same time more personal, and frequently more terrifying.

While the virtues of *The House in Paris* are obvious—its intensity, its tender and penetrating scenes involving the children, its evocation of scene—nevertheless, Miss Bowen is less sure when handling the adult characters. The irrational, the obsessive, the subversive—all these qualities are outside what she can examine and control. In children, she can reach understandingly into the crazy quilt of their isolation and their yearning, but in adults the same method falls short of definition.

The problems that underlie Max's suicide go further than the superficial motivation the author provides. Max leaves the scene abruptly, as though Miss Bowen were compelled to get rid of him without too much explanation. Yet the manner of his death, the cutting of his wrists, is so different from what one expects of the man that the reader wonders if he has really met the character. Miss Bowen fails to provide precisely those objective correlatives that would make Max's suicide plausible. He does not seem committed to Naomi in such a life-and-death manner that breaking from her to marry Karen would cause suicide. Even the strange hold that Mme. Fisher retains over him does not justify what he does, despite her ability to upset his equanimity.

So too, Naomi Fisher. Evidently, she feels in excess of what is presented—in her silence, inner turmoil is dammed below the surface—and yet, Miss Bowen's reticence or inability to probe further leaves Naomi undefined, merely a cold woman whom everybody can use and misuse. Naomi seems cut out to die for others, but the intense undercurrents that must be coursing in her are rarely tapped. Her desires are reduced to nothing. She seems to justify suffering, in some inexplicable way, as a mode of life.

Curiously, this very kind of authorial reticence in handling emotive characters works exceptionally well in *The Death of the*

Heart, for here there are simply lonely people, not suicides or martyrs; the emotions are deep but well contained. Miss Bowen picks up the "lonely child" theme in the career of Portia, another "ridiculous" creation whose presence demands not only love but also logistics: what to do with her now that she is here.

The novel is also about living: how to organize one's life, how to live up to situations that one's personality and style have created, how to come to terms with other people, how to recognize their differences and uniqueness—how, in short, to be a person. All this is from the point of view of Portia Quayne, a gawky, gauche, charming but exasperating, innocent but knowing young lady of sixteen. Portia is the center of what everyone eventually talks about, and she is the one through whom we find out about the others. They, the others, gain their direction and substance from the way they react to Portia; this shift in focus is indeed one of the triumphs of the book.

This frail, concave girl has the kind of innocent mind, guileless, yet frightening in its penetration, that can disentangle motives and actions and probe the center of people. Huckleberry Finn, perhaps the indirect ancestor of these "innocent" adolescents, has a mind of this sort, although his innocence is somewhat different from Portia's. Like her, he is wary and understands motives, but he is able to act for himself and protect his interests with shrewd counterthrusts. Portia shares his awareness but little of his deftness.

Portia is really what Virginia Woolf must have been as a child. Mrs. Ramsay (*To the Lighthouse*), moreover, is Portia grown up, and Mr. Ramsay is a composite of Thomas and Anna, Portia's half brother and his wife. Like Mrs. Ramsay, Portia reaches out for love and understanding and encounters reason, logic, barriers. Her position as an unwanted love-child denies her what she desires; her origin—she is the offspring of Thomas' father at an advanced age by a not very bright younger woman—would be humorous, indeed, the stuff of farce, if not for the presence of Portia herself.

Like any person who desires love, Portia has an idealized conception of the world: that is, since she is ready to offer love herself (it is, obviously, the only thing she has to offer), she interprets the world in terms of the love it can offer her. People are either loving, understanding, and sympathetic—either they are this kind of human being—or they are not human; there is no room for compromise. According to Portia, Anna and Thomas are less than full human beings, although we as readers may feel they are human in their very inability to understand this child. Nevertheless, so much do we accept Portia's view of life, as well as her desire for love, that we are tempted to apprehend life through her eyes.

One of the brilliant turns of the novel comes when we realize that Portia tortures everyone she comes into contact with, until he either offers her what she wants or brutally rejects her. Acting as conscience for all, she is an emotional scapegoat, a purge for their best and worst. The opening passage, with its superb evocation of frailty and evanescence, foreshadows the whole: "That morning ice, no more than a brittle film, had cracked and was now floating in segments. These tapped together or, parting, left channels of dark water, down which swans in slow indignation swam." The brittle ice of the Quayne home has been split apart to allow the figure of Portia, that indignant swan, to swim through. Later, the swans—like those indifferent birds in Yeats' "The Wild Swans at Coole"—become a kind of leitmotif indicative of Portia, indignant yet gentle, rejected yet full of warm emotions, isolated yet hugged by others' thoughts.

As Portia reaches out for love, she is juxtaposed to one character after another, each of whom is represented by the way he reacts to her. The first is Eddie, the least likely person to offer anything to her or to anyone else. Eddie is self-oriented, unaware of many things, directed by the feeling that he is irresistible, but mostly compounded of a mixture of disillusion and expedience that is a direct counterpart to Portia's trust and sincerity. Eddie is after the Fall, Portia before. He seems never to have been either a child or an adult; he rarely trusts anyone and rarely has an ideal or a thought not self-directed. He hangs on to anyone who will support him, and he is attracted to Portia *because* of her innocence, *because* of her sexlessness. Portia is necessary for Eddie simply because she provides no problems: her body is a child's, her mind an adolescent's. She is company without conflict, and she is not supposed to question him. The mere fact that he could never go to bed with her gives him some relief; with her, he hopes to relax into self-importance.

Eddie is another of Miss Bowen's useless young men having nothing but a kind of devilish charm. Like Markie Linkwater, Eddie seems to have sold himself to the devil at birth, and to have obtained little in return. Although he uses Portia for his own comfort, he completely misunderstands her need for him. He does not realize that Portia has idealized him, that his physical being is not for her that of a man, but of a father figure her own age. Even when she tries to kiss him, to Eddie's disgust, she wants to demonstrate love, not physicality in itself. When Portia kisses, she is awkward, sexless, unphysical, the embodiment of innocence; she can only be a sweet sister or a loving daughter, not a woman with a woman's functions, as Eddie cruelly impresses upon her. Her lack of physical attraction is simply another way of isolating her, as much as Eddie's uselessness and obsessive insincerity isolate him.

Portia's rejection by Anna and Thomas, although on somewhat different grounds, partakes, however, of the same frame of mind. The death of the heart penetrates to every aspect of Portia's environment, but especially to her home with her half brother and his wife, Anna, who does not love him. All of Anna's love, or what she is capable of, was directed toward her former lover, Robert Pidgeon, whose name constantly turns up as a mockery of her marriage to Thomas. This was her sole passion, although Pidgeon would not marry Anna, or even take her seriously. The memory from the past unsettles her relationship with Thomas, and the elegant house at 2 Windsor Terrace is a loveless one. Curiously, Thomas is almost as much a stranger in his own home as Portia. Whenever a situation is about to develop that he cannot handle, he retreats to his study and putters around under the illusion that he is doing important work. Then, when the situation has cleared, he re-enters the life of the house, released, so to speak, from his room.

Anna herself has been isolated by her marriage—through a juxtaposition of characters, Miss Bowen is able to show how they overlap and share the problems of each other—and would, if she were able to feel, find consolation in Portia. However, their meeting sympathetically would mean that "heart" were possible, that a connection could take place; but the tragedy of the novel is that people similarly isolated and alone cannot reach each other even in their most fundamental needs. Anna wanders the large house alone, befriended only by St. Quentin, the Jamesian novelist, and he himself manifests an Olympian coldness, a kind of aloof sympathy which is not designed to warm anyone's heart.

Portia's very background has been one that has forced the strangeness of present familial relationships. Her father was divorced from his wife late in life and then isolated from his former wife and from his son, Thomas. He circles around the group, unwanted, no one knowing what to do about this wandering old man who fell into a passionate affair with a weepy woman who is now, somehow inexplicably, his. Living in shadows, creeping up on Thomas' home, he has been exiled from his own past life. Irene herself is an exile for having lived with Mr. Quayne and caused the divorce. The offspring of such a marriage can be nothing but an excrescence—what does one do with it? where does one put it?

With the sins of her father visited upon her, Portia is attracted by the only people she can associate with: the marginal, statusless ones, like Major Brutt, a friend of Robert Pidgeon's who materializes from nowhere, and Matchett, the imperious house maid. Her one attempt to connect with "solid" people outside the household is a complete failure; her visit to Seale on the sea to stay with Mrs. Heccomb and her two stepchildren only points up her inadequacy when faced by vulgar reality, her inability to experiment with life on any terms except her own. Portia is lamed, so to speak, by her innocence as much as lack of heart cripples Anna and Thomas, lack of social grace Major Brutt, vulgarity the Heccomb stepchildren, and an unfeeling serenity Mrs. Heccomb. At Seale, Dickie Heccomb is unfathomable in his egocentricity, Daphne is all sensuality; neither of course can make contact with Portia, and the situation there is a loose parallel of the one in London with the Quaynes.

The Seale episode, entitled "Flesh," serves almost the same function as the "Time Passes" episode in Virginia Woolf's *To the Lighthouse*. Portia passes on from one experience to another, but the change is imperceptible; she is untouched by the Heccombs' middle-class vulgarity, as she is by the Quaynes' hardness of heart. Although she becomes more aware of her body, sex is still something vaguely foreign to her.

Portia's intransigence in the face of things she does not understand is not, according to the tone of the novel, merely a passing stage in her development. Her innocence and sincerity and need for understanding are an entire way of life, we are led to believe, not simply an episode from which she will advance. What Portia seeks from life is what life can never give her. The adults around her are excellent examples of people who also have sought certain things and have been unable to obtain them. The difference is that Portia has the ability to feel, although ironically this quality is useless in a world in which no one else shares it. Yet Portia is implacable; her values are the only ones she knows, and she resists change with the tenacity of one for whom it means destruction.

When, for example, she returns from Seale, Anna and Thomas are both unable to come to terms with her. While they were away from the house, traveling on the continent, they had momentarily forgotten the response that she demanded, and now that they are back they find her a test they cannot successfully pass. Anna immediately feels inadequate; somehow the trip abroad made her think that the young girl had been expunged from the house, and then when she returns, there stands Portia, all friendliness, greeting, innocent smile. Thomas develops a headache, Anna must have her bath, and they cannot help but feel antagonistic; for the young girl draws upon them in a way that unmasks their inadequacies.

Major Brutt makes demands upon them in much the same way, although they can close their door to him. Brutt is a male double of Portia; recently back from long army service that has kept him out of contact with English life, he, like Portia, is unsettled, without occupation, ready as she to move on from one situation to another, unable to impress people with anything but his integrity, incapable of asserting himself in a competitive society in which his honest stare is unnerving. Brutt sends Portia jigsaw puzzles, monstrously large puzzles that take days and weeks to work out, and the symbolism of his act is clear. They meet across a gigantic puzzle; for him as for her, people seem to be operating according to some secret pact from which he is excluded. Once he gets inside this exclusive circle, he feels, everything will be all right, but at every turn he is denied entrance.

Brutt, again like Portia, never seems to have grown up to the deceptive ways of the world, and attempts to breach directly this conspiracy of adults. Lacking deviousness, he forces situations that create displeasure. He likes Thomas Quayne's home at 2 Windsor Terrace, for there he senses a glow that might rub off on him. Yet, ironically, except for material success, nothing exists there: friendship, warmth, acceptance—all these do not exist. And Portia, in her one cruel act of innocence, smashes Brutt's childish view of the Quayne home, reduces his modicum of happiness by forcing him to see that he is as ridiculed and mocked as she, making him realize that he is tolerated simply because he is there.

"You are the other person that Anna laughs at," she went on, raising her eyes. "I don't think you quite understand: Anna's always laughing at you. She says you are quite pathetic. She laughed at your carnations being the wrong colour, then gave them to me. And Thomas always thinks you must be after something. Whatever you do, even send me a puzzle, he thinks that more, and she laughs more. They groan at each other when you have gone away. You and I are the same. (pp. 309-10)

Portia destroys Brutt's marginal existence, for her innocence cannot tolerate the delusion of which even he is capable, much as later Anna in her momentary identification with Portia smells the nauseating odor of her own deceptive existence.

"If I were Portia? Contempt for the pack of us, who muddled our own lives, then stopped me from living mine. Boredom, oh such boredom, with a sort of secret society about nothing, keeping on making little signs to each other. Utter lack of desire to know what it was about. Wish that someone outside would blow a whistle and make the whole thing stop. Wish to have my own innings. Contempt for married people, keeping on playing up. Contempt for unmarried people, looking cautious and touchy. Frantic, frantic desire to be handled with feeling, and, at the same time, to be let alone. Wish to be asked how I felt, great wish to be taken for granted. . . ." (pp. 335-36)

Then Anna returns to her former state and admits that she of course is not Portia. The insensibility returns; Portia is a burden that she cannot bear.

By asking Brutt to marry her, Portia seeks a father precisely as in her relationship with the maid Matchett she seeks a mother of a sort. Yet everything she seeks—and particularly the marriage—is outrageous because she forces her natural feelings on people regardless of the circumstances. As a figure of innocence amid a world of experience, Portia must ask for and receive unhappiness; the demand she makes upon people will always be in excess of what they can give, what in the course of life anyone can give. The only rapport she can establish in the house is with Matchett, the maid whose sole passion seems to be the upkeep of the house; outside the house, only Brutt can "see" her, simply because he is in the same position.

The long line of Miss Bowen's teen-age heroines reaches its culmination in Portia, for more than any of the others, she fits into a way of life which can both receive and reject her. Miss Bowen achieves the tightness of this life through structuring the novel on character doubles, so that each character comes into the path of another by sharing some characteristics, or by finding in himself the qualities which disturb him in another.

Both Thomas and Anna, for example, identify with Portia at one time or another in the novel; yet the actual terms of the identification disturb elements within them, and they reject her for the very thing she demands of them and they might give. Again, Portia and Matchett curiously come together, for the maid identifies completely with the house, and through her Portia almost reaches some rapport with the large, antiseptic structure. In a different way, Portia and Brutt meet on common ground. As Portia points out to him, both are rejected souls; a conspiracy has excluded them. Another isolated soul hovering in the background is Irene, Portia's mother, as excluded from society as the daughter later will be, exiled because of her passing indiscretion with Mr.

Quayne. The situation at Seale is similar: even with the society changed from genteel upper-class to vulgar middle-class, Portia is isolated by virtue of her extraordinary demands—Daphne, in particular, is incredulous of Portia's innocence and suspects her of having mysterious motives.

The large London house which serves as background for Portia's fluttery existence significantly sets the character of the novel. Sanitary, polished, veneered, the house is a needful reminder of its occupants, and even their trip abroad is geared closely to the cleaning of the house. Working symbolically with the house are the everpresent swans, cool, untouchable, unfeeling, "aristocratic." The swans are, on occasion, identified with Portia, that "indignant swan," but at other times the swans are unapproachable, sailing serenely by despite the turmoil within the house. Swans, house, Brutt, Matchett, Portia, the Quaynes—they raise no moral questions, have no ready answers, reach no solutions, cause neither desperate happiness nor unhappiness, are, indeed, a small world on the surface of the larger one. Yet the coldness and heartlessness implied in their inter-relationship come as symbols of a world gone mechanical and dead. No less than D. H. Lawrence, Elizabeth Bowen indicates that social necessity strips away the very feelings that would save, although, unlike Lawrence, she cannot believe in the possibility of regeneration.

For ten years, Miss Bowen did not publish another novel, not until 1949, when *The Heat of the Day,* a "war novel," appeared. This novel contains one of her most appealing heroines, Stella Rodney, but also some of her least sure characterization of males, Robert Kelway and Harrison. The novel itself is a departure; as a "war novel," it attempts to cover a large space, to take *in,* whereas before Miss Bowen tended to exclude as much as possible so that her characters would stand out in bolder relief. Here, however, Stella and Robert work out their lonely passion against a vast panorama of war, spies, double-agents, bombings, a time when everyone and everything are out of tilt, and normal relationships are almost impossible to obtain.

This novel, like Virginia Woolf's *Mrs. Dalloway,* works on a double plot in which Stella's activities find duplication in those of

Louie Lewis, a wandering young girl who seeks love and affection. Although the doubling is apparent, these two do not complete each other the way Mrs. Dalloway and Septimus together become a whole person. The doubling here works more by touch and feel than by strict use of the *Doppelgänger*. Neither woman, in fact, is aware of the other until their paths casually cross, and then they meet not because of what *they* are but because they both know Harrison, the agent who is pursuing Stella and who is himself pursued by Louie. Both women are trying to derive some love from a world tipped sideways: Stella, through choice and moral decision; Louie, through drifting and floating from one casual relationship to another.

Stella is, in one way, Miss Bowen's teen-agers grown up and still disappointed by the conflict between what they are and what, indeed, they should like to be. Stella's inability to find satisfaction with another individual is reflected in her strange affairs with Robert and Harrison. Here, as in her other novels, Miss Bowen is concerned with the inability of people to meet on their own terms. People move through a nebulous darkness—the wartime blackout is symbolic—never fully understood or understanding, their presence rarely recognized, their feelings unreciprocated. The war background provides an excellent objective correlative in the larger world for what is being fought out in the smaller. Stella's conflicts with Robert as well as with Harrison are like those of two armies clashing by night, struggling hard and yet failing even to make contact. The wounds indicate a battle, but only a minor skirmish has been fought.

The individual's hurts, or the possibility of his being hurt, form the spine of the narrative: Stella and Robert feel pain even while temporarily happy. Stella, in turn, tortures Harrison, rejecting him even when he threatens to turn in Robert as a German agent. Harrison, for his part, rejects Louie. The Kelways, Robert's strange family, rebuff Stella when Robert brings her home. Victor, Stella's former husband, has left her when he found her boring and another woman more exciting. Only Roderick, Stella's son, tries to examine what he really is, so that he can face the future with some hope, although the war might destroy him.

The Heat of the Day becomes Miss Bowen's final statement thus far about her world, the last of her major "trilogy," if one can call it that, which began with *The House in Paris* and *The Death of the Heart.* In this novel, as in the other two, the world is viewed through fractured relationships. In all three novels, there is not a single satisfactory union: unhappy marriages, sad young women, teen-agers unable to find love, older men excluded from society by conspiracy, women forced to reject lovers, relationships that result in suicide (Max in *The House in Paris* and Robert, indirectly, in *The Heat of the Day*), drifting and unsatisfactory love affairs—these are the motifs of her mature novels. No longer is social satire (of a kind) or drawing-room comedy evident. The dialogue itself has become tightened, austere, oblique; rarely has the Jamesian influence seemed stronger. The warped syntax, the taut, packed prose, the indirection of phrasing, the stylizing of word and scene—all these indicate how the language has changed to meet the change in vision. Disintegration is the key to *The Heat of the Day,* and both the winding form and the tense use of language twist and jar the material from a smooth, regular narrative. The conversation is jagged in its irregularity; people speak with a minimum of articles and connectives, as though wartime will not allow wasting a single word and relationships are to be smashed almost as soon as they begin.

The enemy, as ever, is the social group which draws one's energies from the really important matters. Robert's activities as a German agent make it impossible for his affair with Stella to continue, and his "suicide" is both real and symbolic: their affair must end in frustration and violence, for its very terms are false. Thus, social groups (the war, beliefs generated by allegiances, et al.) are responsible for broken lives, exactly as social groups rejected Portia. Yet Miss Bowen's vision is sufficiently mature at this point to perceive that the individual is incapable of doing what he must—that is, exist by himself, since social groups oppose him. He disintegrates either alone or with others; the wise author recognizes the impasse of all her sad women. Unable to exist alone and anxious to form connections that take them outside of themselves, they are rebuffed. Stella's relationship with Robert and with Harrison is indicative of all relationships; with Robert, his allegiances rebuff her; with Harrison, she is blackmailed. With neither is honesty possible.

In *A World of Love* (1955), which appeared six years after *The Heat of the Day,* we return to the world of Miss Bowen's second novel, *The Last September,* a kind of love idyll which takes place in Ireland. Here, however, the "love" elements are abstracted from the world at large, for no civil war exists, only the war within each character's heart. Once again, evil, or what passes for it, lies within the framework of what are considered "normal" human relationships. Although Miss Bowen develops the feelings of the people as far as they will go, their rejection of "mind" is too great to allow significant development, and thus the range of the novel is severely restricted.

Like Joyce Cary and Henry Green, Elizabeth Bowen has been somewhat hurt by anti-intellectual literary movements. Throughout her novels, there is no major "thinking" character; not a scholar, pedant, or intellectual, but simply a person who comes to terms with life both mentally and emotionally. Unlike Virginia Woolf, Miss Bowen does not deride this type of person; she eliminates him. She sensitively depicts her kind of world, but it remains in several of her novels too overly feminine and gossipy, in a final view, shadowy.

Paradoxically, Miss Bowen's virtue of conceiving characters who move like spiders on gossamer webs results in her major weakness: that her women remain static, incapable of development, and, finally, immature in their quivering sensitivity. Her most brilliant work concerns young girls, but the mark of the fully mature novelist is his ability to probe emotionally and mentally developed adults. Otherwise, the novelist limits his range by excluding more than he encompasses. Miss Bowen writes with complete comprehension about her one type of character, but the rest of the world disappears. To ask for more is, of course, to ask for a different novelist, and few contemporary writers do offer greater scope. Nevertheless, the discerning reader is struck by the limitation of range, the fluttery concern with a miniature world, the exclusion of much that makes life exciting and significant, the complacency with which the novelist repeats both characters and themes. That this charge was once wrongly brought against Jane Austen does not vitiate its application to Elizabeth Bowen—the earlier novelist's irony and wit often make all the difference.

VII

Joyce Cary:
The Moralist as Novelist

N o w, shortly after his death, the work of Joyce Cary has become a literary battleground between those anxious to force nineteenth-century conventions on the contemporary novel and those wishing to support the avant-garde, the latter usually defined as work in the manner of *Ulysses* and *Finnegans Wake*. The battles once fought over the acceptance of James Joyce as a major novelist are now being refought on somewhat similar grounds: Cary is idolized by critics who want to snipe at Joyce, and derided by others who find nineteenth-century traditions moribund. In brief, Cary, like Joyce in the twenties and thirties, either has received outrageous praise or been subjected to excessive attack, all less for his work itself than for what he stands for and what he is: a link to the past, a novelist interested in morality, a traditionalist who finds workable things of greater importance than the new and the strange, a conservative who cannot conceive of the darkly irrational superseding the rational (even the tumultuous Gulley Jimson in *The Horse's Mouth,* for example, lives according to his own explicable principles). In a way, Cary is a "didactician" writing novels, and his supporters have lined up accordingly.

How much of Cary's reputation is well founded and how much mere propaganda can be determined by his treatment of themes in the more than fifteen novels he had published since 1932.* The First Trilogy, which includes *Herself Surprised* (1941), *To Be a Pilgrim* (1942), and *The Horse's Mouth* (1944), and the Second Trilogy, consisting of *Prisoner of Grace* (1952), *Except the Lord* (1953), and *Not Honour More* (1955), with their examination of past and present values, constitute Cary's major work. The six novels which comprise the two trilogies indeed pose several questions central to Cary's literary and moralistic aims: What happens when two generations overlap each other, with neither one prepared for the change that is taking place? How can people exiled by their own unique feelings understand or come to terms with others similarly handicapped? Where does politics become self-seeking and expedient, and where does the politician lose sight of public goals in favor of private ones? Similarly, when does private ambition lose its justification? and when is genius an excuse for personal expediency? Must a successful artist destroy himself and his talent in exchange for recognition, or can he continue along the lines of his major development toward something new and different? Is religion a sufficient bulwark against personal ego and the drive of the will? How can the contrasting needs of human liberty and social restraint be reconciled? How, finally, can freedom and authority be brought into harmony?

Anxious to catch an individual at the moment his actions are questioned by another, Cary works out his character relationships without trying to appear a moralist. Yet, despite this effort to be emancipated from dogma and despite the ultra-modern devices that he intermittently uses, there is a curious old-fashioned quality to his work; somehow, his ideas have failed to come to grips with a modern world. The terms of Cary's world, even when he is discussing an anarchic artist like Gulley Jimson, are as ordered as any in the nineteenth century. The world around Jimson proceeds as if only he is out of step; the rest is defined, rational, organized, never dark, unsettled, confused in more than a superficial way.

* *Aissa Saved* (1932); *An American Visitor* (1933); *The African Witch* (1936); *Castle Corner* (1938); *Mister Johnson* (1939); *Charley Is My Darling* (1940); *A House of Children* (1941); *Herself Surprised* (1941); *To Be a Pilgrim* (1942); *The Horse's Mouth* (1944); *The Moonlight* (1946); *A Fearful Joy* (1949); *Prisoner of Grace* (1952); *Except the Lord* (1953); *Not Honour More* (1955); *The Captive and the Free* (1959)

Even Jimson's behavior is predictable, providing one has read and absorbed the ideas of William Blake, Rousseau, and a long line of English and French romantics. Like Rousseau and Blake, Jimson believes that the natural goodness of man has been corrupted by institutions, schools, and academies, and that the only way a man can regain a pure vision of the world is by dissociating himself from society and following the call of his own individuality.

Accordingly, the conflict of *The Horse's Mouth* is created through the pure will of Jimson as it runs against institutions and institutionalized people. However, the conflicts are predictable, and Jimson's apparently haphazard irrationality is well planned. Jimson knows exactly what he needs to survive, and his knowledge of this fact places him closer to a nineteenth-century character of pure will than to the typically destructive twentieth-century figure, who fumbles his way through life. Even Jimson's artistic nature is more organized than chaotic; his late interest in "modern" painting is his way of ordering a disordered universe, an example of his vision of present and future. In brief, Jimson is not self-destructive, irrational, or in contact with underground devils; rather, like his nineteenth-century predecessors, he perpetuates himself through the only means he knows: the expression of his individual will through art. For in Cary's world, the individual still thinks his will can conquer and prevail.

Gulley Jimson aside for the moment, Cary's other major characters (Tom Wilcher, Sara Monday, Chester Nimmo, Jim Latter, and Dick Bonser) often seem to be irrational, but their actions too are charted predictably. These characters operate according to an inner logic which both orders and defines the world for them, a world not too different from that of the nineteenth-century characters of George Eliot and Thackeray, with of course a freer attitude toward the relationship between the sexes. Every now and then, Cary does catch some meaningless and inexplicable aspects in the lives of his minor characters, but despite external eccentricities his major characters live within a reasonable ordered framework.

It is precisely this reasonable "rounded" property of Cary's characters which gives the old-fashioned quality to his work, making him seem closer to the major nineteenth-century novelists than to those of the twentieth century. Moreover, Cary's castigation of "modern" looseness and aimlessness seems like an echo from a moralistic past, in which directions and goals were more significant than individual deviations. His characters' anarchy is superficial, their lack of control only external, their loss of purpose only partial. Even if they destroy in order to re-create, they destroy with a definite end in view. Their actions are motivated by things they understand: self-interest, ambition, the need to create, the urge to fix a particular design on life.

The only area in which Cary tries to break this pattern is in his creation of female characters, who become, as it were, buffers between the various males and the rest of society. Only his women seem really chaotic, but even they come to operate according to certain principles of behavior imposed from without. The most famous—Sara Monday of the Gulley Jimson trilogy—is herself a representative of the female principle that destroys man while strengthening him. The model for his best work, she, in her sexual blowziness and sensual manner, gives Gulley some of the happiest years of his life. Nevertheless, her intention is to emasculate Gulley by turning him from his work to her, by trying to destroy the very artistry in him which constitutes his attraction. Sara tempts and seduces and then tries to reform. Her great need is to domesticate Gulley, to make him precisely like other men, and to clip his artistic wings so that he can no longer fly above and beyond her.

In Blake's "The Mental Traveller," which is important to an understanding of Cary's female characters, a man is figuratively destroyed by a woman: "And if the Babe is born a Boy / He's given to a Woman Old, / Who nails him down upon a rock, / Catches his shrieks in cups of gold. / She binds iron thorns around his head, / She pierces both his hands & feet, / She cuts his heart out at his side / To make it feel both cold and heat." Blake writes that "she grows young as he grows old," and as he bleeds, literally a martyr to her, she becomes a "Virgin bright." Thus, Cary's women too exist to make slaves of the men who originally attract them. They turn sexual charm into a moral asset, and although they seem as caught up emotionally as the man they seduce, actually their use of sex is for a predetermined purpose. Still, they are attractive and often seem more sinned against than sinning. In a way, however, they are personally to blame for their downfall, for they operate behind a disguise. Theirs is a vision of the world in which man will be securely tied to the woman of his choice, and his horizons will not extend beyond the family hearth.

Characters of this type, whether male or female, overwhelmed as they are by Cary's moral views and comic sense, cannot go too deep or too far. Accordingly, Gulley Jimson is a typical romantic artist, with none of the deeper vision which would make him more than a picaresque hero. As attractive and as alive as he is, he is, paradoxically, too routine and prosaic in his reactions: he soaks the rich whenever possible, he despises academies, he mocks his own calling as an artist, he steals in order to paint, he flaunts bourgeois mediocrity, he condescends toward those who try to understand him or his art, he uses people whenever necessary; he is Rousseau's natural man with a brush in his hand, a man driven by the need to express himself; in brief, a romantic cliché. Somehow, Jimson remains too lovable, and we have been led to believe that artists are not lovable; somehow, he is too predictable, and we have been led to expect that artists are not predictable.

All this is not to claim that either Gulley Jimson or Cary's other characters lack vitality and warmth. These qualities are certainly welcome at any time, and especially now when various theories of the novel predicate robot-like desiccated characters or caricatures whose eccentricities of behavior preclude their existence in a real world of moral choices. In certain ways, particularly with respect to agitated characters who try to come to terms with life, Cary is akin to Graham Greene and Elizabeth Bowen. However, when real dramatic decisions are at stake, he leaves the company of his two contemporaries, for Cary, with his indecisive characters, seems unable to prolong any actual moral tension. Perhaps the hit-and-run humor in his characterizations precludes the analysis and drama necessary to a serious novel. And because humor often dissipates the moral earnestness that should be present in his themes his fiction often loses intensity and becomes an excuse for marginal comments and feelings.

This attitude is particularly true of the political trilogy which features the fortunes of Chester Nimmo, who, as a man high in the government, is constantly beset by personal conflicts: where to separate personal ambition from public good, how to distinguish between principle and self-interest, when to draw the line between sincerity and expediency. As Chester himself is a composite of opposites, Cary is able to portray him as a man obsessed by the need to advance his fortunes even at the expense of dignity, personal happiness, and his public reputation—all under the guise of his doing the public good. His flexibility is his genius; his ability to duck and bob, as called for, is his sign of political talent. His ideals are viable only as long as they are those of his electors. Within this framework, obviously, most dramatic tension is lost because Chester seems unaware of the forces driving him alternately to success and destruction.

Like many other Cary characters, Chester rarely seems to operate within the area of decision; rather, his choices are dictated by mysterious forces generated in his childhood, and without self-knowledge he can be neither profound nor even interesting. Accordingly, the real drama of this conflict between the public and private man remains largely inconsequential because Cary rarely stops long enough to create people at their moment of decision; for him, they are fixed by what they are, and they are unable to change or grow. Therefore, despite his interest in character, Cary never comes to grips with people in whom real choice is involved. And although his main themes are concerned with the demands of conscience, ambition, and duty, Cary, unlike C. P. Snow, only infrequently surprises us with the conflicts implicit in a character's awareness of these qualities.

A kindred fault of Cary's novels, already suggested, is the easy acquiescence of his characters to whatever befalls them. In *The Moonlight* (1946), for example, even those characters in rebellion rarely show the real tension between what they want and what they have to accept. If the characters acquiesce to the roles that have been marked out for them, there can be little conflict and little drama. Amanda is pliant, yielding, flexible to the point of will-lessness; her sense of responsibility permits nearly anything to happen. Therefore, while the theme calls for some direction, the will-less Amanda succumbs to her fate—seduction by Harry —without forethought, desire, or even dignity.

Similarly, in *A Fearful Joy* (1949), Tabitha Baskett is completely compliant to Dick Bonser; like Sara and Amanda, she is carried away by her feelings and unable to come to terms with her plight. Soft and maternal, she is the eternally forgiving female waiting to receive into her arms an erring man who is weak and childish. According to Cary, woman is both weaker and stronger than man: she can endure where he would fail, but also she succumbs to enslavement when her emotions are seriously engaged. She becomes, in one way, a plaything of man, who has the stronger will and can conquer her; in another, the controller of man who is helpless to resist her charms.

Tabitha is really happy only with Bonser, and yet he is the source of much of her misery. Without him, she would have had no life, while with him she has both misery and happiness. Her own pleasure, then, derives not from *her* desires but from man's will, which directs her to do what *he* wants. Similarly, Sara Monday, in the first trilogy, cushions (in both senses) Jimson, as do the other women in his life; and, likewise, Tabitha protects Bonser, who deserts her, cheats on her, shows no interest in their child, borrows money from her, and even strikes her—the picaresque hero who resists domestication. Yet, since punishment and suffering seem the lot of woman, Tabitha loves Bonser for all that; he is the only person to give her real joy, and therefore the title of the novel, a fearful joy.

With males cut off from any real power of decision, and females easily acquiescent to the power of the males, dramatic conflicts naturally diminish in interest. Arranging his material around male-female antagonism, Cary does not engage the mind or even the deeper emotions. This novel (*A Fearful Joy*) is a running episodic history, humorous in patches, but overall not comic, or tragic, or serious. By sifting the entire novel through Tabitha, Cary gives the work a frivolous air. This focus lessens intellectual content, for by definition woman is for Cary not intellectual, but emotional in her attitudes. Consequently, Tabitha's intellectual limits seriously circumscribe the few conflicts and ideas expressed in the book.

Most of these strictures against Cary tend to destroy his answers to the questions his novels raise. That is to say, important questions are suggested in the narrative: Is genius an excuse for personal expediency? Can freedom and authority be reconciled? How can human liberty and social necessity complement and not conflict with each other? But these questions are rarely answered in terms of the characters, who lack the depth to confront such issues. The answers seem presented, instead, in terms of drifting and sliding characters or hit-and-run comments by the author. The questions, in a way, are in excess of what the answers can possibly be.

This conscious avoidance of thinking characters considerably reduces and thins out Cary's themes; and yet he is evidently more than a simple humorist. We recognize that the scope of his novels is often huge, comprising, in *To Be a Pilgrim,* for example, several layers of society, diverse social groups, numerous professional types—in effect, a microcosm of English society. Like several of Cary's longer works, this novel is a dramatization of the differences between the two generations before and after the First World War. As neither generation is able to understand the other, Cary derives from this confusion both the humor and pathos of life: each is exiled by its own selfish feelings, and each is unable to connect with things outside itself. Basically, this is a large conflict, and the intention is obviously serious. So too, the political trilogy featuring Chester Nimmo attempts to catch the political temper of England when important social and economic changes are taking place. The conflict between Chester and Jim Latter is one between flexibility and rigidity.

Nevertheless, in these novels, as well as in several others, intention is weakened by the lack of analysis, by the author's failure to remain still long enough to create a lasting impression. In many of Cary's novels, including one of his best, *The Horse's Mouth,* the pace is so fast and the change of scene or line of thought so rapid that single impressions become strung out like sections of bamboo. In his effort to be humorous—and Cary is often that—he turns novels into episodic picaresque narratives even when the subject matter calls for different treatment. Furthermore, the humor rarely involves social criticism. Gulley Jimson himself, one of Cary's most effective humorous characters, does not by his powers of creativity become a critic or effective opponent of bourgeois or any other kind of society. Jimson may mock the philistines, but both are, as we meet them, at a standoff. Similarly, characters like Chester Nimmo, Jim Latter, Dick Bonser, and Tom Wilcher are also insubstantial as critics of society, for the humor that describes them is often close to caricature. The result, obviously, is characters who do not operate smoothly within society and are insufficient outside.

There are of course exceptions. The novels in which the exceptions occur, however, are usually not considered Cary's best fiction, although often they contain the seeds of major works. *Mister Johnson* (1939), one of Cary's earlier books, is a slight novel that has an emotional and intellectual honesty at its center which sets it off from both of the trilogies. This basically humorous novel has as its main theme the disorientation of African natives like Johnson who, because of changes occurring in their world, are placed in a no-man's land between two cultures, one too backward to be embraced and the other too complicated and alien for them to be received into. Johnson is a native who likes white man's ways, and in his desire to gain white man's possessions, he embezzles, steals, commits fraud, and finally murders. Yet he remains an innocent, a pawn in the hands of a European culture which makes use of him, and, having tempted him, must kill him.

Johnson has most of the qualities that the native traditionally has in romantic fiction; but here, Cary, unlike Kipling, does not romanticize him or his fate: Johnson dies sadly, not heroically, becoming tragic only in his pathetic desire to retain his dignity. Although he is a joke both to the natives who surround him and to his bush wife who cannot understand his "new" ways, as well as to the whites who call him "Mr. Wog," Johnson retains through it all his innocence and appears, even after an unmotivated murder, a pure being. The murder is inconsequential, and Johnson's part in it is so meaningless in terms of what he really is that his punishment seems supererogatory. Johnson's basic innocence rests on his lack of knowledge—he indeed wants knowledge (of white man's ways), but he still remains identified with the bush, and his acquisition of the new culture is merely superficial. Caught between the two societies, he is a kind of pure fool, anxious to do good and yet careful of his own comforts and sense of respect.

Shifting worlds have made him expedient; yet throughout his transformation of values, he retains his ability to seek and find joy, the one thing the new civilization cannot take from him. Thus, in his way, Johnson remains superior to those he is trying to imitate and transcends the baseness surrounding him.

The novel's humor is created by Johnson's attempts to climb, his exaggerations, his lies, his petty thievery (in a society in which everyone steals), his give and take with the other natives who hate his success and yet are awed by his lavish nature and big talk. Removed to a more civilized country, Johnson would be a typical nouveau riche without malice, impressed by his new friends and anxious to impress others, living above the style to which he has been accustomed and among people who could not possibly accept him. Possibly, *Mister Johnson* seems effective as a novel of ideas because the main character forces himself on a well-defined society, and while his destruction is caused by this, nevertheless he does not suffer from the aimless wandering between anarchy and order that troubles Cary's other characters.

In his Clark lectures, later published as *Art and Reality* (1958), Cary speaks repeatedly of the artist who goes against his own point of view and his own tendencies because the immediate scene calls for this contradiction between long-range beliefs and immediate effect. Cary tries here to demonstrate that an art work sets its own rules, as it were, which the artist must obey once he has put the work into motion; and because the work of art does generate its own momentum, the artist must let it, rather than himself, prevail. Cary gives as an example Ivan's argument with Alyosha about God in the "Pro and Contra" section of *The Brothers Karamazov;* for despite Dostoyevsky's own feelings, Ivan has the better of the argument. Dostoyevsky, Cary comments, undoubtedly could see the logic of Ivan's argument and could not counter it even though it contradicted his own. Therein, lies the great artist.

Nevertheless, this injunction to artistic consistency was one that Cary himself often ignored. The inner radiance that should emanate from his characters and make them incandescent is missing from his conception. As I suggested above, even Gulley Jimson fails to come to terms with himself. Cary's method of presentation eliminates complexity: the Jimson of the famous Sara Monday paintings is no more, and the Jimson we encounter as the novel begins is now old and tired, experimenting with a new style that confuses him and makes it difficult for him to finish anything. We meet him *after* his views have changed and he is out of fashion, caught as he is between two worlds which, in the long run, manipulate him more than he manipulates them. Jimson really has little effect on anyone except Nosy, his loyal young friend, and such are the terms of Gulley's existence that he is unable to move anyone not already amenable to his position. Cary catches him between prison and hospital, and despite all of Jimson's vitality and verbalized sense of rebellion, his energy is vitiated; he is, in the main, one who acquiesces to the role the world expects from him: to be a clown, an entertainer, a mad genius, to perpetuate a romantic image of the artist, to flout convention, and to suffer from frustration.

It is, we have seen, his characters' failure to feel conflict that causes the softness and dormancy in a Cary novel. People usually seem the products of their surroundings or of influences upon them, and even his well-rounded successes "arrive" more because of circumstances than inner will. As a philosophical view of the world, this is, of course, perfectly acceptable. One may claim, as several major novelists have, that inner will is less important than the confusion that characterizes life, and success itself therefore is fortuitous and dependent not upon principle but upon expedience. However, such a view must be dramatized so that the author seems to control his characters. What Cary's characters impose upon the scene is usually less than what is willy-nilly imposed upon them. Unlike Virginia Woolf, for instance, Cary presents distinctly neither the will of his characters nor the muddle of life, and the result is a blurred outline of rapidly moving events.

Cary, we remember, praised Dostoyevsky's ability to let his characters follow their own paths without interference even though they pass beyond the author's own sense of proportion. Nevertheless, in precisely this area, Cary failed. Chester Nimmo, for instance, who in his sense of the world's disorder and the need to impose arrangement upon it is somewhat akin to Gulley Jimson, seems to operate in swirls and cascades. His decisions are based upon motives that remain hidden in the author's rush to describe political events and his relationship to them. Cary often substitutes successive short and choppy episodes for the kind of analysis that would give meaning to the individual scene, as if his inventive skill were running ahead of his interpretive powers. In the political trilogy, for instance there is a headlong rush of episodes, one following fast upon the other, one scene breathing, so to speak, down the neck of the one ahead, so that the reader is rarely permitted to focus on the immediate situation. The characters themselves seem to be dashing toward the end of a requisite number of episodes, several of which, taken individually, are humorous and effective, but with their overall sense of dramatic inevitability lost along the frenzied way.

To compare Cary once again with C. P. Snow, a writer clearly lacking the former's verbal facility and sense of wit, we can see that Snow has an essential quality that Cary fails to demonstrate: the ability to convey intellectual content in characters who are supposed to have minds. Blake's influence, among others, on Cary evidently made him scorn his characters' thinking side, while Snow, trained as a scientist before he began to write novels, is concerned principally with the mind, although not to the complete neglect of the rest of the person. Cary, in contrast, lacks balance. Jimson's doctrines, direct from Blake and Rousseau, so deride man's rational powers that one is almost convinced great painting has nothing to do with the painter's brain and is merely a curious noncerebral reflex. Despite his protests to the contrary, Jimson uses his head; his nerves and bones and blood perhaps give him direction, but his mind helps him distinguish between the rightness and wrongness of his conceptions. When he feels, he also thinks, and for Cary to eliminate one at the expense of the other is to falsify in a way that even D. H. Lawrence, the prophet of man's "blood consciousness," rarely did.

At this point, to contrast Cary with Lawrence, whom he superficially resembles, is to see where Cary failed and Lawrence succeeded. Lawrence claimed that he was not denigrating the mind as an instrument of salvation and that the mental faculties should remain in clear balance with the physical. Thus, several of Lawrence's prophets—Birkin, Don Ramon, Mellors—are directed by thought as much as feeling. They only *seem* to scorn mind when they inveigh against those who deny body altogether or those who are unable to fully utilize their bodies. Actually, they are "philosophical" characters with carefully thought-out views of life. It is ideas that they try to impose upon the world, ideas which their passions embody. In *Women in Love,* for example, Birkin clashes with Hermione not because he wants to denigrate mind, which is all she has, but because she overemphasizes it and denies body.

Cary's characters, besides operating on a lower plane of existence, lack almost completely this intellectual striving after balance. More imposed upon than imposing themselves, they move as the current dictates and appear less individualized than what their roles call for. Thus, there seems to be a dichotomy between the role and the person; the character fails the role cut out for him. This is a dramatic, not a philosophical, failing; and, accordingly, the novels often lose their emotional center because the characters are too compliant to the demands of others. A Lawrence character, on the other hand, must impose himself, and while he may intermittently bore with his views of the way the world should be run, he nevertheless is able to generate a great deal of excitement.

Although, admittedly, one may find much wrong with Lawrence's excessive preaching, still the relationship between characters on the one hand and between characters and things on the other is always alive and vibrant. This vitality results, surely, from the incandescence that emanates from the inner being of every Lawrence character. In a Cary novel, where the basic philosophical aim may be somewhat similar, the inner radiance is rarely apparent, and then only briefly, as in someone like Gulley Jimson or Chester Nimmo. The lack of inner radiance results in a loss of visual sharpness; the only memorable characters in Cary, despite his wit and verbal facility, are those who fit into a long tradition available to the reader. Jimson is *the* romantic artist, almost a cliché in his predictable reactions, effective though many of his mannerisms are; and Sara Monday is *the* warm-hearted, sensual, blowzy temptress, whose aim is not seduction and love but a cozy hearth.

Moreover, Chester Nimmo, even with three volumes devoted to

his activities, remains shadowy, just as Cary's description of Nimmo's pastoral childhood (in *Except the Lord,* 1953) is indecisive and weak in comparison with Lawrence's vivid and forceful one of Paul Morel's or the Brangwen girls'. Nimmo rarely emerges with clarity from his religious background, again despite individually effective scenes. The method of narration itself effects a loss of spontaneity, for Nimmo is relating the story as an exhausted old man waiting to die. Even in *Prisoner of Grace* (1952), which is concerned with Nimmo's public career at the center of English political life, he fails to attain individual status or to stand out against his contemporaries. His central philosophy—to fit himself into events and to act as *they* dictate—works against him, for it makes him a puppet of fate rather than a unique individual.

Cary is the not so curious phenomenon of an author with tremendous gifts of language and characterization whose point of view hampers him. The difference between Blake's greatness as a poet and the equivocal position of Cary as a novelist is one of size and dimension. Blake's reputation remains with his shorter poems, the lyrics, the concise, graphic poems which float on music; while his longer works are read for the brief, luminous passages which intermittently appear. Cary's work, however, is all long, and the kind of lyric vision he had was insufficient to transport the reader the distance he is expected to travel.

When Cary recognized that Dostoyevsky was carried away by Ivan's arguments against God in *The Brothers Karamazov,* he saw that the Russian novelist could not forsake a character to whom ideologically he was antipathetic. This honesty is the mark of a great artist. Yet, in nearly every one of Cary's novels where a figure antipathetic to his own views of order, tradition, and rationality appears, he is ridiculed, caricatured, and made to seem morally confused in contrast with the character who stands for something in which Cary believes. It is precisely this lack of mature conflict between characters that one sorely misses. Even Lawrence, who often seems carried away by the verbalizations of his spokesmen, is able to undermine them; Birkin is important for Lawrence, but he is also a fool and a bore, and Lawrence realized this. The conflicts working in the character and in the author thus supplement the conflicts implicit in the narrative. In a Cary novel, this clash is not present; the conflicts in Jimson, for instance, are non-existent—he thinks in only one way, and nothing makes an impression on him. Similarly, Chester Nimmo never comes up against an issue in which we see him really moved. The result is dramatic waste.

What, then, is left? Is Cary as minor as his detractors would have him? Or is he, despite the above qualifications of his talents the major novelist his admirers believe him to be?

Among novelists developing from the 1940's on, vitality has not been a prime characteristic, nor has variety of characterization, nor, until Kingsley Amis and John Wain, has humor. Many novelists of the 1940's and 1950's have been concerned indirectly with the history of the times and, accordingly, are astringent and baleful. Cary, with his light and graceful style, is of course an exception to these authors. Even as early as *Aissa Saved* (1932) and *The African Witch* (1936), he was writing an assured and witty prose, quiet in its mastery of unobtrusive, pathetic humor. The novels themselves, evidently, are not weighty or important, but the assured technique and grasp of language are apparent from the beginning. These qualities remained with Cary throughout his career; parts of the two trilogies are truly funny, although rarely as pungent and incisive as Waugh's early work. Nevertheless, a novel like *The African Witch,* with its heavy overtones of Conrad's first two novels, promised a great deal, while not achieving significance itself.

The promise, however, was not fulfilled, and while the technical grasp continued unabated, even improved, the point of view rarely varied enough to allow an appreciable change in content. Then, as later, there was the need to jump around and avoid analysis, the need to keep the episodes moving rapidly on a large canvas that included a great deal without defining anything clearly. Cary was already a novelist whose philosophy and technique were fixed, one who, unlike Conrad and Lawrence, was not to develop as he aged in his craft.

His strength, throughout, rested on his exuberance, his vitality, the vibrancy of his prose, the variety of his characters. All these virtues are real. But while one should not castigate Cary for having failed to expand the novel form any further, one can admonish him for not having availed himself of what existed. Although he reworked many techniques with which Joyce and Virginia Woolf had experimented (*The Horse's Mouth,* for example, is full of interior monologues and attempts at stream of consciousness), nevertheless his novels are full of old-fashioned ideas and characters.

Even C. P. Snow, who seems old-fashioned with his straightforward narratives and moral use of the novel in the manner of John Galsworthy, was able to gain modern rhythms and meanings by arranging his subject matter around contemporary problems. His characters may deal with twentieth-century problems in a nineteenth-century manner, but, notwithstanding, their conflicts and their tensions are ours. The conflicts of Cary's characters, however, seem part of the author's winsome nostalgia for a world that no longer exists. Cary himself, despite his man-of-the-world exterior, was a romantic for whom the dream was more important than the reality. Similarly, his dreaming characters, while also his best, belong less to this world than to one they would like to regain. It is as if Dickens had continued to write *Pickwicks* for the rest of his literary life. Therefore, even though the method is "modern," it clashes with the characters. The stream of consciousness of a romantic artist like Gulley Jimson is anachronistic, especially when the stream is full of modern expressions and idioms imposed from without; for example, the opening lines:

I was walking by the Thames. Half-past morning on an autumn day. Sun in a mist. Like an orange in a fried fish shop. All bright below. Low tide, dusty water and a crooked bar of straw, chicken boxes, dirt and oil from mud to mud. Like a viper swimming in skim milk. The old serpent, symbol of nature and love.

As an artist possessed, Gulley is in a direct line from the nineteenth-century "accursed poet" (as he himself advertises), but in speech and thought, in his art itself, he is modern. Even in creating Gulley Jimson, Cary reveals the dichotomy that runs through all his work: the verbal gifts that remain consistently modern contrasting with the vision that is outdated and passé.

When we realize this fact, we see that Cary fails to be a major novelist in the same way that Rachmaninoff failed to be a major composer. Their creative line is in a once major idiom that has been exhausted or brought close to depletion, one no longer practical now that new areas have been suggested or opened up. This certainly does not mean that a novelist or composer working in an outdated idiom cannot say important things; however, had Cary spoken to his own age and said things that that age, as well as all time, would have understood, his work would have been more moving. In the final analysis, Cary repeats to us what Dickens and a whole host of nineteenth-century writers have said, just as Rachmaninoff adds little to what had been said by the major romantic composers. The result, for Cary, is to be categorized as a minor novelist with the gifts of a major one, a minor humorist lacking the sweeping vision of a major satirist or ironist, a minor artist simply because he remained, for one reason or another, a minor thinker.

In one way, Cary, as we saw also in Elizabeth Bowen, is paying for the sins of the romantic movement. In denigrating mind in practice as well as theory, several romantic writers lost sight of the fact that major work is the outcome of a balance between mind and emotion, and that to scorn mind is to strip oneself of a major tool. Where they succeeded, they did so, as Coleridge reminded Wordsworth, despite, not because of, doctrine. The thinness of much of Cary's work may indeed be, paradoxically, the result of his doctrinaire devotion to Blake and Rousseau. For while Blake may have been a good influence on another lyric poet, as a philosophical guide to a novelist, who must fill three or four hundred pages, he perhaps misled more than he helped. Cary himself quotes Blake's advice: "The angel that presided at her birth / Said, little creature, born of joy and mirth / Go love without the help of anything on earth." Nevertheless, even the accomplished novelist stripped of everything but love is bound to become thin and uneven, eventually repetitious and tiring.

VIII

George Orwell:
The White Man's Burden

MORE THAN ANY of his contemporaries, George Orwell (born Eric Blair) became, as V. S. Pritchett called him, the conscience of his generation. It is sometimes irrelevant, therefore, to talk of his "sub-literary" novels as if he consciously sacrificed his "art" to history or journalism. Often, for Orwell, they were one and the same. The novel was for him a way to discuss the issues of his day while providing a maximum of instruction for a large audience.* In "Why I Write," he told his intentions:

What I have most wanted to do throughout the past ten years is to make political writing into an art. My starting point is always a feeling of partisanship, a sense of injustice. When I sit down to write a book, I do not say to myself, "I am going to produce a work of art." I write it because there is some lie that I want to expose, some fact to which I want to draw attention, and my initial concern is to get a hearing. But I could not do the work of writing a book, or even a long magazine article, if it were not also an aesthetic experience. (*Such, Such Were the Joys,* p. 9)

* *Down and Out in Paris and London* (1933); *Burmese Days* (1934); *A Clergyman's Daughter* (1935); *Keep the Aspidistra Flying* (1936); *Coming up for Air* (1939); *Animal Farm* (1945); *1984* (1949)

He comments further that in all his books, even the most propagandistic, there remains much that the politician would find irrelevant, and this "extra" is the aesthetic experience that his novels provide. What he says about his work rings true: once the reader moves away from the message and sermon proper, there is still a great deal that Orwell has seen with the eye of an artist; for he was not forced by his dogma into blindness about reality. His ideas in fact gain substance from being based on sharply seen details, and the latter often remain after the abstraction has been lost. In *1984,* for example, long after O'Brien's speeches about the coming world have been forgotten, the reader remembers Winston's ordeal in the rat cage when he loses all dignity and self-possession.

Orwell does frequently fail us, however, in not clearly indicating what belongs to literature and what is proper to history. History demands, among other things, blinding clarity, while literature can be impressionistic, frenzied, symbolic, romantic. Between the two, as Aristotle remarked in his *Poetics,* there is bound to be a clash, for the intention of one differs crucially from that of the other. Thus, we often feel that Orwell as a topical writer has not integrated the two elements sufficiently, so that one frequently gains at the expense of the other. There is no "conscious sacrifice" on Orwell's part, but there is an evident lack of imagination, the synthetic process capable of wedding dissimilars. Having accepted Naturalism as *the* mode for his type of novel, Orwell forsakes those techniques that might have projected his political ideas into deeply felt literary experiences. Lacking Zola's tremendous intensity, he cannot compensate for what he loses through unadventurous methods.

Nevertheless, because Orwell so cherishes middle-class comforts —although he can forgo them and survive—he conveys, within his limitations, the pathos and terror involved in a man caught between what he wants for himself and what the political system has to offer him. The prison life of *1984* merges with the enclosed life of the private school he attended as a young boy, both visions of what life offers. If the reader recognizes that for Orwell, as for Kafka, the nightmare is an inner one, then he can see the political matter as secondary to the personal content. This is not to relegate Orwell's politics to a less important position, but to retain perspective on the man's talents. Less able than Kafka to project a fully rounded inner vision, Orwell nevertheless sees much that is internal even while seeming to be a reporter.

He is a great reporter simply because he reports impressionistically and does not attempt false objectivity. At his best, he merges history with literature. He reports as he sees, but he recognizes that what he sees is tinged by what he is and by what he chooses to look at. Yet despite the subjectivity of much of Orwell's reporting, we are struck by the compelling clarity of his vision and the sharpness of his images. The Naturalism of his method affects both his novels and journalism; he started with an interest in large issues before the novelist took over, and then he became immersed in the truth of small things.

Part of Orwell's naturalistic equipment is his ability to catch the smell and taste of objects. Like Céline and Beckett—his brothers in literary squalor—he can make anything seem revolting, not only garbage, excrement, soiled clothing (his heritage from Zola), but also pleasant things like books, money, food. In *Keep the Aspidistra Flying* (1936), Orwell's fourth novel in four years, Gordon Comstock remarks the Darwinian struggle in the world of books, which symbolizes all struggle: the novels fight the poetry, the poetry fights the histories, the social tracts fight the novels. All are in a battle to stay in a prominent place in the bookstore; and all seem futile if one has no money. Books, which one has hitherto taken for granted, now appear shoddy and useless, as Orwell handles them, untouchable products of a sterile society. Without money, he tells us, one cannot love; without money, one cannot even read.

The quality of an Orwell "hero"—Gordon Comstock, among others—is measured by his ability to strike through cant: his own and society's. Orwell is not particularly troubled by what his protagonist is or what he tries to do; he is, however, much concerned with what society prevents him from doing. As in the naturalistic novels of the nineteenth century in which the "hero" is caught in a trap of cause and effect, so here, the "hero" is caught by forces which reduce his desires and needs to those of an animal. He is brought to subsistence level, and few elements of civilization can do him good, for to have enough to eat is the sole luxury in which he can indulge.

The nineteenth-century *Bildungsroman* and *Künstlerroman,* charted the poverty of a young man who was inevitably to rise in the economic scale as he improved himself. Implicit in his temporary poverty was the knowledge that he would improve himself and alter his status through struggle. In brief, poverty was simply a base from which he would rise. The person who was born pure and achieved wealth after privation was a better man, so the tale ran, than the man who had always known wealth. As Dickens reminds us in *Great Expectations,* Pip must expect nothing from the outside, only from within. Self, the will, initiative, ambition —all these operate to create a character who will then impose himself on the world. Pip must recognize that only he can help himself, that all his other expectations are based on false assumptions.

Such a view of the hero and of the world could be posited only at a time when order and control were assumed. Dickens, like his contemporaries, obviously recognized the changes that were taking place in mid-Victorian society, but nevertheless he believed, with what now seems to be minor quibbling, in a universe that was basically good, one that was responsive, so to speak, to the touch of a good individual. Orwell, who wrote sympathetically of Dickens, turns this entire vision upside down. Unlike Dickens, who often associates moneyed values with success, Orwell associates money with the defeat of the spirit. He faces the familiar paradox that money is necessary in order to be human, while to make money is dehumanizing. The one area in which Orwell and Dickens meet is in their common recognition that poverty destroys the sexual urge. The poor man feels inferior and loses his potential as a male (Pip with Estella, for example), for without money or means he is, as it were, demanned. Gordon Comstock says, in *Keep the Aspidistra Flying:* " 'It isn't that I don't want to make love to you. I do. But I tell you I can't make love to you when I've only eightpence in my pocket. At least when you know I've only eightpence. I just can't do it. It's physically impossible.' "

The physical impossibility of the sexual act under these conditions marks Gordon as a sensitive young man, one worth saving. Similarly, in *Down and Out in Paris and London* (1933), Orwell's first novel which paralleled his own experiences sometime after he returned from the Burma police service, the narrator perceives in himself and others the nearly complete loss of a sexual self under the exhausting conditions imposed by poverty or by inhuman working conditions. Furthermore, the worker recognizes that he is doing an essentially meaningless job that in no way fulfills himself; and this knowledge of his own uselessness acts as a deterrent sexually.

All this is fairly obvious, yet how infrequently it appears in the English novel. Orwell—along with Henry Green and D. H. Lawrence—is virtually alone among twentieth-century novelists in discussing poverty in this manner. Against a background of Orwell's description of poverty, Zola's seems romanticized; his sensual characters retain energy despite lives that destroy their will. Orwell's characters appear real, with their exhaustion, their lack of interest in anything but a meal and a place to sleep, their indifference to the future.

I suggested above that the quality of an Orwell protagonist is his ability to perceive the hypocrisy of the world and to react to it so that his own aims become clouded. An Orwell "hero" rarely has any hope for the future—except perhaps for his next meal. He has few ambitions, and his chief emotion, when not hungry, is the sexual itch. Thus, in *Burmese Days* (1934), Flory pursues Elizabeth, the sole available white woman in the area, despite the fact that he and she have nothing in common. Flory fails to see her as she is, and this lack of clarity on his part is a measure of his agony. Everything Flory believes in is vitiated by his feeling for Elizabeth, but nevertheless because of his own weakness he becomes a fool of love.

Consequently, when hypocrisy does appear, it results from a character's need for something that scorns his true feelings. Were Orwell a comic writer, this grim irony would be a subject for social comedy in the manner of Evelyn Waugh, or for playful banter in the style of Henry Green. Flory's ordeal—one that he cannot possibly sustain—is to discover the depth of his self-deception and to lose Elizabeth in the bargain. An honest man is unable to survive self-deceived, and Flory commits suicide. Like one of Conrad's solitaries, Flory cannot exist outside the community of men, although to exist inside would be self-corrupting, for the community itself is rotten.

A Conrad hero must recognize the terms of his existence and immerse himself in the illusions that will eventually destroy him. As a psychological novelist, Conrad is interested in the phenomenon of a man who by some act of indiscretion cuts himself off or is cut off from society. As a social novelist, Orwell is less interested in man than he is in the society that has infected him. He has shifted emphasis from *the* man to the social group. Like a good naturalist, Orwell "gets" at people through the accumulation of social detail and external phenomena. This method defines both his success and failure. As a way of realizing a particular milieu, such a method has proven successful; as a way of developing people, the method leaves much to chance.

Unfortunately, Orwell's chief characters frequently exist only as social animals. They are indicated in terms of status, race, caste, tradition; and their place in this scheme is more important than what they are. The novel as developed by Joyce, Virginia Woolf, Conrad, and Lawrence is not the novel that Orwell is interested in. By way of Gissing and the French naturalists, he returns in some oblique way to Dickens. In these novelists, the main characters gain their life from their social function, and frequently when their social function no longer exists they are in serious trouble. Dickens' middle-class "heroes" and "heroines" manage best when they recognize that personal success means that they remain fixed social creatures.

It is in this line of novelists that Orwell fits, even in his first novel, *Down and Out in Paris and London*. The truth in that novel, accordingly, is the truth, or falsity, of the social system. The world of the first novel is an economic nightmare to the individual, not much different in kind from the nightmarish quality of Orwell's last novel, *1984*. In the first, the economic trap in which the narrator finds himself is equivalent to the political trap in which Winston Smith (of *1984*) is ensnared. Both systems leave little freedom for the individual; the lack of money in *Down and*

Out is, as it were, like the telescreen in *1984*. Both "watch" the individual, deprive him of his freedom, and are everpresent in his mind.

There is no denying that these nightmares are true: the greatest of nightmares, fictional or personal, are those which the individual finds real enough to project upon the actual world. The point is that he must make these personal nightmares seem dramatically cogent, that is, the nightmares of all of us. In this sense, Orwell does fail, for his nightmare works out in social and economic terms, not psychologically. The novelist cannot successfully convey a twentieth-century nightmare solely in nineteenth-century terms. The central character, be he Flory of *Burmese Days,* Gordon Comstock of *Keep the Aspidistra Flying,* the narrator of *Down and Out in Paris and London,* Dorothy Hare of *A Clergyman's Daughter* (1935), or even George Bowling of *Coming up for Air* (1939), is himself not fully developed, even while his social progress is. Often, he can avoid personal horror by making a social decision that resolves an inner conflict. Gordon Comstock, for example, must make up his mind about money, and once he decides to earn a living he can enjoy home, family, and love. There is really little desperation to Gordon's plight; if he can decide what to do and thus effect his destiny radically, then the quality of his nightmare is relatively unfrightening.

Similarly, the narrator of *Down and Out* is waiting for a situation that will change his future. His downness and outness are contingent upon his securing a job, but the point is he can obtain one and will: his appearance, education, and enunciation all mark him as a man virtually playing with the idea of poverty. As long as the narrator retains an escape, the reader transforms his social agonies into the adventures of a picaresque. The episodes themselves are full of interest, as were those of the typical eighteenth-century traveler who went from inn to road, but they are not compelling for the very reason that they remain almost entirely external experiences, not inner ones. The victim can survive this sort of thing with resignation if he knows that his circumstances can and will change. Orwell's narrator has a friend to whom he can apply for money, exactly as Gordon Comstock has the fantastic Ravelston. For both the narrator and Comstock, the future holds dreams; for both, there is an illusion that can be sustained; for both, the experience can be changed.

George Bowling of *Coming up for Air,* Orwell's fifth novel in seven years, is somewhat different from the general run of Orwell protagonists simply because he holds his fate in hand, although he too feels that the future will crush him. Now in middle age and with the clownish ridiculousness of the fat man, George is anxious to recover his lost youth, which is attached to his pre-marital, pre-fatherhood, pre-fat, and pre-middle-aged period. In returning to Lower Binfield, Bowling makes the familiar return of every dissatisfied adult to his childhood when purity was possible. And like all those sentimentalists anxious to recall a happier and fresher time, he is disappointed when he finds that his memory has falsified all: the dream can now be recovered only through a drunken fog. The romanticism of such a view is patent, and for Orwell to return to this kind of theme indicates his alienation from major twentieth-century literature and also acts as indirect comment upon his kind of socialism. In his dogged, straightforward manner, Orwell tried to re-create a conflict between hopeless present and hopeful past, between the fat Bowling and the attractive, slim young man, between a time of potential doom and a time of freshness which even the First World War did not appreciably dampen. But the conflicts, such as they are, cannot be dramatized except through psychological analysis. The tension must work out in Bowling himself, and its failure to do so is, ultimately, the failure of the novel.

Unlike Bowling, Flory of *Burmese Days* is permanently marked, both literally and figuratively. His ugly birthmark that glows or fades according to his emotional needs is indeed the mark of Cain: it identifies him and disallows his escaping his fate, which is, obviously, to be marked from birth for some role. Each time he sets himself in position it must be with his "good" side to the person he wishes to impress. It is, clearly, a physical manifestation of a psychological weakness, and it follows Flory through every emotion, lighting up and announcing the disconcerted man.

Burmese Days is surely the most successful of Orwell's novels because Flory is securely tied to his condition. There is no escape for him simply because his character is his destiny. In this novel, whose atmosphere derives in part from Conrad's "Heart of Darkness" and *Lord Jim,* character and theme are cemented together: the fact that a marked Flory has left England to escape himself indicates the man. In Burma, he avoids, or tries to avoid, all the unpleasantness of England; as a "superior" white among natives, he has money to spend and influence to dispense, even though he knows the system is wrong. Thus, in exchange for temporarily gaining his self-respect, he must shamefully know that his type of life in Burma is an escape and an acceptance of a demeaning existence.

Caught by what he is, marked by his ugly sign, psychologically weakened by his inadequacy, he has conflicts which can be resolved only by suicide. The tensions in Flory are those he creates by trying to gain a kind of happiness impossible for one of his character. In reproducing many facets of his own Burmese service, Orwell enables Flory to see the perversion of his motives as well as the rottenness of English rule in Burma. Committed to allegiances which he cannot possibly accept, Flory is on a rack. His position in English society derives from his vocal approval of English prejudice, English experience, English misrule, all of which he loathes. The only man with whom he has any kind of intellectual contact is, ironically, a Burmese doctor vastly superior in sensitivity and intelligence to his English compatriots. Yet to be friendly with any native but a paid whore is to be ridiculed.

Beneath the English assumption of superiority is the great fear which underlies all imperialistic action, an anxiety which Orwell prophetically catches. This fear dictates that the conqueror deny completely the natives' intelligence. Accordingly, the English colony demands that the Burmese be ignored or treated as servants; for the Englishman is aware that the natives are biding their time. Flory, who knows the nature of such self-deception, cannot live the lie of his daily existence. His course of loyalty to the English colony demands what only an Ellis, with his racial rabble-rousing, can offer. Thus, Flory is sapped within and without. Too weak to aid his Burmese friend when he knows the doctor needs help, Flory cannot face himself.

Torn by self-doubt, he sees in Elizabeth, the young, foolish girl who has come to Burma looking for a husband, much more than she can possibly offer. As commonplace as the other members of the English colony, Elizabeth seems to be more than she is because she carries with her wisps of England: freshness, a white complexion, youthful vigor—all the things that go dead in Burma. She is a relief from native women and from the boredom of drinking in the local club, the center of white superiority. But beyond this, she is nothing; and Flory half recognizes her inadequacies while he woos her with his agonized plea for her "cultured" companionship.

Almost alone of Orwell's novels, from *Down and Out* through *1984,* sixteen years later, *Burmese Days* contains conflicts sufficiently dramatized to raise social protest to literature. A small novel in its accomplishment, despite the importance of its theme, it creates a character of some substance and affords a look at minor tragedy. As Orwell recognized in writing this novel, tragedy must be conceived in individual and not social terms.

Orwell was caught in the difficult position of standing strongly behind the individual and yet trying to create through his novels a mold in which individuality is frustrated. He never clearly resolves the conflict between his point of view—individualistic and atomistic—and the naturalistic bent of his technique. C. P. Snow has also faced this problem, and he solves it, at least at his level, by allowing his individuals to realize themselves to some extent. Snow's social matrix, unlike Orwell's, is rarely powerful enough to stifle his characters: the individual will can prevail. Orwell, however, starts with the premise that the system traps the individual, and although he may want the individual to succeed, the latter—Flory, for instance—is cursed from birth. This type of frustration has of course been the stuff of great literature, from Cain on, but only when the author has been able to project and intensify his material imaginatively. Otherwise, the novel becomes merely another demonstration of society's attempt to crush its dissenters.

Even Orwell's ability to evoke disgusting sights and smells suggests his need to root everything in definite time and space. And yet this man whose novels seem based so solidly in modern rot is nostalgic for an irrecoverable Eden. Like Cary, Green, Waugh, and Elizabeth Bowen, writers with whom he otherwise has little in common, he tries to recapture the idylls of the past, a golden age that he is too realistic to believe ever really existed. George Bowling of *Coming Up for Air,* with his return to Lower Binfield to recapture childhood memories, attempts to get momentarily outside a world that is becoming increasingly chaotic. In *1984,* also, there is a longing for the world, bad as it was, before Big Brother took over and granted his murderous paternalism. The world of ordinary wars—when peace did exist between wars, unlike the world of 1984 when war is the same as peace—seems nostalgically and sentimentally pleasant.

Among Orwell's contemporaries, only Greene and Snow have attempted to deal with the present world *without* any significant nostalgia for the past. For Beckett, of course, past and present cannot be separated. Ivy Compton-Burnett perhaps speaks for the rest when she says that the world she is familiar with ended about 1910, as though events after that have unloosed the forces of confusion which must somehow be avoided. Greene, however, accepts the evils of the modern world and imposes upon his characters "guilt" which will hold their individual wills in check. Snow tries to meet each decision as it must be made and suggests that only compromise and flexibility will arrest the forces of anarchy. Both, however, Snow as well as Greene, are aware of the chaos that lurks behind rational decisions, of the bad feelings that go into sincere beliefs, of the ironies and paradoxes involved in apparently rational resolutions.

Orwell, though, presents the paradox of a heroic figure who tries to face every major moral decision that the age offers, and yet remains a man with a wistful nostalgia for the days when life was better, or less obviously bad. Even in *Homage to Catalonia,* that cataloguing of deceit and treachery during the Spanish Civil War, Orwell glances back at the time when alliances were just that, and a man at least knew whom he was fighting for before he died. Now, although men continue to fight for what they believe in, they find that their heroics are hopeless and that they are being undermined at the very moment they are dying for what they think is a worthy cause. In *Homage,* Orwell might have had the tragic theme which eluded him in his other works. But here, where he had perhaps the strongest material of any of his books, he turned to journalism, albeit of a superior kind, which precluded characterization and drama. The human drama of the Civil War was partially lost in the urgency of the experience and the necessity to transmit a political message. Ironically, the "novel" went unrecognized for several years, and even Orwell's journalistic intention was blunted.

This piece of reportage and personal narrative came in an intensely political period in Orwell's career when, except for *Coming up for Air* the following year, he was to desert the novel. Even Orwell's political pieces, however, are not completely felicitous, as though the novelist were fighting the political writer, and the politician fighting the fiction writer. Orwell's political writings ultimately fail because of their lack of theory; so that Orwell's politics, built as they are on deep personal belief, seem somewhat sketchy, the result of day-to-day pragmatism rather than of a fully thought-out system. Curiously, Orwell's political ideas are not sufficiently theoretical or imaginative, while his literary ideas are often too political.

Prior to *1984,* Orwell often kept his ideas in separate containers, although at times his literary values invaded his political ideas, and vice versa. In *Homage to Catalonia,* for example, he writes of personal experiences in one section and then in another switches to an examination of political expedience. One indeed misses the political novel that Orwell *might* have written, in which literature and politics become intertwined, what Conrad tried in *Nostromo, The Secret Agent,* and *Under Western Eyes,* what C. P. Snow is attempting with less success in his *Strangers and Brothers* series. Unfortunately, English fiction has not been noted for its great political novels, and the tradition itself is not particularly strong, Disraeli, Trollope, and Meredith notwithstanding. Perhaps with a relatively stable government and a relatively enlightened electorate, the English cannot generate the kind of violence and hatred that result in effective political literature.

Evidently, Orwell, with his blistering rationalism, was not the man to write this kind of novel. The political novel at its best— *The Possessed, The Magic Mountain, Nostromo, The Red and the Black*—requires an imaginative projection in which characters are trapped, almost smothered, by forces that remain inexplicable and subterranean. Dostoyevsky was of course capable of creating characters of this sort, Mann and Conrad less able; Orwell could not at all, if we cite *1984* as his attempt to integrate literature and politics. Perhaps Orwell believed too strongly in the bourgeois tradition for him to suggest successfully the irrational behavior that must exist in the good political novel. Likewise, Joyce Cary tried to create large-scale political novels in his Chester Nimmo trilogy, and he too failed because he substituted episodic development for dramatic confrontation and comic action for the frenzy of obsessed people.

The political novel demands the author's imaginative obsession with his material. Furthermore, Orwell's technical simplicities— his manner of narrating a non-abstract, straight-forward story— precluded the broad development that usually accompanies the all-inclusive political novel. Orwell's own method was perhaps too well grounded in creating immediate action for him to effectively wed narrative with theory.

In *1984,* Orwell attempted precisely such a union, but here his power to astonish replaces the ability to create meaningful characters in a dramatic situation. Orwell's characters are not individualized people but all mankind caught in a state that exploits and crushes them. As a terrifying vision of the world, *1984* is effective propaganda against encroaching centralization, a natural outgrowth of the author's desire to retain a simpler and purer life, like George Bowling's childhood vision of Lower Binfield. *1984,* in a way, is a culmination of Orwell's vision of life in all of his novels, and particularly of his school days depicted in *Such, Such Were the Joys.*

In Orwell's earlier work, all society was a prison, whether the prison of Flory's Burma, the prison of London and Paris, the prison of living on a pound a week in *Keep the Aspidistra Flying,* the prison of working in the coal mines in *The Road to Wigan Pier* (1937). *1984* seems a logical outgrowth of these books, the work of a man more interested in analyzing crushed human beings than in placing the individual in conflict with other people. Orwell's characters are generally in struggle against a system, sometimes against themselves, but rarely against other people. One thinks of Orwell's having thrown his characters into a circular machine and then noting their struggle against the machine, their attempts to escape it or compromise themselves with it.

The loss in mature contact is great. Perhaps the thinness apparent in all of Orwell's fiction is the author's failure to provide dramatic confrontation for his chief characters, so that the latter would seem to move in a world of people as well as of events. Since Orwell makes events predominate, people always appear less than what they actually are. The result suggests the same faults contained in the naturalistic novel—the system catches and drains the individual so that his own actions become ultimately meaningless.

Orwell's method is possibly a logical extension of the contemporary trend to eliminate the hero. The first group of major novelists presented protagonists who took central roles but who had nevertheless lost all trace of heroic action. These novelists, however, provided conflicts for their characters so as to convey their human stature. As a literary Marxist making the outside predominate over the inside, Orwell has reduced his protagonists to isolated elements in an atmosphere that will swallow them. Unlike Orwell, a naturalist like Zola could compensate for this loss by integrating particular images into universal mosaics and by intensifying concrete details into symbols.

If we look momentarily at an Orwell novel in which just such human relationships were attempted, *Keep the Aspidistra Flying,* we see how weak they actually are. Gordon Comstock has as his chief foil the aristocratic Ravelston, who with his easy air and rich manner is everything that Gordon is not. Ravelston is a socialist through belief, Gordon through necessity. Ravelston can speak against the Establishment even though he possesses everything the system has to offer; Gordon, however, must fight the system as one who is tempted by what it can offer to those who succumb to it. Ravelston has no great conflicts and finds socialism intellectually necessary while he enjoys capitalism; Gordon has to come to terms with a capitalism which he knows is wrong but which provides the comforts he desires. Between the two, obvious as the relationship is, there might have been a powerful conflict, for here the two classes, upper and shabby middle, come together in a common cause but for entirely different reasons and with entirely different points of view. Potentially, there is real tension. Orwell, however, makes Gordon into a wheezing crank and Ravelston into a benevolent friend whose manner derives from a storybook, not from life. A Gordon could possibly exist, a Ravelston never. Orwell is interested in Gordon as a victim, not as a human being, and the novel proceeds from there. Gordon is running away from a world which demands economic competition to insure one's survival, and Gordon defines himself by his negative response to this world. This kind of literary character is self-defeating, not because he denies the world but because his answer to whatever the world demands is simply the opposite, *despite* what he is or wants to be. A character who is merely contrary and whose beliefs become the opposite of what others believe, is generally as lacking in substance as those he opposes. Gordon, moreover, is a chronic complainer, and his difficulties seem to emanate as much from what he is as from the social ills he suffers. Consequently, Gordon seems himself as much at fault for his misery as society, and when he reconciles himself to a prosperous middle class future, he resolves problems that exist in himself rather than those that stem from his social milieu.

In several of his novels, Orwell is caught in this no man's land between the individual need and the social demand. The novel ostensibly appears to be concerned with social conditions, but the character who is used to represent them seems to generate his own type of problem, and the two are confused. Thus, in *Burmese Days,* Flory is marked at birth, and no matter what he does or how he reacts to the situation, he cannot escape the evident mark. Accordingly, his response to the circumstances of English colonialism is as much a result of what he is as it is a consequence of the conditions themselves. Orwell frequently confuses private neurosis with social ills, though if the two are connected, as he evidently feels they are, he has insufficiently presented them.

A piece like *Animal Farm* (1945), with its mockery of Stalinism, was perhaps so successful because Orwell did not have to write about people as such, and therefore could avoid the confrontation between the personal problem and the social sickness. *Animal Farm* catches in miniature the world that Orwell was to project later in *1984,* but it fails as successful satire, despite scattered brilliant passages, by virtue of its predictability. The final result is not so much an exposé of man's iniquity as the lesser conclusion that animals would react like men were they to be given the choices that men have; and this conclusion is not so weighty as many of Orwell's admirers would have it. *Animal Farm* gained its fame because of its timeliness as a political comment—Orwell wrote it while the West strongly accepted Stalin as an ally—and not because of its power as satire. Compared with *Gulliver's Travels,* especially Book Four, it lacks the variety and pungency of Swift and indicates little more than that power corrupts whether man or beast wields it.

In *1984,* Orwell was also concerned with demonstrating how power corrupts, and perhaps the most brilliant part of his novel is that devoted to rhetoric. Once the reader forgets the characters and their daily horror, he still remembers the powerful use of language as a way of controlling society. Here, Orwell recognizes that language, whether used by the poet, the journalist, or the dictator, suggests the quality of a society. And a manipulation of language, particularly at present, affords a manipulation of the society itself. The ramifications of this idea can, of course, be horrible, as the novel indicates. Newspeak, the language of the 1984 "Utopia," eliminates all nuances of meaning; the language of a scientifically controlled future, it attempts to avoid all poetry of expression, all imagination. For by excluding any possible confusion, Newspeak also eliminates the beauty of ambiguity in which suggestions exfoliate from a core of simple meaning. Parts of speech are dropped, all abstractions simply cease to exist, and words are compounded to avoid duplication. *Goodsex,* for example, is chastity, and *sexcrime* covers all kinds of perversions as well as normal intercourse; rape is equivalent to regular intercourse in a society which frowns on sex of any sort. Consequently, the mind is controlled by the word—the word, theoretically, is to act as stimulus, and the response elicited is to be complete obedience to the state.

Just as language in this society will crush the human spirit by making it react scientifically, so too the state will control all forms of sexual activity, making chastity the highest ideal. Sex is considered a form of irrationality which the state cannot control directly; therefore, the state attempts to limit the sexual act by making intercourse punishable by death. In a society in which man is to become mechanical, in which indeed he is to function without thought or feeling, sex must be almost immediately eliminated. The Puritanical code merges with the dictatorial code; both attempt to restrain the uncontrollable. Orwell recognized that he who controls his sex controls a good part of himself; and if the state can control it, the state controls mankind.*

The whole point of *1984* is that the future state will allow man no outlet, so that his entire existence is for the state. In the society of the past, that of the 1940's, for example, indulgence was the rule. To eliminate such laxity is the task of any state that seeks complete control. This emphasis on sexual chastity seems to be Orwell's direct comment on Soviet Russia, in which a Puritanical spirit appears to be the answer to Western profligacy, but the application to the West should not be lost. The repression of real sexual feeling with the substitution of the false and the titillating, responses that D. H. Lawrence spent a lifetime fighting, is ingrained in Western culture; so that Orwell's attack on sexual control is the traditional humanist's plea that man's natural instincts should not be stifled, or the result is a nightmare, a *1984*.

Orwell's vision has always been connected to the humanistic and romantic tradition. His books suggest a kind of civilized pastoral in which man fulfills himself through work and sex without regard for money, competition, and self-seeking. Like William Morris's Utopia, Orwell's socialistic state is tinged with this nostalgia for a past that the latter is surely too astute to believe ever existed outside of man's imagination. Orwell argues what seems a tough brand of socialism, but actually his socialism, once the economic machine is controlled, insists on the possibilities of man's goodness. His socialistic project is not the world of *1984*, as many critics antipathetic to socialism have claimed. Orwell's Utopia, tinged by its author's optimism, is too permissive to seem

---

* A similar idea appeared in Eugene Zamiatin's *We* (1924), a novel which foreruns much of Orwell's *1984*, as well as Huxley's *Brave New World*. In Zamiatin's mythical state of a thousand years later, the state controls every aspect of life, and especially sex. The novel is based on the idea that the way to rid man of criminality is to rid him of his freedom; control his desires, and you can make him a slave of the state.

possible, too idyllic to make sense in an industrialized society. *1984* for Orwell does not represent the socialistic future, but what will appear if world socialism does *not* triumph over both capitalism and communism.

Yet despite his strong commitment to a political system and his desire to see reason brought directly into political thinking, Orwell could recognize another position. In a long essay on Henry Miller's *Tropic of Cancer,* called "Inside the Whale," Orwell remarked what for him was Miller's greatness: the attempt to allow man to do what he wants, what Orwell labeled the "passive noncoöperative attitude." According to this view, Orwell writes, "Progress and reaction have both turned out to be swindles. Seemingly there is nothing left but quietism—robbing reality of its terrors by simply submitting to it. Get inside the whale—or rather, admit you are inside the whale (for you *are,* of course). Give yourself over to the world-process, stop fighting against it or pretending that you control it; simply accept it, endure it, record it." (*Such, Such Were the Joys,* p. 198)

In this comment, Orwell suggests a tragic theme that might have effectively summed up what he believed had he been able to develop and expand it. As it is, the conflict between fighting for what one knows is right and the desire to retreat into passive acceptance is never fully dramatized in Orwell's fiction. Instead, it is discussed in an essay in praise of someone else. Miller's way was not of course Orwell's, it was diametrically opposed; yet both shared some common vision of what the world should be: a private place where a man can realize his own aims with decency and propriety.

This ideal is what the reader comes away with after going through Orwell's writing. No single work predominates, no single idea is clearly remembered, no theory has been set up for future expansion or discussion. What cannot be doubted is the sense of decency of this man who was often wrong, often unjustifiably opinionated, but who in his anger tried to become the moral conscience of his generation. Orwell lived through one of the most chaotic periods in history, and he saw radical changes occurring in the world, unprecedented ones, but he chose to retain hard-gained truths and human dignity. Perhaps more than any of his contemporaries, Orwell has to be read as a whole, or else the keenness of a mind which saw through the falsity of his day will ultimately be forgotten, or at best remembered by over-praised works like *Animal Farm* and *1984*. Possibly, he was better as a man than as a novelist.

It is one of the paradoxes of literature that someone like Orwell, a spokesman for liberalism and a destroyer of cant, was unable to provide satisfactory fiction although his mind saw clearly a world full of conflicts. Perhaps the very clarity of the vision made impossible the "confusion" and "fumbling" which his less politically liberal contemporaries bring to bear upon the novel. Perhaps the very directness of his attack upon the body politic precluded the large novel that Orwell should have written. Once again the specter of Naturalism rises up, and Orwell is ensnared in a literary trap, precisely as his characters are caught in the trap of life.*

---

* A worthy successor to Orwell in this respect is the American writer Clancy Sigal, whose *Weekend in Dinlock* (1960) recalls Orwell's *The Road to Wigan Pier*. Sigal's book is a mixture of novel and journalistic detail—what has more recently become the novel-as-fact in Truman Capote and Norman Mailer—the result of Sigal's two weekends in Dinlock, a coal-mining town in Yorkshire. Like much of Orwell's work, the book is often more interesting as report than as novel, especially for its insights into the love-hate relationship of working men with their labor, for its graphic picture of the way a community forms its own mores apart from the larger society, and, finally, for its delineation of forms of survival in a subculture. The reader interested in the broader implications of such subcultures should consult Richard Hoggart's *The Uses of Literacy* (1957).

IX

The World of Evelyn Waugh:
The Normally Insane

TO PASS from George Orwell to Evelyn Waugh is like moving from eighteenth-century rationality to *Alice in Wonderland* fantasy. Orwell's portrayal of a decaying society in which regeneration is possible through democratic socialism appears naïve juxtaposed to Waugh's world of self-seeking Bright Young People, expedient and dissolute playboys, ineffectual soldiers, and irresponsible aristocrats.* To expect regeneration from such a crew is to imagine the impossible. However, unlike Orwell, Waugh at his best is not concerned with results.

In presentation as well, the two novelists seem sharply divergent. Orwell's world of poverty and social distinctions is directly observed and represented: as we have seen, for Orwell the best method is the one that remains simple and unobtrusive. For Waugh, the more imaginative of the two, the story is itself secondary to the way in which it is presented. Indiscriminate in its attacks, his humor annoys and disturbs, avoiding personal comment; in a way, it imitates the masks that several contemporary

* *Decline and Fall* (1928); *Vile Bodies* (1930); *Black Mischief* (1932); *A Handful of Dust* (1934); *Scoop* (1937); *Put Out More Flags* (1942); *Work Suspended* (1942); *Brideshead Revisited* (1945); *The Loved One* (1948); *Scott-King's Modern Europe* (1949); *Helena* (1950); *Men at Arms* (1952); *Love Among the Ruins* (1953); *Officers and Gentlemen* (1955); *The Ordeal of Gilbert Pinfold* (1957); *Unconditional Surrender* (1961).

writers have assumed. At first, lacking an assemblage of narrators, Waugh could, with ironic wit, observe dispassionately, even
cold-bloodedly; later, he began to experiment with a new and
more personal style. Orwell, on the contrary, is himself in every
line and page, pushing his argument, exhorting, pointing, making
sure the reader misses nothing. Waugh permits the reader to for-
get what he pleases.

Two writers, accordingly, could not appear more different, and
yet, curiously, the unabashed Tory and the rigid Socialist meet
across an apparently uncrossable chasm. If we assume that Guy
Crouchback (of *Men at Arms,* 1952, and *Officers and Gentlemen,*
1955) is something of a literary surrogate for Waugh—his experiences generally parallel many of the author's—then we see
that his growing disillusionment approaches that of the Orwell of
1984. Both Orwell and Waugh remained patriotic, Orwell more
diffuse, Waugh more focused; both, however, justified man's commitment to a good cause. Guy himself joins the service after eight
years of soul-searching in the wilderness, the war having provided
some use for his inert energies. In the war, Guy hopes to be re-
generated; as his Catholicism serves God, so his secular being will
serve England—there is for Waugh an explicit identification between the two. Guy accepts several setbacks, embarrassments,
and indignities, but for good or ill, *"Serviam* both God and country." Eliminate God, and one returns to the Orwell of the Spanish
Civil War, the Orwell who felt that Spanish soil was providing the
battleground for the struggle between right and wrong. Commitment was both necessary and respectable. Orwell was in Spain
while Guy Crouchback was passing through his eight years of
agony, in which he did nothing, felt nothing, had nothing happen
to him. Then came the war, his own Spanish Civil War, in which
issues seemed relatively clear. It became another Holy Crusade.
Later, however, Guy sees his ideal for what it is, a world of deception and of evil, self-seeking mechanical men, the world of
1984. Waugh writes:

It was just such a sunny breezy Mediterranean day two years before
when he read of the Russo-German alliance, when a decade of shame
seemed to be ending in light and reason, when the Enemy was plain

in view, huge and hateful, all disguise cast off; the modern age in arms.

Now that hallucination was dissolved, like the whales and turtles on the voyage from Crete, and he was back after less than two years' pilgrimage in a Holy Land of illusion in the old ambiguous world, where priests were spies and gallant friends proved traitors and his country was led blundering into dishonour. (*Officers and Gentlemen*, p. 325)

The world that Guy now recognizes is one that no longer allows Bright Young Men or expedient and dissolute playboys to move about casually. When the priest to whom Guy confesses turns out to be a spy and when Ivor Claire, the man whom Hitler had not taken into account in his plunge toward total conquest, proves a coward and traitor, then Guy knows that no ideals are possible. The future leads to Orwell's *1984,* a nightmare of personal frustration. Waugh, however, did not stop or begin there.

What Orwell attacked by rational argument, Waugh in his early novels parodies and makes farcical. Close in their nihilism to Firbank's fruity nonsense and Huxley's despairing comedies of the twenties, Waugh's early novels also suggest the indifference to the larger world of Fitzgerald's playboys and Hemingway's dissolutes. His clearly is not the kind of humor or comedy that attempts to create balance by purging nonsense. One might well argue that Waugh's sympathies lie with these Bright Young People—certainly Basil Seal has his own brand of charm. Only to a limited extent do social institutions come under his attack, and the people whom he mocks appear to be the only ones who count. In escaping them, apparently, one embraces the commonplace and tedious. Waugh's humor obviously is far from the comic spirit of Meredith.

In Moliére, in the Shakespeare of *A Midsummer Night's Dream,* as well as in Meredith, the comic helped expunge the distinction between classes and momentarily closed the social gap. As such, it served a moral purpose. In his use of the comic, however, Waugh ignores the moral purpose intrinsic to Meredith's and Molière's view. Waugh avoids issues, decisions, controversy, for all the world is the object of his farce. Nothing is sacred, not even the Catholic Church, which he joined in 1930, almost at the very start of his literary career. That perhaps explains why *Brideshead Revisited* (1945) falls flat, for here Catholicism is to be taken seriously as a powerful but ambiguous force. Possibly that is why all of Waugh's doctrinaire works are slight and unrewarding. His comic approach precluded his worshiping at any altar, and when he did so, method clashed with subject matter. Among his recent novels, *Men at Arms* and *Officers and Gentlemen* are weak for perhaps the same reasons: Guy's religious spirit prevents him from changing or growing. He remains what he is: a boring, well-meaning, ineffectual young man on the brink of useless middle age. Caught midway between humor and seriousness, Guy is tedious.

When, however, Waugh does not restrict himself by considerations of doctrine or qualms of religious conscience, he is his own man; and his very strength as a humorist—his kind—is his freedom to attack in every direction. When he tries to become serious, like Orwell he makes what he defends seem dry and flat. Waugh has often been called a satirist, but satire presupposes belief, doctrine, dogma. Clearly, in his early and most effective work, Waugh is defending no one and nothing. Possibly the only belief that comes through plainly is his defense of the sanctity of the individual, as in *The Ordeal of Gilbert Pinfold* (1957).

Larger issues rarely count in early Waugh, and not until his later work does the reader become aware of the impingement of the world. In the thirties, he was interested in people whose social attitudes mark them as egoists, eccentrics, expedients. In describing their special kind of behavior, he revels in the fact that insanity is the norm and sanity the anomaly. Later, when sanity, or the search for it, becomes his norm, he appears dull. To demonstrate that insanity can seem normal is the basis of Waugh's farcical style. For farce, fantasy, caricature are all related, and all assume that immoderate elements give impetus to society. Here Waugh in one way follows Dickens; the world of *Bleak House*, for example, is completely irrational, and it is this world which predominates, and seems to be the *only* world.

At his best, in *Decline and Fall* (1928), *Black Mischief* (1932), *A Handful of Dust* (1934), *Scoop* (1937), *Put Out More Flags* (1942), and *The Loved One* (1948), Waugh is able to present chaos and disorder as the very fabric of a universe out of tilt; and each time a chaotic character attempts to gain purchase in a sane world, he is re-tipped off balance, as though the norm itself has gone crazy. Here, misidentification can result in knighthoods, people can be incinerated as sheep, boots as well as fiancés can be eaten—and enjoyed, schoolmasters can be jailed for spreading white slavery.

In this kind of world, Waugh catches with a few marks of almost irrelevant identification the idiocy of individuals and their institutions. In *Put Out More Flags,* for instance, Peter Pastmaster is anxious to get married, the girl herself not making much difference to him; he has narrowed his choice to three:

> Since he was marrying for old-fashioned, dynastic reasons, he proposed to make an old-fashioned, dynastic choice from among the survivors of Whig oligarchy. He really could see very little difference between the three girls; in fact he sometimes caused offence by addressing them absent-mindedly by the wrong names. None of them carried a pound of superfluous flesh; they all had an enthusiasm for the works of Mr. Ernest Hemingway; all had pet dogs of rather similar peculiarities. They had all found that the way to keep Peter amused was to get him to brag about his past iniquities.

The brilliant touch is, of course, the phrase about the girls' lack of superfluous flesh and their enthusiasm for Hemingway: through the description, Waugh contrasts these somewhat asexual girls, lean and astringent, with Hemingway blowsiness and sensuality. The girls, in brief, make no sense, follow no rule or principle, are, in their way, mad.

As I have suggested, Waugh, like Henry Green, is at his happiest when his theme is confusion. He is weakest when he deliberately attempts to turn chaos into order, hysteria into sanity, madness into normality. In *Scoop,* he has a theme made to order —the wrong Boot is sent to Ishamelia to report the local war, and then the wrong man is rewarded for what the wrong Boot has not really done.

The tendency of Waugh's early work is to present a man-centered universe, in which values have no moral meaning outside of what they signify to the individual. Legal punishment, as that of Paul Pennyfeather in *Decline and Fall,* results from misidentification or confusion—the real criminals go free unsuspected. Waugh assumes that everyone can be bought, everyone can be made acquiescent to any idea, no matter how ludicrous. The more ludicrous it is, in fact, the more chance of its being believed. People always misidentify what they are: Mr. Joyboy (*The Loved One*), who works on dead bodies, thinks of himself as an artist; Margot Beste-Chetwynde (*Decline and Fall*), a white slaver, conceives of herself as a mighty social power and carries herself like an Eastern Potentate; Agatha Runcible (*Vile Bodies*), an enormously annoying young woman, moves through society as if ultimate power were hers. Waugh's characters, rarely recognizing their limitations, and never apologizing, throw themselves fully into life. When they meet obstacles that they had not dreamed existed and their ultimate power is questioned, then Waugh has a comic situation.

The basis of Waugh's comedy, if it can be defined, is confusion compounded by human presumption. Waugh's characters usually assume more, or less, about themselves than they are intrinsically worth, and then, suddenly, they are thrust into zany situations: Boot in *Scoop,* Paul Pennyfeather in *Decline and Fall,* Basil Seal in *Black Mischief.* Another aspect of Waugh's comedy is the characters' ability to throw off one role and assume another, as the situation calls for it. His characters adjust, merge, reshape themselves. Their substance is protean, their natures flexible and melting: they can do whatever life forces them to do, and, often, they are only too willing to re-make themselves. The bizarre, the eccentric, the idiosyncratic all appear normal to them.

The disparity between what the character accepts and what the reader knows is right often provides the comic element. We can immediately see how different Waugh is from socially conscious comic writers like Jane Austen, Fielding, and Meredith, who used comic situations to redress injustice. Waugh at his best is an entertainer, not a moralist, while the above three are moralists who entertain as a vehicle for their ethical ideas. There is no such purpose in early Waugh, and when he tries to provide one, as his recent work from *Brideshead Revisited* (1945) indicates, then his method no longer suffices, and the comic elements give way to commonplace ideas.

Waugh's ideas, as we derive them from his later books, are too unconsidered to stand successfully separated from the comic devices which mask, strengthen, and give substance to them. Stated directly, his attitudes—politically and socially reactionary, prejudicial, contentious, snobbish, aristocratic—are no more effective than those of the outrageous newspaper magnates he guyed so unmercifully in his early novels. When he could lampoon all ideas, his own as well, Waugh had secure purchase on ground that was his alone; but when either because of age, success, or artistic belief he let down the comic mask and spoke personally, then his novels lost their style. Possibly at some point, Waugh felt that the manner of the early novels would not suffice for a world on the brink of annihilation, and he decided to become "serious." His change, however, from one kind of fiction to another, it must be made clear, is not a development in which the artist's powers come to maturity, but a diminution.

The change is apparent in *Brideshead Revisited* from the second word, "I." There are intermittent passages, particularly at the beginning, reminiscent of the former Waugh, but here, whether his power has weakened or his intention simply changed, irony is lost. The story is a kind of *Pilgrim's Progress* for our day, a Graham Greene morality drama. Charles Ryder, an agnostic, mingles with Catholics and comes to understand their point of view, gradually seeing why they suffer as they do in order to gain God's pity. As Julia says in self-depreciation:

. . . or it may be a private bargain between me and God, that if I give up this one thing I want [marriage with Ryder] so much, however bad I am, He won't quite despair of me in the end. (p. 309)

To marry Ryder would mean giving up God, and she finds that she cannot shut herself off from His mercy—she would have to be considerably worse than she is to set up a rival good to that of God's.

How unusual for a Waugh character to depreciate herself! Once she would have exulted in what she was, and let the rest of the world burn. With moral consciences, his characters become tedious. Christianity smothers laughter, and from ludicrous amoral people come institutionalized hypocrites. Julia allows her ideal of God's goodness to destroy her chance of happiness on earth, or at least she exchanges one kind of happiness for another, and yet how false and pretentious her conversion seems.

Earlier, Cordelia, Julia's somewhat nondescript sister, says of Sebastian, another convert:

One can have no idea what the suffering may be, to be maimed as he is—no dignity, no power of will. No one is ever holy without suffering. It's taken that form with him. . . . I've seen so much suffering in the last few years; there's so much coming for everybody soon. (p. 281)

A great deal of the suffering stems not so much from the world itself as from the very thing that is to give eventual peace: the religious beliefs of the characters. The mother of the Flyte family, Lady Marchmain, is referred to as a saint. Cordelia states extravagantly that ". . . when people wanted to hate God they hated Mummy. . . . Well, you see, she was saintly but she wasn't a saint. No one could really hate a saint, could they?" Lady Marchmain's semi-sainthood consists of transforming Sebastian into a dipsomaniac, turning her other son, Brideshead, into a prig who marries a vulgarian, leading Julia into an absurd marriage, reducing Cordelia to a secular nun, and sending her own husband into exile from England to Italy. Her religious obsession makes of life a kind of purgatory in which souls are judged as either heaven- or hell-bent. Wandering through the country estate at Brideshead, she haunts her children with her goodness and frustrates all life with her viscid martyrdom.

Waugh seems to be indicating that people should be Catholics, as though no alternative existed. It is not curious, then, that unlike Graham Greene's characters, their beliefs appear grafted upon them. There, religious belief is at the individual's core, and his obsession with it defines him. Both authors nevertheless agree that suffering is preferable to pleasure and that badness rather than goodness brings one close to God. Further, both concur that religious beliefs must be trumpeted, not permitted to lie quiescent. Ostensibly, belief is so powerful that it must force itself into every word and action. Finally, one must not expect to derive joy from his faith.

As we have noted, this hovering presence of belief and disbelief forced Waugh into a commitment to his material that was for him a radical departure. With various degrees of cogency, several critics have argued that from the beginning of his career there was a tragic element in Waugh's work and that his values were there long before he began to dramatize them. This argument, which runs parallel to the one that sees the seeds of Eliot's *Four Quartets* in "The Love Song of J. Alfred Prufrock," tends to make a social critic of vintage Waugh. Once this point is established, the reader can come to terms with the "serious" *Brideshead* as a continuation, with variations, of early Waugh.

This argument seeks to make Waugh into a writer in the grand comic tradition. It suggests that in *Vile Bodies* and *Decline and Fall* Waugh was on the side of the angels and was only attacking the pushers, the newly rich, the tasteless ones; stressing that, on the contrary, he really liked those with style, those born to the role of frivolity, those who could carry off their high jinks with charm and aplomb. However attractive this argument may be— and it does contain a partial truth—nevertheless the very power of these novels derives from Waugh's "be damned" attitude toward everyone. By 1930, Waugh had converted to Catholicism, and yet in *Vile Bodies,* the Jesuit priest with the Jewish name, Father Rothschild, is a kind of superspy. Rothschild knows all, sees all, understands all, is always in the background snooping for information. Waugh never informs the reader how Rothschild obtains his information, or even if it is true—the joke is that the priest is a Jesuit, and Jesuits have the reputation for prying into everything. Therefore, Rothschild knows about everyone and seems to glide through the dark night of misunderstanding with his Pandora's Box of gossip and helpful information.

What Waugh does here in *Vile Bodies,* he continues in his first six novels. Nothing is sacrosanct. Waugh often takes groups, races, classes according to their reputation—Jesuits are spies, Jews are coarse, foreigners are communists or political agents, society women are secretly disreputable, schoolmasters are sadists, journalists are amoral, Negroes are semi-civilized, often cannibalistic, politicians are pirates beneath the social veneer, business magnates are moronic, Armenians are salesmen even when there is nothing to sell—Waugh accepts these tags for the sake of his comedy and then writes as though they were valid. Accordingly, he can have it both ways: he can castigate, often viciously and heartlessly, these aspects of modern life, and at the same time he can derive humor from the fact that people do believe such things. In *Black Mischief,* for example, Basil Seal is successful as Minister of Modernisation in Azania, a Negro Empire off the coast of Africa, simply because he treats the natives as savages, despite their aspirations for freedom and Western culture. Waugh accepts as true the nonsense he has heard about natives; and he can then lampoon all those who want to treat the natives as civilized.

With these attitudes, it is no wonder that Waugh has been treated with disrespect by the liberal press, at the same time his qualities as a humorous writer have been recognized. Too often, however, we tend to look for social enlightenment in a humorous writer whose very humor depends on his parody of those who accept and strongly believe in social enlightenment. Disagreeable as Waugh frequently is, especially when he attacks the reader's own sacred cows, the terms of his comic intention must allow him free play. For the true humorist, and Waugh is often that, nothing can withstand close examination. If the only truth is human truth, as Waugh seems to accept in his first six novels, then every belief is fallible and every point of view vulnerable. Waugh posits no position, suggests no better morality, offers no solution, does not define any problems. He does not even seem to disdain this wasteland and therefore set the tone for a later leap into religious fervor. Undoubtedly, like the rest of us, he prefers sensitivity to crudeness, intelligence to boorishness, honesty to deceit, but values as such are not dramatized and conflicts not presented.

The terrible truth, perhaps, is that Waugh like D. H. Lawrence is much less powerful and dramatic when he becomes consciously cerebral. Guy Crouchback with his ineffectuality is as much a bore as Birkin (*Women in Love*) with his prophetic rantings. Scott-King (*Scott-King's Modern Europe,* 1949) in his attempt to impose honesty is as false a character as Don Ramón (*The Plumed Serpent*) endeavoring to exploit his vision of the unified serpent and bird. Scott-King's statement that "it would be very wicked indeed to do anything to fit a boy for the modern world" may perhaps be cogent as an idea, but as a dramatic consequence of an unbelievable narrative it is implausible.

We turn again to *Brideshead Revisited* because it reveals so much about the author's assumptions. The sections devoted to the Marchmain home and to life at Oxford in the 1920's show Waugh at his best, but these parts are peripheral to the main intention. The principal lines of the novel are wrong because the pretentious people that Waugh takes seriously are the very ones he once would have unsparingly taunted, and he is unable to make the transition from parody to belief convincingly. Charles Ryder, the narrator of the novel, is a "typical" modern agnostic who for 300 pages inveighs against religious belief, particularly the dogmas of the Catholic Church, and then in the last ten pages is sufficiently impressed to suggest a conversion, or at least a different attitude. A modern Pilgrim who must find the right path through suffering, Ryder wanders between worlds, aimless, unrooted, unanchored to any metaphysical belief, a Scott Fitzgerald sad young man looking for his Virgil. Only the Flytes can give him direction, although he must not realize that they are exempla. In fact, in their weakness—they are hypocritical, complacent, drunken, priggish—they seem the opposite of moral exempla, but nevertheless they are struggling toward some religious ideal, dim as it may be to them and Ryder.

The final step in Ryder's inner conversion is the demonstration of faith on the part of Lord Marchmain, a staunch anti-believer, an anti-Catholic, a man who has lived for the things of this world. Now dying, he gives the sign of the cross and receives the last rites of the Church: he is saved. The worst, then, can gain salvation, for Lord Marchmain had fought all aspects of the Church, vowing never to return to England as long as his wife lived. Even Cora, Lord Marchmain's sedate mistress, speaks sagaciously, like a latent nun whose role is to save her master. She considers Lady Marchmain a good and misunderstood woman, calls the lord a man who must be protected from his own innocence, and feels that everyone must be defended from himself—a philosopher as well as lover, she sees deeply into human motives.

All this attitudinizing becomes fake. People exist to make a point, not to illustrate the way they actually live. Ryder must be converted, Lady Marchmain must triumph through the final conversion of her husband, Cora must hover as a protectress, Sebastian, the drunkard, must achieve a kind of sainthood through inner suffering, Julia must renounce the possibility of earthly happiness, Cordelia must remain plain and unambitious, a servant to those who need her. Everyone recognizes that there is some role cut out for him, and for him to exceed or underestimate the demand made is, in some way, for him to fail God. The Flytes are modern martyrs, those willing to forgo the chance of happiness in order to furnish moral warnings. And that they do. They provide examples at the expense of Waugh's art.

In his first six novels, Waugh's comic detachment gained effects similar to those achieved by his major earlier contemporaries. Through parody, fantasy, burlesque, Waugh attained objectivity and impersonality. Instead of a time technique, Waugh had a comic technique which gave him distance from his material, and as long as he maintained this method, there was little danger of his smothering the comic spark.

As we have seen in Waugh, a comic author can simplify his material in order to gain a comic effect. When he accepts stereotypes common in everyone's mind and then presents characters who fit perfectly into those stereotypes—the Armenian, for example, who will sell anything, including his own wife—he is of course simplifying life by reducing it to categories. In a comic sequence, this simplification is necessary, is perhaps the sole way. The author gains comic force by making fools of characters who accept stereotypes, at the same time making the stereotypes themselves seem perfectly plausible. Consequently, he can create forces of sanity and insanity, with the reader caught between both, accepting the stereotype for the sake of the novel and rejecting it as he sees it embodied in the characters.

In the more serious comic novel, works that approach the tragic mode, such simplification is detrimental; for tragedy is nothing if not the character's awareness of the complexity of life and the impossibility of his fully solving his problem or even coming to terms with it. The tragic mode suggests complication, infinite complexity of motive and action; it is similar to the comic only when the comic itself serves a deep social or psychological purpose, as Nevil Beauchamp's tragic-comic career in Meredith's novel, or Bloom's sad journey in Joyce's, or the idealist's mad egoism in Molière's *The Misanthrope*. Here, vast "beyonds" are suggested, and in the amplitude of this world, the character runs into possibilities to which he is unable to respond adequately. Waugh's characters, however, do not really grapple with anything, not even with themselves. Frequently, circumstances make them what they are—Paul Pennyfeather, for instance, is sent down because some rowdy undergraduates have stripped him of his clothes, and college officials see him walking naked through the campus.

Waugh's simplification of his characters means that he frequently created them will-less: we have, for example, Paul who drifts into anything suitable, or Basil Seal who expediently looks for situations that will provide power and comfort. There is no question of their seeking something that might give their lives purpose—Waugh is not concerned with the aspect of the will which leads to ambition, goals, purpose. As long as the comic writer is not concerned with purpose, he cannot approach a tragic mode, and the simplification of his material is inevitable.

Therefore, when Waugh, with almost the same equipment, tries to measure a modern dilemma in *Brideshead Revisited, Scott-King's Modern Europe, Men at Arms,* and *Officers and Gentlemen,* he ultimately fails to be convincing. The latter two novels, for instance, attempt to show an almost cosmic disillusionment on Guy Crouchback's part, as he sees in the war a chance for England's resurging greatness and then finds his hopes to be illusory. The war will not solve any problems; it will, instead, merely create new ones. His innocence is purged, although stoically he continues the good fight. Clearly, this wandering, aimless, naïve individual—a Tony Last now converted to Catholicism—is too will-less to sustain a tragic apparatus. He is still a figure of fun, and although Waugh does derive some humor at his expense, he is nevertheless supposed to stand for all the fumbling not-so-young men of his generation who will, we are led to expect, save England in the coming struggle for power.

The alternative is not solemnity, neither that of a Graham Greene nor a C. P. Snow, and surely not that of a George Orwell. For Waugh, it seems, two opposites presented themselves: the wild, savage parody of his early novels, or the vapid seriousness of the later ones, with momentary glimpses of humor that seem intrusions. In *Men at Arms,* for example, there is a long episode in which Apthorpe's "Thunder Box" is the source of a conflict between him and his commander. The "Thunder Box" is a private, sanitary portable toilet, but Apthorpe cannot use it in peace, for Brigadier Ritchie-Hook follows wherever he hides it, uses it, finally spirits it away, and then has it blow up when Apthorpe sits down. The extended joke—almost a music hall parlay—is like a comic aside, not integrated into the point of view of the novel.

In Guy Crouchback, Waugh was perhaps trying to create a "hero" who is really an anti-hero, the ineffectual character who means well, tries to do his best, is devoted to God and man, but commits follies whenever he acts. Modeled possibly on Ford Madox Ford's Christopher Tietjens of *Parade's End,* Guy retains his faith and personal morality despite the upheaval of war and the disappointments of an unrewarding life. This type of person, for Waugh as well as Ford, must be exposed to temptation—sexual, religious, moral—but must not succumb through any weakness of his own, although he is not a particularly strong man. He must demonstrate the muddle of the anti-hero, while retaining the staunchness and integrity of the hero. He is potentially an everyman, however a little weaker than most, but perhaps because of that very weakness a person who can demonstrate an exemplum.

Guy fits this general description. He is ineffective in nearly every operation, and when he does complete a successful mission, he does so inadvertently. He means well, but gets into difficulty because of his good intentions. He is involved in an illegal operation in Africa at Ritchie-Hook's instigation, and acquires a black mark although he follows orders and acts bravely. On another occasion, hoping to relieve Apthorpe, he gives him whisky and kills the man. Guy never does anything wrong through conscious error; as his religion demands, his intentions are pure, even though the consequences of his acts are often disastrous. Guy is a typical Waugh wastrel who has found a cause, a Basil Seal who has effaced himself and gained social responsibility and religious fervor and is now trying to find a place in a scheme that excludes him. Like Basil, Guy tries to get in when all the entrances are shut to him, but unlike Basil, he never learns the ways of the great world.

This kind of novel, in which the central character is purposely ineffectual—a "guy" like you and me—can only exist if the minor characters are sufficiently different to provide distraction and contrast. Two Guys in the same novel would be soporific, and here Waugh recognizes the task he has set himself. In Apthorpe, the man who gets by as though the army were civilian life, and in Ritchie-Hook, the man who rises to magnificence under stress, Waugh attempts to sketch the destructive element in which Guy is immersed. Each man is as eccentric in his way as Guy is normal in his: Apthorpe demands his comforts, Ritchie-Hook his schoolboyish exploits. Neither man has grown up, and contrasted with each, Guy is supposed to gain in stability.

Waugh apparently admires both Apthorpe and Ritchie-Hook. The former is made almost the center of *Men at Arms,* while Ritchie-Hook pervades both novels with his Kiplingesque practical jokes. Waugh evidently finds in the latter's élan the kind of energy which has given the English army its high rate of successes, yet to the mature reader the Ritchie-Hook type perhaps seems a retarded adolescent. For some mysterious reason, most critics have accepted these and the other characters as lovable, but they are visible frauds, with their successes and failures straight out of melodrama. For instance, Tommy Blackhouse, another Basil Seal-like playboy, has the stuff when it is needed; Ludovic, an effeminate artistic type, comes through with heroic action when least expected. Waugh has retreated to a novelistic atmosphere in which an unexpected character, almost the villain, suddenly gains strength from the righteousness of his task and develops the necessary fortitude to carry him through. Such a view of the novel and of character cannot possibly provide mature work; these characters prove a point—indeed, they prove that the English character is capable of great deeds when tested and that its flexibility will cause the enemy's undoing. Such a view projects good propaganda, but poor art.

Waugh's last work of fiction, *The Ordeal of Gilbert Pinfold* (1957), is an account of an artist, strikingly close to Waugh himself, whose creative powers dry up. To purge himself of his malaise, the hero takes a long sea journey but the combination of drugs, rolling sea, and personal illness provides hallucinations, which themselves comprise the novel. As a novel, this is scarcely vintage Waugh, and is of interest only for its portrait of the artist himself in middle age. Surfeited by civilization and all the unwarranted incursions into his privacy, Pinfold-Waugh has retreated into private hallucinations as a means of escape.

Once the most worldly of writers, Waugh is now anxious to pluck himself and his characters out of the world. Retreating not into the wilderness but into a private universe, his latest work has come almost full turn: from the Bright Young People who immerse themselves in the foolishness of existence, who, indeed, help to create its folly, Waugh has turned to Gilbert Pinfold, who can gain stability only through retreat. The passage of Waugh from immersion to withdrawal is also a retreat from those things which gave his novels their piquancy. Always a superb stylist, Waugh now writes stories which make points, underline dogma, elicit positive responses, take moral positions—these postures, however, do not seem to be his forte. At his hilarious best, he would have thumbed his nose at the "artist in middle age," the Waugh of *Gilbert Pinfold* who must explain himself to his readers. This element of sentimentality would have seemed outrageous to the creator of Paul Pennyfeather, Basil Seal, Adam Fenwick-Symes, Agatha Runcible, Mrs. Beste-Chetwynde, John Beaver, and "Black Bitch." One can imagine two or three of them sitting and discussing Waugh; one suggests that he will have to be eaten——.

X

Normality Defined:
The Novels of Henry Green

LIKE CHAUCER, Henry Green (born Henry Vincent Yorke) tries to define degrees of normality. In his nine novels,* from *Blindness* in 1926 through *Doting* in 1952, he has created people who are neither particularly important nor savory, but who live through the power of their individuality. And under the guise of eccentricity, they represent, for Green, a stable world.

Again like Chaucer, Green defines his people through their manner of speech. Language is as much a key to Green's work as it is to the work of any novelist or poet concerned with details. In *Blindness,* a much neglected novel of Green's youth, written while he was still at Oxford, John Haye loses his sight early, and from that point his reaction to the world depends on how words interpret it to him. The story is told in a stream of consciousness, its focus upon Haye as he tries to visualize what he has lost as a result of his injury. Blinded, he depends upon hearing, and he even wonders what would happen if he had lost hearing instead of sight; for words, by the end of the novel, represent the medium of his profession.

Through Haye, Green writes: "Art was what created in the

* *Blindness* (1926); *Living* (1929); *Party Going* (1939); *Caught* (1943); *Loving* (1945); *Back* (1946); *Concluding* (1948); *Nothing* (1950); *Doting* (1952)

looker-on, and he would have to try and create in others. He would write slowly, slowly, and his story would drift as the country drifted, and it would be about trivial things." (p. 181) Perhaps more than any of his contemporaries except Samuel Beckett, Green exploits the trivia and minutiae of life. His characters react to life in terms of basic needs, the most basic of which is how to relieve boredom or dispel loneliness. The need for conversation, the need to verbalize, is of course attached to one's desire to avoid tedium; and Green's characters frequently talk not for the sake of communicating particular ideas but rather to occupy themselves.

Green's titles themselves, notorious for their laconic quality— *Blindness, Living, Party Going, Caught, Loving, Back, Concluding, Nothing, Doting*—are mostly verbals; and one must examine the quality of a verbal to see how the titles define what the novels are. A verbal describes when it is a participle, and when a gerund, it is a noun truncated in its active role. In either usage, the verbal is a verb that fails to be a verb; a verb *manqué,* it does not fulfill its function to do something directly. It is a verb diverted from committing action, a verb turned into becoming (a verbal) a thing or a description; a verb, to mix a metaphor, emasculated of what a verb should be. It is, in another way, a verb that circles around: *Party Going* (1939), Green's most representative prewar novel, is just that—a circle of activity that works its way into the corners of a railway station as the party attempts to depart for the continent. The novel has to do with the party's inability to go, with the not getting there. In brief, the verbal makes activity impossible; it merely describes a group caught (another Green title) in a social trap, frivolous people going nowhere actually and symbolically.

The verbal defines the creatures of Green's world: people who intend to do things and never get to them; people who start out and are held up; people who have no real plans and merely pass time, letting things happen to them; people who have lost their active functions, often, and have become, like the verbal itself, emasculated, descriptive, passive subjects or objects.

The titles, in another way, by their very curtness suggest language cut off abruptly. A long title encompasses language by what it says; a short title suggests an infinity of things it might have said but does not. Thus, the short title fits Green's theory of the novel, which he expressed in two radio broadcasts in 1950 and in an essay in 1951. At this point in his career—he had already published seven novels over a twenty-four-year span—he defined what was to be for him a partial departure in the form of the novel.

What Green did, in effect, was to present a theory of the novel that he had been working with; it only seemed a departure in its emphasis on dialogue. Green claimed that all artists attempt to create a "life which does not eat, procreate or drink, but which can live in people who are alive." Art, he repeats in an echo of all major twentieth-century novelists, is not representational. The novelist exists to create life through words, the only way, of course, in which he can possibly work; and the quality of words themselves, as well as the silences and spaces between them, becomes the justification and the definition of the art work. In this sense, Green, along with Beckett, is the obvious verbal successor of Joyce. *Ulysses,* we remember, appeared only three years before Green started to write *Blindness,* whose method approximates the Joycean stream of consciousness.

If we compare Green's statement of purposes with Conrad's in his famous Preface to *The Nigger of the "Narcissus,"* we see that both emphasized the non-representational quality of the novel, both stressed that naturalistic details must be heightened into symbols, and both tried to blend impressionistic methods with realistic backgrounds to define their own brand of normality in a world out of tilt. Of course, Conrad is a more consciously moral novelist than Green, but, nevertheless, their intentions in gaining their effects are not dissimilar. Now diverging from Conrad, Green claims conversation is the most significant form of communication, and that, therefore, dialogue pre-empts all other ways of gaining knowledge about people. Only the writer arrogant about his godly powers will attempt to portray people through his own eyes. The less pompous author will let his characters reveal themselves, uncontrolled, as it were.

Green attempts to maintain the reality of fiction, to isolate it from the larger world outside the novel itself. He attacks those novelists, particularly the Victorians, who stepped between reader and narrative and led the former to the right conclusion. This method, Green claims, obviously destroys all sense of reality. Once a character is created, he has to define himself and the world he lives in, precisely as Joyce suggested when he remarked, following Flaubert, that the novelist like the God of creation must sit above his handiwork. To claim that the novel has an autonomy of its own, as Green does, is of course to indicate that every act is symbolic and that every conversation as well is non-real. Green recognized this problem, pointing out that dialogue, however real it may seem, must also be non-representational, that is, not an exact record of the way people talk. Green in his earlier work nevertheless accepted the validity of the stream-of-consciousness technique despite the assumption behind it: that the novelist is controlling all. In his last two novels, curiously his least felicitous work, he applies the theory stated at the turn of the decade. *Nothing* (1950) and *Doting* (1952) are created almost solely in conversational terms, with little or no comment by the author and little or no description. The novelist apparently has forsaken control of his characters.

The fallacy here is that a novel *is* evidently a fiction, and that the novelist can only pretend to ignore this fact. All attempts at disguise are merely attempts to mask an obvious condition. Characters have no substance and narratives no meaning without the novelist. Green theorizes as if the novel springs into being through a spontaneous creation and then lives on its own terms.

Green's theories do not define the best of his work, and whether they were formulated to describe what he thought he had been doing or to indicate a new direction in the fifties is eventually immaterial. His first novel, formulated and written, surely, before any theory had fixed itself in his mind, is perhaps his freshest and most touching. *Blindness* catches the physical quality of a world which was to concern Green in all of his work. John Haye is attempting to learn about himself in a boys' school when, suddenly, he loses his sight, blinded by broken glass in a meaningless accident (a boy throws a stone through a train window against which Haye is pressing his face). Haye is literary, different, sensitive, and his blindness suddenly makes him dependent in a way that would have revolted him before. Once blind, he must re-make himself and his world. This circumstance affords Green the opportunity to examine a world of sensations from the viewpoint of one who "sees" differently from the ordinary person. John Haye's inner eye becomes, then, a measure of his sensitivity and his originality.

That Green, at barely twenty, should have been concerned with such a theme is an indication of his fresh approach to the novel, for Haye's blindness gives him and Green an original point of attack upon reality, one that the author was to maintain, in one form or another, for much of his writing career. *Blindness,* to a large extent, fixed his style, although as he became more experienced, the prose gained in grace and the content in sophistication. The world of the blind, however, with its self-enclosed area of observation, predominated; and accordingly Green's novels rarely project into a social, political, economic, or religious world. These aspects of life do not exist once the novelist centers his consciousness on the essentials of people; clearly, no one more than a blind person is concerned with his whatness.

To convey his difference from others and yet to see it against a normal world of people with their daily boredom and their daily attempts to resolve anew their nagging problems—to catch this sense of life is the measure of Green's art. But often his novels become bogged down in the triviality they are attempting to define. Frequently Green's characters appear insignificant and attenuated rather than important. The chance that Green takes is that his point of view may fail to transmute boring and trivial detail into life, and that he remains boring and trivial himself.

Cast almost solely in dialogue, *Nothing* and *Doting* lose the authorial comments that relieve the early novels from triviality. While Green admittedly does have a sensitive ear for common speech and can reproduce it comically, this emphasis on dialogue is the least interesting part of his work, unless it derives from an original character like Raunce of *Loving* (1945) or Rock of *Concluding* (1948). Frequently, his characters' triviality—although conscious and planned—precludes significant dialogue, and the meandering of these semi-articulate characters becomes irrelevant.

Green, however, in his concern with the trivial tries to heighten it in the manner of an expressionist, carefully avoiding flatness and insipidity. If we compare Green's exploitation of minutiae with C. P. Snow's, we can see two sides of the problem. In Snow's treatment of the trivial, one is always aware of large issues, of which the relatively trite detail is merely a manifestation. There is, in the background, a world of complication, a sense of impending events and foreseeable complexity. In Green's major novels, like *Blindness, Party Going,* and *Loving,* the trivial is heightened to make it seem appropriately all. Green can treat a detail so that nothing beyond it appears important, so that nothing else comes to mind. Thus, John Haye's blindness literally shuts out the world; and his inner world, his only substitute for what he can no longer share, is of sole significance when all light has disappeared. A literal fact as well as a symbol of what man must go through, the blindness effectively defines the areas in which man must make his peace and come to terms with his own kind of reality.

In *Party Going,* the group of upper middle-class party goers at the station pre-empts all other life: this group frustrated at every turn by the fog which holds up travel is, again, a literal and symbolic fact. It includes all frustrations, and combines sickness and health, sick love and healthy love, death and life—it becomes a complete world in itself. Even the title is indicative of the scope of the novel: Party Going may mean that the party is about to leave or is already leaving on the train; or else that the party is going away, leaving altogether for an unknown destination; also, that a party is going on at the station; or, finally, that someone is going to a party, as a young girl does a lot of party going. Thus, the title of the novel sends out further waves to include increasingly more, although the events themselves remain inconsequential.

In *Loving,* the trivial is obvious in the mise en scène. Once the prerogative of the aristocracy (in fiction), "loving" is now the chief activity of servants sitting out the war in an Irish castle. What was once a marginal episode at best has now become the focus of the narrative, and trivial loving treated humorously suddenly becomes important enough to sustain a medium-sized novel. Green's emphasis on Raunce, the butler with a fine sense of his own importance, is equivalent to Dickens' writing a novel with Sam Weller or Mark Tapley as central character, or Fielding with Partridge, or Cervantes with Sancho Panza. And Raunce's world is as trivial as it is expected to be, with his eyeing the maids, his sentimental letters to his old mother in England, his fear of a German invasion, his desire to cut in on as much graft as he can, his attempts to blackmail visitors to the castle. All his operations emanate from a small mind and a small frame of reference; nevertheless, through exaggeration and through language comically wielded, Green is able to make Raunce seem sufficient, at times even overwhelming.

The comparison of Snow with Green becomes acute when we recognize that Snow, through naturalistic detail, is attempting to create order, while Green, through exaggerated detail, is trying to revive chaos in the novel. As the direct literary descendant of Sterne, Dickens, Lawrence, and Joyce, Green is interested in chaos for itself, the chaos of people who revolt against control, symmetrical shape, and order. Green is interested in the flotsam and jetsam of the human character, the stuff that floats up from the unconscious past and haunts the present. His manner of working, itself, is to run obliquely against the material of his novel and gradually unfold it less on paper than in the reader's mind.

Thus, the opening lines of *Party Going,* through choppy language and indirect statement, achieve the disorder that characterizes the entire novel:

Fog was so dense, bird that had been disturbed went flat into a balustrade and slowly fell, dead, at her feet.

There it lay and Miss Fellowes looked up to where that pall of fog was twenty foot (feet?) above and out of which it had fallen, turning over once. She bent down and took a wing than (then?) entered a tunnel in front of her, and this had DEPARTURES lit up over it, carrying her dead pigeon.

Disordered punctuation, language leaping and straining, thoughts rushed together—here we have the entire paraphernalia of a novelist out to confuse the order of experience. This is stream of consciousness, of a sort, from the novelist's mind rather than from a character's. The association of the sick Miss Fellowes with the dead pigeon—both frustrated by the fog—sets a tone which will prevail in the novel, the latter as ridiculously jumbled as the lives and the activities of the people involved. The dead pigeon which Miss Fellowes carries around is a manifestation of behavior that lies too deep for rational explanation; the dead pigeon defines Miss Fellowes' unconscious needs as much as the party itself defines the conscious needs of the main characters. This juxtaposition of irrational and rational elements is characteristic of Green's style: the dead pigeon contrasted with the frustrated party goers who are caught by a fog representing their entire existence.

Juxtaposing the irrational to the rational is a mark of the comic writer, and Green's work is full of these parallelisms. In *Concluding,* for example, Green's last serious novel, the farm animals of Rock, the old scientist now himself out to pasture, are juxtaposed to the girls' home; and the warm snousiness of the animals is a constant contrast to the cold inhumanity of the school, which subverts the girls' real selves to the wishes of the repressive schoolmistresses, Miss Edge and Miss Baker. The animals, like Rock, signify life and fertility, while the schoolmistresses indicate denial, repression, ultimately death of the spirit. Rock himself, for whom the animals are everything—with a mentally sick grandchild on his hands, they become his healthy children—retains the enduring values of life: singleness of purpose, recognition of human qualities, emotional generosity. The animals and Rock will survive all calamities, for they are close to the earth, while the schoolmistresses' lives are founded on a lie: they deny life. In Green's hands, the tragedy of life is a comic matter, and accordingly the farm animals, not the author himself, are comments upon the school.

Green's work, then, becomes a clearing house for right reason and common sense—qualities which stem from the viscera rather than the mind—and in this way he is close to his contemporaries, Joyce Cary, Elizabeth Bowen, even Samuel Beckett. Like them, Green is didactic, although not overtly. His is a campaign for those elements which allow full life, and an ironic attack upon what precludes and destroys it. There is not in his work a single "thinking" character who can come to terms with life through his intellect as well as through his blood, bones, and nerves. Green's characters are emotional creatures whose needs place them "above" a world of mentality. In technique and method of attack, he follows Joyce, but in content and point of view, Dickens is clearly his master. Compare, for instance, Dickens' *Hard Times,* and its life in a factory town, with Green's *Living* (1929), set against the same kind of locale eighty years later. Like Dickens, Green works the double plot: the upper life of the factory represented by Dupret and his son, the lower life represented by the workers. In Green's novel, the didacticism is less manifest, the sense of happiness far less conclusive. Romance is systematically killed, but life remains, and here Green joins with Dickens. For both, intellect by denying feeling is a destructive villain, while reliance on emotions saves.

Happiness is not everyone's lot, but life teems for the lower classes. Craigan, the old foundryman in *Living* now ready for his pension, seems like Rock of *Concluding,* in possession of some life-truth denied his fellowmen. Representing continuity of life, pride in craft, moral purpose, he hovers over the others making their demands seem foolish and immature. Although slowed by age, his senses somewhat dimmed, he is still the best caster of steel in the factory, a man who retains a love for his work. He recalls Conrad's Singleton, that aged prophet of *The Nigger of the "Narcissus,"* whose tenacity and sense of purpose prevail over the do-nothingness of James Wait and Donkin. Both Singleton (singleness of purpose) and Craigan represent the old order of men, those who recognize duty and discipline and gain strength from their work, as opposed to the new order who grumble at their duties and plan to escape from them.

Green catches the world of rock-like Craigan as, now deaf, he drifts further into himself and away from the outside world, attached only to his work and the young Lily Gates. The latter, the new generation, has a sense of loyalty, but her mind wanders to entertainment and enjoyment at the lowest level. A girl who must be entertained to be won, Lily runs off with Bert Jones to get married, only to be deserted when Jones cannot locate his parents and becomes ashamed of the Liverpool streets where he thinks they live. Green is fully aware of the psychological debilitation of poverty, the de-sexing quality of being in need. This theme is of course one that George Orwell dealt with at length, but since it is better suited to the naturalistic novel than the impressionistic one, twentieth-century novelists have largely overlooked it.

Green manages to avoid the didactic and the sermonistic by making the factory into the bones and blood of the novel, so that the workers are not simply employed there; they become part of its rhythm. It is these rhythms of life that Green more than most of his contemporaries is able to duplicate; so that even when his novels are not particularly significant, there are waves of tiny unseen particles which seem to emanate from his themes, and these waves floating in the reader's memory convey, often, the value of the novels. Green forces the reader into "making" the novel himself, by bringing together the various bits and *quanta* that the narrative throws out.

Green's exclusion of definite information—there are no de-marked social classes, religious ideas, political beliefs or figures, intellectuals, or people of definite professions in his novels—gives everything the roundness of generality and incompleteness, even though observed details are profuse. To avoid a naturalistic frame of reference, a novelist like Green is concerned more with what his characters are than with what they do, more with their inner fears than with their external behavior.

This method can of course fail, and fail it does in *Caught* (1943), Green's tribute to the Auxiliary Fire Service which did heroic work in putting out fires during the German blitz of London in the early years of the war. The particulars of the firemen's lives indicate the shallowness of Green's method when applied directly. He achieves his greatest success with the oblique presentation of characters whose substance gains from being seen indirectly. Since Green is concerned with essences and not particulars, he does best when he stresses those attitudes common to all men. In *Caught,* however, Green probes a world of particulars, and the men so caught are too puny in stature and intrinsic interest to sustain the novel. Roe himself is one of Green's least attractive characters, and the other major figures are characterized generally by how much they grumble against their lot. Pye, with his klepto-maniacal sister, his fears of having committed incest with her, his attempt to handle a job for which he is unequipped, is a potentially interesting character. But Green's psychologizing of Pye is rarely convincing, and the attempt to clarify the past by citing an incestuous relationship is a shortcut to what would have to be a long process of explanation.

Even so, Green evidently knows how people talk, especially people involved in trivial everyday jobs who have only themselves, not ideas, to express. He conveys this quality in *Caught,* pinning down his characters at the same time, and in his particularity achieves the unrelieved monotony of the routine naturalistic novel. As if recognizing this very failing, Green wrote *Loving* the following year, moving from the fire service to an Irish castle and imposing over all the mantle of romantic love.

Several critics have remarked, and rightly so, that Green is almost alone among English novelists in writing successfully about sex. Even in D. H. Lawrence's novels sex usually seems an outgrowth of the doctrine that sex is good and should be encouraged, and therefore the right characters practice it because they are expected to do so. Despite Lawrence's courageous attempts to deal with it maturely, sex seems superimposed from the outside, not the natural process that Green conceives. From *Blindness* through *Doting,* twenty-six years later, from the novelist barely into his twenties to the successful novelist and businessman in his mid-forties, Green has treated sex as a natural part of the rhythmic flow of life, as an outgrowth of people's attachment for each other. Women are attracted to men, and men to women, as natural as that. There are here no perversions, no eccentricities, no abnormalities—simply the natural response of one sex to the other. In this sense, Green is virtually unique among twentieth-century English novelists.

In *Doting,* the characters pair off in varying (heterosexual) combinations, an almost endless procession of affairs and near affairs; several scenes resolve themselves with the characters going to bed with each other. Even if people cannot love, Green suggests, they can dote. With love made impossible by the fragmentation and uncertainty of life, then the only thing left is doting. Doting is enough, however, for one can dote and fall into bed without any attacks of conscience.

In Green's world, sex perhaps seems natural because it is rarely intertwined with the sentimentality of love. In a comic writer, love and sex do not have to go together, although in the tragic author they of course must. Green allows sex when love is not involved, and in so doing he eliminates a great deal of hypocrisy. His naturalness with the sexual relationship is part of his over-all avoidance of the sentimental: people fall into bed because they like each other; they need not love or even feel attached to one another. The irony of this attitude, however, works two ways: first, the natural processes are triumphant, but, second, the tensions implicit in a love relationship are lost to the novelist.

Sex is circumambient in a novel like *Concluding* (1948), in which only the presence of Rock, that almost senile scientist, seems to hold the world together. The state school for homeless and orphaned girls is like a volcano, with the girls' passions ready to explode and engulf the entire community. Two girls have run away, and several of the others sneak out at night to indulge sexually in any way they can. Green emphasizes the unnaturalness of holding mature girls together under repressive conditions even without constant sexual temptation. The two schoolmistresses, particularly Miss Edge, with their desire to force the girls into something they are not, actually make the girls think of nothing else. The teachers suspect even Rock, now in his eighties, of having sensual designs on their charges.

Like Dickens, Green in this novel recognized that officials in order to justify their roles must balk life, and the first thing they systematically try to bar is sexual naturalness, since it is chaotic, disorganized, furious—something they fear because it creates circumstances outside their control. The outer man can function under their direction, but the inner one, particularly his sexual desires, cannot be checked. And therefore, the fear! Because of the repressive quality of Miss Edge's personal life (even in this respect Green follows Dickens), she must survive by bending others to her will, and thus she tries to control the uncontrollable. In such an atmosphere, the girls' sexuality will be all the stronger, simply because it is denied. When given outlet, it dissipates its potency; when dammed, it penetrates everything.

The overt sexual activity of Rock's granddaughter, Elizabeth, and Sebastian Birt, a Wildean schoolmaster, permeates the novel. They cavort and gambol in the bushes, while Miss Edge and Miss Baker sneak around looking for the runaway girls. Birt and Elizabeth lie naked in each other's arms: the scene is symbolic as well as real, for they express themselves in natural surroundings and, masked by the green, hide from those who proscribe sex. Elizabeth and Sebastian, grotesque, unlovely, unattractive physically, fulfill themselves despite the proscription against satisfaction. They work out realistically everything that Rock stands for.

In several ways, *Concluding* takes on the quality of a "sex novel" in a way that Lawrence's *Lady Chatterley's Lover* curiously does not. Even animals in the Green novel move according to the rhythmic pace of life that one identifies with sexual drowsiness and intermittent satisfaction. The animals, like their keeper, Rock, provide a paean to life; his pig, Daisy, is the only thing that matters in a world in which Miss Edge under the dizzying influence of a cigarette can propose to Rock in order to secure a cottage for life. Her repressed sadism is transformed, in her struggle for survival, into a kind of masochism. When such things happen, only Daisy can answer: a squeal at the ludicrousness of human beings.

Like Lawrence's much younger Mellors, Rock is a rightful descendant of those romantics, following Rousseau, who indicated that communion with nature and a simple life is a form of salvation. Thus, this novel becomes, in one way, an idyll, what with the abundant grounds, the wandering farm animals, the heavy shrubbery, the luxurious undergrowth; an idyll doubly potent because the girls are forbidden to enjoy the fruits, sexual and otherwise, of the surroundings. Rock, as his name implies, is firmly rooted to the earth. Initiated by the girls into secret rites in a room far under the school, he burrows into the very nature of things. No longer the scientist who once looked at things as revealed by reason, he now seeks the meaning of life through his feelings. Like Forster's Mr. Emerson (*A Room with a View*), whom he strongly recalls, Rock knows what life is, and he endures by the very knowledge that he will outlast the schoolmistresses, the school, and all the forces that seem to have him on the run. He destroys his mail and lives simply while the outside world attempts to trap him, and his avoidance of its snares is a measure of his intention to survive.

Concluding is only one of Green's novels in which feeling and emotion become the whole of life. Published two years earlier, in 1946, *Back* contains one of Green's most attractive females, Rose, although we never see her. Like Joyce Cary's Sara Monday, Rose is a female principle who "directs" the novel even when she is not present. Unlike Sara, however, Rose does not try to change the man she has attracted. Sara, in her way, is destructive: she wants to domesticate Gulley Jimson once she has enticed him into her bower. Rose does not domesticate, Rose merely exists, the woman principle embodied, fleshed out.

Thus, Rose and roses, the words used as nouns, adjectives, and verbs, dominate the novel. Green is working with an obvious gimmick here—to bring Rose back to life through the use of her name as a part of speech: prices *rose, rise* up, *rose* up; voices *rose,* my gall *rose,* as red as a *rose.* One of Green's triumphs is to have the reader become aware of the word even when it is not explicitly mentioned, to have him alerted to the possibility of rose and roses at every turn. Green has, as it were, the reader working for him, speculating on how important Rose is and was for Charley Summers.

The novel ends with a great image of Rose:

Then he knelt by the bed, having under his eyes the great, the overwhelming sight of the woman he loved [Nance, whom he has confused with Rose, her half-sister], for the first time without her clothes. And because the lamp was lit, the pink shade seemed to spill a light of roses over her in all their summer colours, her hands that lay along her legs were red, her stomach gold, her breasts the colour of cream roses, and her neck white roses for the bride. She had shut her eyes to let him have his fill, but it was too much, for he burst into tears again, he buried his face in her side just below the ribs, and bawled like a child. "Rose," he called out, not knowing he did so, "Rose." (p. 246)

Party Going and *Loving,* although quite different in intention and execution, are both pervaded by a similar stream of sexuality. The love affairs of the servants in the latter novel fill up the gigantic castle, more than matching the illicit love enjoyed by the owners. Raunce and the beautiful flirt Edith; Paddy, the filthy, ignorant pheasant keeper, and Kate—these two couples play out their passion at every opportunity, until the novel is imbued with soft glances, secret kisses, lightly touched bodies, until sex drowns out all other considerations. Even the pheasants, the everpresent and untouchable pheasants, seem to accentuate the air of sexuality. Paddy, the keeper who lies in filth in the dark, watches the furtive pheasants in their daily rounds and keeps guard over their eggs, the ever-fertile pheasants that have become part of castle life.

Again, in *Party Going,* the group that has congregated at the station to go to France has as its intention a sexual adventure to relieve the tedium of daily life. The center is Max Adey, apparently one of Aldous Huxley's or Evelyn Waugh's marginal and bored young men, who calls the party together as a whim, not even sure himself that he will go along. Chased by Amabel, he in turn chases Julia, and provides an eligible man on the trip to interest Amabel so that his own way is left open to Julia. Their relationships are, like the atmosphere, foggy; but their purpose is clear—for lack of anything else to do, to drift in and out of sexual affairs, as the desire moves them.

Behind Green's presentation of these effete young people (a typical Waugh crowd), there may be a moral purpose, but Green does not deprive them of their enjoyments in order to castigate their way of life. Green makes sex pleasant, despite the nihilism motivating it. There is no guilt attached to a relationship that affords pleasure; there are no agonies of conscience if one is unfaithful. For the character, there is only the realization that he will have to countenance faithlessness in his partner as well, and in a comic novel this is no great ordeal. Unlike his contemporaries, Green does not torture his characters sexually; sex is available, at times super-abundant, and it is rosy.

For Green, then, sex is a way of attaining joy. Even his most unattractive people gain stability and a measure of order through sex. Rather than depriving them of reason, it defines their needs. They talk about sex, participate in it, and find pleasure through sexual fulfillment, for there is little exploitation, little guilt. If one believes that honest fulfillment of natural needs is superior to intellectual accomplishment, then one must equate the natural with the sexual, something that Green recognizes and acts upon.

By dissociating sex from love, Green escapes sentimentality; similarly, to avoid sentimentality in his language, he eliminates necessary connectives in his sentences. For example, to avoid baby sentences—the way people do talk—Green cuts out articles, sometimes prepositions and conjunctions, connecting sentences through substantives hooked to each other. The result is a packed prose which expresses what might be sentimental ideas and thoughts in unsentimental, rather tough, language that is almost a parody of Hemingwayese.

In *Living,* his second novel, Green tried to approximate the processes of thought in which one image blurs into the next, the connectives between them unclear, disappearing rapidly as still another image appears. Green in the following passage is writing about the son of Mr. Dupret, the factory owner now too ill to manage the business:

Standing in foundry shop son of Mr. Dupret thought in mind and it seemed to him that these iron castings were beautiful and he reached out fingers to them, he touched them; he thought and only in machinery it seemed to him was savagery left now for in the country, in summer, trees were like sheep while here men created what you could touch, wild shapes, soft like silk, which would last and would be working in great factories, they made them with their hands. He felt more certain and he said to himself it was wild incidental beauty in these things where engineers had thought only of the use put to them. He thought, he declaimed to himself this was the life to lead, making useful things which were beautiful, and the gladness to make them, which you could touch. . . . (pp. 6-7)

Such prose works effectively in a passage like this, wherein the images flit past one another; and the son of the factory owner, with his youth and uncertainty, is juxtaposed to the "purity" of steel, which he thinks about in a way that had never before occurred to him. He sees in the factory a kind of terrible beauty, sensing in the steel an untouched quality which expresses the savagery innate in man. This kind of prose fails, however, when it narrates, for often it distracts from what is being said because of its odd form. Prose without the connectives that we expect and without the punctuation we look for calls attention to itself. With such prose, the author can *describe* ordinary things without falling into clichés, for the language itself dominates and the content becomes secondary. Joyce of course worked in this way, turning trivial details into poetic elements through the use of "eccentric" language. In both writers, there is an obvious attempt to approximate the thought pattern itself. But the style fails when the thought pattern does not lend itself to this kind of prose. When factory workers talk without connectives, the author is imposing a literary style upon them; their thinking without connectives is something else. Joyce triumphed, where Green partially fails, in his use of "disconnected" language almost solely as interior monologue; when his people do talk, they speak in the expected manner. With Green, however, thought and conversation sound alike. The two should of course be different, for in transforming thought into speech, the mind creates the order that makes connectives necessary, as well as pauses, and punctuation marks.

Nevertheless, Green uses prose artistically, in fact, somewhat like the abstract painter whose canvas hints without representing the object or divulging his intention. Green's use of disjointed language also suggests that his characters must go their own way once the novelist has sparked them to life.

Disjointed language works with titles laconically clipped short to convey, paradoxically, the roundness of life as well as its incompleteness. The titles, as much as his subject matter, suggest Green's attitudes. Somewhat arrogant in their curtness, they imply a prophetic tone that is almost pompous. *Concluding* is offered as if nothing more exists; *Loving* as if *that* is love, and nothing else can be; *Back* as though coming back and looking for Rose, who is also "back" through her half-sister, are all of life; *Doting* is suggested as a modern form of love, and nothing but doting can and does exist; *Nothing* indicates that nothing does count and anything that does seem to matter is inconsequential; *Living* comes as if *this* were life, and only this; *Blindness* prevents the author's seeing the world from any other point except that of blindness. There is a finality to these short titles which gives a finality to the world they represent. They are, almost literally, the final word.

Green, we remember, is a comic novelist, and before we are carried away by his apparent arrogance in offering the final word on things as pretentious as loving, living, blindness, concluding and nothing, we must remember the wit which he acquires from playing with this sense of finality. Green's humor undermines any possible pomposity, as though the author were laughing at himself for writing about such vast things as living and loving. Green can have it both ways: he can make these things sound grand, and at the same time he can through humor reduce their grandiosity to the small world in which people live. Thus, "living" is all life, but "living" is also what Green's "little people" do. Both the large and small world are suggested, both the large and small world filled in. Probing all is Green's wit which balances the ambitiousness of the title. If wit is a measure of stability and normality, then wit brings a mad world into focus, and Green, almost alone among his contemporaries, tries to define a normal world that has roundness and shape. What Joyce Cary attempted to do through twisting and turning reality to suit his purposes, Green does without apparent effort. He leaves the world as he finds it, but through some alchemical artistic process he has transformed chaos into a semblance of order, even though at times he seems to have transformed order into chaos.

XI

The Intimate World of
Ivy Compton-Burnett

MISS IVY COMPTON-BURNETT is a family chronicler whose late-Victorian homebodies become possessive, sadistic mothers, destructive, self-willed fathers, and persecuted children who try to murder their parents. For her, family life is a jungle in which no holds are barred; tooth and nail are preferable to persuasion, and verbal wit helps one gain what rightfully belongs to another. Only the fittest survive throughout the in-fighting; the battle goes to the strong-willed and the deceptive. The weak and honest lose their fortunes as well as their self-possession, while the winner cheats with all the resources available to him.

Her large Victorian families, with their intertwining relationships of numerous cousins, aunts (fewer uncles), and grandparents, are predatory as sharks, their teeth out, their fins, so to speak, always in someone else's pocket. Everyone—usually a small army of relatives—is dependent on one or two others, and the latter are systematically bled until they have little left to give. Then they can be abandoned, although some spark of vestigial feeling usually keeps the family together. Perhaps it is not feeling that finally unifies, but the law of the jungle.

The morality of Miss Compton-Burnett's work* involves ma-

---

* *Dolores* (1911) (juvenilia); *Pastors and Masters* (1925); *Brothers and Sisters* (1929); *Men and Wives* (1931); *More Women Than Men* (1933):

terial values—how does one sustain himself in what amounts to a predatory jungle? The family is not a reservoir of sympathy and feeling but a miniature of the larger world in which self-interest is the sole motivation. A person survives in the family group through conniving and competing. Frequently, the forces are divided: the children on one side, the parents or adults on the other. Neither side is restricted to gentleman's weapons. Nagging is raised to an art, and each side dogs the other, looking for an advantage, trying to thrust in a verbal dagger. For in the destruction of the other person, whether actual or figurative, the individual gains his own life.

In nearly all of Miss Compton-Burnett's novels the stories take place before the turn of the century, a period wherein the family was still strong enough to be central in a character's life. Her large family groups, like so many armies fighting off the enemy and then breaking down into civil war, allow ready-made relationships. There are few friends of the family involved in these struggles, and when they do appear they are peripheral. The friends for the children are their own brothers and sisters, but even here cruelty is not precluded. Siblings, however, are rarely as cruel to each other as their parents are to them: they have less to gain. Parents work out their guilt, insufficiencies, vanity, and frustrations through the vicarious torture of their children, and the latter are fully aware of what is happening. They react with their only weapons: conspiracy and deception, for they too must survive.

Thus, in *Bullivant and the Lambs* (published in England as *Manservant and Maidservant*, 1947), Horace Lamb's two children (age twelve and eleven) allow him to approach a bridge that they know is washed out; they are aware that he is walking toward his death, and yet they hesitate to warn him until it might be too late. Horace has reformed himself from what he was—a tyrant in the home—but the boys agree that no father at all is preferable to what Horace formerly was, and he might regress at

---

A House and Its Head (1935); *Daughters and Sons* (1937); *A Family and a Fortune* (1939); *Parents and Children* (1941); *Elders and Betters* (1944); *Manservant and Maidservant* (1947); *Two Worlds and Their Ways* (1949); *Darkness and Day* (1951); *The Present and the Past* (1953); *Mother and Son* (1955); *A Father and His Fate* (1957); *A Heritage and Its History* (1959)

any time. Their decision is simply one to insure survival; the former Horace, with his nagging criticism and his inability to let anyone else breathe, was suffocating them.

The situation in *Bullivant and the Lambs,* in which the father tries to restrain his instincts and feelings, is less insidious than in several of the other novels. For Horace's actions are at least in the open: everyone sees him for what he is. Far more dangerous is the person who hides behind a mask and gains his ends without revealing what he actually is, or one who disguises his trail by revealing just enough to keep his real motives hidden. That type of person treads a path of destruction and, in Miss Compton-Burnett's world, will find himself rewarded. In *Elders and Betters* (1944), a key novel in Miss Compton-Burnett's charting of late Victorian manners and morals, Anna Donne destroys her aunt's original will and becomes sole heir in the new will, which her aunt did not want to stand. Then she proceeds to lie her way to success, driving to suicide a second aunt who had expected the money, getting engaged to her cousin, whom she can now support, and acquiring everything that money, no matter how ill-gained, can buy in the way of happiness.

In this world, money can indeed buy happiness, for social morality is attached to self-gain, both material and psychological. There are no real heroes: one is a hero or heroine only in his own eyes. One survives in fact by becoming, through vanity, his own hero, and then trying to impose his role upon everyone. There is no salvation, no repentance (there are few visible crimes), no chance for redemption. As Miss Compton-Burnett suggests in *A Family and a Fortune* (1939), to sacrifice oneself may seem fine for others, but it is horrible for oneself.

Miss Compton-Burnett has of course taken the Victorian family novel and turned it inside out, revealing the dirt behind the romantic exterior. Although her subject matter seems close to that of the mid-Victorian novelists, unlike many of them she recognizes that below normal social behavior lies a swamp of discontent, mixed motives, and deception.

In *Mother and Son* (1955), Rosebery Hume is so closely attached to his mother that no other satisfactory relationship is possible for him, and after her death he throws himself indiscriminately at every available female, only to find that his sole company for life will be children two generations his junior. In *Brothers and Sisters* (1929), Christian and Sophia Stace have become the parents of three children, although they are half brother and sister. In *Darkness and Day* (1951), the reader first believes that Edmund and Bridget Lovat, now long married, are father and daughter, only to discover that they are merely half brother and sister. In *The Present and the Past* (1953), Cassius Clare attempts to become the center of family activity by a false attempt at suicide; when he does die, everyone thinks it is another false suicide attempt and ignores him. In *Two Worlds and Their Ways* (1949), each member of the family has something to hide: the two children have cheated at school; Sir Roderick Shelley has fathered a son who works in the house as a servant; Maria, Sir Roderick's wife, has almost "destroyed" her children trying to make them shine in their father's eyes.

In nearly every one of the novels, there is movement toward a revelation that will, inevitably, make the characters aware of what they are and what the situation is. The revelation takes the form of a recognition scene (many critics have thus compared Miss Compton-Burnett's novels with Greek tragedy), but the recognition itself does not appear to change the characters. In Greek tragedy, the recognition was the climax of the rising action, entailing a meeting between the protagonist's past and future—for what he has been will now determine what he will be. After the recognition scene, the character passes into a decline that is in some ways the equivalent of Christian contrition, except that there is ultimately no salvation. His exile is from his self; he must pay for the rest of his life for something he was unable to control.

This, obviously, is not the pattern in Ivy Compton-Burnett's novels. True, she shares with the Greek tragedian his awareness of the importance of the recognition scene, but she has reworked the materials of the tragic vision so that further comparison is valueless. Frequently, the revelation amuses the reader more than it changes the character. Instead of facing the revelation, the character merely tries to hush up the news and live with it. The incestuous pair in *Brothers and Sisters* are treated comically, as they are in *Darkness and Day*. First, we are led to believe that

Edmund and Bridget Lovat are father and daughter, but later we find they are half brother and sister—and thus their marriage should not seem outrageous. If only Oedipus and Jocasta had been siblings! Meanwhile, their incest has become a source of common gossip among the children and servants. No one, however, is particularly upset, for incest serves as well as anything else to gossip about.

Furthermore, in Miss Compton-Burnett's world there is no repentance, no Christian charity which will reward the good person, no Christian revenge which will punish the bad. There are no amenities whatsoever. If one has been incestuous, it is discreet to keep the news to oneself and continue living. If the news does get out, then one hopes that the other fellow has done something even worse so that incest will not disturb him. If one has had illegitimate children in the past, then he usually finds that his husband or wife has committed a similar folly, and the two indiscretions cancel each other. If one loves his brother's wife or fiancée, he finds that another woman can be provided for the brother, perhaps a maid or governess.

Governesses in Miss Compton-Burnett's world are extremely expendable; the supply appears inexhaustible, and they are usually available for whatever the household requires of them. While they teach the younger children, generally an older child (one about fifty, the product of a previous marriage) is measuring their suitability for marriage. The governess, frequently, becomes a competitor with the mother for the affection of the children, and in this scheme the father is excluded, unless he himself makes a play for the governess. When he does, he finds his older son in competition. One need not be a hypocrite to survive in Miss Compton-Burnett's world; cruelty and expedience are sufficient.

The lack of repentance and salvation makes possible the comic play of the novels. If the amenities are meaningless, the law of the jungle must prevail. And all this against the background of a Christian society! The surface of behavior is impeccable, but beneath lie arrogance, vanity, jealousy, and excessive pride—all the characteristics of normal people. Miss Compton-Burnett's characters are always themselves. And just as no force from within can change them (only circumstances change, they remain the same), so no force from the outside can alter them. They are fixed by their characters and doomed, to some extent, by their heritage. They resist progress with the fierceness of people who recognize that change means death, although not to change is also a kind of death. Their death throes, however, are often comic.

The chief weight of this amoral world falls on the children. They are the beneficiaries of the muddle that adults make of their lives; but rather than learn from their sad experiences, these children perpetuate similar lives in their own children. The cycle of infamy is endless. For someone to have learned from his experience would be for him to deny what he is. His individuality consists of denying that his children's claim on life might be superior to his own; the struggle between the two, consequently, becomes one of life and death, with the children hanging on through desperation.

Lest the reader feel sorry for these children, Miss Compton-Burnett has made them monsters who speak and understand in an adult way. Unlike the Victorian children who had to be seen but not heard, Miss Compton-Burnett's children are constantly uttering witticisms to dissipate their parents' evil. In a society in which even the family becomes an institution supporting injustice, the children must conspire with each other to float above the backwash of their parents' past. Like Dickens' long-suffering youngsters, they too must endure the absurdity of their elders, but they have weapons and armor that Dickens could not have conceived. By hiding beneath couches or in doorways, they become aware of everything; and, with the servants, provide a chorus-like comment upon their parents. Their revenge comes from understanding exactly what is happening to them, and at a suitable time they torture the adults by withholding affection and love. Precisely as their elders use love to gain what they want, so the children themselves form alignments and use love, withdrawn or extended, as an offensive weapon in their struggle for survival.

In a tragic or semi-tragic novel, the child must become the victim of adult duplicity; in the comic novel, however, the adult becomes the child's victim. And yet the weapons of each side in Miss Compton-Burnett's novels are so fierce and the moves so predatory that comedy gains a new dimension. This is comedy based on torture, cruelty, and selfishness, in which no one can afford to relent because to survive he must continue being what he is. Graham Greene's dialogue between man and God, with the ensuing conflicts, becomes in Ivy Compton-Burnett's hands the everyday conflicts between the generations, between parents and children, between grandparents and their children, between aunts and nephews and nieces.

The construction of Ivy Compton-Burnett's novels is essentially the same in the seventeen she has published from 1911 (*Dolores* is juvenilia) to 1959, with *A Heritage and Its History*. The departures from a common structure are fewer than the adherences: Miss Compton-Burnett has marked her originality not only in the conversational idiom but in the form of her novels. The reader is first introduced to a family, usually one with numerous children. The father may be senile or else in vigorous middle age, and there is often a disparity between the ages of the younger children and the older one(s)—an age gap of twenty years is not uncommon. Thus, the older children, in their twenties and thirties, form one band, while the younger ones, usually around ten or eleven, form a second. The two bands often join in order to fight the parents, but frequently their problems differ in degree (not kind—they are all persecuted by the parents) so that there cannot be full agreement on a course of action.

The elders themselves are not united; an old relative—father, aunt, or uncle—will ally himself with one of the parents to form a conflicting band. The patriarch or matriarch is often in his eighties,* and during his lifetime he casts gloom over the entire house; even those who do not hate him wait for his death. He knows, however, that he is useless and employs his great age as a way of obtaining sympathy and deference. An old person is indeed a scarecrow upon a stick, but nevertheless a voluble one—being unwanted does not hush him. His isolation, in fact, seems to act as goad for further intrusion in what does not concern him. Although no one has love for the elder statesman, there is, neverthe-

* In *Memento Mori* (1959), Muriel Spark has collected some typical Compton-Burnettian octogenarians and revealed the dog (or cat) that lies beneath their withered skins. Several of Miss Spark's novels, in fact, follow the pattern of merciless wit that has been Ivy Compton-Burnett's trademark for the last three decades.

less, a primitive connection that has nothing to do with love—what savages must feel for their elders who have attained an untouchable situation within the tribal hierarchy.

Within this family, there may be an alien member who belongs to a second family, and this latter group is then presented in similar terms. These two interrelated families, with perhaps a third, or with fragments of other families (brothers and sisters, aunts and nieces, mothers and sons), constitute Miss Compton-Burnett's "society." There is no other "group" in her novels: outside the family lies a shadowy substance, the great world, which has no bearing on that primal relationship. One achieves something, or is destroyed, not because of the world but because of the family; and a son or daughter reels from family to family seeking a haven. The rebel does not run off to London to find solace in material success; such things do not exist. The family is his all: it dominates, circumvents, encloses, frustrates, and provides one with mates (so many cousins marry in these novels that the hundreds of characters in the seventeen books must somehow all be related as second and third cousins). In *Elders and Betters,* for example, there is such extensive intermarrying contemplated among cousins that congratulations are in order for the first person to marry outside the family, and he weds the governess's niece.

It is this tightness of family structure—the family both gives sustenance and destroys what it maintains—which causes the claustrophobic quality of Miss Compton-Burnett's novels. With the family blocking its members on every side, the latter are repeatedly thrown back into the caldron, which burns with a heat that must nullify everyone within its confines. What a hideous revenge society has planned for itself: its sole unifying unit is a group that tortures its members for pleasure and gain. What a vision of the world: a vast network of relatives who do the work of the devil; and there is no escape. Without families, they would have to work, or give up their education, or search for a mate, or stand on their own feet. And since no one desires such pursuits, he inevitably falls back on the family, which provides all these essentials in exchange for sucking dry his soul and spirit.

Miss Compton-Burnett's method of narration is perfectly coordinated with the subject matter. By bringing two or three families together as the whole of society, she makes their interplay the sum of all essential forces in the world, until nothing else seems to matter. Her conversational method creates, as it were, an external stream of consciousness, in which the characters overtly voice what the traditional novelist usually explains about them. Consequently, in a literal way, we see what they are—there is nothing to hide, for the very nature of their communication forces complete disclosure of their thoughts. Only infrequently do the characters enter into a conspiracy to withhold information. More often, the characters reveal everything they know, and their disclosures suggest the limits of their cruelty.

This aspect of the method is effective, for its very freakishness becomes a way of complementing the eccentricity of Miss Compton-Burnett's characters. The stream of consciousness has been transformed into a spray of epigrams. The conversational method that Henry Green was seeking in his last two novels, *Nothing* and *Doting,* has been a staple of Miss Compton-Burnett's work for thirty years. Most novelists assume that their characters will hide certain things about themselves, since they are ashamed of their iniquity. For Ivy Compton-Burnett, however, iniquity is not a marginal characteristic of a chosen few but the substance of the whole world. To feel shame indicates a commitment to a morality of good and evil, but to be unaware of shame is to show allegiance to an amoral world in which a generous action is repaid not by kindness but by retribution, in which a sympathetic word is offered—for a gain, in which the old must survive by fighting their children for their rights.

The method suggests, then, that if a character has a thought of any kind, he will shape it into words. And even more, into an epigram. The conversational idiom, however, does result in emotionally flaccid people, although this consequence does not disturb the author. Her characters are not emotional beings under any circumstances; they react with reason, and reason is their only god. For the reader, nevertheless, there is a curious sameness of character and narrative, perhaps because we tend to remember literary creations by their emotions. In these novels, however, no survivor grieves for the deceased, no one is horrified to see what his children have turned into, no one questions that a mother has the right to destroy her son(s), no one is particularly upset to discover incest or infidelity. The emotions are so well controlled that the most startling revelation will not elicit surprise. Life itself seems frozen.

The conversational idiom of the characters helps establish their complacency. Their epigrams are rapier thrusts cleaned of all sweat and all effort—the thrust is cool and straight to the mark, as though they had spent their lives polishing their marksmanship for precisely this situation. Even the children are untouched by the grossest of deceptions. In *Daughters and Sons,* for example, the daughter of John Ponsonby, a popular novelist, accepts unquestioningly that her father's writing career is finished, and that he must be protected from this knowledge. Accordingly, she turns her own novel over to a publisher, receives a large sum of money, and then pretends that the money has been sent her father by an admirer. Mr. Ponsonby inadvertently thinks the money comes from the family governess and marries her, setting off a whole series of misunderstandings. Yet, Frances, the novelist-daughter, calmly accepts that her father is written-out and that she must sacrifice herself for him. An ancient ritual is carried out in modern dress.

This very lack of emotion or surprise creates a good part of the horror—a kind of intellectual sport—which an Ivy Compton-Burnett novel generates. The glitter of the conversation helps form a tight wall around the characters, as the novelist herself has built precisely such a wall around her society. The epigrams convey an exclusive quality, as though these are special people who cannot react or speak in any other way. In *Two Worlds and Their Ways,* these sallies occur on every page. For example:

"Is your family musical, Mr. Spode?" said Juliet, with no suggestion of a change of subject.

"My mother is one of those people, who do not know one note from another. That means that they do not concern themselves with notes. I do not know about my father. He died when I was born."

"What?" said more than one voice.

"It appears to have been the case. There is a primitive people, whose men take to their beds, when their wives have children. It seems that my father followed that course, and never rose again."

"So your mother is a widow?" said Mr. Bigwell.

"That is one of the consequences."

"We must remember that Mrs. Cassidy is present."

"I did remember it. I was trying to cause her some amusement."

"Thank you so much," said Juliet. "You have quite taken my thoughts off our disgrace." (p. 179)

This is a special language, one that is sheathed and unsheathed like a sword or dagger, a language that, so to speak, lies in wait for its victim, scores a light hit, and then moves away preparatory to another strike. Consequently, because the children in these novels can survive only by answering back, their conversational abilities are phenomenal. They speak like adults, indeed like special adults—like Henry James and La Fontaine. Their use of language stylizes them, gives them the brittleness and nervousness one expects of children whose parents "use" them. They rebel without illusions, conspire without shame, and survive without love. And while they fail to gain our sympathy, they do win our amazement.

Despite the virtues of the conversational method—its literalness, its sharp definition of issues, its penetration into the thoughts of the characters—despite these, its deficiencies are apparent. Miss Compton-Burnett's characters all seem cut from the same mold; the children all have the same awareness of evil, and the parents and grandparents all demonstrate the same predatory expedience. When a mother in one novel says, "My good, dear children," or something similar, she is preparing to sacrifice them at the first need, and the mother in the next novel is little different. A widower makes a "wife" of his eldest daughter, and a widow makes a "husband" of her eldest son. To gain a life, one must crush a life. A flat sameness is evident both in character development and plot, and it precludes Miss Compton-Burnett's being a creator of memorable characters.

Another factor, and one that drives to the heart of the creative process itself, is the lack of motivation in her characters. Here the novelist allows the surface to be definitive: either the character explains himself or he does not. There is no "background filler" to provide the explanatory material which the character himself is unaware of. Part of the unreality of the conception is that the character maintains almost total awareness of himself: what he is, how he got that way, what direction he is to take. There are no uncertainties. The author assumes that the background of the elders was the same as that of the children, and that the cycle perpetuates itself.

An almost total reliance on dialogue further weakens characterization by making people float, as it were, on the rhythms of their speech. Miss Compton-Burnett's characters seem to have no substance except what their words give them. They are little more than mouthpieces, wits, talking heads, disembodied streams of words. And yet strikingly, despite the brilliant flow of words, there are no characters who are expert in their work. Her writers are second-rate, her professionals marginal and uninvolved in their work, her "intellectuals" uninterested in pursuing ideas. Every ideal is in decline.

There is of course little doubt that Miss Compton-Burnett is indebted to the fiction of Henry James, perhaps more so than to that of Jane Austen. Like James, she is interested in late-Victorian attitudes, and, again like him, she is concerned with revealing the hypocrisy that the age has disguised as hearty materialism. Both have placed limitations on the range of the novel so that they could probe in depth, and both have emphasized characters whose lives are built on sand or based on misconceived relationships that are no longer viable.

Miss Compton-Burnett's restrictions on the range of her novels seem an epitome of the contemporary English novel, which has forsaken adventurous forms and broad content for the small, intensive work. Often like the Greek tragedian in her attempt to convey the doom that waits for the successful man, she is unlike him in her inability to project individual ills upon the social framework. The "sickness" of her characters is theirs alone, a condition of their lives, and there is no other life. Perhaps this is her main point. Despite her fierce brightness, the inner world of her typical characters is as moribund as that of a Beckett bum; for both, love, hope, faith, and desire are meaningless values in a world that only language can define.

Of the seventeen novels in Ivy Compton-Burnett's canon, the **two** that have gained the widest popularity, *Bullivant and the*

Lambs (1947) and *Two Worlds and Their Ways* (1949), best illustrate her values and the kind of world she is involved in. They, along with three others, *Brothers and Sisters* (1929), *Elders and Betters* (1944), and *Mother and Son* (1955), demonstrate the author's main themes: the stifling of the child by the parent, the nature of successful deception, and the great secret which slowly and silently destroys.

Bullivant, as his truculent name suggests, is a bull of a servant in the house of the Lambs, who, however, contain a fierceness of their own. One expects them to be Lambs, but Horace is anything but that: a domineering, self-centered, egotistical man who has nagged and terrorized his children until they plot his death to insure their own survival. Bullivant and the servants in the kitchen serve as a sub-plot countering the life and death struggle between Horace and his children. They act as chorus, gaining all information as soon as the reader himself knows it. In this way, *Bullivant and the Lambs* recalls Henry Green's *Loving,* which had appeared two years earlier (in 1945). The servant has his masters cowed: the initial description indicates the relationship:

Bullivant was a larger man than his masters, and had an air of being on a considerable scale in every sense. He had pendulous cheeks, heavy eyelids that followed their direction, solid, thick hands whose movements were deft and swift and precise, a nose that hardly differentiated itself from its surroundings, and a deeply folded neck and chin with no definite line between them. His small, steady, hazel eyes were fixed on his assistant, and he wore an air of resigned and almost humorous deprecation, that suggested a tendency to catch his masters' glance. (p. 4)

In small, the theme of the novel is here. The relation between masters and a servant as feared as Bullivant—in Dickens, the servant has an eye, here he has a glance—can be nothing but comic. Servants, like their masters, are interested in power: Bullivant's power is over the Lambs, while Horace's is directed toward his children. Horace's use of power, however, is more brutal, because it takes advantage of ties based on trust. The servant's future depends on the fear he can build around his demands, but the child's depends on the love and sympathy he can obtain.

Horace offers neither love nor sympathy: he demands obedience.

The result is that the five children, whose ages run from thirteen to seven, have set up a war camp of their own, and find solace in the kitchen with the servants. There they escape Horace's dictum —reminiscent of Meredith's Sir Austin Feverel's—that " 'Civilised life consists in suppressing our instincts.' " Horace imposes on them the burden of being adults while they are still children; he denies that they should want anything—Christmas stockings, for instance—which he is unwilling to provide.

The children, however, reject both the wisdom and the man, and Horace gradually becomes a stranger in his home, doubly so when he recognizes that his wife, Charlotte, intends to run off with his cousin—both, evidently, feel about him the way the children do. After a severe illness, Horace reforms. He becomes the opposite of what he was: sympathetic, yielding, flexible in his wishes, and discreet in his demands. He becomes a model father and husband, and wins back to some extent both his children and his wife. Residual fear, nevertheless, remains: he may return to what he was, and after the respite, that would be more than the family could bear. So the boys reason when they think Horace is walking toward his death—" 'It would be better for him to die, if it was the only thing to prevent that.' " When Horace returns, as if from the dead, he questions his boys sadly, and they answer:

"We are afraid of you. You know we are," said Marcus [age 11]. "Your being different for a little while has not altered all that went before. Nothing can alter it. You did not let us have anything; you would not let us be ourselves. If it had not been for Mother, we would rather have been dead. It was feeling like that so often, that made us think dying an ordinary thing. (p. 227)

Kafka's own appeal to his father was not more bitter. The words of the boy come with the force of a judge's reprimand to a criminal awaiting sentence. Horace answers that he will be careful, that he will not stumble back into what he was, but also that he will always remember their capacity for evil. Nevertheless, he sadly perceives their act was little more than self-defense. If the children recognize that their parents want to suck them of life, they have the moral right to retaliate in kind. Murder itself becomes a relative thing, and at times one must murder (it must, however, be matricide or parricide) to maintain life. Both Horace and his sons have been initiated into the real world in which fear has transformed a possibly loving relationship into one of hate and desire for revenge. Unlike Kafka, Miss Compton-Burnett's "sons" do not write letters to their father: they plot his death.

As a counterpoint to this theme of parent-children brutality, there is the presence of the third power group in the Lamb household, the servants. Ever-aware and ever-hovering, the servants maintain their independent existence despite the presence of tyranny in the house. Bullivant burns with his own type of dominance, but there is within him a sense of proportion, something almost akin to kindness. In his dealings with Miss Buchanan—a storekeeper whose great secret is her inability to read—Bullivant displays tact and discretion, the very qualities that Horace Lamb failed to show toward his children. The two halves of the book work as complements: Bullivant, despite his bull-like independence, is able to demonstrate kindness toward those who are helpless, while Horace Lamb attacks his children because of their helplessness. The "moral" of the book is that Horace must learn the lesson that Bullivant has known all along; the penalty for refusing to learn it is to be re-condemned to death by his children.

In *Two Worlds and Their Ways,* which appeared two years later, the attitude is similar: the two worlds of the title are primarily those of the children and the adults. Also, there are the two worlds of the differing generations, the former and the present, and the two worlds of Sir Roderick Shelley's two wives, the first now long dead and the second, Maria, who wishes to best her in Sir Roderick's eyes. Maria's ambition is that her two children, Clemence and Sefton, should surpass their half brother, Oliver, Sir Roderick's child by his first wife, Mary (the similarity of the wives' names is not fortuitous—the two maintain a constant rivalry).

Since the childrens' own wishes are not represented in this intra-familiar competition, they feel that whatever they do is permissible. There is no moral question involved, for if one is to obey his elders, then he must not scruple over base action in order to fulfill what is expected of him. Therefore, when Maria requires a high standard of the children, they feel obliged not to disappoint her, for her disappointment may return to them in the form of subtle changes of attitude: withheld love, declining affection, diminishing interest—all of those intangible areas of which the parent thinks the child is unaware.

The children, who had been protected by being educated at home, are sent away to boarding schools run by Sir Roderick's two sisters. Once at school, each child is thrown against older children, who add to their sense of inadequacy and act as goads to their need for success. The competitive children at school, no more monstrous than children at any school, maintain their high places through systematic cheating and gain congratulations for accomplishments that were expected of them. In their own eyes, they are doing no more than they are supposed to do.

Their experiences are the same; both are caught cheating, both are disgraced at school, and both return home at vacation guilt-stricken, humiliated, and ashamed, waiting for the knowledge of their actions to reach their parents. What makes it unbearable is that the owners of the schools are their aunts, and they must live with the very people whom they have cheated. The shadow of their guilt is present in their homes, present in every aspect of their lives. Truth is no longer of any consequence. Their childhood, their youthful aspirations, their own quest after personal goals—all these aspects of their individuality have been lost. They were expected to compete unnaturally, and now they find themselves awaiting punishment for having fulfilled their mother's expectations. The basic immorality is clear: the parent tries to gain personal status by bending his children to his will instead of letting them follow their own course.

What makes this a comic and not a tragic novel is the fact that the children themselves treat their cheating as normal behavior. Furthermore, the comedy gains momentum when the parents and the aunts accept the cheating as unfortunate but not serious, and they gossip about it as if it will have little bearing on their lives.

In addition to their relative insouciance in this matter, the parents reveal striking things about themselves—Sir Roderick has fathered an illegitimate son who works as a manservant in the home, and Maria has deceived everyone about earrings she had sold to gain money. These revelations place the parents on the same level with the children; nearly everyone in the household turns out to have been a cheat.

The burden that Sir Roderick and Maria have placed on the children is humorously dismissed by Oliver, Sir Roderick's son by his first wife:

"Children are always reproached for doing what we do ourselves. What else could they be reproached for? They must have some bringing-up, and that consists of reproach. A term as a schoolmaster shows you that. And without it they would yield too much to their instincts." (p. 291)

And the children themselves ponder the situation, ruing that they ever went to school:

"Of course it is a pity. No one is in any doubt. Now we think Mother is odd and shabby; and Father is simple; and Miss Petticoat [their governess] is on the level of matrons; and none of them is different from what they were. And they see us as children who would get things by cheating, if they could. They do not think of us in the same way. And that is hardly an enrichment of our family life." (p. 308)

All this chaos has resulted from sending the two children away to school. In the home they might have survived without difficulty, for there nothing was expected of them; as soon, however, as they were sent out into the world, for which they were entirely unprepared, they compromised their aspirations, although not tragically. As much as Ibsen, Miss Compton-Burnett accepts that the sins of the parents are visited upon the children, even though, like Molière, she has turned melodramatic tragedy into the stuff of "serious farce."

The basic conflict is worked out, then, in terms of the two

worlds. The home has provided the children with no resources for living outside it, and as soon as they must manage alone, they capitulate to the worst part of their natures. They struggle to survive at the lowest level of their instincts; by cheating, lying, and deceiving, they have assumed the values of the world. When we view this novel against the background of Miss Compton-Burnett's others, we can see its trenchant humor: the home itself in most of her novels destroys, but even at its worst it provides a framework for behavior. Her characters, children as well as adults, are trapped. In the home, they remain semi-developed, immature, clinging, and protected, but at least alive; outside, where the wicked world awaits them with an entirely different set of values, they can hope for no solace whatsoever. The conflict cannot easily be resolved: the children can stay at home where the parents determine all courses of action and crush all spirit, or go out into the world where in different terms virtually the same occurs. To be caught between the two worlds, as Clemence and Sefton are, suggests humor, but of the grim sort that characterizes all of Miss Compton-Burnett's novels.

As her characters soon discover, life is destructive no matter how it is conceived; this is the one central truth that runs through Ivy Compton-Burnett's work, from her first mature work, *Pastors and Masters* (1925), to her most recent, *A Heritage and Its History* (1959). In her first novel, we meet several people of little or no accomplishment who think themselves extraordinary figures of great personal achievement. Their basic hypocrisy is immediately established, and in their way they are humorous monsters, deceiving themselves as to what they are and deceiving, or trying to deceive, everyone they meet, including each other. This is the chief pattern which runs through her chronicle of late-Victorian England, a chronicle that catches much of the worst that people can say and do. And yet behind their monstrous motivation and evil intentions, there is an energy that enables them to survive and to maintain the kind of strength that most characters in fiction no longer have. Miss Compton-Burnett's characters avoid nothing in order to assert themselves, and while they lack self-knowledge of a profound sort, they do know enough about life to recognize that to relent is to give themselves over to other equally monstrous people. They fight for what they are and for what they want with a tenacity that marks them as people for whom nothing has come cheaply. In their struggles, they revert to primitive passions, and for a novelist to bring back the primitive in a late-Victorian character indicates a special talent for the comic.

XII

The Angries:
Is There a Protestant in the House?

THE NOVELS of Kingsley Amis, John Braine, William Cooper, Thomas Hinde, Peter Towry, John Wain, and Keith Waterhouse are frequently more significant as demonstrations of certain social phenomena than as works of fiction. As literature, the novels are too limited to allow the kind of projection that results in satisfactory art; although even as social commentaries, they are generally too narrow to make possible the range of experience we expect from fiction, light or otherwise. Narrow range, superficial analyses, irresponsible and aimless protagonists, anti-heroic acts, anti-intellectualism, slapstick comedy—these are the qualities suggested by these novelists of the 1950's.

The term Angry Young Men* has been arbitrarily imposed upon these novelists' protagonists, but the word "snivelling" would perhaps have been more appropriate. For those accustomed to

* I repeat this popular phrase simply in order to group several writers whose "heroes" share certain characteristics, although the term is itself not descriptive of all the work of the novelists in question. I use it only for the sake of convenience, rather than as an artificial tag from which the writer cannot escape. The words themselves gained currency in connection with John Osborne's Jimmy Porter in his play *Look Back in Anger* (1956), but they had appeared as early as 1951 in the title of Leslie Allen Paul's autobiography, *Angry Young Man*. With the growing popularity of Kingsley Amis's *Lucky Jim*, the phrase Angry Young Men has become part of the language despite Amis's and Osborne's angry disclaimer of it.

real protest, this kind is strange indeed. It consists of pot shots at vainglorious individuals and at institutions which reward hypocrisy. It also means gnashing one's teeth, burning holes in mattresses, fighting in pubs, testing one's endurance with gin and beer, making ridiculous faces; it allows for little wit, little intelligence, little analysis of society in anything but black and white. In brief, it cuts off nearly every area of life that gives sustenance to human beings, and, accordingly, it makes a circus sideshow of the comic novel. Although these novelists are often akin in theme to their eighteenth-century predecessors—in common, they ask how an "honest" lowerclassman can move into genteel society with its sophisticated and frequently phony tastes and retain his innocence—their over-all performance dissipates the seriousness of the intent.

Primarily, the protagonists of these novelists are not really angry. They are, however, disgruntled—with themselves, with their social status, with their work, with their colleagues, with the shabbiness of daily life, with their frustrated aspirations for self-fulfillment, with the competitive spirit, with the inaccessibility of women and drink, with all the small activities whose pursuit takes up their depleted energies. If we want genuine anger, we must turn to the continental novel. An angry man, if his protest is to have significance, must react in terms beyond his own wants and dislikes. When he is angry or when he rebels, ideas are set into motion—he must stand for something significant, inarticulate though his feelings may be. When, however, Lucky Jim is angry, he is a fool; for his anger often manifests sour grapes, chances offered and withdrawn, opportunities lost. What a small world he is allowed to enter! How minuscule his desires! How petty his aims!

Even so, there is still room for a point of view if the author maintains ironic distance, giving perspective and proportion to Jim's pettiness. But Amis nowhere makes it clear that Jim's level of revolt is not also his; the focus that irony would provide is missing. Jim seems to become in his creator's eyes admirable rather than puny. The reader has little choice but to think that Amis accepts Jim's vulgar protest as a healthy sign in a drab society that forces conformity, competition, and goal-seeking. It is, however, debatable whether Jim is preferable to the society; both obviously must be rejected. And for Amis to identify his aims with Jim's is for him to accept protest at almost its lowest possible level; to strip protest, anger, and rebellion of their positive qualities and to substitute music hall farce for social analysis.

Lucky Jim (1954) is perhaps the best illustration of this kind of novel not because Amis consciously started a school or even created a fixed pattern, but because his Jim is representative of the younger "heroes" of this decade. Jim is part of the petty bourgeois world of librarians (John Lewis in Amis's *That Uncertain Feeling,* 1955), teachers (Jim himself, Edgar Banks in Wain's *Living in the Present,* 1955), civil servants (Joe Lampton in Braine's *Room at the Top,* 1957); as well as William Cooper's Joe Lunn (*Scenes from Provincial Life,* 1950) and his Leonard Harris (*Young People,* 1958), Keith Waterhouse's Billy (*Billy Liar,* 1959), William Camp's Mark Andres (*Prospects of Love,* 1957), J. D. Scott's Margaret Warriner (*The Margin,* 1949), and Hugh Thomas's Simon Smith (*The World's Game,* 1957). These are people who professionally must get what they want by moving slowly toward clearly defined goals. To move slowly, however, is precisely what they want to escape, although to move rapidly toward the same goal is also inadequate. They need to break out, to seek new landscapes in which they will be defined as individuals, to escape the confines of an organized social structure with its pressures and false admonitions. Their protest in the fifties is similar to the American gangster's revolt in the twenties, as the motion pictures have presented him: a man trapped by social forces which are themselves corrupt. In order to be "honest," he must deceive, lie, steal, even kill. He must work his way to margins and peripheries. Eventually, he must throw himself against the very structure which will eventually crush him. Nevertheless, in destroying himself, he achieves a certain kind of perverted purity.

These Jims of the fifties feel anger as much against themselves for being trapped as against those who have trapped them. Educated to discontent, they find nothing in society that appeals to them, except perhaps female breasts and buttocks. Despite their intellectual pretensions, their intellect bores them.

People generally are appalling; values are nonexistent, or else they exist only for the advancement of the Establishment—the hated hierarchy of institutionalized hypocrisy. Accordingly, the class lines have been drawn. One must attempt to break out of his class altogether and seek communion either with the working classes or with other social eccentrics, all of whom can FEEL. So far, this kind of attitude can lead in several directions potentially fruitful for the novel. The author can mount a cosmic attack against the order of the universe, although pomposity may result. He can generate situations in which moral decisions must be made, although melodrama may develop. Or he can use this information as a way of developing character, although this too may prove to be cliché-ridden. Notwithstanding, whatever the author chooses to do, numerous possibilities for fiction are involved. Developed seriously, these themes could lead to the new novel of manners and morals, catching a society in change, as Jane Austen and Dickens did. However, to avoid most of the implications of these attitudes, as the novelists above have done, is consciously to thin down the substance of the novel.

When the reader stops to examine what Jim is angry about, he finds straw dummies which the mature person would reject outright. Jim is against the hypocrisy and vanity of his department chairman, Professor Welch. Who would favor the man? Jim opposes pseudo-artists who pose as the real thing and offer temperament instead of craft. Who likes pseudo-artists? Jim rejects neurotic unattractive girls and prefers lush, buxom, more simple ones. Who would dispute his taste? Jim is against fakery, phoniness, and pomposity. Once again, who would argue with him? What Amis has done is to take superficial incidents and characters and make them the center of the novel, as though even farcical comedy can proceed this way. Dickens, as well as Chekhov, who covered this ground dozens of times, knew much better. Professor Welch, for example, becomes the focus of Jim's rancor all out of proportion to what he is worth. As a peripheral character, the Professor might awaken momentary interest, but as a center of attraction, with his useless learning and his meaningless patronage of the arts, he fails to justify the thousands of words expended upon him. Similarly, his son, Bertrand, is someone who should be caught and dismissed in a few pages; instead, he persists as a thorn in Jim's temper. At every stage of the novel, what should be merely a minor item assumes undue significance. Jim, consequently, is found in a series of episodes which initially attract the reader and then become tedious as they fail to develop.

The reader soon recognizes that Jim is little more than a music hall character attached to a university by some cosmic error. As a comedian, Jim would make an excellent minor character. As a rebel, however, even as a rebel in a Restoration comedy, he fails almost completely. Everything that Jim revolts against is understandably obnoxious, but Jim's aim is not opposition so much as it is to seek a niche for himself. Like the rest, Jim is a pusher; only he cannot make it in their terms. Cast this way, Jim's revolt is meaningless, merely another form of social and economic expedience. Yet for Amis, Jim can have his childish antics and still succeed as an honest non-hero. As long as there are rich saviors like Gore-Urquhart, the young man's revolt against hypocrisy will continue to be confused with the real thing.

The alternatives for the novelist are not necessarily romantic heroes or figures like those in C. P. Snow's novels who make control and discipline the touchstones by which they live. The alternative to a hero and an administrator need not be a Jim Dixon, as Amis seems to feel, any more than the alternative to a Greek protagonist and an organization man must be Beckett's Murphy.

John Wain's *Hurry on Down* (1953), published shortly before *Lucky Jim,* contains more substance than Amis's novel, but is marred by a basic sentimentality that compromises its point of view. Charles Lumley does not fit into ordinary life, although he admits that he would like to do so. Lumley in his various anti-social acts is not a simple rebel against the commonplace and bourgeois; as he says, " 'I never even got into it.' " His acts, consequently, are ones of survival on any terms that life can suggest; he drifts until he finds something acceptable—writing for a popular entertainer—and then wins what he wants, the hitherto unobtainable girl and monetary reward.

Reaction to class stratification is clearly the key to Lumley, as it is to Amis's Jim. Lumley comes from the bourgeoisie, and while he is imprisoned there by virtue of his education and his speech, he does not share its aspirations. Sufficiently educated to detest his own class, he nevertheless rejects the tastes of the effeminate highbrows and the factitious sophisticates. He must, accordingly, make his own world in which class will not be significant. His aim is to be neutral and classless—emotionally, socially, and economically. Caught between two worlds, neither of which is palatable, he becomes, in turn, a window cleaner, truck driver, smuggler of narcotics, and chauffeur—all attempts to disgrace his class and wipe the past clean. For a short time, he even becomes a bouncer in a combination night club and whore house. All his jobs are calculatingly on the margin of society; all are socially reprehensible. His only socially acceptable job is as a hospital worker, and that too is a form of escape. Immersed among the sick and injured, he is left alone. There, society can make no demands upon him.

Lumley is more interesting than Jim because he actively attempts to create order out of chaos, while Jim is satisfied with making chaos out of unacceptable order. The latter way works well in episodes, but is too short-sighted for a full novel; while Wain's way—to create order—could possibly have sustained the novel provided the author had been able to maintain mature invention. Lumley is characteristic, however, of most of the Angry protagonists. They rebel and then find some niche for themselves that fails to accommodate their former intention. The honesty of the intention becomes transformed into the expedience of reality.

Originally, each protagonist wanted to create his own kind of earthly paradise in which the individual could float free of the hypocrisy and restrictions of class. The paradise he longed for would not of course be free of restrictions, but he at least wanted them his own. None of these protagonists, however, becomes *déclassé* in the sense of Camus' rebel: the former's desires ultimately are too close to those of the average citizen to allow for the sacrifice of props that rebellion entails. When he finds that things of this world strongly attract him, he adapts himself to some situation which, like a deus ex machina, miraculously saves him. The result is frequently a sentimentalized compromise.

The author, whether Wain, Braine, Amis, Cooper, Scott, or Thomas, assumes that natural man in his natural setting is ideal, the closest thing to an egalitarian social structure. Their protagonists, whatever their differences, must return to the source of their strength and express their freedom from conventionality. Every move they make in the name of self-expression, however, is a gesture to the society they are trying to circumvent, but the irony is lost upon them. They confuse their own natures with their masks, and while they deceive themselves, society determines what they are. Trying to be Rousseauistic natural men, they only superficially break away from organized humbug, and often they end up nourished by the very institutions they have mocked.

The search for values that these pseudo-rebels undertake is invalidated by their selfishness, and the author rarely indicates whether their egoism is condemnable because it is generated by a competitive society which squeezes out all naturalness, or admirable because it enables the protagonists to survive. The reader recognizes that they do not really want values; they simply desire to find a place for themselves—to find room at the top, in the middle, at the bottom. Anyone who seriously gets in their way is, therefore, a fool, a moron who can be used for the protagonist's expedient purposes. Right and wrong are blurred not by the ambiguous quality of life itself but by the desires of the protagonist, who makes value judgments based not on mature evaluation but on personal need.

The shallowness of the "hero" results naturally from the shallowness of the novel's conception. The prose in these novels, with few exceptions, is short and choppy, the dialogue of men who do not have the time or will to develop a more mature outlook. A protagonist who lacks all ambition will not be disturbed by language that communicates only at a basic level. The prose, such as it is, indicates that everything can be said in language that has few nuances and that yields only superficialities. The prose indicates the tone of the protagonist: his fluttery uncertainty, his lack of depth, his easy resolution of his problems, the superficial look he takes at himself and society. The following passage from *Lucky Jim* suggests these qualities, even though Amis is perhaps the most felicitous writer of the group and surely the funniest:

While he [Jim] followed Welch next door, wondering whether the subject for debate was the sheet [which Jim had burned], or his dismissal, or the sheet and his dismissal, Dixon reeled off a long string of swearwords in a mumbling undertone, so that he'd be in credit, as it were, for the first few minutes of the interview. He stamped his feet hard as he walked, partly to keep his courage up, partly to drown his own mutterings, partly because he hadn't yet smoked that morning. (pp. 83-4)

Jim simply seems silly after one experiences his repertory of jokes, faces, and facetious remarks. His substance is dissipated in meaningless gaffs. Despite his obvious intellectual gifts, Amis fritters away nearly every major issue that his material might suggest, even when the resolution could be in comic terms. Often, he heads directly for farce when satire would better serve his purposes. Dixon's drunken speech on "Merrie England" before the assembled notables is too long and lacks verbal sharpness. His burning a hole in the bedding at the Welch home is a funny routine from the music hall, but it is merely an oddity without real focus. Frequently, a scene is, as it were, interpolated—merely a sequence that serves no purpose in the development of character or situation. Amis's strength as a writer—and at times he can be hilariously funny—has been identified by the English critics as that of a parodist, but the parodist gets at issues and does not hurl thunderbolts at straw gods.

One often wonders, against the grain of the novel, whether Jim Dixon with his "honesty" is better suited for the academic life— or any kind of life—than his ridiculous Professor Welch. If Jim's very unfitness perhaps causes him to be placed with a man like Welch, then how can he act as a criticism of the older man? Both basically are fakes cut from the same cloth and coming from the same basket. In a world of masks, Jim too holds up his head through various disguises; his faces, his veneer of culture, his standing as a university teacher, his patina of smart talk are all deceptive ways of hiding what he is. If Bertrand, Welch's son, is a pseudo-artist and a bore, then Jim, his chief antagonist, is a pseudo-intellectual and a pest. His insight into his own motives does not necessarily make him a better person than those whose disguises are inseparable from what they are.

The values of Amis and Wain are not, of course, the only ones in this general movement identified, or misidentified, as the Angries. As I have suggested above, these authors are allied solely by the general tone of their novels and the general attitudes of their protagonists. Aimless, will-less, lacking moral stature (either good or bad), the characters of Amis and Wain stand out simply because these authors were among the first with this contemporary version of the picaresque novel. Their protagonists, along with Joe Lampton of Braine's *Room at the Top,* find their distant literary ancestors in Julien Sorel of Stendhal's *The Red and the Black,* Rastignac of Balzac's *Père Goriot,* Fredric Moreau of Flaubert's *A Sentimental Education,* and are related to every British and American young man on the make or on the run, from Butler's Ernest Pontifex to Dreiser's Clyde Griffiths and Saul Bellow's Augie March. In the immediate background are the disillusioned young men of Aldous Huxley, Waugh's Basil Seal, Anthony Powell's Nicholas Jenkins, and Willian Cooper's Joe Lunn.

The differences among these figures obviously are huge, but there is a general thread of identification. They are more or less open characters in a closed society, or at least a society closed to their particular style. They may merely want comfort, or perhaps power; notwithstanding, their surface rebellion is a manifestation of egoism. Clearly, they do not rebel for the sake of society. They are, in fact, nauseated by the moral demands that society makes upon them, and, as we have seen, they stride the fringes of law, morality, and respectability. Their rule of thumb is that what is good enough for them is sufficient for society. Obviously, they do not multiply their actions several-fold in order to see how their collective behavior determines what society is. Introspection itself is often alien to them. Give them money, education, and background, give them status, and they would fit, as several readily admit.

Lest one chide them harshly, these young men, whether French, English, or American, do not have much choice, cut off as they are by drabness on one side and privilege on the other. Educated to positions of minor power, they are nevertheless outside the puritanical injunction to seek private gain through hard work, and one can scarcely moralize about that. They are also, to some extent, outside the hypocrisy that is required for one who wishes to make his way within the "respectable" world. And, further, they simply lack the staying power and will necessary to continue at something until it begins to yield money and prestige. Like Beckett's Murphy, they are of the little world. And they know all this about themselves. They are not fools, although some of them —Julien Sorel, for instance—confuse romantic visions with expedient gestures and thus destroy themselves. By and large, however, they attempt what they think they are capable of completing, and this self-knowledge within a small frame is certainly valid for the character. Their existence, their identity, depends on a sharp questioning of established values. Had they lived in the twenties, they might have become tribal members of the Lost Generation, gaining focus through exile. Otherwise, they may kill outright, as Clyde Griffiths in *An American Tragedy,* or indirectly as Joe Lampton in *Room at the Top,* or merely commit the childish indiscretions of Jim Dixon in *Lucky Jim.*

Joe Lampton of Braine's first novel (1957) illustrates the difficulties of the slow rise to the top of one who has the will and desire to succeed. Part of his dissatisfaction with ingrown society is that he wishes to immerse himself in its nonsense while recognizing its insufficiency. Unlike Wain's Lumley, however, who wants to justify his identification with the lower classes and then finds himself writing for a popular and rather vulgar entertainer, Joe Lampton does not confuse means and ends. He heads straight for the big money, a girl named Susan, who says things like, " 'I won't be cold. Cross my heart.' " or " 'If you love me up, I'll be as warm as toast.' " and refers to her parents as Mummy and Daddy. Joe admits to himself, honestly, that accepting Susan's money involves accepting the girl as well, but without much inner difficulty he finds attractive her youthful beauty, her cleanliness, her wealthy background.

Not that Susan is unattractive; she is simply boring in a spoiled-child way; and this is evidently not the girl cut out for a hustler like Joe. The alternative is Alice: much older, less directly attractive, not wealthy, married, and neurotic. On the credit side, Alice is a woman while Susan is a girl. When Alice "commits suicide" on the road, a direct result of Joe's choice of Susan, Joe considers himself guilty, although nobody blames him. Nevertheless, the novel ends as Joe has risen from his class and convinced himself that he has also found love.

Like Defoe, whom he often resembles, Braine allows his predatory hero to confuse love with money. Joe Lampton is, as it were, a Robinson Crusoe carving an empire for himself on the island of England, dropping and picking up love as his need may be, acutely aware of the demeaning power of a love that does not pay off and the exultant power of a love that does. Marriage to Susan is rewarded in every possible way except that of self-fulfillment; but Joe chooses her.

Room at the Top evidently has within it the seeds of a good novel. Braine writes succinctly and to the point. He has the phrases necessary to catch a situation and a character without waste. The only difficulty, however, is the quality of the content. The novel posits a choice between real love and fake love; and much as the reader hates to say it, he has seen it before and seen it with more profound variations and more interesting embroidery. The decision as posed this way is a cliché of novel planning; the conception itself unfortunately precludes any original large-scale comment. Distinct weaknesses are apparent in the minor characters who fulfill their functions but rarely come alive—for example, Jack Wales, Susan's rich boy friend with all the advantages, as well as Alice's husband and Susan's father, small-town businessmen who act the way such men are supposed to behave.

Braine's second novel, *The Vodi,* published two years later, is less sharply focused than *Room at the Top* and consequently disappointing. Dick Corvey is tubercular, and while others of his generation are having fun and making their way, he must lie in a sanitarium. The Vodi, a figment of his imagination, have condemned him to torture. Dick's struggle, then, is against himself. He must come to terms with these internal torturers and virtually will himself to life. The novel settles down to resolve this conflict, with its main setting, reminiscent of *The Magic Mountain,* in the sanitarium. Braine attempted through flashback to create dramatic tension between life inside and life outside the sanitarium by sketching in Dick Corvey's past and then focusing on the contrast between his hopes then and his hopelessness in the present. Eventually, to everyone's surprise, Dick does recover and enters the world to begin another kind of struggle to survive.

The idea of the novel, while not original, poses several possibilities for development; but, handled unimaginatively, the material becomes sodden and formless. Unfortunately, Dick's adventures prior to his hospitalization as well as his encounter with a nurse within the sanitarium are tirelessly realistic. Braine obviously is endeavoring to express something important about the human will to survive and about the apparently inconsequential things that make one endure existence. In *Room at the Top,* Braine was also concerned with important issues: the clash between love and money, feeling and reason, temporary satisfaction and long-range ambition. In that novel, as in *The Vodi,* however, the conception of character and situation was too limited to allow for significant projection. The trivial details of the narrative diminish the theme and make it too commonplace to convince us. The problem with Braine's work—and this is true of many "young" novels in the 1950's—is not in his intention but in his execution, not in his ideas but in his inability to "see" his material before publishing it.

Most of these novelists have published too rapidly after initial success with a first novel. After *Lucky Jim,* Amis published within four years two novels even sketchier than the first, when evidently he had nothing new to say. *That Uncertain Feeling* (1955) replaces Jim Dixon with John Lewis, changing his vocation from lecturer in a provincial university to small-town librarian. The roll call of fools remains more or less constant, and John, like Jim, gains happiness by finding a job that removes him from middle-class life. Jim identifies with money, while John merges with the worker, neither solution quite convincing in the format Amis allows. Amis's third novel, *I Like It Here* (1958), was made possible by a Somerset Maugham award (Maugham had himself once called the Angries and their kind scum). The work is barely a sketch for a novel, as though Amis felt obliged to break into print as rapidly as possible, regardless of what he had to express. *Take a Girl Like You* (1960) is a more workmanlike job than the previous two novels, but it merely repeats from Jenny Bunn's point of view what Jim Dixon and John Lewis have already said.

One also gets this feeling of duplication about John Wain, who gave up his academic post to write professionally. He followed *Hurry on Down* with three short novels that appeared within four years, *Living in the Present* (1955), *The Contenders* (1958), and *A Travelling Woman* (1959). Wain is a serious novelist, as he suggests in his statement in *Declaration,* but the three novels that followed *Hurry on Down* are full of the conceptual clichés and examples of unimaginative planning that flawed his more artistically successful first novel. In *Declaration,* Wain described *Hurry on Down* simply as an examination of the conflict between education and life; he was concerned with "the young man's problem of how to adapt himself to 'life,' in the sense of an order external to himself, already there when he appeared on the scene, and not necessarily disposed to welcome him; the whole being complicated by the fact that in our civilization there is an unhealed split between the educational system and the assumptions that actually underlie life." Further, Wain emphasized that in Lumley's attempt to solve his problems there is an implicit moral point —"something to do with the nature of goodness." The intention, then, was of the highest, an intention that has motivated some of the finest apprenticeship novels of the last hundred years. Dickens, in fact, was concerned with the same problem, and in *Great Expectations* grappled with the nature of success and morality. Only the writer willing to project his material imaginatively, however, can properly dramatize the major conflicts implicit in this type of novel.

Nevertheless, in accordance with the author's serious intentions —whether successfully carried out or not—one expects more than *Living in the Present,* with its pretentious epigraph, "Death destroys a man, but the idea of life saves him." Such a tag is more appropriate to a Max Beerbohm parody of Conrad's fiction than it is to the shenanigans of Wain's novel. Edgar Banks' initial problem seems valid enough—he despairs of life, sees its pettiness, and rejects its shallow success and intermittent failure. Banks is no madcap revolutionary or under-the-counter anarchist but a basically social chap repelled by cant. Out to make his own peace in a world captured by morons and directed by schizoids, where can he, a sane man, fit? The existentialist situation generates clichés and frail humor.

The same thinness recurs in *The Contenders* and *A Travelling Woman*. In the former, relating the futile struggle between two successful people, Wain concludes that it is better to be outside the arena, or "inside the whale," as Orwell put it. The latter novel is full of the "Look, pa, I'm sleeping with a woman" type of humor that often passes for pseudo-Restoration comedy. Once more, however, Wain suggests an important theme beneath the surface of his trivial characterizations. Is he indicating that in a world of hypocritical values even sexual intercourse, the one realistic and stabilizing factor in a relationship, is futile? Is he indicating further that all human relationships, no matter what their basis, inevitably prove fruitless when mass values are petty? These questions are valid, but Wain's weak humor, his thin characters, his lack of imagination in the love scenes, his failure to define where his characters leave off and he begins (the entire question of attitude or tone in the narrative) preclude his fulfilling the promise of the theme.

The tremendous need to rush into print with a short novel surely hinders these authors from developing their talents. Has the novel for them replaced the hastily written political pamphlet which the eighteenth-century writer composed in his spare moments? Their "protest"—such as it is—perhaps at first forced them into hurried statements, but even their subsequent books show no development in craft or content, and as well no desire to slow down and see what the novel really entails. Whatever anger or feeling they may have had was released by them before it became art. Their anger turns into an ineffectual protest against a counterfeit society.

I have mentioned in passing the names of Thomas Hinde, Peter Towry, William Cooper, J. D. Scott, and Hugh Thomas, whose relationship to Amis, Wain, and Braine is that of distant cousins who with or without direct recognition cross each other's paths. William Cooper is often thought of as the "father" of the Angry Young Men, although he is the least angry of the lot. In *Scenes from Provincial Life* (1950), his Joe Lunn moves to the fringes of society, even while maintaining his position as a school-teacher. Joe is a typical anti-hero or non-hero of the fifties. He obtains his freedom by week-ending in a cottage with Myrtle, who is good to sleep with but not to marry. Marriage, for the male, means prison, while the cottage on the week-ends means escape. Also, Joe writes novels, another form of escape from petty routine at the school. Joe's chief worry in life is to maintain the privacy of his week-ends. He is irresponsible in everything except his art, but even that has no power to cloud his euphoria. He sees life superficially and arranges his time so that he is his own man; he feels no ties and wants to feel none. Of course, later he will settle down, as Cooper demonstrates in *Scenes from Married Life* (1961).

Distantly allied to Joe Lunn is J. D. Scott's Margaret Warriner (*The Margin,* 1949), who finally escapes her "intellectual" job and trivial milieu by running off to Brazil with Colin, an impetuous film maker. Hugh Thomas in *The World's Game* (1957) was to repeat a similar theme; his Simon Smith, while a romantic idealist in the Foreign Service, is an anarchist toward institutions and traditions. Similarly, Keith Waterhouse's Billy (*Billy Liar,* 1959) must create illusions to live by and thus through tricks and false assumptions break out of his spirit-crushing daily routine that requires mind and attention. In a somewhat different kind of novel, *City of Spades* (1957), Colin MacInnes also demonstrates the fatuity of intellect when it is opposed by feeling. Against a back-ground of the Negro influx into England, MacInnes cleverly charts the career of an attractive and not so ingenuous African, Johnny Fortune, who upsets preconceived notions and disarms those who would contain him.

Towry's *It's Warm Inside* (1953) appeared only a few months before *Lucky Jim* and in certain ways helped set the pace for many of the "young" novels that followed. Towry was concerned with an important question that has troubled his generation, the question of how one should live when only personal values exist. However, instead of raising the answer to a significant level, he lowered it to inconsequential farce. Using post-Restoration pas-tiche, Towry chronicles the bedroom athletics of his characters, none of whom either feels love or enjoys satisfaction. Richard almost loses Silvana, his wife, when she returns unexpectedly from vacation to find him in bed with Daisy, a girl he had known and "lost" ten years before in Paris. From this point, Richard must decide what he is and what he wants. He decides that he wants Silvana, but she is not sure that she wants Richard. He must win her all over again. Richard finally effaces his "sin" and falls into the waiting arms of Silvana, and even finds financial success in work he started at Daisy's encouragement. Love and success are joined once again in a tandem.

Richard's charm is difficult to place, except perhaps for a devil-may-care attitude that types him for Daisy as a source of fun. He is willing to corrupt whatever talent he has as an artist, flexible as he is to the point of disbelieving in everything. He sways with the winds of immediate passion and falls into any situation that proves temporarily exciting. He is the complete opposite, obviously, of the self-willed young man of the nineteenth century who saw his goal and sacrificed his comfort in order to pursue it. Richard has no goals, except perhaps a fleeting sense of pleasure. He resolves decisions on the basis of what will give him the greatest happiness in the shortest time.

In 1957, Thomas Hinde published *Happy as Larry,* whose protagonist is a typical Angries anti-hero. He makes passes at a writing career, drinks heavily, and drifts from job to job. His episodic adventures form the substance of this new version of the picaresque. Larry, however, is the kind of character who generates almost no interest because he operates on such a small and insubstantial level. Since he is drunk most of the time, his mind, manner, and language are below the level of full awareness. He claims to be creative, but demonstrates no talent. The trouble with Larry is that he should be a minor or marginal character, not the central figure in a novel of three hundred pages. After two or three pages, the vapid Larry yields little but fumes and childish desires.

In common, these novelists wage obvious war on convention. Like Anthony Powell's Nicholas Jenkins, who looks out of all-seeing eyes at social breakup, their protagonists resist the heroic gesture and the idealistic commitment. Rejecting the larger world, they wish to be left alone in the smaller. Their irresponsibility is to them a sign of honesty, selfishness an indication of freedom. Their values center around the illusions they have created for themselves, in particular their success in isolating their interests from society's. Unfortunately for the novel, their creators too frequently accept these illusions as their own, and we have a truncated fiction that says far less than the theme suggests.

There is, of course, a great deal to be angry about. It is no solution, however, merely to substitute egoism for guilt and altruism, selfishness for the humanitarianism of the thirties, or self-gain for a sense of responsibility. Conservative critics have attacked the Angries, claiming that the rigidity of the Welfare State —which gave them whatever they wanted without a struggle, so the argument runs—has resulted in their puerilities. This is the gist of the *Time* magazine article in 1957, in which the Angry Young Men were handled as a group who ridiculed and denied all allegiances, as though this in itself were condemnable.

The rejection of all allegiances is potentially fruitful for fiction—it forms the basis of many significant novels: Goncharov's *Oblomov,* Conrad's *Victory,* Camus' *The Plague* and *The Stranger,* Sartre's *Nausea,* among others. As a theme, it is obviously capable of important ramifications, but it takes shape only if the author is honest with himself and his material. By curious reasoning, *Time* hit upon the important theme, but the fact is that the Angries themselves have not faithfully accepted the implications of the idea. They have not declined all loyalties, although their material seems to call for precisely this. Instead, they have temporized and sentimentalized. They are, for example, loyal to expedience, to lower-class "honesty," to the power of physical sensations.

It is in failing to see their material completely that these younger writers, their individual talents aside for the moment, are found seriously wanting. Even if they reject gentility, upper-class imposture, middle-class pettiness, the inner-directed dedicated man, the organization man of C. P. Snow, the guilt-stricken invalids of Graham Greene, the sensitive young women of Elizabeth Bowen, the "effeminate men" of Lawrence Durrell, the old fogies of Ivy Compton-Burnett, and the gushy artists and politicians of Joyce Cary, even then, they still have themselves to cope with; and here they have little to offer. We have come full circle: one can reject the world only if he can replace it with himself, as the French existentialists have indicated. The arrogant anti-heroes of the Angries, swilling beer in the corner pub, have nothing to draw upon; as empty as the people they attack, they too are parasites.

Possibly the semi-hysterical rantings of Jimmy Porter in *Look Back in Anger* are more acceptable than the childish nonsense of Colin Wilson's *The Outsider,* with its call for religious greatness; but neither work moves us past the point that Conrad reached sixty years ago in "Heart of Darkness" and *Nostromo* or attained later by D. H. Lawrence and Aldous Huxley. One needs protest, let us agree, but the protest must cut all the way through; it must not stop at comfort, expedience, and individual stability. It must contain ideas, and it must have range.

In the hands of these younger writers, the English novel has become de-internationalized and insular. While this generation of French existentialists has probed man's fate, their English contemporaries have analyzed his comforts and temporary needs. This critic is antagonistic toward many of these novelists precisely because they have limited themselves to trivialities when there is so much to be angry about. Neglecting the whole scene, they have pecked at the periphery; this is simply drawing-room comedy turned inside out. Even the problem of class, which is central to an understanding of their kind of protest and vulgarity, does not receive adequate handling. Like their protagonists, they have retreated to the provinces, and, accordingly, their short, restricted novels are provincial.

XIII

The Still Comic Music of Humanity:
The Novels of Anthony Powell,
Angus Wilson, and Nigel Dennis

Anthony Powell's *The Music of Time*

UNLIKE C. P. Snow's series of novels, Anthony Powell's *The Music of Time** is concerned not with the decisions that people must make but with those they try to avoid. Snow's earnest men of will who desire personal power become in Powell's five novels (so far) objects of ridicule for breaking the upper class code of relaxed leisure. Powell's "new men," like Widmerpool and Quiggin, push their way rather than swim along with the tide; and consequently they are traitors to their upper-class friends, whose code demands that no one work hard or accomplish anything. The pushers make good in the City, while someone like Stringham, who is loyal to his heritage, dissipates his substance in wasted opportunities and drink. Thus, emerging from this ooze, the offensive and mechanical Widmerpool becomes a hero of our time, the vulgar buffoon and clown now making his way through sheer will.

Powell's narrator, Nicholas Jenkins, who is a more relaxed Lewis Eliot, provides the focus for about two dozen characters whose zaniness passes for normality in the England of the twen-

---

* *A Question of Upbringing* (1951); *A Buyer's Market* (1952); *The Acceptance World* (1955); *At Lady Molly's* (1959); *Casanova's Chinese Restaurant* (1960)

ties and thirties. If Snow's purpose is to relate how relatively normal men come to decisions that affect themselves and their country, Powell's concern is to prevent his "normal" people from sinking from the weight of their eccentricities. Their lives are tales told by one of themselves of successive marriages and divorces, of constant re-formations and regroupings, of lost opportunities and wasted chances. At one point, Jenkins recapitulates the world in which he moves (*The Acceptance World*, p. 213):

I had enacted scenes with Jean: Templer with Mona: now Mona was enacting them with Quiggin: Barnby and Umfraville with Anne Stepney: Stringham with her [Anne's] sister Peggy: Peggy now in the arms of her cousin: Uncle Giles, very probably, with Mrs. Erdleigh: Mrs. Erdleigh with Jimmy Stripling: Jimmy Stripling, if it came to that, with Jean [Jenkins' own mistress]: and Duport [Jean's husband], too.

The re-alignments of these couples—and this listing is only partial—leave them little time for other activities; and in this comic format, Powell charts the course of the upper classes as they weave their bored way through the years between the two great wars. Everyone seems to know everyone else; in fact, everyone seems to have had an affair with everyone else. The combinations are virtually endless, and the oddity of a particular person does not preclude his finding a mate. Jenkins himself is like a sideshow barker—those who come under his purview perform their act and then become part of his memorable collection, to recur at intervals.

Powell's material is perhaps reminiscent, in one way, of Ronald Firbank's, in another, of Evelyn Waugh's in the thirties, but the comparison holds only superficially. In Waugh's world, as in Firbank's, people exist only for themselves, possessing egos that preclude any real accomplishment. Waugh rarely indicates how society does keep going, for his characters are either upsetting society or removing themselves from it. Powell, however, gives his characters enough freedom and sense to operate within the great world, although most expend a minimum of effort. Powell's concern with their personal failings and private lives notwithstanding, they continue to function in a public way; they do keep the world operating despite their neglect, ignorance, and flightiness. The result is a "true" social fiction, and in this sense Powell is a finer social critic than Waugh.

The latter, like Sterne, is capable of delineating the ridiculousness of human action, but Powell, here like Fielding, is able to merge the ludicrous with the necessary and show people in the round. Waugh eliminates the question of how people sustain themselves when they are involved in senseless situations, while Powell is constantly aware of it. A Waugh character attempts to escape from what he is by allowing outside forces to mold him as *they* will; a Powell character differs in that he has some sense of what he is, but almost complete lack of will negates his chance for self-fulfillment. When someone does accomplish something—Jenkins writes a novel, for example—it is passed by almost without notice, as though achievement were itself a mockery in such a world. And when Widmerpool pushes his way through London financial life on his road to success, we see him as a man without gentility, dignity, or humanity. He is an obsessed inner-directed man who can be only a figure of fun for his tradition-directed contemporaries.

There is in Powell's comedy a generous awareness of the sadness of life, an awareness to which his characters (except perhaps for Jenkins himself) remain almost totally blind. Against a vast background of depression, coming war, and moral chaos, they seek entanglements and fruitless re-alignments. Ennui leaves them little time for anything but self-gratification, and often their charm lies in their powers of self-deception.

The cast of Powell's novels would seem to recall the typical Aldous Huxley novel of the twenties, for both are writing about similar worlds. In Huxley, though, everyone is odious, even the people he appears to favor; while in Powell, we have the unique comic novelist who can write with wit and subtlety and still create not simply personality but character. A typical Huxley (or Waugh) figure is too insubstantial to function outside of a Huxley (or Waugh) situation—he would disintegrate as soon as the author removed pressure. A Powell sophisticate, however, has substance that carries beyond the immediate circumstance, and he has reactions which reveal that he can be touched. A Waugh character is motivated by forces that remain outside explanation; he is innately insane. A Powell character, Widmerpool perhaps excepted, has human desires no matter how driven he is by forces he cannot understand. Even Mona—the elegant toothpaste model who gravitates from man to man—feels that each successive mate is unsuitable for her, and we see how Templer, Quiggin, and Erridge, in turn, cannot relieve her enormous sense of boredom.

In a world ready to explode, Powell takes up Snow's ambitious middle class and makes it ridiculous; examines Thackeray's upper middle class and demonstrates its flaws; probes Waugh's upper class and while cataloguing its antics shows its unfitness not only for positions of power but for life itself. Powell instills his picture of this apparently innocuous and superficial group of people with his realization of their tragic inadequacy in a world demanding moral fiber. In *The Acceptance World,* he speaks of the meaning of the title and its application to life in general:

"When in describing Widmerpool's new employment, Templer had spoken of 'the Acceptance World,' I had been struck by the phrase. Even as a technical definition, it seemed to suggest what we are all doing; not only in business, but in love, art, religion, philosophy, politics, in fact all human activities. The Acceptance World was the world in which the essential element—happiness, for example—is drawn, as it were, from an engagement to meet a bill. Sometimes the goods are delivered, even a small profit made; sometimes the goods are not delivered, and disaster follows; sometimes the goods are delivered, but the value of the currency is changed. Besides, in another sense, the whole world is the Acceptance World as one approaches thirty; at least some illusions discarded. The mere fact of still existing as a human being proved that." (p. 170)

The five novels in *The Music of Time—A Question of Upbringing* (1951), *A Buyer's Market* (1952), *The Acceptance World* (1955), *At Lady Molly's* (1959), and *Casanova's Chinese Restaurant* (1960)—have, then, under the puckish humor a solid foundation of tragic event. The process of growing old is obviously intrinsic to the series; one grows old while nothing seems to change, and age and growth themselves become hallucinatory. Powell's concern with the relationship between present and past time forces an inevitable comparison of his work with Proust's, although he is not interested in the functions of memory itself. For him, things in the past continue to well up; events come back as though eternally recurrent, "like those episodes of early experiences seen, on re-examination at a later period, to have been crowded together with such unbelievable closeness in the course of a few years; yet equally giving the illusion of being so infinitely extended during the months when actually taking place." (*A Buyer's Market,* p. 23.)

In Powell's series, the pressure of time, while lacking the intensity conveyed by *Remembrance,* does create a sober undertone despite the author's subtle humor. Time becomes a Fury which pursues his characters and makes them feel guilty for not changing internally as they are altered externally. In their need to avoid boredom, in which they often consciously demean themselves, the one thing they cannot escape is time. Consequently, the seriousness pokes through despite what seems to be Powell's neutrality toward his characters.

His humor itself depends more on the characteristics of normality than on eccentricity. And unlike Waugh, Powell does not rely on prejudices or fixed beliefs in order to be funny. There is little savagery in his attitude. Even to those people whom he does not like he allows moments of hesitation and fumbling which make them human. His is a civilized voice of sympathy and moderation which might, if applied with greater intensity, be called wisdom.

Nicholas Jenkins' Uncle Giles, whose scattered appearances take on legendary significance, is not so much an eccentric as the type of person who operates marginally and must disguise what he is and where he has been. Giles might appear anywhere and at any time, make a relevant comment about his nephew's style of life, divulge something about his own, and then more or less sink into the ground until the next visit. Giles' appearances are symbolic of the whole series, for much of Powell's humor derives from the fact that people re-appear from the past, as though there are only a few individuals in the world who keep turning up all the time. The past is ever present, and whenever anyone is mentioned, Nicholas has met him or knows about him. No one in this exclusive group ever totally disappears; like Giles himself, he merely slides temporarily from view, only to re-appear when least expected. Accordingly, as the series continues, the reader becomes increasingly aware of the music itself, of the frequent variations and modulations on a basic theme, of the counterpointing of motifs and characters, of the rich harmonic chords suggested by the author's close orchestration, of the subtle melodies that result from precise notation.

Nicholas Jenkins himself—the conductor of these orchestral selections—provides an interesting example of the kind of man who survives, integrity intact, amid this social waste. Jenkins is what American writers call "cool" or "hip," possibly an angry young man with less muscle and more manner. That is, Jenkins seems neither strongly in favor of anything nor strongly against; he moves with the political tides and flows with the social current. He presents a façade of complete compromise, although he maintains values of his own. Little will surprise him, he suffers few agonies of conscience or feeling, and his personality seems protean enough to adapt itself to any situation. Further, he can tolerate unpleasantness without becoming a boor. He lacks a strong will, or more likely is able to control it, even though he does have some indeterminate ambitions, which he knows he must hide. For he would break the code that keeps him cool were he to reveal his goals to others.

There are, then, very severe rules to remaining cool in upper-class society. Widmerpool, of course, is the opposite of cool, smothered as his reason is by ambition. With him, ambition is so strong that he cannot mask his will, and the thrust of his limitless energy forces him into awkward situations and gauche actions. His powerful will to power also makes him unaware, or careless, of the figure he is cutting. Jenkins, on the other hand, with his characteristic insouciance is conscious of how he looks, and carefully looks cool. He antagonizes no one by what he is, and does not try to impose himself. He lives, so to speak, without excessive noise, and consequently finds nearly all doors open to him. No one apparently considers him very able, but neither does anyone find him reprehensible. He remains, in effect, his own man within a relatively small area of operation.

Unlike the angry young men of Kingsley Amis and John Wain, Nicholas wants more than merely a suitable niche for himself, although like the others he is willing to let the rest of the world work out its own problems. For the Angries, to be cool is to live without powerful convictions of any kind, while for Nicholas it means transforming his convictions into a style of living. In a period when despair and chaos render impossible any significant individual action, to protest loudly is itself a hypocritical and pretentious imposition of will. Nicholas must, instead, maintain his integrity and try not to injure his contemporaries while protecting his own interests.

This realistic, yet moral, point of view is both attractive and sad. The individual will matters little; the social order has contained and baffled it, and now the will, like the order itself, must slowly decline. Withal his attractiveness and basic integrity, Nicholas Jenkins has inadvertently thrown away his individuality. His is the paradox of the man who, while trying to retain his individuality despite social pressures, succumbs to what he thinks will be the lesser danger, the loss of his own will; this is, indeed, the paradox of the vapid age Powell describes. And whenever he suggests this paradox with all its sadness, he is writing the best type of comedy; for he has revealed the tragedy that lies beneath all serious social comedy.

A Question of Morality: Angus Wilson

In *Anglo-Saxon Attitudes* (1956), Angus Wilson has written one of the most mature novels of the fifties, although maturity, we are reminded, is not always commensurate with artistic excellence. The characters of the novel are varied, the range of comment wide, the point of view, as always, sophisticated, and the verbal gifts as abundant as ever. These are qualities that few other novelists of the past decade have been able to muster. Wilson's work, nevertheless, fails for several reasons to realize its potential, most of the faults being embedded in the conception of the material.

If we look back to his first novel, *Hemlock and After* (1952), we can perhaps see why, despite his obvious gifts and evidently large accomplishment, the potential has not been fulfilled. One must discuss Wilson's fiction in large terms, for he is attempting the "big novel," the broad canvas, the major work. He cuts across social classes and includes a wide variety of characters who are solidly rooted in English life; unlike many of his contemporaries, he does not restrict himself to one kind of person or one kind of reality. In his first novel, Wilson tried to convey the inner experiences of an aging novelist whose work has been acclaimed, but who finds that the creative urge has become stilled. The creative urge, in fact, has been diverted into new sexual tastes, and Bernard Sands, now with an old neurotic wife and two children, identifies with a smart set of young homosexuals. Wilson, however, probes none of these momentous changes in Sands; and the aging novelist, despite the long comments about him by the author and other characters, remains shadowy and unexplained. For such a character to be portrayed successfully, Wilson must somehow forgo his Zola-esque reliance on outside detail and analyze from within, or else indirectly suggest relationships, as Zola did, through images and symbols.

Several characters and scenes, furthermore, have nothing to do with Sands' situation, as though Wilson, the expert short story writer, had material that he tried to force into the novel despite its unsuitability. *Hemlock and After* remains a series of isolated vignettes, with little sense of life as lived or experience as experienced. Like much of Aldous Huxley's fiction, it is brittle, superficial, and lacking in depth of character—perhaps the qualities that Wilson was endeavoring to reflect. But then where does a supposed heavyweight like Sands fit? What is he attracted to in this other life? In answering, Wilson might have dispelled some of the problems the novel raises.

In *Anglo-Saxon Attitudes,* which appeared four years later, much of the brittleness remains, but here it is at least partially integrated into a view of life. Gerald Middleton, an historian, an aging scholar who has not lived up to his promise, is now surrounded by the wreckage of his family—a wife he cannot tolerate, three children whose attitudes range from suspicion to hatred, and a mistress who alternately repels and attracts him. Middleton is neither a particularly bad nor good man, for these qualities are incidental to Wilson's purpose, which is to show the muddle of life that results when different interests cross and re-cross and often cancel out the meaning of an entire career. Here, as in an Ivy Compton-Burnett novel (Wilson seems as much influenced by the Ivy Compton-Burnett type of novel as he is by Zola's and Dickens'), family relationships both sustain and destroy the characters.

Paralleling the chaos of Gerald's family life is the chaos in the academic world among medievalists concerned with a possible fraud: that of Professor Stokesay's discovery of a bishop's tomb containing a pagan fertility symbol. (The suggestion for the fraud might have come from the Piltdown Man disclosures.) Gerald's suspicion that the great Melpham find is fraudulent permeates the novel, although his closeness to the Stokesays keeps him silent. To discover the facts in the case, Gerald follows each clue, driven by his duty as a scholar and yet horror-stricken at what he may find.

The point of the novel, which follows the pattern of a search, is to disclose the monumental deception that occurs in all aspects of human relationships, in public as well as private life. Most of the private material is commonplace enough, except that Wilson can write witty and direct dialogue; and his portrait of Gerald, baffled by feelings which recur to torture him, is far more effective than that of Bernard Sands. Gerald is caught between worlds, public and private, which have rarely given him personal satisfaction, although his reputation as an historian is high. He is afraid that he has grown old without having grown wise. As he daydreams over the twists of the present and past, he finally sees a gleam in the darkness all around him:

An odd freak of Anglo-Saxon history was faked. What did that matter to the general study of the subject? An hysterical unhappy woman had been guilty of an act of cruelty to a small child [Gerald suspects that Inge deliberately caused their daughter's hand injury]. It had not made the adoration of the girl and young woman for her mother any less. It seemed to him suddenly as though he had come out of a dark narrow tunnel, where movement was cramped to a feeble crawl, into the broad daylight where he could once more walk or run if he chose. (p. 184)

Gerald can now walk or run because he has come to see himself with clarity and recognizes the inevitability of human life. The only other person who cannot be deceived is Gerald's former mistress, Dollie, who nevertheless must disguise reality by drinking and making caustic remarks. Inge herself hides the past, and wins the children by deceiving them. As for the children: John is a childish hypocrite; Robin deceives his wife and then thinks of atoning by joining the Catholic Church; and Kay hates her father for having left her mother even when she discovers that Inge had in anger pushed her (Kay) into the fire. Robin's mistress, Elvira Portway, is a superficial young woman who associates with sophisticated intellectuals, deluding herself that their smart talk has rubbed off on her. And John's boy friend is an adolescent criminal whom he hopes to "save."

The undeniable virtue of this novel derives from the sharp focus Wilson brings to bear upon character and theme. The lines here have become firmer than in *Hemlock and After,* and the mature wit gives tone and shape to the material. After this book all that Wilson needs to become an important novelist is a greater reliance on imaginative creation, with a corresponding de-emphasis of the specifics of character and plot, a rejection of his Zola-esque stress on catalogued detail. There is lacking, even here, an imaginative awareness of things that cannot be expressed in dialogue.

Wilson's third novel, *The Middle Age of Mrs. Eliot,* appeared two years later, and although its length indicates an ambitious undertaking, it does not live up to the expectations raised by *Anglo-Saxon Attitudes.* It is a somewhat fussy novel, with a narrow range despite great amounts of detail and comment. There is a thickness not of event—the novel is almost static—but of observation, much of it excessive or commonplace. The loss in dramatic intensity and narrative urgency is clear. Unfortunately, one gets the feeling that, once saddled with Meg Eliot, Wilson had no choice but to carry out her uninteresting career to the bitter end.

Meg Eliot is a smart, attractive, somewhat selfish and domineering woman of forty-three who suddenly finds herself without her husband and her previous position. Her former life having vanished with her husband's accidental death, she must salvage what she can without depending on anyone else. The problem of the novel, then, is to show how a woman who had rarely relied on herself before must suddenly survive through her own devices. At first, her decisions result in a series of near disastrous setbacks; under the new and trying conditions, she meets successive defeats, whereas previously she had been successful. The road back is long (the terms of the novel suggest just such a cliché), even longer for the reader who finds Meg Eliot unattractive both as a popular matron and as a woman trying to regain her self-confidence.

The chief difficulty with the novel centers around the main character. A book of close to 150,000 words based on the problems of one person must generate some excitement around the character or else everything fails. Meg Eliot simply does not have the reserves or depths to elicit such a response. Her former position as a society matron deeply in love with her ambitious husband does not augur well for her new situation in which she must perform heroically. Perhaps her abiding superficiality (even when she "grows") might have been disguised had Wilson surrounded her with more diverse individuals. However, the chief complement to Meg is her brother, David, whose life, while different from hers, is equally uninteresting.

While Wilson catches quite effectively the life of a lonely widow as she drifts from one dingy place to the next, these are simply vignettes. The center of the novel is the woman herself, and even though Wilson's regard for her struggle is affectionate and sympathetic, and his feeling for the nightmarish quality of her life is evident, nevertheless these virtues are not sufficient to salvage the novel. The wit and sharpness apparent in the previous novel have been dissipated; the style here is dogged and earnest—"honest" would best describe it. Possibly irony would have given the author distance on his characters and allowed a greater variety of feeling than the direct approach permits. Despite its ambitious design, this book returns us to the infelicities of *Hemlock and After* and isolates *Anglo-Saxon Attitudes,* with its great promise, between two intelligent but not very effective novels.

Nigel Dennis's *Cards of Identity*

Cards of Identity (1955) contains the imaginative projection so sorely lacking in most novels of the forties and fifties and is one of the few recent works of fiction to suggest a broad range of satire. Dennis's first novel in 1949, *A Sea Change* (or *Boys and Girls Come Out to Play*), offered little basis for the present work. That book was concerned with political life in the Polish Corridor on the eve of the second world war as it affected Max, a political writer, and Jimmy Morgan, a callow young boy seeking his identity. Dennis ironically draws the contrast between the heroic Max of the newspaper world and the puny Max as seen by Jimmy. Only in this way—in the shifting Maxes—does Dennis suggest the theme of the later novel, concerned as it is with changing identities.

With *Cards of Identity,* however, Dennis obtained a sharp focus for his ironic view of the world, although to probe identity as such is of course not original. Nevertheless, Dennis has returned to the theme of the great novelists of the earlier part of the century, Kafka, Joyce, Conrad, Lawrence, and Mann, in whom the search for one's identity is the cosmic quest for what one is. The form the search takes is a metaphysical confrontation of man with the universe, and the novel that successfully catches this encounter moves into an imaginative re-creation of man's potentialities.

The Identity Club offers a unique service to its members. It recognizes that " 'Identity is the answer to everything. There is nothing that cannot be seen in terms of identity.' " What makes the Club unique, however, is that, unlike the psychiatrist, it does not reveal an identity already latent in the individual. It does not need the individual's past at all; it provides an entirely new identity. This identity is, so to speak, already fixed, a known quantity in every respect, and all that is lacking is the person to assume it. Yet while the Club is certain that its constructed identities are superior to the present identity a person has, it must suffer anguish at the slowness with which people step forward to assume these new selves.

Identities are created in the form of case histories, which explicitly are not to contain any eccentric material: they have to be typical and plausible. "The invented people," Dennis writes, "must sound like real people. Any personal whims must be properly contained, not only within the theory but within the bounds of possibility." Eccentricities, absurd paradoxes, ironies of behavior or misbehavior, and excessive individuality must be curbed or presented with such brilliance that the eccentricity itself appears to be the norm.

The purpose of burying an individual's own unsure identity and pursuing a ready-made one is to put as great a distance as possible between what a man believes and how he lives. The measure of this distance, in the modern world, is a measure of his ability to survive. The individual courts disaster, indeed virtual destruction, if he confuses his beliefs with his way of life. The Identity Club serves the function of creating symbols for the individual which will not impinge upon his real life; he lives solely for the symbols.

The constructed case histories concern nationalistic, sexual, and religio-political man: the entire spectrum of contemporary man's most significant activities. Nationalistic man operates according to a set of symbols which rarely, if at all, intrude on reality, and is therefore the simplest. Sexual man, however, creates a special problem for the Identity Club, because sex at present is difficult to determine. This problem is exemplified by the case history labeled simply "Dog's Way: *A Case of Multiple Sexual Misidentity*." The patient once heard his father tell his mother: " 'Let's always speak frankly about sex before the child, so that we don't give society a maladjusted dwarf.' " These words the child took to heart, fearing, obviously, that lack of conversation about sex would result in his becoming a maladjusted dwarf. He wanted to grow normally, and so sex assumed the proportions of religious salvation. Dennis writes of the patient, "I think I imagined sex as a kind of doctor sitting on a cloud. . . ." Church service was confused with sexual relief. When the applicant signs up for war service, he writes for his sex: Church of England. The problem only increases as the patient goes out into the world and faced by sexual deviations cannot determine what sex he is. To make a decision one way or another, he is warned, is to return to the Dark Ages. His modernity is measured by his sexual ambivalence. And so he, or she, goes on.

The third case history, concerned with religio-political man, outlines a modern monastery devoted not to religious aspirations but to ex-communists working on anti-communist pamphlets and histories. In one way or another, they are all busy on a giant *Encyclopedia Penitentia,* a rewriting of history according to the doctrines of anti-communism. The brothers are known not by name but by the year they broke with the party. The nature of their dictatorial social organization was obviously indicated by Orwell's *1984,* although with the allegiances reversed from political to religious, a matter of no great importance, Dennis is quick to suggest.

The novel ends with a long Elizabethan drama in blank verse, called *The Prince of Antioch* or *An Old Way to New Identity* by William Shakespeare. The theme of the play is, of course, identity. Who is the dog that lies beneath the skin? is it man or woman? is it prince or slave? The play is a comment on the entire novel in that it sustains the artificiality of a life in which identities can be assumed at will or personalities dredged up that bear little or no relationship to the person possessing them. The actors in the play, to move the illusion one step further, consist of people who have surrendered their former identities and stepped into those offered by the Club. Consequently, people with assumed identities act out before the Club a drama in which the principal characters themselves are disguised. By the end of the play, no character can be identified, for he has appropriated the composite semblance of three or four people.

At this point, Dennis takes over the frame of the novel. A policeman comes to the hitherto deserted house now serving the Club. For within the play, a murder has taken place, or has it? Acting in self-preservation, the Club tries to cover its track by assuming new identities. It begins to transform itself, and we meet a duke showing his ancestral home to tourists. And so on through several reversals of character and identity. The end returns to the beginning, but is it the end? and what is the beginning?

Dennis's novel is a comic tour de force, and unlike the work of the Angries, with whom inexplicably he has been misidentified, it is not narrow. Striking out fiercely in several directions, Dennis's attack is clearly upon all aspects of life. He joins with the major satirists of the past, Voltaire among them, as a fearless castigator of social and political nonsense. As satire or comedy, *Cards of Identity* is trenchant, but unfortunately its ideas are projected not so much from people as from other ideas. Satire has of course always been concerned more with ideas than with character, and on this very ground Dennis leaves something to be desired. The satirist has to avoid the temptation to caricature. This pitfall Dennis fails to escape, and the novel, for all its breadth and incisiveness, becomes an intellectual sport, a literary eccentricity.

This drawback—a large one, indeed—is doubly unfortunate, for Dennis reveals the verbal and mental gifts as well as the ability to perceive levels of hypocrisy which are the essence of great comic novelists. We find some of these qualities in early Waugh and others in Anthony Powell, especially in the *Music of Time* series, but neither Waugh nor Powell has been fully able to generate important situations. Of the three, Dennis seems at the moment the best equipped. In *A Sea Change,* he demonstrates the ability to write about people, although the novel fails to succeed for lack of sharp focus. In *Cards of Identity,* he has the focus, as clear as anything in the novel of the last two decades, but lacks the humanizing quality which would give concrete significance to the material. To combine the two qualities, the ability to probe individual human beings and yet to keep all society in focus, is to write the large novel, comic or otherwise, so sorely lacking since the death of Joyce, Lawrence, and Conrad. Of contemporary novelists still working seriously, few seem better qualified than Dennis to catch satirically the major currents of contemporary life; in brief, to become a comic conscience. As we see from the past, the effective satirist is able to turn nonsense into metaphysical concepts and hypocrisy into philosophical speculation. How much more mature this is than the protests of the Angries or the puerile antics of their "heroes" in rebellion against forces they are too arrogant or limited to understand!

XIV

The Novel as Moral Allegory:
The Fiction of William Golding,
Iris Murdoch, Rex Warner, and
P. H. Newby

The Metaphysical Novels of William Golding

THERE IS LITTLE QUESTION of William Golding's originality as a novelist. He has not been afraid to experiment with form or to attempt daring themes: for instance, life amid a predatory group of stranded boys in *Lord of the Flies,* 1954; the decline and death of man's immediate predecessors on earth, in *The Inheritors,* 1955; the struggle for survival of a shipwrecked sailor, in *The Two Deaths of Christopher Martin* (in England, *Pincher Martin*), 1956; a man's attempt to trace his guilt and his subsequent fall from grace, in *Free Fall,* 1959. In each of the novels, the manner is indirect, the symbols rarely clarified, and the method of narration uncondescending and stringent. Golding is obviously striving to move behind the conventional matter of the contemporary novel to a view of what man, or pre-man, is really like when his façade of civilized behavior falls away.

Like Graham Greene in his religious novels, Golding is interested in the metaphysics of behavior. He is not simply a social novelist attempting to see man's response to a given society, but a metaphysical writer interested in states of being and aspects of survival. In a broad sense, his work is existential, and the similarity of his last novel, *Free Fall,* to Camus' *The Fall* is not fortuitous.

Both writers are interested in pride and its damning consequences; both have created contemporary Fausts—for what nugatory reward does modern man sell his soul? and both treat their main character with irony and an awareness that guilt is greater in a world that does not punish transgression than in one that severely penalizes. In this respect, both Camus and Golding are moralists.

Free Fall is concerned with the limitations of man's rationality. Like Camus, Greene, Mauriac—his obvious literary compatriots—Golding is interested not in the superficial capabilities of man but in those long-buried responses the latter can suddenly evoke in order to satisfy or preserve himself. It is not surprising that three of Golding's four novels are directly concerned with man's struggle for survival, with his attempt to maintain not only body but also soul. For under these circumstances, man loses his superficial social mask and becomes man reduced to any course that will insure his life. At this point, Golding, like the other three writers, can speculate about man's relationship to the universe, ultimately about his final aims as a human being.

Sammy Mountjoy in *Free Fall* narrates the story of his fall from grace. At what stage, he asks himself, did he lose his soul? At what stage, he asks all men, do they lose their souls, religious or otherwise? While the outer frame of the novel is religious—the title itself is obviously so—Sammy's concerns are both religious and humanistic. Similar to a Greene character up against a problem he feels too weak to resolve or even face, Sammy writes:

Mine was an amoral [world], a savage place in which man was trapped without hope, to enjoy what he could while it was going. But since I record all this not so much to excuse myself as to understand myself I must add the complications which makes [sic] nonsense again. At the moment I was deciding that right and wrong were nominal and relative, I felt, I saw the beauty of holiness and tasted evil in my mouth like the taste of vomit. (p. 226)

In an amoral world, Sammy has behaved rationally, unaware that rationality can be a kind of devil, especially when it is attached to a voracious ego (Sammy is an artist, a successful painter). In an amoral world, the Sammys are supreme until they develop moral consciences, and Sammy's relentless pursuit and seduction of the virginal Beatrice (like her namesake in Dante, she is a visionary ideal) indicate his attempt to enjoy whatever his appetites find desirable. Sammy is a proud sensualist who assumes that all people possess his power and emotional flexibility. According to Golding, Sammy has sinned against the design of the world by "mounting joy" before all other considerations. Sammy, however, is not unregenerate; like Greene's whisky priest, he lives expediently according to a relative and shifting morality but is nevertheless haunted by "the beauty of holiness" which he finds himself both too weak and too strong to accept.

Sammy has lost his freedom by choosing the way of self-gain at the expense of the rest of the world, just as an army of contemporary protagonists has lost its freedom by pursuing dreams outside the range of what the world will allow. The archetype for this kind of self-destructive anti-hero is Conrad's Jim (*Lord Jim*), the man of pretentious claims who is unable to fulfill the role he has envisaged for himself and who is hounded by his own insufficiency until he destroys himself. Sammy's problem is perhaps more directly religious than the secular Jim's, but the terms of their salvation are not dissimilar. Just as Jim exorcises his guilt through suicide (an aimless gesture that resolves nothing but his uneasy conscience), so Sammy assuages his feelings by visiting the now mad Beatrice and hearing the doctor blame him for her hopeless condition. How much this affects Sammy we do not know; we do recognize, however, that the drive of his will to destroy others has been momentarily blocked and that even if he does not feel cosmic guilt, he realizes the nature of his transgression.

What seriously weakens Golding's novel—similar to what flaws Greene's *The Power and the Glory*—is the appearance of a predetermined deus ex machina that suddenly resolves the conflict. In *Free Fall,* Sammy has avoided his problem until Golding shifts the stress to the helpless Beatrice; then the thrust of destructive will in Sammy is checked by a force external to him, the very kind of force, we are led to believe, to which he is impervious. For Golding unexpectedly to make Sammy into a social being responsive to the consequences of his deeds is for him to ignore the main direction of the entire narrative. Golding, here conventional at the expense of artistry, must not let amorality prevail even if it appears that the latter is ascendant. And although Sammy is amoral, even immoral, by any Christian or humanistic standard, Golding is anxious to indicate that he can be reached and transformed. This he imposes upon a character who earlier admitted that "I had lost my power to choose. I had given away my freedom. I cannot be blamed for the mechanical and helpless reaction of my nature."

As in Greene's novels, there are beliefs and values operating in Golding's fiction that must dominate despite the main thrust of each novel toward disbelief. For most of his narrative, he seems to be concerned with moral aimlessness: the stranded boys in *Lord of the Flies,* for example, almost entirely shake off their civilized behavior. Under certain conditions of survival, the primitive element predominates; residual savagery lies barely below the surface and is controlled only under the right circumstances. Remove these circumstances and the boys are amoral, vicious, chaotic, murderous. What Golding senses is that institutions and order imposed from without are temporary, but that man's irrationality and urge for destruction are enduring.

The stranded boys under Ralph's leadership divide into two groups, those who will supply the food and those who will keep the fire, their only hope of attracting attention. In a way, the fire-keepers are the poets, the contemplative ones, while the hunters are the doers, the men of action. As in the real world, so here, the hunters begin to woo the fire-keepers, for to do is more glamorous than to be. Having first aimed at their common salvation, the two groups soon divide into warring factions. Ralph, however, possesses the conch shell (a symbol of his "poetic" power), which attracts some of the boys to his side, but even that piece of magic is eventually destroyed when the hunters become violent. Physical force comes to smother magic, religion, creativity, humanity itself.

The boys become caught by the chaos of violence and its accompanying quality: fear. They begin to stalk Ralph across the island, and they viciously attack and kill Simon when he comes to tell them of a rotting skeleton at which the lord of the flies has picked away. As the skeleton has been eaten, so is Simon, in a kind of ritualistic death, torn to pieces by boys screaming " *'Kill the beast! Cut his throat! Spill his blood.'* " The blood thirst of their chant has poked through the veneer of civilization, and they are helpless within the throes of a primitive passion.

Finally, a rescue force comes to the island before Ralph is killed, and the boys are chided by the officer in charge for their failure to put up a better show. The officers themselves are engaged in an atomic attack of some sort, and the implication is that while the adults are disappointed by the boys the former are themselves of course little better. Ralph himself is torn by tears which indicate that his childhood and innocence are gone forever, that he has been initiated into a malevolent adult world from which escape is impossible. Crying for a childhood lost beyond redemption, he recognizes through his tears what he must face for the rest of his life.

When the boys on the island struggle for supremacy, they re-enact a ritual of the adult world, as much as the college Fellows in Snow's *The Masters* work out the ritual of a power struggle in the larger world. Snow, however, gave his characters the knowledge attendant upon adulthood, while Golding by treating the boys' imagination as childish dilutes the seriousness of the theme. Without gaining the possible irony he intended, he partially dissipates the tremendous force of his narrative; the power that conflicting passions have generated dribbles away in the resolution.

There is in all of Golding's work this crucial avoidance of subtlety, and that is perhaps why his novels are concerned almost solely with primitive struggles for survival. Both *The Inheritors* and *The Two Deaths of Christopher Martin* (*Pincher Martin*) reduce life to precisely such a struggle. Washed up on a large rock formation in the Atlantic Ocean, Martin attempts to stay afloat in a world in which he has already drowned. The entire novel, Golding suggests, occurs in the split seconds it takes Martin to drown, and his exertion on the rock is the equivalence of his personal hell; in brief, his repentance for an amoral life. The weakness of the piece, despite its exciting and vivid prose, stems from the author's stress on survival only—Martin is reduced to unthinking, instinctual flesh. He has nothing left over beyond the sheer will to live and his belief that he will be rescued. This lack of intellectualization, the very return to the primitive, leaves the novel flat;

thrown back entirely upon Martin, the reader finds him insufficient. Had Golding been more interested in Martin's psychology than in his instincts, he could perhaps have created a real hell of these few seconds, one that convinced us of Martin's cruel drama.

Similarly, in *The Inheritors,* Golding's concern with survival and the instincts destroys all conversation and virtually all intelligence. Since his characters are pre-men and almost pre-language, they must talk in some approximation of the way primitives speak; and we have, " 'Now is like when the fire flew away and ate up the trees.' " or " 'It is heavy to be the woman.' " Everything is reduced to this level, and once the reader has insight into the situation, he has little left to engage him. What is true of this novel is also true of *Lord of the Flies:* the boys become semi-civilized, and consequently they converse and act at a level that precludes mature thought. Once the originality of the allegory and language wears off, we see merely a number of semi-articulate boys having a savage romp.

The idea of a Golding novel invariably is superior to the performance itself. Ironically, the idea, often so engaging in the abstract, is self-defeating, for it forces an artificial method. Golding is an allegorist whose allegory pre-empts the realistic level; often, only the allegory is of interest and when that begins to wear thin, there is insufficient substance to grapple with.

Golding's novels, then, seem more attractive in their parts than as wholes. His inability, or lack of desire, to give intellectual substance to his themes, and his didactic intrusion in nearly all of the narratives, lessen the power of what still remains, however, an original talent. His eccentric themes, unfortunately, rarely convey the sense of balance and ripeness that indicate literary maturity: a shipwrecked sailor is interesting only if *he* is interesting; stranded boys are compelling only if their behavior indicates something significant about them and not merely their similarity to adults; an obsessed "loner" (like Sammy Mountjoy) is relevant only if he works out his problems in his own way without external influence, once it has been established that he is that kind of person; and pre-civilized people are attractive as literary material only if the author makes them act in some way that transcends their daily boredom, or if he can write about them ironically. To present all of these characters and situations "straight" is to take them as they are, and this evaluation simplifies them all out of proportion to what Golding's serious intentions demand.

To end a discussion of Golding's work on this note is, however, to lose sight of his importance to the contemporary novel. Even if his didacticism makes him resolve what should be unresolvable, he nevertheless indicates in nearly every line that he is an artist seriously interested in his craft. And even if he seems prone to surprise the reader with gimmicks, he nevertheless has demonstrated a sharp enough awareness of his material to overcome this defect before it permanently damages his fiction. When literary values overcome the moralist, Golding's potential may well be realized, and he will become an outstanding novelist.

Iris Murdoch

Although honest, intelligent, and well written, the novels of Iris Murdoch nevertheless lack clear definition. Hers seems to be a talent for humor, but she appears unable to sustain it for more than a scene or a temporary interchange. Her first novel, *Under the Net* (1954), fits into the humorous pattern set by Kingsley Amis in *Lucky Jim* (1954) and John Wain in *Hurry on Down* (1953). Her Jake Donaghue of this novel is akin to Amis's Jim Dixon and Wain's Charles Lumley, in that he maintains his own kind of somewhat dubious integrity and tries to make his way without forsaking his dignity, an increasingly difficult accomplishment in a world which offers devilish rewards for loss of integrity and dignity.

Jake is an angry middle-aged man who mocks society and its respectability. He moves playfully around law and order; he does small things on the sly—swims in the Thames at night, steals a performing dog, sneaks in and out of locked apartments, steals food. His is a puerile existence in which he remains "pure" even while carrying on his adolescent activities.

The dangers of this type of hero, indeed of this kind of novel, are apparent, for when the humor begins to run low, the entire piece becomes childish. In *Lucky Jim,* we saw that as the humorous invention lost vigor, the novel became enfeebled because it had nothing else to draw upon. In her first novel as well as in *The Flight from the Enchanter* (1956) and *The Bell* (1958), Miss Murdoch unfortunately was unable to sustain the humor, and the novels frequently decline into triviality.

Another danger that Miss Murdoch has not avoided is that of creating characters who are suitable only for the comic situations but for little else. When they must rise to a more serious response, their triteness precludes real change. This fault is especially true of the characters in *The Flight from the Enchanter,* a curious mixture of the frivolous and the serious. The characters are keyed low for the comic passages but too low to permit any rise when the situation evidently demands it. The comic novel usually is receptive to a certain scattering of the seed, while a serious novel calls for intensity of characterization and almost an entirely different tone. In her four novels, Miss Murdoch falls between both camps; the result is that her novels fail to coalesce as either one or the other.

This is not to gainsay Miss Murdoch's substantial qualities; and her recent novel, *The Bell,* is indicative of both strains in her work. *The Bell* contains the same mixture of serious and ridiculous material that characterized her previous books—the sense of hokum, the world of the practical joke, the need to pierce the pompous and the pretentious. For Miss Murdoch, there are basically two kinds of people. There are those for whom life is desperate; they are deeply committed to whatever they are engaged in, and they can see nothing else. In their steadfastness, they may become grim and morbid. Then there are those for whom life has not settled into any fixed pattern; they are flexible and mobile, desirous of variety and willing to make changes. In the first group, we have Michael Meade, the leader of a lay religious community located near an Anglican Order of nuns. In the second group, there is Dora, an easily distracted young wife, a female Jim Dixon, who comes to the community with her youthful friend, Toby Gashe.

The conflict in part of the novel concerns the relations of the spirited, sensual, and unintellectual Dora with her husband and later with the community, whose spirit is so completely different from her own. Dora's attitudes represent this world, while the community's are a microcosm of the other. The clash between the two is inevitable, and Miss Murdoch chooses to define the conflict in terms of burlesque—a practical joke will demonstrate Dora's need for self-expression at the expense of the community. The joke centers around a bell, a bell that comes with a legend from the past. In the legend, the bell of the then Benedictine order of nuns fell into the lake, the result of the Bishop's curse. The curse itself derived from the infidelity of a nun and her refusal to confess. When the bell flew into the lake, the guilty nun, overwhelmed by the demonstration of God's power of punishment, flew from the Abbey and drowned herself in the lake.

The present community at Imber is planning to install a bell of its own, and it occurs to Toby Gashe and Dora that a bell they have located at the bottom of the lake should be substituted for the new one. The one at the bottom, they feel, is the bell of the legend; the substitution will provoke astonishment and also provide them with entertainment. The intention is to shock, at least on Dora's part; on Toby's, the aim is to prove himself a man, especially after Michael has kissed him and cast doubt on his masculinity.

Running parallel to this course of action, in which Dora seeks fun in order to escape from her boorish and possessive husband, is the attempt of Michael Meade to find his own depth without destroying himself. Tempted by young men until he forgets both his principles and his position, Michael is tortured by the knowledge that what he wants he cannot have. Earlier in his career, he had wanted a young boy, Nick Fawley, and that venture had ended in embarrassment and dismissal; now he sees and wants Toby Gashe, and Michael again is unable to resist. There runs through his position in the community the disparity between his public and private life; he tries to be a good man—he does have an ideal of behavior—but his emotions preclude his aspirations. In both instances, with Nick and Toby, Michael is persecuted as a sodomist, although with neither has his demonstration of feeling gone past the initial stages.

Thus, Michael, the spiritual leader of the community who takes his turn preaching the weekly sermon, is something of a figure of fun. His passionate twists and turns, in which his emotions are directed first to God and then to young men, parallel those of Dora, who is both attracted and repelled by her husband. Her marriage is just such a combination of duty and discipline on one hand, and a need to break out into chaotic excitement on the other. She is caught in a typical Lawrentian union—she, bouncey and full of verve, her husband lost in his work, although not lacking in a narrowly focused sensuality of his own. She is vigorous and physical, while Paul burns more finely; she is a person of whimsy, he of planning and discipline. Accordingly, they hate each other except in bed, and their "modern" marriage is a compromise that Dora is unwilling to maintain.

Miss Murdoch attempts to gain her chief comic effects by juxtaposing the calm surface of the religious community with the turbulent and effervescent emotions boiling beneath, by contrasting the ideals of the community with the reality of people's lives. The entire conflict, however, is softened so that neither comedy nor an indication of tragic event is evident. That Michael is found out whenever he transgresses against his better sense is not funny, although it might be, and it is not sad, although it could be that also. That Dora is caught in several situations which might be built into real comedy is certainly possible, but this too does not happen. The comedy, when it does appear, is in terms of details and small incidents; one, for example, that occurs when Dora steps off the train at Imber with a butterfly in her hand and forgets her baggage; or the scene when she cannot find her shoes in the grass and the entire community is alerted to the search.

The resolution of a deep conflict with a long practical joke— a practice that Miss Murdoch shares with several of her contemporaries—can be excellent indeed if the writer has the bite of a Waugh or the playfulness of a Henry Green, both of whom can sustain the long comic scene necessary to this type of resolution. But the episode with the bell in this novel, as with similar episodes in *Under the Net* (for instance, the long scene on the motion picture location) and *The Flight from the Enchanter,* loses interest for the reader precisely as the characters themselves lose interest in it. After a while, Toby Gashe thinks it silly and beneath his effort; and this is what the reader has also felt—the joke now seems to be carried out simply to fulfill the plot line and not to complete the characters.

In her third novel, *The Sandcastle* (1957), Miss Murdoch forsook all attempts at comedy and wrote a romance against the background of an English school. Mor, a schoolmaster long unhappily married, falls in love with Rain Carter, an artist commissioned to do a painting for the school. Rain, as her name suggests, conveys all the freshness that will conflict with the staleness of Mor's marriage. But she is half his age and has been bred to a life completely different from his. Nevertheless, they find common sympathy and plan to run away, although his obligations to his wife and family finally force Mor to renege on his promise to Rain.

Again, this novel, like the others, is low keyed. The theme is familiar enough, concerned as it is with a temporary romance which lifts a middle-aged, complacent man from his smooth-running life onto a different plane; an affair, incidentally, which reveals to him another, more dangerous world which his own way of life has blinded him to. In the temptation are all the desires of romance and excitement missing from long years of marriage. Mor recognizes that Rain is what he wants, but the pull from the past is too strong and back he goes, good father, loyal husband, safe man. His personal happiness gives way to duty, obligation, and social expedience. In a way, fear triumphs.

The lack of sharp focus, however, keeps everything undramatic to the point of tediousness. Miss Murdoch has presented so much realistic detail to give background to her characters that there is little difference between her novel and real life: the photographer has been victorious over the creative artist. If her aim has been to flatten out all existence to a set pattern, to present a perfectly ordinary situation, then in this novel she has succeeded, but at the expense of the extra dimension that transmutes trivial detail into artistic forms.

In *A Severed Head* (1961), Restoration bedroom farce is transformed into a modern cultural drama. Through her delineation of various patterns of love, both normal and perverted, Miss Murdoch is evidently trying to explore contemporary boundaries of freedom and restriction. As one critic has commented, she is attempting to transcend reality, in *The Bell* through religious symbols, here through a metaphysical examination of love. At this point in her career, Miss Murdoch appears to be questioning whether a breakthrough to inner freedom can be gained in secular terms, or whether it is possible solely as the result of a religious quest.

Verbal skill, incisive conception of some characters, ability to convey humor and sadness, awareness of the large world, a philosophical point of view—all these qualities are admirably present in Miss Murdoch's work. Nevertheless, through her first five novels, they have remained merely potential, or else only sporadically realized. Her themes take forms that yield less than her skill warrants, which suggests that she could do much more than she tries. The obvious fact that she does this well with her off-beat material indicates that her talent places her high above many of her contemporaries, several of whom have been more widely publicized and read. These five novels, with their mixed quality, seem to be preparation for the big work which will synthesize the comic and tragic.tones in her fiction and establish her as a major novelist.

Rex Warner

Warner's type of allegorical novel works best when it is brief, and therefore *The Aerodrome* (1941) is a better book than *The Professor* (1939), and the latter more effective than *The Wild Goose Chase* (1938). In the shorter work, Warner seems able to sustain the realistic level so necessary for allegorical projection, while in the two others the allegory pre-empts the surface, which is diffuse and attenuated. The first rule of the allegorical novelist should be to construct a persuasive surface of action and then project from it. *The Wild Goose Chase,* on the contrary, has a soft surface, with semi-surrealistic effects that themselves suggest further layers of meaning: the nature of justice, the limits of freedom, the meaning of political man. To chase the wild goose is to seek an ideal of justice, but the events of the chase must themselves be sufficiently compelling and lucid so that the reader, as the author, is aroused to pursue the elusive animal.

In *The Professor,* the ultimate aim is to create a state in which justice and equality will prevail, and to this end the Professor devotes his life. Warner focuses on the European political situation before the Second World War when a country (for example, England) has to choose between fascism and democratic socialism. The Professor idealistically believes that the latter can be attained, and, armed with humanitarian ideals, attempts to meet the opposition: the killers, the treacherous, the tyrannical. He believes that reason and learning can prevail once they are understood, although he recognizes finally that only force can make these values viable. By this time, however, it is too late, and the Professor is treacherously shot dead.

In this novel, as in *The Wild Goose Chase,* Warner is less interested in people than in the ideas they stand for. The Professor, consequently, with his belief in Greek democracy and with a classical allusion on his lips, is a stock figure of righteousness in a world that viciously rejects what he stands for. The people around him—his idealistic son, the deceitful police chief, the philosophical lower-classmen—are all standard characters from political fiction, simply allegorical representations of justice, socialism, democracy, humanitarianism, equality, decency, or the lack of these qualities. In themselves, they are not compelling, and precisely here the novel flounders. Even in an allegorical work, if the people involved fail to engage the reader, then the theme, despite its importance, degenerates into the obvious.

As though recognizing the problem, in *The Aerodrome,* the latest of these three novels, Warner tries to work with three-dimensional figures; and although he does not create rounded characters, at least they are rooted in an everyday world that gives them substance. Once again he is interested in making a serious statement about the world, here through the conflict between the village and the aerodrome. Those attached to the latter are authoritarian and brutal, a new race of men who base their actions on reason and who mock emotions. The village, as a counter force, preserves the amenities and retains a moral conscience, although its morality is often a mask for hypocrisy. The village is by no means perfect, and it is to Warner's credit that he demonstrates how the old world of the village crumbles not only through outside pressure but because of the weight of its own corruption. The conflict, nevertheless, is between two ways of life: the airmen are efficient, the village wasteful of human talent and human activity; the airmen cut through a great deal of social nonsense and head for the heart of a problem, while the village dallies and allows sentiment to strap its movements. The choice is between an efficient dictatorship and a bumbling democracy, a clear warning, Warner suggests, for those who have missed or questioned the real issues of the war.

In the foreground of the death struggle between the two ways of life is the personal element in the novel: the attempt of Roy, a young man of the village, to decide between village and aerodrome. In brief, to decide what kind of person he will be. Roy is at first contrasted to a Flight-Lieutenant who personifies the brutal values of the aerodrome. When the military takes over the village, the Flight-Lieutenant is appointed chief clergyman, and while he slowly begins to gravitate toward the village's values, Roy becomes increasingly interested in the Air Force. Consequently, the village gains one recruit while the Air Force gains the other. In the background is the question of Roy's parentage; paradoxically, he turns out to be the son of the Air Vice-Marshal himself, whose influence brings him into the air cadet program. Roy's father is a dictatorial man who runs the airfield by sheer strength of his perverse will, a man for whom ends are everything and his means of little matter. When the Flight-Lieutenant sabotages the Vice-Marshal's plane, the new order of the military dies with him, although the old order of the village cannot be resurrected. As the novel ends, the village is caught in a world that it does not and cannot understand. At least, however, it has rejected dictatorship, even while its own form of government remains unshored and wobbling.

Unfortunately for this novel of considerable power, there are frequent conflicts of style. Certain scenes are life-like but involve people who are barely real; or else certain scenes are unlife-like and involve people who are real. Warner's object here, as though in response to the defects of his earlier style, was to fill the allegorical canvas with living people who had living problems. Allegory, however, must entail a consistent style, not one in which a human situation will conflict with an idea or figure who exists only allegorically. The Air Vice-Marshal, for example, tells Roy in some detail that discipline inevitably leads to a kind of power, as well as to a type of freedom. Yet is Roy the person with whom one discusses power and freedom and discipline, really the metaphysics of behavior? Roy shows little sensitivity or feeling—he is an average physical youth—but the allegory calls for the Vice-Marshal to speak of freedom and power, abstractions that are meaningless to the young Roy.

Accordingly, the abstraction of the allegory and the reality of daily life clash. Perhaps a conflict between styles was to be the verbal-literary equivalent of the struggle between village and aerodrome, with everything pertaining to the village as real and everything to the airfield as allegorical, supra-real. For instance, Roy in the village exists, but the Air Vice-Marshal shrouded by a mysterious past is de-humanized, as is everyone in contact with the aerodrome. However, if the two elements are to clash, as they do, how can they meet? They would remain on parallel levels, the substantial never mixing with the insubstantial.

It is of course in Warner's favor that he was deeply concerned with the world at a particularly dangerous time. He warned specifically against the obsessed Vice-Marshal who will do violence and kill for an idea, who will put men in chains to secure some future freedom, who will, like Greene's lieutenant in *The Power and the Glory,* destroy in order to preserve life—the paradox of the dictatorial mentality which ignores human rights in order to save them. Furthermore, it is to Warner's credit that he recognized the weakness of the ideology that tries to resist the Air Force. The village is better, we admit, not absolutely but only relatively. It contains the seeds of its own deterioration; its feebleness, in fact, makes possible the strength of the Air Force. For the latter has power only in relationship to the weakness of the village.

The political warning is obvious, too obvious, however, for an effective piece of literature. For Warner, the urgency of the message over-rode the need to transform it into art, and, consequently, the message suffered. This fault, indeed a large one, is one that underlies George Orwell's work as well, and made the substance of *1984,* possibly a deeply felt personal conflict, into a political tract. The long discussions on freedom and power in all of Warner's novels come baldly and undisguised to the reader, and the latter recognizes them for what they are—the didacticism of an author who wishes to preach without fulfilling the primary concern of the novelist: to create life.

The Search for P. H. Newby

The qualities that P. H. Newby demonstrates in his first novel, *A Journey to the Interior* (1946), are characteristic of all his serious fiction: the discovery of a man's self through a journey or quest that he forces himself, or is forced, to take. During the quest, some mysterious or alchemical process occurs that rejuvenates the character and makes him fit for himself and for society. In *A Journey to the Interior,* Winter (perhaps seeking the spring) goes to Rasuka, a semi-civilized piece of land owned by his company, to recuperate from a serious illness. When he arrives, he is hardly fit for any sort of relationship, for in addition to his illness, he has been brought low by his wife's recent death. Clearly, he is a "modern" man who has lost his will, and the novelist's task is to show how he may be brought back from his interior self, where the death wish has prevailed over the desire for life. How Winter is saved, or saves himself, provides the substance of the novel.

The atmosphere of Rasuka has been long familiar, principally from Conrad's "Heart of Darkness," Orwell's *Burmese Days,* and several of Graham Greene's novels. Images of dissolution and despair abound. Dirt, waste, insects, discomfort, deception, lack of moral posture, and even madness are the stuff of such an atmosphere. Into this, Winter, himself in severe decline, enters after an ocean voyage when he had listened nightly to a woman bewailing the sudden death of her husband. The trip is a fitting augury of his future in Rasuka, a typical Greene territory in which good and evil are personified. Presiding over all in the independent colony is a sultan, as corrupt and self-seeking as we have been led to believe sultans usually are.

Far in the background is a fellow named Rider, who had journeyed to the interior of the country, never to return. His memory, like Kurtz's in Conrad's novella, has been kept alive, however, and his deeds or misdeeds return to Winter's ear. Rider becomes something of a saint to Winter, although exactly what he is is never defined. Definition is unnecessary, though, because Rider is meaningful only to Winter, not to the reader. Rider becomes an obsession to the sick man, and he recognizes that he can regain his health only by a journey to the interior in search of this mysterious double. Not that Winter really expects to find Rider, for the latter has disappeared six months ago, and disappearance in Rasuka is tantamount to violent death.

Winter somehow must make the same search that Rider made into a death-situation, and in this way he will have searched into himself to discover his identity. Paradoxically, he will gain life (recovery) through facing death. On the journey, he is almost killed on several occasions by members of his own party or by marauders, but he manages to return before anything serious occurs; and he has found himself. He returns bearded and with a new sparkle. The illness is gone; his search for Rider, God, or whatever has given him health. A new man emerges from the interior, a man able to love, feel, and communicate, a man cognizant of his identity.

In several ways, the characters in Newby's later novels, even those in his comedies, follow this pattern with varying degrees of success. In *Agents and Witnesses* (1947), Pierre Bartas chances death in a weird sort of political commitment, and is shot for almost no reason. In *A Season in England* (1952), Tom Passmore feels compelled to visit and remain with the parents of a man, now dead, whom he had never liked. And even though the parents remain mysteriously undiscovered to Tom, he stays with them, drawn by some force which will eventually clarify aspects of his own life. His trip to the Passmore home is a journey to the interior of himself, and while what he finds is not monumental, it is nevertheless essential for his own stability. In *The Retreat* (1953), Oliver Knight must explore the semi-mad existence of Jane Hesketh before he can return to his own wife, whom he loves and desires. Once purged of the enigmatical Jane, he will be free to join his wife. Newby indicates in this novel that in the general disruption caused by a war situation, all relationships are affected; even the kind of love one is sure of becomes uncertain.

While the outlines of Newby's novels seem promising, their substance is less rewarding. Despite his high critical reputation in England, Newby's is a small talent, with his best work indicated in realistic dialogue and effective movement. Unfortunately his characters are not sharply drawn; frequently, the details of their movement predominate and block any larger significance. What should be intense is often flaccid or unfocused. Returning to *A Journey to the Interior,* we find that Newby treats Winter's objective almost casually. To suggest that he journeys to the interior to find himself is to signify a massive drama. Yet Newby makes Winter approach the venture without emotion, as though he were journeying to the corner grocery store instead of seeking his identity. Obviously, there is a severe lack of dramatization, of intensification. This failing is true of nearly all of the novels, carrying over as well into the comic ones. In the latter, Newby tones down the humor to such a degree that often a supposedly comic sequence remains flat throughout its narration. And the characters themselves, like those in the more serious novels, are indefinite and curiously one-dimensional.

The so-called Egyptian novels, *The Picnic at Sakkara* (1955) and *Revolution and Roses* (1957), are only mildly comic. The reader thinks of Waugh's *Black Mischief* of twenty-five years earlier, which made hilarious the pretensions of an unorganized nation as it attempted to become modern overnight. Newby does have humorous situations here and there—the accidental shooting of Yehia in *Revolution and Roses* and the ever-recurring

Muawiya Khaslat in *The Picnic at Sakkara,* for example—but there are long passages throughout that are nondescript. In the later novel, Elaine Brent is a bumbling newspaperwoman caught in the middle of an Egyptian palace revolution: Farouk is out, the army is in. Potentially, this is a comic situation, but Newby lacks Waugh's touch of the ridiculous as well as the verbal gifts of the parodist. The result is low-keyed comedy written with taste and modesty, but too inconsequential to be effective. In *The Picnic at Sakkara,* concerned with Egyptian nationalism, Newby is traveling a well-worn path, combining the social ideas of E. M. Forster with Waugh's sense of confusion.

Part of the difficulty with Newby's comic novels is the fact that they derive from Waugh and Powell and inevitably seem second hand. For colonial satire, Waugh, Cary, and before them, Forster, hog the field; for city comedy, Powell is there with his *Music of Time* series. As for his serious fiction, Newby is intelligent, unpretentious, and in command of an acute shaping talent; but he has set his sights so low and has so minimized his characters that his novels lack vitality and intensity. He writes about love and sex, but one rarely senses them as significant forces; he is interested in eccentric and mysterious situations, but one rarely feels that he is willing to explore them; he is drawn to characters who have important problems, but one rarely finds that the characters come alive beyond the settling of their problem. Their lives are circumscribed by the problem itself: how they react to it, how they will attempt to solve it; as though they have achieved reality only through identification with a conflict. Often, there are forces in their background which haunt them like furies and which must be exorcised, but these forces, like the characters themselves, lack definition.

A novel like *The Young May Moon* (1951) brings together material that might have proven provocative. An adolescent is hit in succession by the death of his stepmother, the desertion by his father, and the death of his real mother. The workings of his confused mind under these blows could well provide the material for a sensitive novel, but Newby fails to probe the young boy sufficiently. The events cause things to happen, but the happenings are always less than the causative shocks themselves. The problem here is not one of melodrama but of under-suggestion. So carefully has Newby tried to avoid the large scene and the large character that he has curiously cut himself off from the very areas that would have given life to his novel. All this is doubly curious, for Newby has several of the gifts necessary for the effective novelist; but despite his inventiveness, he has stayed too close to his sources and failed to find his own depth.

XV

Composite

I INCLUDE HERE several novelists whose work warrants mention although for many reasons they have not been or are not yet in the first rank. Some are young and have not proven themselves, even though their early work both in the novel and short story indicates promise of serious achievement; for example, Alan Sillitoe.* Others, somewhat older, have not suggested any clear direction, and their fiction, while satisfactory in part, as a whole seems unfocused and unrealized; for instance, Gerald Hanley, William Sansom, and Roy Fuller. Still others have not lived up to the promise of early work, or else have aimed too low in their later novels to be judged serious—I have in mind Christopher Isherwood. The fourth group, and largest, consists of those who aim at the well-made novel which neither surprises nor disappoints: *Pamela Hansford Johnson, Nancy Mitford, L. P. Hartley, Rosamund Lehmann;* also, *Elizabeth Taylor, Olivia Manning,* and *Muriel Spark.**

The novels of the last group are clearly well above the typical fiction of women's magazines or popular men's magazines. Their fiction is mature, polished, worldly, and, despite its limitations, it does create a life of its own. Its lack of intensity, daring, and range, however, immediately places it at a disadvantage for the reader who wishes a solid and complete engagement from fiction.

* An asterisk indicates that the author's later work is discussed in Chapter XVII.

Often these writers have aimed at no more than sophisticated entertainment, and to discuss them as more weighty would be a disservice. If, as Horace claimed, poetry or fiction is to instruct and entertain, then these authors have ably fulfilled the second of their roles.

The novels of Pamela Hansford Johnson are the basic material of the publisher looking for a well-made, intelligent novel that stands the chance of a book club selection and will go well with a public that wants its fiction neither light nor heavy. It is the kind of fiction that keeps the novel going in between the valleys and the peaks. It handles ideas in terms of the people involved; it rarely aims at abstractions, and the conflicts themselves are those one encounters in daily life. Emotions are of course played down; there are few powerful climaxes, few dramatic intensities that would weight the novel unduly. In brief, the novelist makes no attempt to exceed the tight, well-controlled world over which he or she is a master.

The themes of Miss Johnson's novels demonstrate the ordinary world in which her characters are immersed. In *An Impossible Marriage* (1954), for example, she is concerned with a marriage that does not work; the situation, the characters themselves, the incidents that display their incompatibility are all commonplace. What significance the novel does have is simply its toned-down, day-to-day cataloguing of why and how a marriage fails—the direct appeal to a middle-class female audience is clear. In *The Sea and the Wedding,* published two years later, Miss Johnson centers on the relationship between Celia Baird and Eric Aveling, principally their hopeless love affair while Eric's wife is slowly dying, their inability to marry once she has died, and Celia's attempt to find happiness at any price, which she does by marrying a homosexual friend, Junius. This novel is somewhat spicier than the previous, including as it does the illicit affair and the homosexuals around Junius.

To take one more of Miss Johnson's novels, the one with perhaps the most exotic content: *The Unspeakable Skipton* (1959) features a rogue who lives in Bruges and tries to cadge his way through life, much as Cary's picaresque Gulley Jimson in *The Horse's Mouth*. Miss Johnson has turned the painter Gulley into the writer Skipton, a man who must live by his wits. The central character is a man who believes so strongly in himself that he will do anything to insure the opportunity for his art to mature. In presenting Skipton and his world, however, Miss Johnson avoids the larger issue suggested by the introduction of a confidence man: that is, coming to terms with the confidence man as he tries to disguise his various shifts from illusion to reality.

To read Nancy Mitford is great fun. Considerably different from Evelyn Waugh, she nevertheless reminds the reader of his work because of the similarity of their characters. But while Waugh devastates with parody, Miss Mitford lets her characters speak for themselves, and they, as true English eccentrics, are hilarious. Perhaps in her ability to permit people to be what they are, she is closer to Anthony Powell than to Waugh, but even here the comparison must not be stretched. Unlike Powell, she suggests no point of view, rarely judges, and allows no one to triumph. Her great virtue is her amorality.

The people who inhabit Miss Mitford's main novels, *The Pursuit of Love* (1945), *Love in a Cold Climate* (1949), and *The Blessing* (1951), are members of the wealthy ruling class who are responsible to no one but themselves. They take their pleasures and comforts seriously, for in their indulgences, they find their hobbies and vocations. While trying to enjoy themselves, they exert their real force not in political life but in the social whirl—bringing out a daughter, steering her into a suitable marriage, and then welcoming her home when the marriage no longer works. They detest foreigners, consider England the cynosure of the universe, and in their eccentricity allow nearly anything to prevail, provided, of course, it is English. They may seem fools to the outsider, but they speak with the accents of real people.

Miss Mitford's charm lies in her naturalness. Without forcing her talents into areas that obviously are not for her, she writes about what she knows with energy and verve and a striking ability to catch the cadence of preposterous talk. She makes the outlandish seem natural, and the natural sound bizarre, a twin talent necessary for any comic writer. Her novels swim with unlovable characters many of whom would like to be malicious if they knew how; but part of their attraction is their inability to be anything but themselves, to be inadvertently comical without trying for more than personal satisfaction.

L. P. Hartley has a high reputation in England and deservedly so. What he starts out to do he accomplishes admirably; his novels are models of intelligent writing, good sense, sharp feeling for proportion, and clean design. His world of upper middle-class gentility unfolds without fuss or affection. Hartley is that rare novelist who knows what he wants to do and goes about it with a minimum of waste.

Eustace and Hilda, consisting of four pieces he wrote during the forties (*The Shrimp and the Anemone,* 1944; *Hilda's Letter,* 1945; *The Sixth Heaven,* 1946; *Eustace and Hilda,* 1947), is Mr. Hartley's major work and an impressive piece of writing it is within the limitations he places on his novels. Hartley's fiction is a continuation of the late-Victorian novel which, while satisfying and rarely mediocre, lacks incisiveness and real wit: the work of a gentleman-novelist who is not squeamish or prissy. Principally, there are overtones of Trollope and even Henry James, although Hartley lacks Trollope's comic sense and James' intensity and sense of evil as well as his pungent and witty dialogue. There is also something of Arnold Bennett's *Old Wives' Tale* in this slowly-paced novel that moves according to its own rules.

The main relationship in the novel between Hilda and Eustace creates the dialectic: between her asceticism and his hedonism, her puritanism and his lack of sexual definition, her need to direct and his need to be directed, her compulsive stress on work and his desire to drift, her need for satisfaction through personal effort and his lack of goals, her separation from life and his attempt to seek life, her inflexibility and his tractability. They are truly antinomies, and yet the characters find satisfaction only in each other.

In this novel as well as his others, Hartley is somewhat akin to John Marquand, both writers possessing a sharp eye for the social fact and the individual weakness. There is, however, an obvious distinction between this kind of novel and the real creative thing. Lord David Cecil in his introduction to *Eustace and Hilda* overrates Hartley's accomplishment, claiming that some of his pages are among the most beautiful in all modern English literature. A great deal depends on how one defines beauty, but if the word includes a response that is more than what we mean by memorable, striking, or in good taste, then Hartley is less than a "beautiful writer." There is no doubt that he can evoke tones and colors, but he almost completely misses the world of deeper feeling and action.

In his other fiction since this long work, *The Boat* (1949), for example, or a recent novel, *My Fellow Devils* (1959), Hartley brings the same even intelligence and good taste to quite different themes. *The Boat* concerns the attempt of a writer, Timothy Casson, to understand life in a small English village, all his efforts centering around his desire to launch a boat in waters the town fishermen forbid to rowing or sailing. In *My Fellow Devils,* Hartley charts the pilgrimage of a self-willed young lady toward faith in the Catholic Church. Margaret Pennefeather breaks her engagement to the man she should have married and marries Colum McInnes, a film actor, by admission a "bad Catholic," who turns out to be a thief, a liar, and psychologically a child. He charms her until gradually she almost accepts his values; what saves her is her growing interest in the Church, which dwarfs her other feelings. Hartley's manner, however, belies Margaret's great need; her growing belief, narrated with English good taste, lacks cogency.

Hartley, then, is at his best when he deals with quiet situations and calm characters. Timothy Casson (*The Boat*) sitting and writing in his house or arguing with the intractable maids, is the kind of person whom Hartley catches authoritatively. He is most successful when he centers on man woven into his social fabric, caught by everyday detail, neither heroic nor cowardly. When an author who does this excellently tries to do more, then method and tone conspire to defeat the larger ambition.

Rosamund Lehmann is as good in her way as L. P. Hartley in his, which is effective indeed within the limitations suggested above. Almost against the grain, one is tempted to raise Miss Lehmann's work higher in the scale and compare it to Jane Austen's, Katherine Mansfield's, Virginia Woolf's, or Elizabeth Bowen's. However, her novels do lack intensity. While she catches agony and suffering in a phrase or sentence, she is unable to integrate these qualities into the development of her characters; often they appear as sharply-conceived fragments.

Miss Lehmann's most effective novel, *The Echoing Grove* (1953) recalls Elizabeth Bowen's *The Heat of the Day* (1949), for both are concerned with fitting a triangular love affair against a social and political background. Miss Bowen's novel partially failed because her hero was unbelievable, although the disjointed nature of the novel's structure and language successfully conveyed the incoherent quality of the period. Miss Lehmann's book partially fails not as a result of her male character, Rickie, but because her characters are monotonous and fail to develop.

In two of her early novels, *Dusty Answer* (1927) and *The Ballad and the Source* (1945), Miss Lehmann brought to bear upon her themes the same polished craftsmanship manifest in *The Echoing Grove.* In *Dusty Answer,* there is an arrangement of characters that Virginia Woolf was to follow to some extent in *The Waves,* published four years later. In Miss Lehmann's novel, Judith, a sensitive young girl, is the center, and around her revolve Charlie, who marries young and dies in the war; Martin, who loves Judith and is rejected by her, drowning shortly afterward; Julian, who wants Judith as his mistress, a role she rejects; and Roddy, whom Judith loves, but who cannot return her feeling for he is homosexual. The novel does not lack sensitivity or feeling, but it does fail to generate sufficient ideas to justify its length of almost 400 pages.

Elizabeth Taylor at first seems a member of the group that also includes Jane Austen, Katherine Mansfield, and Elizabeth Bowen, but she lacks their undertone of irony. There is, consequently, a flatness to her novels that even her careful prose and subtle plotting is unable to disguise. This flatness is characteristic of *A View of the Harbor* (1947) and *A Wreath of Roses* (1949), although it is less noticeable in a short novel like *Hester Lilly.* Miss Taylor has keyed emotions and actions so low she dissipates the intensity which should be below the surface of the character. And while there is an effective sense of mood, chattiness often replaces real dialogue, and her scenes lack clear definition.

Olivia Manning gains her most effective moments when she concentrates on the trivialities of daily life. In *A Different Face* (1957), she effectively catches the shabbiness of life in a coast town in south England. Hugo Fletcher, a man with a past, returns to Coldmouth to try to find himself, only to discover that all the money he has invested in a school has been lost. Miss Manning, however, succeeds less well with Hugo than with the town itself. As its name suggests, Coldmouth offers little but seediness; its former splendor is now tarnished and tawdry, and its inhabitants survive as though in purgatory. It is not Hugo but Coldmouth we remember, as terrifying in its way as Greene's Brighton.

In *The Doves of Venus* (1956), Miss Manning juxtaposes a romantic young girl's dream of London with the reality of the city itself. Once again, the sense of place is more effectively presented than the main character. Miss Manning writes gracefully and her characters are well limned, but their activities rarely rise above the ordinary. Were she to retain her ability to convey the spirit of place while increasing the emotional and intellectual range of her characters, she might develop the qualities which her novels now merely suggest.

Muriel Spark's four novels—*The Comforters* (1957), *Robinson* (1958), *Memento Mori* (1959), and *The Ballad of Peckham Rye* (1960)—are so involved with the eccentric event and the odd personality that they have virtually no content. *Memento Mori*, for example, is concerned with octogenarians who reveal their former vagaries, and *The Ballad of Peckham Rye* revolves around the fortunes of a modern-day Panurge. Miss Spark's novels are a sport, light to the point of froth. She can write about murder, betrayal, deception, and adultery as though these were the norms of a crazy-quilt society. In several ways, she reminds us of Ivy Compton-Burnett and Evelyn Waugh, although she lacks the penetration of the former and the sense of parody of the latter.*

Alan Sillitoe:
(Francis King, Brian Glanville, and Mervyn Jones)

Several young writers have published serious novels in the fifties which indicate the possibility of even finer things ahead. The best-known of this group is Alan Sillitoe, whose *Saturday Night and Sunday Morning* (1958) was praised by the press as the best proletarian novel since the thirties. Actually, the novel is less than that, although it is effective on a small scale and in a minor key. Sillitoe's Arthur Seaton is an angry young worker, a "heel," who, on weekends, escapes from his factory job by going on drunken sprees. The cataloguing of Seaton's picaresque adventures forms the spine of the novel, as he goes with great vitality from drink to female-cushioned bed, and then returns to drink.

Far more impressive is Sillitoe's novella *The Loneliness of the Long-Distance Runner* (1959). This long story concerns a Borstal boy, Smith, who gains his personal liberty by losing an important foot race the governor of the Borstal expects him to win. For Smith, running is a source of freedom; he becomes one with nature as he swiftly races along the path outside the prison walls. In running, he denies his class and his criminal status. He has become so good that the governor of the Borstal enters him in a big race, for through Smith's triumph he hopes to gain praise from the authorities. Smith understands that running for the governor means simply this: praise, a medal, a pat on the back, a more comfortable future. To win the race is tantamount to playing society's game, and Smith decides to run and deliberately to lose.

Sillitoe has in operation here two conflicting ideas of society: the social "normality" of the governor, with his corrupted values, and the personal defiance of the angry young Borstal boy, with his integrity and purity. Smith must prove to himself that he is really a free individual, that the governor, as a member of the state, might imprison him, but he alone controls the ability to run. Smith knows that his fortune is made if he wins the race, but he also recognizes that in another way he will be completely imprisoned if he plays the governor's game. He prefers social ostracization to the loss of inner liberty, and by refusing to win revenges himself on a society which has nothing to offer him. In losing the battle, he wins his war.

In writing this kind of novel, Sillitoe indicates that he can raise class struggles to mighty warfare and, through dramatic conflict, can portray a large range of social relationships. *The Loneliness of the Long-Distance Runner* remains one of the best short novels of the decade. In the next year, Sillitoe published *The General,* an allegorical novel concerned with the conflict between man's savage instincts and his civilized manners, specifically between war and art. The novel completely fails because Sillitoe embodies his ideas in virtual robots. In his previous fiction, he carefully placed his characters in their milieu; here they are abstracted from the social world, isolated as allegorical figures acting out the eternal struggle between art and war, between disorder and discipline. His characters have no motivation beyond the intellectual distinctions placed upon them by the author. As allegory, *The General* is too simple; as fiction, its characters are insubstantial.

Originally encouraged to write by Robert Graves, Sillitoe seems, like several of his contemporaries, to be publishing too rapidly. Three works of fiction in three years and a volume of poetry in 1961 would indicate a desire to rush into print. Certainly, *The General* is a disappointment after the picture of the Borstal boy seeking freedom in his long runs outside the prison walls.*

Among writers who began to publish steadily in the 1950's, Francis King, Brian Glanville, Mervyn Jones, Edmund Ward, Frank Tuohy, and Emyr Humphreys are worthy of mention. King's two novels about Greece, *The Dark Glasses* (1954) and *The Man on the Rock* (1957), demonstrate a keen sense of place and the ability to probe man's infinite capacity for corruption. Although projected on a small scale, they are, as far as they go, incisive and mature.

In Brian Glanville's *The Bankrupts* (1958), Rosemary Frieman resists corruption in seeking her identity in Jewish upper-middle-class life. Like C. P. Snow's *The Conscience of the Rich,* published the same year, Glanville's novel concerns the war between the generations. Jewish life offers comfort and *Gemütlichkeit* to Rosemary while attempting to destroy her image of herself. In pursuing the latter, she cuts herself off from her parents and their way of life. The Bankrupts, on the other hand, are those who have lost all ideals and have nothing to offer but their money and lavish possessions. Glanville's novel does not have the authentic flavor of Snow's book, but, in embryo, it contains the elements of mature conflict.

Mervyn Jones's *The New Town* (1953) is based solidly on a social and political world but partially fails because of its wooden central character, Harry Peterson. Peterson is involved in setting up New Towns to provide adequate housing for those who work within a radius of London. He is noble and self-sacrificing, but his private life allows him no peace, surrounded as he is by corruption. Like Ford Madox Ford's Christopher Tietjens, Peterson is long suffering, but refuses to capitulate despite his defeat. Were Peterson himself to come to life, this ably written novel might have more adequately projected the relationship between his personal life and his political and social ambitions.

None of these talented authors have yet written a novel that fulfills their promise. Either they have not trusted their own ingenuity, or else they have not seen their material clearly enough to overcome its shortcomings. There is, unfortunately, a sameness about their work, as though they were not developing from one book to the next. Nevertheless, for all of these novelists, especially Doris Lessing, Alan Sillitoe, and Francis King, there is the possibility of major work if they were to slow down and allow their powers to mature before becoming depleted.

William Sansom, Gerald Hanley, and *Roy Fuller:* (Denton Welch, V. S. Pritchett, and Anthony West)

Judging by a sampling of their fiction, the reader can see in William Sansom, Gerald Hanley, and Roy Fuller the potential for first-rank novelists if they were to expand the range of their intentions. William Sansom, for instance, expends much talent on themes that are basically trivial, or on characters who are unduly shallow. In *The Body* (1949), the short-story writer turned novelist has caught the note of middle-aged frustration, but by stressing details at the expense of the whole, his skill is partially vitiated.

In *The Loving Eye* (1956), the theme is no less than the distinction between illusion and reality, between the girl Matthew Ligne sees behind her window and the real girl who works in a night club. *The Face of Innocence* (1951) is concerned with a similar theme. Eve Camberley derives pleasure from an imaginary life that she recounts in detail. Having never had anything substantial, she continues to lie about her past even after she marries into money and a position. On a trip to the continent, Eve is partially cured after an affair with a French mechanic, an affair that seems to embody one of her own lies. In a more recent novel, *The Cautious Heart* (1958), Sansom strikes a compromise between style and theme, and a charming small novel results. The love affair between a night club pianist and a girl who is attached to an old wastrel is the kind of thing suitable for Sansom's colloquial style, full as it is of good-humored slang and nervous energy.

Sansom's comic talent is obvious, although his themes often dissipate it. He is interested in sensitive people: in frustrated individuals seeking happiness, artistic people mocked by reality, drifters who must find some workable order in a blundering universe. But often his interest in them makes them less, not more, than what they are, and reduces their scale until their lives and their problems seem unimportant.

The alternative of course is not solemn dialogue and ponderous philosophizing; nor is it parody and removal of the author from the interests of his characters, à la Waugh. The alternative is possibly something close to the work of Henry Green, whom Sansom resembles in several superficial ways. Neither Green nor Sansom writes on a grand scale, but Green, through density of social detail, nevertheless makes the world seem large, and consequently under his treatment his characters expand. Sansom's characters, on the other hand, often appear to contract, with their world diminishing commensurately as they diminish. Despite his gift for narrative and colloquial dialogue, despite his urbanity and civilized point of view, Sansom has not yet written a novel that provides a gauge of his talent.

Gerald Hanley writes workmanlike novels whose themes force inevitable comparison with those of Conrad, Hemingway, and Graham Greene. His *The Year of the Lion* (1953), for example, is a typical initiation novel in which a young man goes out to Africa to seek his fortune and there after surviving several tests grows up into the ways of the world. The overtones are obvious, and although this is a neatly written novel, the theme adds little to what we already know of such people and their initiation rites. Hanley has placed a Hemingway young man in Graham Greene territory and then enveloped him in Conrad's world of illusions.

The initiation novel has traditionally taken two courses: that in which the protagonist has to overcome obstacles before he can be accepted into society, or that in which the young man, more aware than most, must seek those personal values by which he can live, whether they are inside society or not. The first kind is physical, the second sensitive and occasionally arty. Conrad's initiation novels, at their best, straddled both worlds, while those of the Angries pretend to the second type when they are actually closer to the first. Hanley's Jervis is more physical than sensitive—he goes out to Africa to make his way—and therefore he must prove his manhood with blood and thunder.

The opposite side of the coin is Denton Welch's *Maiden Voyage* (1945) in which the Alastor-like Denton searches the world for Life, and in searching will find himself. His voyage is that of a maid (he is a tender homosexual) or a virgin who seeks experience. Like Proust's Marcel, he is super-sensitive to odors and tastes. Once exposed to life in China, he tries to avoid nothing and embrace all. The sole difficulty, however, is that Denton merely flirts with experience, and this kind of novel is meaningless unless ultimately the protagonist develops under the pressure of events. In another novel that followed shortly afterward, *In Youth Is Pleasure* (1946), Welch is again concerned with maturation, here a young boy who runs away from school and recognizes he is homosexual. The novel, though, is too slight to convey the agony of such a monumental discovery.

In another schoolboy novel, *That Distant Afternoon* (1959), the poet Roy Fuller turned to the typical English theme of the impressionable young boy out of step with his classmates. Fuller's novel is neatly written and appropriately spare, but the theme has worn somewhat thin, and his portrayal of institutionalized injustice adds little to what Orwell indicated in *Such, Such Were the Joys.* . . .

Despite their virtues, these novels are partially unsatisfactory because Hanley and Fuller have not demonstrated where they begin and where their sources end. In *Without Love* (1957), Hanley's Mike Brennan is a fallen Catholic, a killer out of Greene territory who finds in the Spanish Civil War some use for his destructive talents. As a child of the century, he will fluctuate to any ideology which offers him temporary identity. A victim of his times, Brennan is also guilty: he is not merely victimized, he seeks his fate.

This type of creature beyond the pale of God and man is truly frightening, for he embodies a nihilism suggesting that life is so meaningless that a man is free to dispose of his own as cheaply as he wants. Whether he lives or dies is irrelevant. Greene perceived that man must accept this possibility unless he mitigates it by belief in a supreme being. This idea even as Greene handles it, however, is not new; Conrad and the Existentialists, Christian or otherwise, have been poking around in these corners since Dostoyevsky's *Crime and Punishment, The Possessed,* and *The Brothers Karamazov.* By the time Hanley picks up the theme and applies it to a modern situation, there is little left to add.

The same might be said of Fuller's *Image of a Society* (1957), a slight but efficient novel of the inner workings of a Building Society. As a poet, Fuller is capable of the apt phrase, and this effective use of language often prevents the novel from becoming naturalistically monotonous. This is the kind of book that C. P. Snow writes, for it depends upon those power struggles within an organization that typify the major conflicts outside. What Fuller has started out to do, he has ably accomplished. One wishes, however, that he had grafted this theme on to a more ambitious narrative and gained greater variety of character and situation. Without such expansion, the book seems imitative of several others, particularly of dozens of American business novels which have appeared throughout the fifties.

V. S. Pritchett is an excellent short story writer and critic who turned to the novel, but was partially unable to fulfill his talent in the genre. As we would expect, *Mr. Beluncle* (1951) is a novel in good taste and with a strong literary background. Pritchett's protagonist is a composite of the "heroes" of Defoe, Fielding, and Dickens, with overtones of Thurber's Walter Mitty. Pritchett captures ably the various fakes and fanatics who surround his central character; at the same time, he projects Mr. Beluncle's superstitions and shows him as a typically confused modern man who has no command over his mind. Beluncle, nevertheless, is inadequate to support the apparatus of class structure, and the book goes soft whenever the author's invention flags.

On the basis of his four novels thus far, the Anglo-American critic and novelist, Anthony West, deserves mention. In his first novel, *The Vintage* (*On a Dark Night,* 1950), West attempted a *Faust* for our times in which characters already dead must come to terms with choices they made during their lives. Like the characters in Sartre's *No Exit,* West's remain in a hell which is a duplication and perpetuation of what they were in life.

West undoubtedly tried a tour de force, but failed for several reasons: the episodes themselves, the substance of the numerous flashbacks, are too commonplace to bear the weight of such a large design. The imaginative projection of the material is often admirable, but the imagination must itself be rooted in the real before it can soar, and the real here is not sufficient to allow significant thrust. There is the suggestion of a grand design: a conflict between God and the devil; the psychological doubling of two apparently dissimilar characters; an allegory of England and Germany in war and peace; a large panorama of battles, troop movements, and war crimes trials; a small army of willing females; numerous love affairs of varying intensity. To sustain what this pattern suggests, the author would need the ground plan of *War and Peace.* Nevertheless, despite its faults, this first novel demonstrates an awareness of what contemporary fiction badly needs: the synthetic imagination which would keep the novel large and significant.

In *Heritage,* published five years later, West wrote a persuasive and charming novel which lacks the size of *The Vintage* but gains in cogency what it loses in range. Modeled on H. G. Wells, Max Town is an intensely energetic figure described by his sensitive son with affection and occasional antipathy. As seen through the eyes of the son, the narrative traces the boy's years of shifting from one parent to the other, and his attempt to grow up in a world which does not pretend to understand him.

Heritage fits generally into the type of society novel familiar from Nancy Mitford's *The Pursuit of Love* and *Love in a Cold Climate* and repeated in Sybille Bedford's *A Legacy* (1956), although West lacks Miss Mitford's diabolical humor and avoids Miss Bedford's historical chronicling. Nevertheless, this picture of upper-class artistic life has a vivid existence of its own. Perhaps the somewhat light touch precludes any significant inner development in Richard Savage, but West is not interested in creating a novel of agonized adolescence. He is concerned more with the understanding that Richard has for his parents. Rather than rejecting the parents, as the novel of adolescence takes for granted, Richard accepts them after realizing what they have to offer. Then he takes the step into maturity by recognizing that what they offer is not sufficient to sustain them and him, and that he must seek his own identity despite the famous father and the exciting mother. In effect, he rejects his heritage at the moment of understanding it, and this combination of rejection and knowledge provides the substance of a novel full of insight and tasteful brilliance.

Christopher Isherwood:

Perhaps no novelist of the last thirty years seemed better equipped than Christopher Isherwood to catch the peculiar tone of his times; he had verbal facility, inventive ability, and a sense of form and movement. What he lacked in his early work was imaginative breadth, and this, the reader felt, would develop as his total powers grew. In *All the Conspirators* (1928), Isherwood was obviously making his gesture of rebellion, and through his artist protagonist, moving off to be his own man. The novel is reminiscent of a great many late-Victorian works, especially Butler's *The Way of all Flesh,* but nevertheless it is, despite its slightness (Isherwood was only 23), an honest statement of the conflict between an individual and his family.

Instead of maturing into a novelist, however, Isherwood demonstrated that his real skill lay with the short sketch, the vignette, the brief portrait, the episode. His verbal facility and grace of movement remained, but they were placed at the service of basically trivial characters. In *The Last of Mr. Norris* (1935, published in England as *Mr. Norris Changes Trains*) and *Goodbye to Berlin* (1939), Isherwood was concerned with personal breakdown and corruption against the backdrop of pre-war Berlin. Perforce, his characters are trivial, for they bend with the times and corrupt easily. Nevertheless, his kind of corruption is slight: it is closer to seediness.

In *Prater Violet* (1945), Isherwood is concerned with the making of a motion picture and particularly with its director, Friedrich Bergmann, but certain attitudes turn the novel into soap opera and dispel the force of the somewhat attractive Bergmann. In his two other novels, *The Memorial* (1932) and *The World in the Evening* (1952), Isherwood has so well isolated the brassy and the phony that when he tries to penetrate beneath the façade, he finds little more to say. *The Memorial* seems cut from the same fabric as Huxley's *Eyeless in Gaza;* that is, it features several time shifts which themselves cannot disguise the thinness of the material. Like Huxley, Isherwood was trying to capture the vapidity of the postwar world, but he clearly lacks Huxley's bite and the latter's ability to symbolize futility on a grand scale. *The World in the Evening* presents a childish Stephen Monk, who becomes a hanger-on, picking up love with man or woman as he finds it. Had Isherwood conveyed real moral tension in Stephen, he might have made the anguish seem significant. As it is, Stephen voices pity and compassion, but these qualities are so removed from his juvenile character that they appear superimposed.

Perhaps Isherwood is suggesting that "modern" people like Stephen Monk, Sally Bowles, Mr. Norris, and Edward Marsh (*The Memorial*) have been so conditioned by the times that they have no moral sense; for them to feel more would indicate they are more substantial than we can rightfully expect. If this, however, is Isherwood's point, then he has failed to provide the necessary tensions for cosmic ennui; at most, he conveys petty boredom.

XVI

Major Work in the Sixties:
Doris Lessing and Anthony Powell

THE MOST CONSIDERABLE single work by an English author in the 1960's has been done by Doris Lessing, in *The Golden Notebook* (1962). It is a carefully organized but verbose, almost clumsily written novel, and if we were to view it solely as an aesthetic experience, we might lose most of its force. The book's strength lies not in its arrangement of the several notebooks which make up its narrative, and certainly not in the purely literary quality of the writing, but in the wide range of Mrs. Lessing's interest, and, more specifically, in her attempt to write honestly about women.

In this respect, *The Golden Notebook* recalls another compendium of women's attitudes, in a very different time and place, George Eliot's *Middlemarch*. In that novel, Dorothea Brooke is, of course, a less obviously sexual creature than Anna-Ella of *The Golden Notebook,* but Dorothea's main actions do focus upon men, and, indeed, upon men as sexual objects. After her unconsummated marriage with Casaubon, Dorothea's later movement toward Will Ladislaw is a direct response to her continued virginity, an attempt to complete herself with a male. Without losing sight of the delicacy of Dorothea's emotional ballet, one can say that the undercurrents are strongly sexual, and that intellectual satisfaction is impossible without physical completion. By hinting at the unmentionable—that is, a woman's need for orgasm—and by advocating the very feelings normally held to be degrading, *Middlemarch* was a liberating novel for women.

Doris Lessing picks up the attack. While England has not lacked female novelists, few indeed have tried to indicate what it is like to be a woman: the sense of being an object or thing, in a society whose values are relatively liberal. Even Virginia Woolf, of recent novelists the one most aware of women, portrayed women as stereotypes—as emotional and sensuous creatures, as anti-intellectual and anti-materialist—and failed to catch their mundane problems and privations. For *her* portraits, Mrs. Lessing has adopted, indirectly, the unlikely form of the descent into hell, a mythical pattern characterized by her female protagonists in their relationships with men, an excellent metaphor for dislocation and fragmentation in the sixties. Like Persephone, her women emerge periodically from the underworld to tell us what went awry—and it is usually sex. If the Bomb exists *out there* in every Lessing novel, then within each woman who tries to transcend the traditional protection of housewife and mother there exists a comparable bomb, which threatens to explode whenever she tries to live without men, or even when she lives with them.

In a May 1969 interview at Stony Brook, New York, Doris Lessing spoke of the period in which *The Golden Notebook* takes place as a time when "everything is cracking up. . . . It had been falling apart since the bomb was dropped on Hiroshima." Then, in a statement which carries the full force of the self-hatred and driven quality we sense in Anna-Ella, she says: "Throughout my life I've had to support parties, causes, nations, and movements which stink." She states, further: "I feel as if the Bomb has gone off inside myself, and in people around me. That's what I mean by the cracking up. It's as if the structure of the mind is being battered from inside. Some terrible thing is happening." The bomb metaphor recalls Donne's "Batter my heart, three person'd God; for you / As yet but knocke, breathe, shine, and seeke to mend, / That I may rise. . . ." The paradox is similar: One may be either destroyed or resurrected by the same experience. The difference is that Donne felt rape was another form of chastity, and Mrs. Lessing is afraid that rape is the final step. All her women, in one way or another, are raped. As if to confirm the paradox in her desire for experience, she says later in the interview: "Today it's hard to distinguish between the marvellous and the terrible." After *The Golden Notebook,* Mrs. Lessing tried to plumb the terrible, for her next novel, *The Four-Gated City* (1969), is nothing less than a nightmare, the portrait of a city, London, in which all four gates are guarded by Cerberus.

The four gates lead to houses of constriction, nightmare, impotence, not unlike the four notebooks of the earlier novel. At each gate, the protagonist Martha is seeking a path, like Dante's faltering figure at the beginning of the *Inferno.* We remember that the protagonist undertaking the Perilous Journey in her five-novel series, *Children of Violence,* is named Martha Quest. Accordingly, if we are to discuss Doris Lessing's work in the sixties, we must compare two books which converge and move away from each other, *The Golden Notebook* and *The Four-Gated City,* which crowns the *Children of Violence* series.* Like asymptotes, the two books approach each other without touching, all the while utilizing common images and symbols: the gate, the door, the house or room, the descent into hell, the quest. To gain a sense of this underworld, where all quests lead to further frustration, we should begin with *The Golden Notebook.*

At first, it would seem in *The Golden Notebook* that Mrs. Lessing has picked up where Joyce ended, with Molly Bloom's somewhat ambiguous "yes I said yes I will Yes." After all, her women, Anna Wulf and Molly Jacobs, seem to be saying "yes" to themselves and thumbing their noses at convention. But this impression is deceptive. Actually, their uncertain survival fits well into the ironies, paradoxes, conspiracies, lies, and deceptions of the world around them. About midway, in the Red Notebook 2, Comrade Ted tells of his idyllic meeting with the father-figure Stalin, whose wisdom appears to see and know all. When Anna has read

* *Martha Quest* (1952), *A Proper Marriage* (1954), *The Ripple from the Storm* (1958), *Landlocked* (1965), *The Four-Gated City* (1969). Her other fiction includes: *The Grass Is Singing* (1950), *Five* (1953, short novels), *Retreat to Innocence* (1956), *The Habit of Loving* (1957, short stories), *The Golden Notebook* (1962), *A Man and Two Women* (1963, short stories), *African Stories* (1964).

this tale of Ted's meeting with Stalin, she comments: "But what seemed to me important was that it could be read as parody, irony or seriously. It seems to me this fact is another expression of the fragmentation of everything, the painful disintegration of something that is linked with what I feel to be true about language, the thinning of language against the density of our experience."

A tale that can be read either as parody or as slavish devotion to an ideal is, in one sense, like most human experience since the end of the Second World War. Doris Lessing tells us, among other things, that experience is infinite, protean, and messy (neither Sartre's contingency nor Marx's necessity), that all is appearance, that we cannot measure life according to preconceptions, that indeed we cannot distinguish between subject and object, and that, in many ways, we are self-made fools. To make these declarations is not to wallow in guilt about our deficiencies, but to suggest a way of seeing the familiar and the expected. Like Anthony Powell, who views his characters against infinite sweeps of time, even emerging like saurians from primeval swamps, Doris Lessing sees her women as protean, as endlessly trying to re-create themselves, only to fall back befuddled by men like Paul-Michael or Saul Green, who need women for mothers and/or scapegoats for their own weaknesses. The individual is always on the threshold of drowning in the collective consciousness, politically as well as psychologically.

Powell's insistent mythical references correspond to Mrs. Lessing's mighty metaphors. The notebooks, four in number, are obviously facets of Anna's life, both clear affirmations of her attempts to find unity and evidence of her fragmentation. "I keep four notebooks, a black notebook, which is to do with Anna Wulf the writer; a red notebook, concerned with politics; a yellow notebook, in which I make stories out of my experience; and a blue notebook which tries to be a diary." These notebooks perform the same function as Joyce's interior monologue. The source of this novel may be female novelists, George Meredith's feminist tracts, and Simone de Beauvoir's *Second Sex,* but the structural concept is neo-Joycean, much as Powell's *Music of Time* is neo-Proustian despite its patina of Waugh and early Huxley.

These notebooks are outposts of achievement or sanity, a means of holding on when all other paths are blocked; nonetheless, Anna does not triumph through them. Rather, she must always return to her room—like Gregor Samsa's, her room is a fierce refuge from harsh men and events—and in her room she dreams. They are terrible things, her nightmares, almost comparable to Gregor's metamorphosis into a bug. One recurring dream is of going under water, drowning in the very element she is trying to breast. Such dreams make a mockery of Anna's belief that people are like Sisyphus, who put his shoulder to the boulder even knowing that it would roll back. Great men may stand at the top of the mountain and meditate on life and death, but the majority of souls, she accepts, are "boulder-pushers."

Her dreams and her will are always in conflict. In the Blue Notebook 1, Anna tells her psychiatrist, Mrs. Marks ("Mother Sugar"), about her dream of the casket. Instead of the casket holding beautiful things, it is more like Pandora's Box, letting out odoriferous waves of war, blood, bits of flesh, illness. Suddenly, the contents are transformed into a small, green, smirking crocodile, whose large frozen tears turn into diamonds. The precise meaning of the image is unclear, but the sardonic crocodile mocks all of Anna's dreams, hopes, and illusions. One may assume that the casket and the malicious crocodile are Anna's burdens or obstacles, always there when she seeks good faith or release.

This dream is linked to others involving a smirking, dwarf-like old man, sometimes deformed, sometimes with a "great protruding penis," whose original shape was a vase, like the crocodile in the casket. These hollow shapes, whether casket or vase, are surely vaginal, and therefore the misshapen, malicious figures who fill them are symbolic of the men intruding in Anna's life. These men are necessary and at the same time inadequate; the dreams are examples of anxiety. Late in the book, in a part that prefigures the section called "The Golden Notebook," Anna sees herself as the dwarf-figure, as what she calls the "principle of joy-in-destruction." Perhaps she is right. What she means is that her anxiety regarding men is built into her own needs; in some self-destructive way she is bound to seek out men who will remind her of the crocodile and the deformed dwarf with the protruding penis. All this would be consistent with her desire to live existentially, beyond normal supports.

In her Stony Brook interview, Doris Lessing spoke of using her dreams whenever she is stuck. "I fill my brain with the material for a new book, go to sleep, and I usually come up with a dream which resolves the dilemma." Then she says, "The unconscious artist who resides in our depths is a very economical individual. With a few symbols a dream can define the whole of one's life, and warn us of the future, too. Anna's dreams contain the essence of her experience in Africa, her fears of war, her relationship to communism, her dilemma as a writer." While simplified, this is an honest attempt to create literary material out of Freudian analysis, although elsewhere Mrs. Lessing rejects the Freudian unconscious as too dark and fearful a place.

But the dream is a warning, whether it is sugar-coated by Mrs. Marks (a female "Marx") or whether Anna wishes to see it through. The dream always brings her back to the closeness of her room, just as Martha Quest in *The Four-Gated City* is nearly always enclosed in houses and interiors. Anna writes in the "Golden Notebook" section that: "My big room, like the kitchen, had become, not the comfortable shell which held me, but an insistent attack on my attention from a hundred different points, as if a hundred enemies were waiting for my attention to be deflected so that they might creep up behind me and attack me."

This fear of attack or rape, the use of a room as refuge—in the later book, houses are lairs—the insistent need to withdraw into nightmares: all this is part of the descent into hell, that mythical yet personal seeking after self. What Mrs. Lessing insists upon is the imperfection of her female characters, her realization that because of their own frailties they will always seek out inadequate men. Hell is within, and it cannot be exorcised by anything the external world offers. This vision places Mrs. Lessing among the nineteenth-century novelists whose protagonists piece together fragments of experience in an attempt to derive some unity; not among later novelists who take patterns of fragmentation for granted.

For a closer sense of what Doris Lessing is doing—very unlike her generation of English novelists—it is instructive to see her alongside the playwright Harold Pinter, or poets like Ted Hughes and Charles Tomlinson. Clear analogies can be drawn to Tomlinson's preoccupation with whiteness and absence (in "Icos" and "The Fox"), or to his images of annihilation. But Hughes's poetry, in particular, with its dream-like sense of death, its animals whose world is primitive and predatory and uncertain, its heavy weights of rains and rots and winters, provides images appropriate to Mrs. Lessing's vision. Hughes's image of the otter, who "belongs / In double robbery and concealment," shows the artist-poet-novelist who lurks beneath the shards, trying to hold together the only world he knows. In this way we view Anna, who, writing furiously in notebooks, "Re-enters the water by melting," like the otter neither "fish nor beast." Or else we see her in another Hughes image, in "Cadenza": "And I am the cargo / Of a coffin attended by swallows."

In this poem, which is as much about Hughes as about his wife Sylvia Plath, who committed suicide, the sense of destruction and fragmentation of self is the dominant theme, recalling Ella's plan for a novel about a suicide. The tension of the novel, Ella says, would be between his surface sanity and his underlying motive of self-destruction: very close indeed to Sylvia Plath's own career. In such a career, the continuity of a life would only be understood when one saw its inevitability: in suicide. Hughes ends "Cadenza" with "Blue with sweat, the violinist / Crashes into the orchestra, which explodes." Here, too, we have Anna's, and Doris Lessing's, sense of the inner bomb as smashup and death, a metaphor for the postwar years.

Perhaps the closest we come to Doris Lessing's sense of the sixties is in Harold Pinter. At first, the two seem dissimilar, and the coupling of their names may appear bizarre. But both the playwright and the novelist are heir to a development in literature that has become insistent in the last fifty or sixty years. Since Kafka and Proust, there has developed what may be termed a literature of enclosure, fiction in which breadth of space is of relatively little importance. *Space exists not as extension but only as a volume to be enclosed* in a room, a house, or even a city. Joyce's Dublin has this quality—as though the city were not open to the sky but were a series of enclosures of houses and bars and meeting places. Such a city conveys not the sense of something unfolding but of something accruing, like an internal growth which invisibly expands to tremendous size under cover of the flesh.

Kafka's use of rooms and houses is, of course, one prototype of this kind of fiction. Another is the room of Proust's Marcel, where he stifles in heat and frustration and self-hatred. A third is the cluttered rooms of Beckett's Murphy or Watt, where they bitterly deplore their fate but remain immobile. Rooms so used in literature appear to be a direct counterpart to the Freudian description of adult regression and tendencies to return to the womb, that quasi-sacred place where needs are met without effort and without external threat. One wonders whether such a literature could have developed, at least in this manner, without the influence of psychoanalytic thought. To follow this argument—which ultimately is not the major one—is to see that the room is *the* place in which one can dream, where one can isolate oneself in neurosis or withdrawal symptoms, can seek refuge from external onslaughts too severe for the individual to withstand.

But a room or rooming house in Pinter and Mrs. Lessing,* I think we can say, signifies for them an entire culture, in particular England's shrinking in the sixties from its postwar eminence to a minor "enclosed power." In *The Four-Gated City,* for example, Martha Quest uses Mark Coldridge's house as a way of settling her life and at the same time as an escape from a social and political world she cannot control. Just as a medieval family hid behind drawbridge and moat, she hides behind the door, and thus self-concealment is a physical and a psychological fact.

Since enclosure is so significant in Doris Lessing's work, its features need detailed description:

1. Even though the room is a place of refuge, it is also the locale of one's descent into hell.

2. Its physical desolation is a counterpart of the character's psychological state.

---

* Besides *The Golden Notebook* and *The Four-Gated City,* cf. the rooming house milieu of *In Pursuit of the English* (1960) with similar places in Pinter's *The Birthday Party, The Room, The Dumb Waiter, The Caretaker,* and *The Homecoming.*

3. The room serves as a tiny stage for those on a string, a puppet show.

4. The room bottles up rage, leaves no escape for anger except back into the self.

5. The room or house is a battleground—nothing escapes into the air. The family relationship is symbiotic.

6. The lair is a physical symbol of impotence—lack of choice, will, determination. (See Anthony Powell for this also—most of his action takes place in living rooms or at parties; only Widmerpool has will, the rest are virtually impotent.)

7. In such a room, Eros becomes sex, spirit becomes physical, idea or theory becomes fact. The enclosure fixes the limits of sexuality, threatens and reassures within bounds.

8. Whereas space was once used for repetition of a holy act, the act of creation itself, now its repetition is one of staleness, folding anxiety into neurosis.

9. In the room, a dumb waiter serves as feedline, or people themselves are "dumb waiters."

10. The novel becomes personal, subjective, solipsistic even when externals like politics are of significance.

11. The panoramic novel is snuffed out, adventure lost, no struggle.

12. Finally, in the novel of enclosure, the room is the ultimate of the profane world, negating Mircea Eliade's idea of Space as Sacred. The room is geometric space, not the infinite space that Eliade sees as central to a reliving of the cosmogony:

It follows that *every construction or fabrication has the cosmogony as paradigmatic model.* The creation of the world becomes the archetype of every human gesture, whatever its plane of reference may be. We have already seen that settling in a territory reiterates the cosmogony. Now that the cosmogonic value of the Center has become clear, we can still better understand why every human establishment repeats the creation of the world from a central point (the navel). (*The Sacred and the Profane,* p. 45, Harper Torchbook edition)

Keep in mind Mrs. Lessing's "four-gated city" when Eliade writes:

On the most archaic levels of culture this possibility of transcendence is expressed by various images of an opening; here, in the sacred enclosure, communication with the gods is made possible; hence there must be a door to the world above by which the gods can descend to earth and man can symbolically ascend to heaven. (p. 26)

When the room or house was sacred, one's conception was that space was infinite, extending to the infinite space of the cosmos. Breathing in the air of this room, one was, as it were, breathing in something coexistent with the cosmos. Lessing and Pinter, like Beckett, provide rooms whose air is foul; the space is not infinite, but geometric, and it signifies the final vestiges of the profane city.

All literature has had its enclosures, but never before have interiors been so intensely the depository of "normal" illness and anxiety. There is virtually no Nature in Pinter or in the Lessing of these novels, and certainly not Nature as relaxation or renewal. When Pinter wishes to speak of Nature, he puts its joys, ironically, into the mouth of a killer like Goldberg, in *The Birthday Party*. "Because I know what it is to wake up with the sun shining, to the sound of the lawnmower, all the little birds, the smell of the grass, church bells, tomato juice——." Here we have the typical Pinter metaphysics: the juxtaposition of dissimilars as the image or symbol of dislocation. So, too, Doris Lessing. Scribbling away in her notebooks, Anna-Ella tries to deny the outside, to negate possible renewal through alignment with external forces. Just as all anxiety comes from within—after all, nothing very dreadful really *happens* to her—so, also, all surcease must come from within. The modern predicament: caught in our own existential stoicism, we cling to our miseries as the sole form of our salvation.

So much is clear. What is curious is that Doris Lessing has picked up many of D. H. Lawrence's injunctions about mechanical sex, about enervating marriages, about the boredom of non-vital relationships, and yet she has broken with his romanticism, in which human failings, or successes, are worked out in a Natural climate. At one point in *The Golden Notebook,* Mrs. Lessing speaks of the vaginal orgasm, as opposed to the superficial clitoral orgasm, as something "that is created by the man's need for a woman, and his confidence in that need." She says she can always sense when a relationship is dying, for the man begins to insist on giving her clitoral orgasms, and that is a substitute and a fake. The only female sensations occur ". . . when a man, from the whole of his need and desire, takes a woman and wants all her response." The language, as well as sentiment, is Lawrentian. Doris Lessing is speaking about something very important in the human spirit, and she is clearly right when she makes Ella insist on this aspect of her sensations.

But she sidesteps an even larger question when she fails to ask why the male is incapable of eliciting this response. Lawrence asked the question, and spent hundreds of pages trying to answer it. The question, put simply: Is it not possible that we have reached the point in civilization at which the male has been dehumanized and is incapable of responding in wide areas of feeling? Anna wants, through some existential process of choice or search, to deny the historical role of women: a rightful desire to destroy female bondage. But she does not see that the world has itself entered a new phase. And the very qualities of tenderness and satisfaction equally given and equally accepted are no longer possible for men who have sublimated their human qualities to the practical advantages of civilization. Lawrence spoke of dehumanization, and he felt it had arrived. By 1969, with *The Four-Gated City,* Mrs. Lessing appears willing to admit that the question has answered itself. But in *The Golden Notebook* she had only drawn up to the edge.

Nevertheless, *The Golden Notebook* is one of the few English novels of the last few decades to project outward rather than seeking forms of settlement. Anna's quest, already doomed to futility and failure, must continue: as an emancipated woman, as an outsider, she must complete or destroy herself with a male. She cannot be complaisant. Even though she suspects that man is dehumanized —she is familiar with Freud—and is capable of relating only to profession, career, or materiality, she still asserts her choice. To justify her existence, she must deny her historical role. To justify her existence, she must start the descent that most women attempt to avoid or mitigate through marriage and children.

While *The Golden Notebook* stops short of the apocalypse, *The Four-Gated City* embraces it. If the former sketches a kind of limbo, then the latter paints a hell. Yet Mrs. Lessing's statements in *Declaration* (ed. Tom Maschler, 1957) do not prepare us for the sense of doom in *The Four-Gated City*. In *Declaration,* she asserted her preference for the nineteenth-century realists—Stendhal, Balzac, Tolstoy, Dostoyevsky—who "despite their differences, stated their faith in *man himself.*" She said, further, that the writer must not plunge into despair, as Genet, Sartre, Camus, and Beckett have done, or into the collective conscience, as the socialist country writers have done. "The point of rest [for the writer] should be the writer's recognition of man, the responsible individual, voluntarily submitting his will to the collective, but never finally; and insisting on making his own personal and private judgements before every act of submission." Particularly ironic is her statement that "there is a new man about to be born . . . a man whose strength will not be gauged by the values of the mystique of suffering."

By the time of *The Four-Gated City,* twelve years after *Declaration,* Doris Lessing has descended into despair. The four gates are four houses, and the four houses are all various circles of Dante's Inferno. The vision here is especially compelling because it appears to contradict the entire drift of her earlier work beginning with *The Grass Is Singing* (1950). In that first novel, concerned with the struggle between white interests and black survival, she demonstrated that she could write a personal story against the background of complex social and political relationships. In fact, many of the attitudes and situations of that protagonist, Mary Turner, were later grafted on to Martha Quest of the *Children of Violence* series, chiefly the survival, or disintegration, of the individual under collective pressures. Mrs. Lessing catches superbly the degeneration of those whose relationships are based on subterfuge. Ostensibly about Mary Turner, the novel is prophetic: while trying to maintain his supremacy, the white declines, eventually fragments.*

In the *Children of Violence* series itself, Martha grows up amid the distrust between Englishmen and Afrikaners, and their common hatred of blacks, Jews, and change. These tensions, of which

---

* The title comes from *The Waste Land,* V: "In this decayed hole among the mountains / In the faint moonlight, the grass is singing / Over the tumbled graves, about the chapel. . . ." The quotation is a metaphor for the Turner household and beyond that for the entire white African society.

she is aware from childhood, become the major conflicts she confronts in the adult world. Already refusing her mother's self-imposed, constricted role, Martha drifts toward socialism and atheism, becomes pro-black, and attempts anything that will lead to substantial personal values. She is, of course, seeking her identity as a woman and as a person.

The first four volumes unfortunately often become trivial, especially when the main line of the narrative becomes lost in political detail or in inconsequential personal acts. Doris Lessing knows certain things very well—the land, family relationships which have soured, the frustration of meaningless affections, the way parents hang on to their children when neither can really bear the other—but when she details the dogma of the Marxist-Trotsky-Stalin axis, the reader lets go.

There is, nevertheless, in those early novels a curious psychological play: for those blacks hovering like dark presences in the background of white settlements are curious embodiments of Martha's slowly emerging other self. Like the black natives, waiting to break out, she, too, is twisting and turning in her appointed, nonconscious roles as daughter and then wife. As Mattie, she is a girl who will fit into the colonial pattern; as Martha, she is her own woman seeking consciousness.

Closely related to the dialectic of her roles is the recurring image of the black women who refuse to be fragmented by vague choices and who breed contentedly; they are essential women, avatars of Martha's own potential future. But Martha knows that these women do not live in a blissful, untroubled paradise; she knows they are diseased, that they die young, that they have given themselves over completely to a natural process without really wanting to. And yet she envies their instinctual mode of survival, their indifference to consciousness. The temptation is to be Mattie. And yet she also knows how impossible it would be for her to try to emulate the black women.

These first volumes in the series, very much a product of the 1950's in their linear political and social aspirations, were evidently part of Mrs. Lessing's own experience in Southern Rhodesia and parallel in many ways arguments and attitudes put forth by Simone de Beauvoir in *The Second Sex* (1949, 2 vols.). One might go on to say that the *Children of Violence,* except for its ideology, is a working out of entire chapters in the Beauvoir book: "Childhood," "The Young Girl," "Sexual Initiation," "Lesbianism," "The Married Woman," "The Mother," "Social Life," "The Narcissist," "The Woman in Love," "The Independent Woman," etc. "The Independent Woman" is especially descriptive of Martha: "When she [woman] is productive, active, she regains her transcendence; in her projects she concretely affirms her status as subject; in connection with the aims she pursues, with the money and the rights she takes possession of, she makes trial of and senses her responsibility" (p. 639).

Yet as the series continues, Doris Lessing clearly rejects the role of existential female, as later she rejected the polemics of women's liberation for a larger, more political view of life. Her character Martha fears recurring history, knowing that she "could take no step, perform no action, no matter how apparently new and unforeseen, without the secret fear that in fact this new and arbitrary thing would turn out to be part of the inevitable process she was doomed to." This sense of nightmarish repetition, of destiny repeating itself inexorably, is of course very much part of the literature of enclosure. With spatiality, one can avoid repetition through novelty of choice or act, but enclosure negates personal expansion.

The Four-Gated City begins with stiflement and strangulation. The key images in the first pages are of grime, globules of wet, browny-gray textures, oilcloth with spilled sugar, gritty smears, grease, thumbmarks. All these are "inside" images and forerun the theme of enclosure. Mrs. Lessing's continued descent into a fiercely populated hell is very close in effect to Bosch's *Garden of Earthly Delights* or his *Last Judgment.* In the paintings and in the novel, there is the mixture of sacred and profane, of realism and fantasy, of the loving and the obscene, of large vision and carping detail, of panorama and the local. There is no single style, but a comprehensive, somewhat mannered tone. The sexual by-product is a desire to wound and be wounded; to delight in watching others roast over a slow fire and to be roasted oneself over the same fire. The theme of torture, ever present in Bosch, is never far from Doris Lessing. Both put a roof over hell.

Durrell's Alexandria was also a hell, but frantic sensuality was at least a temporary escape. Anthony Powell's seriatim novels are filled with mythical hells, whether from Homer or from Wagner, but his central character, Nicholas Jenkins, remains relatively isolated from the deterioration around him. His descents are pratfalls, while others have indeed fallen. In Doris Lessing's novel, Martha succumbs. The theme is not so much disintegration—unlike Camus's *The Fall*—as it is the struggle to survive schizophrenia. Of the various denizens of Doris Lessing's hell, possibly the key one is Lynda Coldridge, Mark's wife; it is to Mark's house that Martha goes, seeking a refuge from external events which are themselves mad.

Lynda has proven too sensitive for normal contacts—among other things, sexual relations—and her waking hours are spent trying to hold on. As a rule, she survives by eating pills, but periodically she gives these up to seek inner support. In some curious way—she is not particularly sympathetic to others—she is a seer, one who has a sense of impending disasters, and Martha evidently cannot forgo her presence. Lynda's ability to "hear voices" and to experience visions is, in her society, a sign of her sickness. In other societies where such talents are appreciated by the majority, she would not be sick; her extravagances might even serve a social function. One is reminded of R. D. Laing's injunction to those who would work with psychotics: ". . . one has to be able to orientate oneself as a person in the other's scheme of things rather than only to see the other as an object in one's own world. . . ." A man who suddenly kneels down amid a crowd to pray fervently is insane; in church, he is considered devout.

What is of interest here, however, is not simply Lynda. By herself, she is not a compelling person. Doris Lessing has moved beyond trying to create attractive characters with empathic points of view. What is compelling is the fact that Martha Quest has given up the quest. Martha will never reach the Holy Grail, or even continue the Perilous Journey, for she is seeking security at any level, and finds it easier to remain in the Coldridge house—behind that locked gate—and relate herself to Lynda's mad state. As long as Lynda is mad, Martha has Mark, while Lynda herself needs Martha's sense of order. All attachments are symbiotic. Again Laing proves instructive: "Generally speaking, the schizoid individual is not erecting defences against the loss of a part of his body. His whole effort is rather to preserve his *self.*" Martha's effort is by now to preserve her "precariously structured" person: the overall symbol of this is Lynda's tenacious attempt to hold on without returning to the hospital.

There is some warning of this deteriorative process in *The Golden Notebook,* during Anna's affair with Saul Green and shortly after with her dream of the dwarfed man with the protruding penis:

> Sitting there I had a vision of the world with nations, systems, economic blocks, hardening and consolidating; a world where it would become increasingly ludicrous even to talk about freedom, or the individual conscience. I know that this sort of vision has been written about, it's something one has read, but for a moment it wasn't words, ideas, but something I felt, in the substance of my flesh and nerves, as true. (p. 485)

Her affair with Saul Green, destructive in virtually every way, is a forerunner of nearly all relationships Martha has in *The Four-Gated City.*

More specifically, those four gates to the four houses where Martha stays are themselves microcosms of English society, and, ultimately, of the world as Doris Lessing envisages it. This society follows on the holocaust of the Second World War and immediately precedes the apocalyptic vision that will end our present notion of the world and the book. Yeats's rough beast has arrived. Whereas gates were once entrances that one opened while seeking something or someone, they are now barriers which close off exits or prevent egress. The four bleak houses of England are: the restaurant at the beginning, where Martha would be Mattie (a "good fellow") and would be expected to lose herself in a dull marriage; second, the house of Mark Coldridge, a writer somewhat close to the center of power. He is besieged by predatory journalists and the house is a center of madness, inactivity, frustration, as well as some kindness. Third, Jack's house—literally, that Jack built—where girls go to be broken in for their future as prostitutes, where Jack sits like a spider catching them on the fly; and, finally, Paul's house —Paul is Mark's nephew—where derelicts and misfits, sexual cripples and the maimed, as in some James Purdy story, congregate under Paul's protective wing.

The connecting link among all the houses, all the gates, is Martha herself. At the opening of the novel, she visits the restaurant when she arrives in postwar London, a continuation of the earlier *Landlocked.* She then seeks a job as a secretary, but accepts temporarily a post as Mark Coldridge's housekeeper. The house becomes a walled-in medieval fortress which protects her against further action, even further thought, and the job turns into a way of life. The house is Bosch's hell, Gregor Samsa's room, the Invisible Man's basement cell, but it is also a refuge. Perhaps a modern view of hell is no more than this, Sartre's *No Exit,* a place in which one loses oneself, one's will, one's determination, and exchanges choice for a lair. Dostoyevsky pressed this option in the Grand Inquisitor scene, and the contemporary response is clear. Freedom, as Martha once quested after it in the stifling atmosphere of the white man's Africa, is not worth the struggle; we are, she appears to accept, all caught in a larger scheme anyway, and it is better to be besieged than to besiege. Using Mark's house as a base of operations—settling in for the rest of her useful years—Martha occasionally ventures out, to have casual sex with Jack and to continue the debasement of her former intentions. Or else she gravitates to Paul's house, a kind of live-in encounter group, in which the maimed attempt to support each other; all experience there is "tripping," hallucinatory.

Shut in, besieged, surrounded by madness, frustration, sickness, inadequate, furtive sex, gated, with hyena-like journalists howling outside, with nuclear bombs in production, with marches and countermarches, with threats always looming—whether Russia, fission, or personal schizophrenia—Martha has to pull herself together somehow. If she is enclosed in four houses, she is also Janus-faced: the softness of Mattie is the reverse of the questing Martha. The houses are both integrative and disintegrative, much as the notebooks in *The Golden Notebook* represented two opposing strains: those parts of Anna-Ella which could be consolidated and those pieces which defied stabilization. The apocalyptic epilogue of *The Four-Gated City* represents, in some ways, the "Golden Notebook" section in that book. The content of both is seeking form. In geometry, the circle indicates perfection, completion. But Doris Lessing utilizes not circles but fours: four notebooks, four gates or houses, and epilogues or "golden" episodes. The fours indicate all directions, negate completion, baffle expansion, intensify the enclosed quest. There is no magic in four. And the content finally achieves a form that allows no exit, except through the apocalyptic vision of a new, technological world which ends the novel.

The hopeful, striving Martha of the earlier books in the series is clearly very different from the Martha of this novel, and also different from the Anna-Ella of *The Golden Notebook*. Doris Lessing has changed her vision, where formerly political and social action —the image of Sisyphus pushing that boulder—was possible, even though results were minuscule and possibly not even visible in one's own lifetime. Now the world has turned upon itself, in a repetitive cycle of violence: *The Children of Violence* ends in a final disaster in which radioactivity, lethal gas, nerve gas, and the other by-products of a runaway society destroy life as we know it. Like Anthony Powell, as his series darkens, Doris Lessing's story gets gloomier and murkier, heading toward that vision which has rarely been sympathetic to the English temperament. It is chiefly a continental design, the sense of final things in Mann, Kafka, Conrad. Deeply humanistic, Doris Lessing takes up the familiar question of technology in conflict with the rest of life and foresees science as inexorable in striking images of disintegration, while human values, never more than tenuous, are trapped in Atreus-like houses in which people devour each other.

The symbol of breakdown in morality and in humanity is Jimmy Wood, a mild-mannered scientist and writer of space fiction who is a human computer. Jimmy represents the bland forces of military, science, and government which, with velvet glove, offer salvation while they lack a human dimension. ". . . It was as if Jimmy had been born with one of the compartments of the human mind developed to its furthest possibility, but this was at the cost to everything else." Jimmy has been designing machines that can tamper with the human mind, improving existing machines that destroy part of the human brain by electric charges. In addition to developing, on government request, machines to destroy the brains of dangerous persons, Jimmy perfected a machine for "stimulating, artificially, the capacities of telepathy, 'second sight,' etc." Perpetual fuel for the machine was to be provided by governments or the military in the form of a "human bank." Such a human radio or telephone, or whatever, would serve as an extension to the machine and prove more flexible; after that, it was up to the military to find a specific use.

In a way, Jimmy Wood's invention works, for certain people do have psychological reactions as telepaths. The drift is toward the interchangeability of people and machines, until they become indistinguishable. The final sections of the novel concern a letter from Martha, now old and worn out, addressed to Francis Coldridge, Mark's son. At the time Martha is barely surviving in Robinson Crusoe style on a "contaminated island" off the coast of Scotland. Britain has been poisoned; the political center has shifted to Africa and to the Chinese. The time is less than thirty years from now. In her NAR interview, Doris Lessing spoke of *The Four-Gated City* as a prophetic novel. "I think that the 'iron heel' is going to come down. I believe the future is going to be cataclysmic."

In *The Golden Notebook,* the key issue was human relationships, especially the relationships between men and women as a key image of modern humanity or inhumanity. Sexual liberation, from the female side, and sexual restructuring, from the male, was necessary. But in 1969 Doris Lessing says: "I'm impatient with people who emphasize sexual revolution. I say we should all go to bed, shut up about sexual liberation, and go on with the important matters." Her turn upon herself is curious. For this conflict between collective politics and personal matters had been the crux of her work of the last two decades. Anna's psychiatrist, in fact, suggested that her political activity was an avoidance of personal blockage. The conflict was real. Now the conflict has been "resolved." The incredibly difficult question of man-woman relationships becomes "going to bed," and sexual liberation seems an act of conscious choice, whereas before the very question of liberation raised all the familiar problems of identity and will.

The Four-Gated City is, in several ways, a curious finale to the *Children of Violence* series. It appears to cap the "enclosure" theme, so that Martha ends up, in Mark's house, as exhausted and otiose as the narrator in Proust or one of Beckett's dying gladiators. Up to this point, Martha, like Powell's Nicholas Jenkins, had been involved in a Bildungsroman. Far more than Jenkins, however, Martha has rubbed her nose into the filth of events. Observer more than participant, Jenkins moves easily in his own version of the dance of time. But while he waltzes, Martha goes through the contortions of modern dance. Tensing muscles and nerves, her body refuses the easy positions. While Nicholas relaxes into old motions, as befitting someone who glides through an established society, Martha twists her body into brittle shapes, as befits someone who must always create the society in which she is to move.

Self-evidently, she is involved in constant assertions of her mind and body; while Powell's protagonist has a ready-made group into which he always fits. And although he acts as a voice of decency and constraint among those who indulge in desperate ventures, he is too reserved to take any chances for himself. We remember he is Sloth in the tableaux of the Seven Deadly Sins. Doris Lessing, born in Persia of British parents, then coming to England as an alien from Rhodesia, where she had lived from her fifth through her thirtieth year, is herself the prototype of the unsettled artist. Not unusually, her Martha must go through all the awkward, anxiety-producing movements of the dance of time. There is no point at which she can stop to say: "I have arrived, I can see all around me." For her, all experience is a series of new starts. Powell's Jenkins need never start anew, for all the flotsam and jetsam from the past are at hand to create continuity in one fluid, dance-like step. Only events interfere.

In addition to these twists and turns, Martha must struggle through male-female relationships that could stifle her at any given point. In *Martha Quest,* she must deal with a series of narcissistic young men whose need is not for her but to quell some nagging fear in themselves; whose own hesitancy about their manhood shades every aspect of their relationships and turns most sexual episodes into mother-child encounters. With herself unfulfilled as a woman, Martha must avoid her "biological destiny," which would mean the end of all; at the same time, she finds such will-lessness attractive as an alternative to setting herself constantly against her destiny. This feeling is particularly acute, as we mentioned before, when

Martha views the easy compromise of the black women, who give in early to their destiny and live without seething.

Yet Martha fights off the situation in which ". . . men seemed to press a button, as it were, and one was expected to turn into something else for their amusement"; that is, "married, signed and sealed away." In her relationship with her mother, in particular, one sees what Martha has had to fight even before she comes up against young men. She detests her mother as only those can who have translated their hatred into pity. That is to say, she must fight against her mother in herself; she must be aware of sliding back. For Mrs. Quest is a mother, not a human being, and Martha must resist the same role for herself. Not only has Mrs. Quest been destroyed by racism—like most of the other settlers, she accepts a schizoid, paranoiac routine in which blacks both serve and persecute her—but she has been destroyed by her sexual, emotional, psychological repression. Having been miserable, she rejoices in her philosophy of misery; and needing to justify her own choice, she must destroy her daughter's alternatives.

Therefore, Martha's rebellious assertions of will are the substance of the first four volumes of *Children of Violence*. To understand this fact is to see how contrary *The Four-Gated City* really is, for there all relationships are symbiotic. No one stands without using another as crutch; no one is sick or well without influencing the sickness or illness of another. And these relationships are not of the sort that build a whole or unify a group that can stand together; they are an infection, a slow stain throughout the society. A good image of such suppurating love and affection comes when Mark Coldridge approaches his symbiotic other half, the mad Lynda:

He kissed her. Lips, a slit in the flesh of a face, were pressed against a thin tissue of flesh that saved them from pressing a double row of teeth which had lumps of metal in them. Then these lips moved to touch her own slit through which she was equipped to insert food or liquid, or make sounds. A kiss. That part of Martha which observed this remarkable ritual was filled with a protective compassion for these two ridiculous little creatures—as if invisible arms, vast, peaceful, maternal, were stretched around them both, and rocked them like water. (p. 468)

The imagery is remarkable for its quality of lost identity, of sub-mergence in another, of rejection of self. From here, the novel ends with the apocalypse; the ultimate bomb goes off, and a profane society has embraced its doom.

None of this is witty, or even ironic. Perhaps because she was an outsider, Mrs. Lessing has always been earnest and has never traded on the English tradition of social comedy, or muddling through. Both Anthony Powell and C. P. Snow, in their vastly different ways, belong to that mode, as do most of the 1950's "Angries" writers. In her rather grim, relentless manner, Mrs. Lessing has tried to be both panoramic (about racism, communism, bombism, all the "ologies" and "isms") and subjective. Her length indicates as much: *The Four-Gated City* runs one quarter of a million words, and *The Golden Notebook* is about as long. And yet, with all her prolixity, she has almost nowhere to go. She is getting less personal, as she suggests in her NAR interview, and she has destroyed the objective world. There is always science fiction, but in that mode those intense human relationships which are the strength of her earlier work can have no outlet. One wonders, holding these two considerable achievements in hand, if still another novelist is succumbing to apocalyptic visions as a way of settling personal problems.

Anthony Powell

Anthony Powell's fiction alone would suffice to mark the decade of the 1960's, and together with Doris Lessing's work the two provide complementary views of considerable merit. It is perhaps not accidental that both writers were writing a series, creating a cumulative effect by works that taken individually might not seem sufficiently solid. Unlike Mrs. Lessing, however, whose talents blossomed in two long novels in the sixties, Powell has worked at a steady pace since 1951, publishing novels of almost equal length, biding his time until his readers saw the figure in the carpet.

After nine novels and with three more to appear, the figure is now clearer; Anthony Powell has emerged as the most elegant writer presently working in the English language.* He has created nothing less than a chronicle of his times, what C. P. Snow, following Galsworthy, started out to do in his *Strangers and Brothers* series. It is instructive to try to determine why Powell's sequence, seemingly built on upper-middle-class values, succeeds so generously when those values no longer pertain, while Snow's, dealing with the success of a young man of restricted opportunity, appears remote and cloying although his view would seem the present way of the world.

Among the disturbances a writer engaged in a series must confront are the changes within himself over the fifteen or twenty years spent on his project. At some point, the series will call attention to him, attention that may bring about a different sensibility which is bound to be reflected in the rest of the series. Doris Lessing remained relatively unknown, almost a struggling author, throughout most of *The Children of Violence*. Until 1962 and *The Golden Notebook*—possibly the most ambitious British novel since *Ulysses*—she had not been enough in the public eye to cause her own sense of achievement to enter into or distort her fictional values. C. P. Snow, however, moved rapidly into the great world, where normalization tends to deny the value of imaginative fiction; his literary talents, modest to begin with, had little chance to develop separate from his international activities. As Snow's journalistic voice was increasingly noticed in the early 1960's, his fiction became supererogatory.

Unlike Snow, Anthony Powell chose to speak solely through his novels. There is no competition between the public and private man—few interviews, only scattered journalism and reviews, no god-like pronouncements—and his work has had a chance to develop and grow on its own terms. This is a constant in art, as Yeats so often said: the need to grow within the definition of the object

---

* See p. 238ff. for discussions of the first five novels in the series and their dates; subsequent titles have been: *The Kindly Ones* (1962), *The Valley of Bones* (1964), *The Soldier's Art* (1966), and *The Military Philosophers* (1968). The twelve novels making up "A Dance to the Music of Time" will, evidently, bring Nicholas Jenkins and his circle into the 1960's. Volume 10, titled *Books Do Furnish a Room,* published in 1971, covers the years 1945 to 1952.

itself, so that public and private do not clash, or if they do, so that art can act as synthesis. This is not to deny change in Powell: his sympathies have grown, indeed broadened. What began as witty and somewhat superficial, the pre-*Dance of Time* novels* in the mode of early Waugh or Huxley, has acquired darker hues, without losing wit or tone. Social comedy has increasingly become social tragedy: as the old world fades, a vacuum is created, to be filled only by the self-serving Widmerpool, the captious, punctilious technician of our own age. Powell's "new world" is not Eden but Marcuse's reduced cosmos of one-dimensional men, constricted, squeezed, ultimately snared by life.

Several passages in *The Military Philosophers* (volume 9) indicate how Powell's winding, twisting method of burgeoning references has moved him deeper into irremediable social tragedy. About midway through this novel, he begins to look upon the Second World War as a form of doom, and moves in and out of Eliot's *Waste Land* as Eliot himself had moved in and out of history: "Although it was London Bridge to which the poem referred, rather than Westminster, the place from which I had just come, the dark waters of the Thames below, the beauty of the day, brought to mind the lines about Stetson and the ships at Mylae, how death had undone so many" (p. 113). Then comes Powell's roll call of the mythical dead, the talented and untalented, the self-willed and the impotent; the frivolous social events of the past, where names were intertwined like dance steps, have become elements of the dance of death. Later in the same novel, when Jenkins is campaigning in the Netherlands, he looks at a military map, and Powell draws together a series of paradoxes, very intricate dance steps:

As the eye travelled northward, it fell on Zutphen, where Sir Philip Sidney had stopped a bullet in that charge against the Albanian cavalry. One wondered why Albanians should be involved in this part of the world at such a time. Presumably they were some auxiliary unit of the Spanish Command, similar to those exotic corps of which one heard rumours in the current war, anti-Soviet Caucasians enrolled in a German formation, American-Japanese fighting with the Allies. The thought of Sidney, a sympathetic figure, distracted attention from the Field-

* *Afternoon Men* (1931), *Venusberg* (1932), *From a View to a Death* (1933), *Agents and Patients* (1936), *What's Become of Waring?* (1939).

Marshal's talk. One felt him essentially the kind of soldier Vigny had
in mind when writing of the man who, like a monk, submitted himself
to the military way of life, because he thought it right, rather than
because it appealed to him. (p. 181)

Jenkins's daydreaming continues and he thinks of Maastricht,
which recalls the poet Rochester, then the prototype of d'Artagnan,
finally swinging back to Jenkins's contemporaries, all of whom, like
Vigny's soldier, are caught in the figure of a vast dance step in
which personal need must be balanced against that of the public.
And this becomes, in its historical and personal involvement, Powell's way of measuring the individual against the impersonal force
of war, even a necessary war. We are reminded of Powell's remark,
as he stated in *Twentieth Century* (July 1961), that he wished to
be ". . . naturalistic, that is to say never to describe anything that
could not have happened in everyday life."

But Powell's Naturalism is not Zola's or Dreiser's, or even Hemingway's. His great ability is to see social history and individual
destiny as mythical, that is, as part of the recurring patterns by
which we would like to explain human history. From the beginning,
with *A Question of Upbringing,* Powell began to develop the myth
of the artist, loosely Orphic and Apollonian, in conflict with the
myth of technology and war, generally but not exclusively Mars.*
These are not irreconcilable opposites, for Powell, neither Homeric
nor Virgilian, attempts no final resolutions. Nicholas Jenkins, Powell's central intelligence, embodies both opposites, for his father was
a military man and he himself is a novelist of growing reputation.
His surname—for what it is worth—points to that whimsical mar-
tial myth, the War of Jenkins' Ear, between Walpole's England and
Spain (1739–41).

* In *A Buyer's Market* (volume 2, p. 177), Jenkins speculates about the relationship between art and power (Apollo and Mars) and how, inevitably, the
one contradicts the aims of the other: "These hinterlands [the painter
Barnby's preoccupation with Baby Wentworth and Sir Magnus Donners]
are frequently, even compulsively, crossed at one time or another by almost
all who practise the arts, usually in the need to earn a living; but the arts
themselves, so it appeared to me as I considered the matter, by their ultimately sensual essence, are, in the long run, inimical to those who pursue
power for its own sake. Conversely, the artist who traffics in power does
so, if not necessarily disastrously, at least at considerable risk."

The myth of Time pervades this conflict between Orpheus and Mars: not the sophisticated Time of Proust's involuntary memory,* or of Yeats's "Hades' bobbin bound in mummy-cloth," but a Time that resembles the more elemental Greek idea of the Fates, who control not only substance but duration. The sequence of novels opens with the magnificent image of Time from a painting by Poussin, the Seasons dancing hand in hand; there, Time becomes the fated dance of mortality, with the appearance and disappearance of partners, the patterns of associations, the interwoven design and fabric of a tapestry.

The use of mythical structures creates unity and coherence in this long series. Myth, by any definition, is a synthetic power, a general and universal force. Some more apparent than others, both primary and subsidiary mythical forms are utilized to get beyond "social comedy" or "satire" or "historical chronicling"—terms usually applied to Powell's work as if to describe his method. If the idea of the series is dialectic, to play off present against past, individual against history, single movement against dance movement, step against series of steps, personal will against zeitgeist—if the sequence is structured on such point and counterpoint, then the emerging structural element must be mythical.

The conflict between the artist myth and the war myth** works

* Through historical allusion and the thick texture of his densely populated scenes, Powell approaches without imitating Proust's great plan. In Proust, the involuntary or unconscious memory frees time from its historical element, releases it from habit. When a sensation evokes the involuntary memory, time is purified of association and, subsequently, is always present. Powell's dance pattern—the ever-repeated pattern of intentions, acts, and consequences—is *his* involuntary memory.
** The Orphic myth—generally associated with the arts, specifically with the power of music—can also be designated as an Apollonian form, although Orpheus does appear prominently in a Bacchic, Dionysiac scene. Orpheus combined conflicting elements—Dionysiac, war-like, frenzied, willed, and Apollonian, artistic, creative, imaginative, civilizing. In still another way, the Orphic myth fits Powell's scheme, if inadvertently. In its development, Orpheus offered the Greek a personal life style, as opposed to the established social and political order he was expected to follow, a philosophy of behavior and a form of belief which could exist outside the established norms, antihistorical as it were. At the same time its concerns touched the established order at several points. Powell uses the myth to provide a structure for the individual moving in society while also moving, according to his needs or eccentricities, outside of it.

out at many levels and unfolds in several variations that are fundamental to a "dance to the music of time." The Orpheus-Mars myth
becomes increasingly prominent in the later volumes, *The Soldier's
Art* and *The Military Philosophers*. There, art both paralleling and
contravening war is virtually the sole theme. But further aspects of
this and other myths appear in various shapes, here as art, there as
war: in the Venus and Tannhäuser symbolism; in Mrs. Erdleigh,
the Cumean Sibyl embodied as Eliot's Madame Sosostris; in the
imagery of the Seven Deadly Sins tableaux; in the periodically
emerging Uncle Giles, a male Persephone; in Nicholas himself,
again like Persephone, sometimes like Adonis, released from the
underworld; in the numerous painters, composers, and writers, Deacon, Barnby, Quiggin, Members, Moreland, Jenkins; in the
variations of the Isis-Osiris axis, which involves family servants,
hangers-on, and a phalanx of relatives.

Along the way, Powell has also redefined our views of Sisyphus,
who was, in his words, "one of those beings committed eternally to
undesired and burdensome labours" (*The Kindly Ones,* p. 148).
Hitherto, our notions of Sisyphus have been directed by Camus's
definition, more heroic and romantic, perhaps, than would appear
applicable to the fifties and sixties. With Sisyphus in mind, Camus
speaks of the absurd man "who wants to find out if it is possible to live *without appeal*"; he speaks of "no fate that cannot be
surmounted by scorn"; he tells us that in consciousness there is
happiness—"one must imagine Sisyphus happy" even as he is frustrated by his eternal punishment. Sisyphus knows the worst, and
yet his *knowing* frees him.

Powell's interpretation of Sisyphus is unique. Frustration, consciousness of failure, confronting the absurd—these are present in
Powell's work; but they lead to will-lessness, resignation, alcoholic
bouts, aimless marriages and remarriages; to man descending the
human scale, definitely not the embodiment of humanity's finest
moments. Nicholas Jenkins—the conductor of Powell's orchestral
selections—is not Camus's embattled warrior, or even one of
Beckett's dying gladiators; he is a cool cat, a hip operator, a young
man who knows all the byroads past condemned property. Nicholas does indeed carry the burdens of Sisyphus, but with a diminished will. Rather than surpassing his material (except possibly as

a rather shadowy novelist), he permits his ambience to engulf him. He personifies the paradox of the age Powell describes, what Arthur Mizener calls Powell's "deep, quiet sense of the twentieth century as a wrecked civilization grubbing along in the shadow of its greatness's ruins." ("The Novel and Nature in the Twentieth Century: Anthony Powell and James Gould Cozzens," in *The Sense of Life in the Modern Novel*, p. 94.)

While he draws on existing mythical forms, Powell also creates many of his own, which become leitmotifs, variations, interpretations, comic comments. Powell's invented myths usually involve Widmerpool; the best example is the episode when Barbara Goring, a minor figure, pours sugar over his head. Another involves his overcoat at school, a Gogolesque coat that haunts one's memories of the man, a coat that merges first with the schoolmaster, Le Bas, and then with the various images of clothing employed throughout the series. Clothes—serving in the art or the theater of war—begin *The Soldier's Art*. Powell speaks of Nicholas's buying an army greatcoat in a place where "two headless trunks stood rigidly at attention." Clothes come to symbolize Art and War: "One of these effigies wore Harlequin's diagonally spangled tights; the other, scarlet full-dress uniform of some infantry regiment, allegorical figures, so it seemed, symbolising dualisms of the antithetical stock-in-trade surrounding them . . . Civil and Military . . . Work and Play . . . Detachment and Involvement . . . Tragedy and Comedy . . . War and Peace . . . Life and Death . . ."

Powell's mind is a ferocious synthesizing force, and the myths he invents wind around and entwine themselves with the more traditional ones. Powell has quintessential control over his material; in this respect, the orchestration of his dance music recalls the *Totentanz* of both Proust and Mann. The early part of *The Military Philosophers*, for example, with its insistent Wagnerian images, indicates how Powell makes variations and wholes interpenetrate like Yeats's gyres. Doris Lessing has been described in terms of the literature of enclosure. Through his myth-making and myth-using powers, Powell turns war into enclosure. He opens *The Military Philosophers* with the first image from *Siegfried:* Mime, in a rocky cave, at his anvil. Powell's Mime is a British lieutenant crouched over a table deep inside a subterranean enclosure. Wagner's Mime, we remember, grouses about "Wearisome torment! / Meaningless toil!" while hammering away at the broken magic sword. Powell's lieutenant sits over wearisome papers, and the war is defined by this: men moving around like insects above and below ground, without heroics, not an enemy in sight, subjected to haphazard bombing patterns, the future leading either to salvation or to doom, the blows of the hammer relentlessly pounding on the anvil.

Powell embroiders like a ballet master choreographing variations, all within a set theme. Lieutenant Mime's subterranean office is a cave parallel to several others, all similarly inhabited by men crouching over their work in endless, meaningless toil. Powell attempts to suggest the historical processes by the images of recurring enclosures, each with its attendant myth. Within thirty pages, the image recurs when Persephone-Nicholas heads into the bowels of the earth, toward a kingdom comparable to Widmerpool's, which in turn recalls Mime and his fellow Nibelungen. "Here, for example, the unsleeping sages of Movement Control spun out their lives, sightless magicians deprived eternally of the light of the sun, while, by their powerful arts, they projected armies or individual over land and sea or through the illimitable wastes of the air." The images provide a vision of the war and particularly of Widmerpool, a figure from Wagnerian opera, a Nietzschean creature of will and determination, a man even like Wagner himself, calculating, solipsistic, and ruthless. Nicholas speaks of himself here as "Orpheus or Herakles returning from the silent shades of Tartarus."

Moving up from the depths of Tartarus, Nicholas comes into further enclosures, Kafkaesque attics under the eaves, little segments of rooms where elves and hermits and prisoners work on huge problems, a kingdom of bureaucracy commanded, in its financial aspects, by Blackhead. A myth of parsimony, Blackhead rules his kingdom as "an anonymous immanence of all their kind, a fetish, the Voodoo deity of the whole Civil Service to be venerated and placated . . . the mystic holy essence incarnate of arguing, encumbering, delaying, hair-splitting, all for the best of reasons." Blackhead's job, as he sees it, is to scrutinize all requisitions in the hopes of discouraging them. Like Widmerpool, he hopes to make the war come to him and lend itself to his personal needs.

So begins *The Military Philosophers*. Thereafter, the images and metaphors move out, at the same time that they rove back into the other novels as well. The Ufford Hotel, the periodic lodging of Nicholas's Uncle Giles, is such a subterranean place; Giles, an underground man, occasionally "surfaces" there mysteriously, like the figures that rise from the Wagnerian depths. The key image is of something prehistoric, a saurian man. All this fits the philosophy of the book: all movement forward is haphazard, the past is never let go, unforeseen shapes unexpectedly loom up, and one's own self has been repeated and duplicated in myriad forms since time began.*

Man exists really only in various disguises or costumes, at several times in history, and he can never escape role-playing, whether he copies literature or history. At the beginning of *The Soldier's Art,* as I suggested above, theater images predominate when Nicholas outfits himself for the war. War becomes a gigantic theatrical machine, a staging area, an artistic process in which the soldier at every level plays a role. Life is an insistent continuum, and the more man struggles through acts of will to get outside of it, the more he is caught up in process. The images of clothing—quite different from Carlyle's—ironically remind us of Archie Gilbert, the party-going clothes horse of earlier volumes, of Widmerpool's overcoat, of English history with its uniforms, of the doffing of uniforms and the return to civilian dress, finally ending *The Military Philosophers* with the word "underclothes"—whose fashion does not change.

Supplementing the Wagnerian and other mythical references, there are repeated allusions to paintings and painters, so that the Belgians to whom Nicholas is attached during the war, who have touches of Bacchus or Silenus, also remind Powell of figures in

---

* In *Casanova's Chinese Restaurant* (p. 174), Nicholas repeats Moreland's metaphor of the Ghost Railway, the mechanical equivalent of Time and a symbol of man's fate: "I thought of his recent remark about the Ghost Railway. He loved these almost as much as he loved mechanical pianos. Once, at least, we had been on a Ghost Railway together at some fun fair or on a seaside pier; slowly climbing sheer gradients, sweeping with frenzied speed into inky depths, turning blind corners from which black, gibbering bogeys leapt to attack, rushing headlong towards iron-studded doors, threatened by imminent collision, fingered by spectral hands, moving at last with dreadful, ever increasing momentum towards a shape that lay across the line."

Memling, Teniers, Brouwer. These art images then carry us back to the very beginning of the series, to *A Question of Upbringing,* in which men working on the street suggest Poussin's Seasons, whose "dance to the music of time" is a reminder of man's mortality. These associations, murky and ambiguous as they are, in turn recall Nicholas's days at school, and the first image we have is of Widmerpool emerging from the fog and ooze of his daily run. "Widmerpool moved on his heels out of the mist," and we are thrown into the personal depths, subterranean rooms, and disguised motifs of the entire series. We see Widmerpool as an "archetypal figure, one of those fabulous monsters that haunt the recesses of the individual imagination." Change the focus slightly and Kafka's intense world of burrows and moles would emerge. Related images wind and rewind, accumulating as they move on, until they become vast symbols suitable for art or war, peace or violence, diffidence or determination.

The theme of love and sex is never far from these mythological figures slogging around in prehistoric slime. And the primary image of all affairs is based on Venus and Tannhäuser, not Tristan and Isolde. Widmerpool is always involved with destructive types—that is, he is attracted to girls who would circumvent his ambitions: Barbara Goring (who pours sugar over his head), Mildred Haycock (with whom he is impotent), Pamela Flitton (for whom all men are grist for her inner rage). None of these women is remotely suitable for a man of ambition who must make his way passionlessly and calculatingly. Yet Widmerpool seems drawn only to the Venus type, which is to say that our view of him is incomplete, as Nicholas recognizes. There are depths in Widmerpool that contradict everything we can say about him, everything he claims for himself. The swamp out of which fragments of him appear is not unlike the unconscious from which desires emerge haphazardly, indeed not unlike Powell's own view of man and history.

But Widmerpool's antic love affairs are merely one part of the soup-mix of balletic marriages. Only Nicholas remains impervious to the alignments and realignments which occur incestuously in this closely organized group. Like large families in Victorian novels that feed marriageable partners to each other, Powell's society provides an endless variety of connubial provender. Four and five marriages are not uncommon. Nick's wife, Isobel, is one of ten Tollands who catch all types of local fish.

Although the series has so far been discussed in a temporal sequence, we should not lose sight of the visual element, which recalls a closely worked tapestry or Oriental rug. In a tapestry of quality, shadows highlight the prominent figures, so that one's initial view of it is often misleading. A good deal depends on the skill of the design and the weave. Powell's insistence, like Proust's, on shadows and shading is nowhere more apparent than in *The Kindly Ones,* where tableaux are formed and reformed. The key scene in the book comes with the depiction of the Seven Deadly Sins in Sir Magnus Donners's castle. Here, his guests, as forerunners of Fellini's depleted party-goers, work out styles of life in terms of the sins they embody. Their arrangement appears casual, and the equation of a character with a specific sin appears equally casual. But Powell shrewdly assigns various roles in the tableaux to derive the most subtle characterization, that is, to suggest shading, backgrounds, secret wishes, conspiratorial desires, destructive impulses. Nicholas himself is Sloth, a witty view of oneself. Acting as puppeteer is Sir Magnus, the camera eye, a voyeur whose morbid sexual practices run like a leitmotif through the series. When Widmerpool, in full uniform, appears, disapproving, the sequence ends: a symbolic confrontation between "progressive" War and "decaying" Art, the imagery recalling Bosch and *Götterdämmerung.*

This combination of time and space, of sequential and visual, is the particular mark of Powell's style. As a stylist, unlike Doris Lessing, he does not plow on or through; he is balletic, graceful, verbally sophisticated. But Powell's style is more complicated. It is not merely verbal; it is not merely graceful arrangement: it is most importantly the combination of a particularizing force with a generalizing power that makes him unique among contemporary English novelists.

In its combination of the particular with the general, of the rapier thrust with the solid background, Powell's series recalls the great fiction created in the first quarter of the twentieth century: Proust, Mann, Gide of *The Counterfeiters,* Lawrence of *The Rainbow* and *Women in Love,* Conrad of *Nostromo.* Vastly different as Powell is from all these, as is each from the other, he has, like them, conveyed the substance and thickness of a society that has a function of its own. For Powell recognizes the residual toughness of this decaying, disintegrating society, chiefly its ability to provide mutations even as it is hell-bent on destroying itself. And this society does, after all, create Art, in that classic dissension between the dissolute imagination and the manly military, between the slothful, impotent Old People who support creativity and the energetic, ambitious New People like Widmerpool who have no use for art or beauty or even people, only work and war.

Such a summation of themes and references makes Powell appear far more diagrammatic than he actually is. For he has brought back, more forcefully than any of his contemporaries, more convincingly even than Sillitoe and Fowles, the English attention to class. And without giving us more than glimpses of the working classes, he has suggested the sense and stuff of a classed society, not doomed, as some critics have stressed, but mutating constantly into other forms; an England as Proteus, an England after two centuries of surfeit and self-neglect slowly coming to terms with an opened Pandora's Box. It is a grand scheme, a panoramic novel that never loses sight of the details that make fiction possible.

With Doris Lessing, Anthony Powell has emerged as a writer who, despite seemingly intractable material, has conveyed the feel of how a modern, civilized, industrial country stumbles along from fate to fate. Our points of reference may be Bosch, the death of the gods, the "kindly" Furies, and medieval tapestries, but the real center is human frailty, fear, impotence in the face of complex challenge, retreat before the larger questions—that is, the full range of the Modern Spirit.

XVII

Postscript:
1960–1970

I N *The English Novel: From Dickens to Lawrence* (1970), Raymond Williams asserts that novelists in 1847–48 began to explore the "substance and meaning of community" differently from their predecessors. This was a time, he says, when living in a community became more uncertain, "more critical, more disturbing" than ever before in history. The major problem for the mid-century novelist was to understand this sense of the "knowable community"; his creative response was that act of social imagination. He writes: "Indeed it is to just this problem of knowing a community—of finding a position, a position convincingly experienced, from which community can begin to be known—that one of the major phases in the development of the novel must be related."

Williams's is a viable argument about the development of the English novel, but he wisely carries it only through Lawrence (d. 1930). In his final chapter, he hesitantly treats the successors to the socially oriented novelists of the late nineteenth and early twentieth centuries, speaking briefly of Joyce Cary, Orwell, Sillitoe. But the entire development of English fiction since World War II has demonstrated that the community Williams speaks about no longer exists. Even C. P. Snow—committed to a stable, optimistic society —recognizes radical changes in this notion of community and calls his final novel *Last Things*. We can no longer speak of "community"² in any nineteenth-century sense. Community of a certain number and kind has become infinite communities. Society is no more the crucible, the "active creator" or "active destroyer" of values and persons, since no one can be sure what society is or where it can be located. Perhaps this is the new sensibility: that community exists wherever the individual rests.

For the contemporary novelist, the situation is critical. And it is this crisis to which Williams should have directed himself in his conclusion. The fiction writer is faced by breakdown on so many levels, without the compensatory idea of communities explored by the nineteenth-century novelist, that he annually finds his material changing. After the Second World War, the traditional sense of community became outmoded, and will remain outmoded until the novelist discerns new formations. While the fifties' fiction of the "Angries" was a response to fragmentation, the novels themselves were inadequate to express it. Still later, in *The Four-Gated City,* Doris Lessing carried the disintegration of community as far as any novelist working in a relatively realistic vein can, and yet she could resolve it only with an apocalyptic vision of nuclear destruction.

The radical constriction of England's power; its economic isolation even from the Continent; its increasing role, under both Macmillan and Wilson, as an American satellite; its loss, because of its economic precariousness, of an independent political voice; the continued devaluation of its currency; the mediocrity of the top leadership in both parties; the perpetuation of class structure despite its obvious disadvantages in an industrial, modern society—all these issues characterized the sixties even more than they did the fifties, but *they are not the major questions.* The essential question, for England with its pervasive traditions, as well as for America with its much shorter history, is how any society can be held together when it is dividing into subinterests and subcultures. The last time English society hung together was during and just after the war, roughly the same years that American society last saw itself united in a common destiny.

The quality of life is the issue in England. The enfeeblement of England's world role, the creation of a "New People" with no traditional allegiances, the increasing repudiation of custom and the historical process, the radical alienation of a large part of its youth, and the development of a pop counter-culture—these are the facts of life in the 1960's, not just in England but in most nations who overrate their image. The novelist's function—if he functions at all—is to create images and symbols comparable to what is occurring. When C. P. Snow early in the decade spoke of the "two cultures," he meant the humanities and science (or technology); but the "two cultures" in England, as elsewhere, more likely would number 200 or 2,000, given the almost infinite subdivision in both establishment and disaffected. Snow speaks of synthesis when the scene is virtual anarchy. In the feeble later work of the 1950's university wits—especially Amis's and Braine's—their hatred for the old forms and traditions took the shape of beer drinking, rubbery faces, and simpering protest, a response that clearly demonstrates their inability to cope with the loss of a viable community. For all its literary value, Powell's *Music of Time* works best in the past, when England still thought of itself as one nation, one people. This assumption no longer holds, and it will be interesting to see how Powell works in the problems of the postwar decades, especially in terms of his narrator, Nicholas Jenkins, who appears well out of things. Doris Lessing ended her series with the apocalypse; Snow terminated his with an inconclusive awareness that times are changing, but without a sense of the real urgency of the change or its effect on every aspect of English life. The only novelist who still seems politically aware—leaving aside Sillitoe's class consciousness—is Doris Lessing.

It is nonetheless difficult to see how political solutions, even if intelligently proposed, can make much difference. Even more difficult to imagine is that such solutions will come from men like Harold Wilson, Edward Heath, or Enoch Powell, whose policies run the gamut from soporific and ineffectual to odious. George Orwell once said that life in England remained attractive because the English did not run around killing each other; but "killing" takes other forms than physical. It is in these areas that the novelist must assume responsibility, though most contemporary English novels seem distant from the scene: William Golding's insipid *Pyramid;* John Fowles's Victorian novel, *The French Lieutenant's Woman;* Iris Murdoch's social comedies that fail to become even the sum of their parts; Kingsley Amis's rewriting of James Bond adventures and support of American Southeast Asia policies; Anthony Burgess's multilingual nostalgia for the fixed past; and so on.

In my Afterword to the original edition of this book, I spoke of the danger that confronted the English novelist of the late fifties. Faced with the buzzing confusion of a society that offered no conclusions or resolutions, the writer would be tempted to withdraw from the large world into the little one. But the result of such indulgence would be finely wrought insignificant novels, or intelligently presented minor fiction, or sharply etched small books. Though works of this kind are always welcome—indeed, are often more intelligent than large and pretentious novels—nevertheless, fiction needs weight as well as intelligence, size as well as manner, and breadth as well as nuance.

There is no denying the extreme difficulties facing the English novelist as community after community in a tradition-bound country breaks down into subcultures. When Raymond Williams speaks of the Victorian novelists meeting such divisiveness at mid-century, he really must distinguish between what breakdown meant in 1848–68 and what it means in this century. Change is not constant. Whatever the difficulties confronting the Victorian novelist, he knew what his society was; and in whatever ways he opposed his society, he knew what he was opposing. And even when he seemed to be of the devil's party and supported philosophical anarchy, he knew that the goal was still order, balance, moderation. For him, anarchy was a step toward some kind of development. None of this holds true for the contemporary English novelist. If he is completely honest with himself, he will find himself adrift. Only Alan Sillitoe identifies with a distinct community, the working class, all the while hoping that it will provide a revolution based on life, survival, grittiness. But the working class is no longer a class, is not at all monolithic. It too has fragmented into individuals who group themselves, according to common interests and tastes, into subcultures.

Adrift, identity-less, isolated from society and even from community, cut off from viable traditions, his country constricted, its reputation limited, its advice scorned—the contemporary English writer, the emerging writer of the seventies, faces monumental tasks quite different from those of his predecessors in this or the last century. Overriding all, Doris Lessing reminds us, is final destruction, the beast of the apocalypse, Yeats's rough monster slouching toward Bethlehem. Naturalism, Symbolism, Realism, Existentialism—all the old tags and methods—are somewhat beside the point, for the vision will determine the mode, and the vision will determine whether the English novel, like the country itself, will constrict to a tight little island.

Nigel Dennis

With *Cards of Identity* (see p. 249), Nigel Dennis appeared to be the kind of satirist that postwar England needed; but he cut back sharply on his fiction, wrote a brief study of Swift, and published only *A House in Order,* in 1966. This is a beautifully planned and written short novel that curiously dissipates its energies at nearly every turn. It is a parable that cuts through all political, social, and cultural categories. The protagonist, unnamed, is a prisoner throughout most of the novel, a prisoner of war, moreover, in a run-down greenhouse in what appears to be Sweden. He is a cartographer by profession and a horticulturist by avocation. His captors are an assortment of military men and civilians who compete for his talents while trying to prove that he is really a spy left behind by their enemy to chart the country. Lying in the shadow of a POW camp, the greenhouse becomes a way-station for the escape of prisoners, escapes engineered by the mythical figure called MacKenzie, the only character with a name in the novel.

The unnamed protagonist is not only a horticulturist but virtually a plant. In the deep winter, like his plants he freezes in his greenhouse, and in the spring he thaws out, as does his greenery. A whim of his captors, he is also a whim of the seasons and of Nature; all life depends on the warmth of the sun. And in a greenhouse, he gains the rays of the sun in the way that all Nature achieves life. The only thing that keeps him going is his sense of natural preservation, and to this end he tries, with rudimentary equipment, to grow things, to make something come alive. As the oldest of artists—those who embrace Nature in their artwork—he achieves a rare plant not seen for one hundred years. And this work, which catches the eye of a master agronomist, eventually saves him.

A House in Order works by implication rather than by achievement. But while implication is the heart of parable, the *novel as parable* demands more. Large questions about the nature of existence arise, as do equally large questions about the nature of reality. After all, the protagonist sees everything through glass, and in turn is seen through glass; he reflects and is reflected, so that objects are never clearly viewed. The very title of Dennis's earlier *Cards of Identity* suggests similar problems. Also, the protagonist of *A House in Order* is a stranger throughout, referred to by his work as Mr. Cartographer, Mr. Spy, etc. He is a pawn, the subject of controversy among his captors, as well as alienated from the other prisoners. At the same time he is a prisoner who fears freedom and pleads for the protection of his enemies. He especially fears his fellow prisoners, whose walls are within sight, and he despises MacKenzie for making him take a heroic posture he does not feel. He considers the greenhouse a refuge, even though the cold may kill him. His only support is his ability as a horticulturist, Candide tending his garden under conditions Voltaire would have found insufferable.

Perhaps Dennis means no more than this. Certainly the novel has a simple line, like the narratives of Voltaire, without the technical manipulations of *Cards of Identity*. Possibly it is no more than a kind of intellectual sport, itself a reflector of man's condition, modern man immured in a greenhouse, a captive trying to ally himself with Nature and Art (however inconsistent the marriage may be), unnamed, a stranger to all. Ultimately, the novel is a parable about England reduced to plant life, greenhouse, and insects.

Lawrence Durrell

Tunc (1968) and *Nunquam* (1970) form a diptych, Lawrence Durrell's first long fiction since *The Alexandria Quartet*. The cast of characters is familiar: Benedicta here is Justine; Julian is Nessim; the narrator, Felix Charlock, is Darley, now an inventor, and so on. But the characters of the *Quartet* found their place in time and space; and against the background of Alexandria, where anything was made to seem possible, *they* seemed possible. But in *Tunc,* the equivalent tortured and agonized figures, extracted from a place, have no sense of life, and their antics are strung-out trivia, bad puns and jokes.

Felix works for Merlin, a gigantic international cartel with holdings in everything; its executive officer is the tortured Julian, a kind of Howard Hughes, who collects movie stars, companies, inventions, bodies and souls. He has everything a man could want except testicles, which, we discover, were lost in a scene reminiscent of Abelard's misfortune, the romantic object being, in Julian's case, his sister. It all seems like a Kingsley Amis retread of James Bond without the bedroom athletics and other derring-do, a bout of weak camp, an unconvincing instant replay of what once worked well. One character says of another: "He has been slumming among the Gnostics, selling his birthright for a pot of message. He will end by becoming an Orthodox Proust or a monarcho-Trappist." There is no way to relate this to life, either natural or supernatural, only to poor taste and miscalculation of effects.

Durrell has said that the reader should not judge *Tunc* without seeing *Nunquam.* By that, he meant that several of the mysteries of the first novel would be worked out in the sequel, like the plan of the *Quartet.* But *Nunquam* is very thin, material for a tongue-in-cheek short story. The plot hangs on the construction of a life-like model based on Iolanthe, the prostitute-turned-movie-star whom in life Julian idolized from a distance. After she dies, he commissions Felix, like Frankenstein, to build a perfect Iolanthe, a work of art that will improve on nature. The result of modern technology is an Iolanthe who surpasses the original, has perfect skin and sexual organs, exudes only enticing odors, and does everything except eat and excrete, but those functions are in the works.

Durrell has mastered a mock-scientific jargon for these novels and has tried a sweeping satire on modern technology, very different from his reliance on a singular time and place in the *Quartet.* Yet it is difficult to see for what end. The level of wit is indicated in the anagram of *Tunc,* which works out to Cunt after a couple of letter reversals. And *Nunquam* is not much better.

These novels, coming as Durrell's first major effort since the *Quartet,* will inevitably force a downgrading of those earlier books. James Gindin, in *Postwar British Fiction* (1962), after sympathetic sections devoted to Wain, Amis, Waterhouse, and other kindred protesters, includes Durrell in a chapter called "Current Fads." By sifting through for Durrell's more exotic passages, Gindin ridicules the entire *Alexandria Quartet* and says it is possibly even an "elaborate hoax." It does seem strange to deprecate as "faddish" Durrell's attempt to create something—however ornate, even fruity—while lauding Amis's work after *Lucky Jim,* which is tepid, uninspired, flatly written comedy. My comment is cautionary: that hindsight should not judge the *Quartet* by the unfortunate *Tunc* and *Nunquam.* Those novels miss their mark at nearly every turn; they strain after cleverness and modernity, and, in the end, all that is apparent is the rupture between intention and deed.

William Golding

In his two novels of the sixties, *The Spire* (1964) and *The Pyramid* (1966), William Golding continued to stress the isolated individual who must either find ways to restrain himself or else destroy everyone around him. But his demonstration of this almost obsessive idea has become even more singular, so that in *The Spire* Jocelin's compulsion to build the spire, which serves as focus for all his energies, is merely a naked demonstration of will. The spire and apple tree dominate, almost to the exclusion of all other life, and as such they are direct, simplistic symbols that draw life from the novel rather than giving it.

Other readers—notably Bernard Oldsey and Stanley Weintraub, in *The Art of William Golding* (1965)—have seen the spire and apple tree as complex, all-inclusive symbols. In this view, both spire and apple tree lead to the sacred, with the spire poking toward God and the apple tree evoking the Fall, man's expulsion from Eden. But one's quarrel is not with the meaning of the symbols themselves—their texture should depend on what the author imbues them with: however, the main character's one-dimensional response to those symbols tends to thin them out.

This singular attachment to the thing itself, here to Jocelin's sense of purpose, even when purpose is connected to the loss of self or to one's fall from grace, drains the novel, not the reader. The idea of such a man and of his wavering position vis-à-vis God seems more intense than Golding's execution; or, rather, the idea has preempted the creation of the complex terms by which such ideas can be communicated artistically. Golding has combined elliptical language with oblique scenes, often in the style of Robert Browning's poetic dramas, but the aura of significant import is deceptive.

One is reminded of Golding's remark on the BBC that he liked to think of himself as a myth-maker rather than as a fabulist. "I do feel fable as being an invented thing on the surface whereas myth is something which comes out from the roots of things in the ancient sense of being the key to existence." Golding had in mind, evidently, myths rooted in the sacred world, defined by Mircea Eliade as part of the original creation. In such a world and in such terms, the construction of a house—like Jocelin's (Salisbury) cathedral and spire—is symbolic of man's imitation of the works of God, the cosmogony itself. "The house," Eliade writes, "is an *imago mundi*. The sky is conceived as a vast tent supported by a central pillar; the tent pole or the central post of the house is assimilated to the Pillars of the World and is so named."

This distinction between myth and fable is probably a major key to understanding Golding's work, and he feels he has achieved the manner of myth; but the reader remains dubious and senses the factitiousness of fable. In a 1962 interview at Purdue University, Golding admitted that society in the usual sense is not significant in his work, that he is more caught up in the development of the innocent spirit toward greater experience; and yet the myth-making power is rarely neglectful of a society or of social values, while the creature from fable does stand outside, in high relief. Had Golding been able to give Jocelin, in his quest for spiritual power represented by the spire, the mythical strength of a flawed Prometheus—

as the terms of the novel appear to indicate he tried to do—then *The Spire* might have existed in the domain he speaks of.

The second of the two novels, *The Pyramid,* defies discussion. It is a departure from Golding's other works, lacking their tense, anxious presence. Oliver of *The Pyramid* has not fallen, at least not seriously—he is no Samuel Mountjoy—and his career is chiefly a series of vignettes in which he grows to manhood and understanding. The manner is intended to have serio-comic undertones; the characters, except for Oliver, are small-town people reminiscent of those in Wells's *Kipps* or *Mr. Polly.* The book is a strange agglomerate of shallow intentions and unresolved achievements, almost a throwaway. It adds nothing to our understanding of either Golding or ourselves. Wells, clearly, did it better.

Since Golding's work in the previous decade has slackened, it may be time to take another look at *Lord of the Flies,* which is now seventeen years old. No English writer of the last generation has been as closely identified with a single book, and in America only Salinger's *Catcher in the Rye* comes to mind as a comparable phenomenon. Yet the Salinger book has not held up well over the years; Holden has proven too innocent, too romantic, ultimately too much an American Adam. Must we say the same of the Golding novel—that after a decade of acclaim by academic critics, its psychological apparatus no longer engages the mature reader? That despite its evident concern with evil, despite its broad allegorical implications, despite its often striking lyricism of phrase and scene, despite Golding's ability to create a distinct world—that despite all these obvious virtues, the novel does not extend beyond itself and become wedged into our consciousness? Or can we say that it fills out enough of its own myth so that, like *Robinson Crusoe* and *Heart of Darkness,* it generates a power that goes beyond word and phrase?

One of the chief difficulties is, of course, that no single character obtrudes. The counter-argument would be that the island, or the isolated situation itself, is the chief character; but what goes on is too full of people not to produce a protagonist. Furthermore, a book fathering only children has its problems when it attempts to move beyond a children's world. Ideologically, *Lord of the Flies* and *Heart of Darkness* are analogous, and in that comparison perhaps we can see why one remains in a minor genre while the other works for each new generation. We remember that in 1962 Golding said he had never read *Heart of Darkness,* but read it or not, he is treading on Conrad's territory, not only in *Lord of the Flies* but throughout his entire canon.

The essential basis for comparison is that both Golding and Conrad interested themselves in situations that offer no other restraint except what the self may provide. Somewhere one must find it, and it is an individual, not a social, matter. Restraint is a muscular courage not to do, and it marks the difference between civilization and capitulation to savagery. Yet where does it come from? How does one obtain it, especially if it is innate and not social? Conrad's chief example of someone lacking restraint is Kurtz: he goes to the Congo as a missionary and his final solution for the savage is to kill him. It is Conrad's irony that Kurtz is doing the world's dirty work and represents not barbarism but the forces of civilization.

Golding's children, except for Ralph, Simon, and Piggy, become barbaric like Kurtz, reverting to a level of savage behavior that pokes through their civilized veneer. The boys undergo considerable loss of restraint, at the same time gaining some consciousness of their debasement. If Golding had left it at that, he might have had a symbolic action of some magnitude. But the deus ex machina of naval officers saves Ralph from the pack and the pack itself from the fire; this changes all the terms. For with the officers, Golding is saying that the adult world offers the safeguards of civilization, that those officers, with their spotless uniforms and their spick-and-span cruiser, offer an alternative to the boys, who had "let go." Thus restraint is still possible, and it is British; one had simply expected better behavior of the boys.

Conrad had avoided this very point. If restraint or the lack of it is to be taken seriously—and that is a dubious proposition to begin with—then it cannot first be questioned in boys only to be demonstrated in adults. The quality either exists or does not exist. Golding resolves the entire question by falling back on British civilization; while Conrad's Marlow, much chastened, much tempted, almost seduced, goes back to preserve civilization with a lie. Golding has reduced his situation to a preachment, to the effect that these boys have grown up. Ralph weeps for his loss of innocence and for the fall of Piggy and man; but Marlow's lies about himself and about Kurtz are too deep-seated for tears. They embody ironies and paradoxes for which there is no explanation, and they permeate everywhere as a condition of both civilization and savagery. Golding has made the situation into games, savage though they are, while Conrad would suggest that naval officers commit their own brand of atrocities.

Possibly *Lord of the Flies* has been so well received by students because it seems to offer a paradigm of the adult world; but it does no such thing. In Golding's terms, the adult world is a hedge against what the children experience in themselves, and therefore those who read the book seeking a broader statement are bound to be disappointed. A complacent Christian morality hangs heavy on the novel, from the choir boys' doffing of their robes decorated with crosses to Jack's tears of repentance and the gaining of self-knowledge. Golding wants to show that evil lurks beneath smooth surfaces, ready to poke out, not to make a social or political point about children and from them about the adult world. This is another way of saying that Golding's concern with moral issues, with the secular fall from grace, never approaches the intensity of *Heart of Darkness* or Camus's *The Fall*.

Graham Greene

Most of Graham Greene's press* in the sixties has been of the ho-hum variety, implying gently that the old dog is displaying old tricks which have by now become clichés. But often Greene's so-called tricks are richer than the virgin inventions of much better-received novelists. While there is much repetition from book to book, there are, nevertheless, certain things Greene does better than most living novelists.

The weak parts of *A Burnt-Out Case* are apparent: most obvi-

* For *A Burnt-Out Case* (1961) and *The Comedians* (1966).

ously, the striving for a religious allegory and the ridiculous symbolic names (Deo Gratias, Querry-Christ, Marie Rycker, still another, earlier Marie, Father Thomas and Father Joseph, et al.). Here Greene is playing out the conflicting elements of his own dialectic rather than moving toward a new way of seeing or a new way of resolving. But there is something quite alien behind Greene's by-now institutionalized categories of God and the devil embracing, of Marian worship, of the victim-devil as saved; behind this is a sharply felt attitude that Greene projects in appropriate images. A famous architect, Querry, a man who has tempted both God and the devil, now wishes to hide, is trying desperately to find a place, any place, where he can go unrecognized. He is metaphorically a "burnt-out case," a technical term referring to a person cured of leprosy but severely disfigured: Querry is cured of the disease but also of life.

This theme recalls Conrad's *Victory,* wherein Axel Heyst, another burnt-out case, seeks an island refuge. But entanglements follow upon the wish, and there are no hiding places. Heyst and Lena (Magdalene, another Mary) become Querry and Marie. Querry also recalls Kurtz, a second burnt-out case, here victimizer as well as victim. This kind of man operates well in the jungle or at sea; in lesser novels, he joins the Foreign Legion or the Green Berets. His prototype outside literature is T. E. Lawrence, who used the desert, like the sea or the jungle, to seek anonymity. Such a man's motto is stated early on in the novel, a parody of Descartes, "I feel discomfort, therefore I am alive."

Greene has always maintained that this type of character, hiding, moving from one refuge to another, full of hate or whisky or acedia, turned against life, virtually impotent against (self-) destructive forces, has insights into the nature of spirituality or devilishness denied the man who moves normally. This is a psychological assumption that most readers of contemporary literature would share. Pain deepens awareness of surrounding phenomena; stopping in the middle forces recognition; interrogation of self unbalances one's field of force; going underground shifts one's alliances, gives angles of vision denied those who refuse to make the journey. Dostoyevsky pioneered here, Conrad followed, and Greene and Golding are perhaps the last serious heirs in England. In Greene's aseptic view, laughter becomes an alien language, triumph is another form of disgust, love is a physical mockery, and all social relationships smack of loss. He who chooses exalted suffering over cheap happiness is apparently a loser, although in Greene's book he has gained insight, a form of salvation. Any journeyman novelist can tell us as much, but Greene is capable in his best fiction of finding correlatives for such feelings of exhaustion, languor, spiritual death. A period of thirty years in which Greene has been raking over the despoiled ecology of the self culminates in *A Burnt-Out Case*.

At the beginning of Part Six, Marie Rycker breathes in the smell of stale margarine, "which she would always associate with marriage, and from where she sat she could see the corner of the engine-house, where they were feeding the ovens with the husks." Stale margarine becomes a metaphor for a burnt-out Querry as well as for a sexually revolted Marie and, by extension, for all relationships that have no feeling in them. This is, in fact, a novel about staleness, bad odors, stunted forms; and the juxtaposition of the stale smell with the ovens creates a sexual image of nausea. The enticing odor of virgins becomes the sour, vaginal smell of frustrated wives sweltering and rotting, exuding not even rancid butter but margarine.

In *The Comedians,* the Congo, Mexico, or Brighton becomes Haiti under President Papa Doc Duvalier. The burnt-out lepers become both the enervated main character and the burnt-out, soulless Tontons Macoute, the president's bogey-men, who wear dark glasses and commit their violence after sundown. While the landscape is typically Greene, the novel is too diffuse, as though it were a series of interrelated excerpts from his earlier novels. The saint-like Mr. and Mrs. Smith, the forces of evil embodied in the Tontons Macoute, the liar and cheat Jones, the lost, giving woman, the anger at American foreign policy, the aura of Catholic corruption, the dialectic of religion and politics, the tortured narrator who has lost his fortune and his beliefs—all these are familiar. Brown, the protagonist, is brown, as well as "browned-off," and, like another Browne, of Joyce's "The Dead," he serves a function rather than becoming himself. On such a stage, everyone who tries to live, including both victims and victimizers, is a Comedian. But Greene has only begun to demonstrate this rather grand theme of cosmic comedians; it, in fact, requires great satire, not a grim book that is not far from a movie script.

Iris Murdoch

Despite her abundance of ideas and a productivity that results yearly in a novel of good length, Iris Murdoch's achievement remains puzzling.* *The Nice and the Good* and *A Fairly Honourable Defeat,* along with *Bruno's Dream,* are examples of her latest work, and they do prove enigmatic. By now she has become adroit at social comedy, at witty dialogue, especially at suggesting existential situations for people who live rather dully. She makes ordinary people take chances and watches their antics with much amusement, before allowing them to pull back into dull, normalizing situations. What she has presented is a kind of puppet show, created for our amusement rather than for our edification, all brightly done, but rather heavily based on existential notions of freedom and necessity, consciousness and unconsciousness. The dialogues have the brittleness and malevolent perkiness of those in Ivy Compton-Burnett's novels; the latter's presence, in fact, is powerfully felt. The language is crisp, the characters drawn within their social functions as well as their individual talents; the scenes often have great narrative power. Topping all is a piquant, somewhat sadistic need on the author's part to see people perform for the pleasure of others. Withal, styles clash, and something is lopsided.

If Iris Murdoch's philosophy ostensibly celebrates life, one senses an exhaustion, so that even sex is no longer a relief. People now create *roles* around their sexual tastes, or else project illusions that they are participants. Sex itself is willy-nilly, at one time serious, even grim, at another frivolous. *A Fairly Honourable Defeat*

* After *A Severed Head,* in 1961, Miss Murdoch's fiction for the decade has been: *An Unofficial Rose* (1962), *The Unicorn* (1963), *The Italian Girl* (1964), *The Red and the Green* (1965), *The Time of the Angels* (1966), *The Nice and the Good* (1968), *Bruno's Dream* (1969), and *A Fairly Honourable Defeat* (1970).

devotes dozens of pages to two wearisome homosexuals, whose "marriage" is only of interest—and that minimal—because they are both males. The sly bitchiness of one, Axel, is low-drawer Oscar Wilde. Similarly, in *The Nice and the Good,* John Ducane may be AC/DC, or even have all power turned off, and it does not really matter. In Miss Murdoch's "entertainments," people slither through their lives playing to the audience, indifferently having a good cry or a good laugh or a good or bad screw. And around them fastidious, controlled language plays like Mozart sonatas. It is all very unreal, neither altogether solemn enough to give us a sense of futility nor witty enough to give us distance on such puppets, ants, and performing animals. Miss Murdoch appears to be between styles, or else the styles she has attempted have not proven fruitful for her kind of inquiring, philosophical mind. The mind is almost always more compelling than the fiction.

Iris Murdoch's most meaningful fiction was that done at the beginning of the 1960's, with *A Severed Head, An Unofficial Rose,* and *The Unicorn.* From the vantage point of several years and six more novels, it appears safe to say that in those three books she had found her manner. There she wedded symbol or myth with intellectual discussions of freedom and her special kind of bedroom farce. Coming from the more traditional *Sandcastle* and *Bell,* in *A Severed Head* she attempted to probe the orderliness of English society to the anger, violence, passion, and desire for bizarre communion which lies beneath. Whether in a drawing room, a barren castle, or a rose garden, she sought sincerity, good faith, honest commitment; or, at least, forced her characters to recognize their existential states.

In spite of her sympathetic book *Sartre: Romantic Rationalist* (1953), it is a mistake to call Iris Murdoch a Sartrian. But in the course of this short study she worked out ideas that found substance in her three "mid-career" novels, ideas that increasingly take issue with Sartre's reliance on obsessive self-analysis and rejection of the other as object. In the January 1961 *Encounter,* Iris Murdoch further attacked Sartre's views on contingency and necessity: "We are not isolated free-choosers, monarchs of all we survey, but benighted creatures sunk in a reality whose nature we are constantly and overwhelmingly tempted to deform by fantasy.

. . . Simone Weil said that morality was a matter of attention not of will. We need a new vocabulary of attention." Literature, Miss Murdoch says, can serve this function, arming us against fantasy and helping us "recover from the ailments of Romanticism."

As a novelist, Iris Murdoch weds British empiricism with quasi-Sartrian ideas of free will. She is concerned not so much with self-analysis as with its consequences, specifically with the translation of self-knowledge—however imperfect—into forms of action, really into the act of love. Love is the great mystique, and its forms, she observes with wit and sadness, are virtually infinite. "What if we realise," she writes in her book on Sartre, "that value is a function of the movement or yearning of our consciousness?" She then asks, "Is man condemned to the same fruitless pursuit, even in his very realisation of its fruitlessness? . . . Can the self-aware unillusioned consciousness take itself as a value, or must the valuable be always the transcendent something by which it is haunted?" These questions are crucial, particularly to *A Severed Head,* where the manipulation of characters superficially appears to be mere drawing-room comedy.

Martin Lynch-Gibbon, a wine dealer, sets the dialectic ajar from the first, as a male narrator in a novel written by a woman. The sexual transference is further intensified by the introduction of Honor Klein, a Japanese sword-wielding anthropologist, a Medusa-like woman of great ugliness and magnetism, the Sibyl of Cumae in mufti, a more vigorous Tiresias. "I am a severed head," she says with authority, "such as primitive tribes and old alchemists used to use" for uttering prophecies. Through her hair, her sword, her Fateful appearances, she is the female Martin has feared (he had married a woman many years older than himself).

The situation is typical Murdoch. A solipsistic person who has treated others as objects of convenience suddenly finds his self-enclosed world threatened. His life must undergo a change that will radically alter his view of himself. His ego, which he had accepted as determined and fixed, must be reformed to accept the existence of others, and he must learn to love. At the very end of *A Severed Head,* to illustrate her point, Iris Murdoch cites the tale of the friends Gyges and Candaules. At Candaules' insistence, Gyges peeps at his friend's naked wife, while she, subsequently, because she has been seen, asks Gyges to kill her husband and assume the throne. Martin, like Gyges, has seen Honor in the embrace of her half brother and is now ready for the throne, an experience that will turn an impotent Fisher King into someone worthy of "Honor Little."

After *A Severed Head,* Iris Murdoch moved into a more objective phase in which her models were nineteenth-century English fiction. In her various essays on novel-writing, and especially in "The Sublime and the Beautiful Revisited" (*Yale Review,* XLIX, Winter 1960, pp. 247–71), she has demonstrated her preference for writers who allow their characters to exist apart from the author; in this group, of which two members are Shakespeare and Tolstoy, she includes the major nineteenth-century English novelists, Scott, Austen, Eliot. Iris Murdoch opposes the moderns, whose work is either "crystalline": allegorical, generalized, subjective, deliberately ambiguous; or "journalistic": political, contemporary, thin, even documentary. In both crystalline and journalistic fiction, the author "uses" his characters, instead of giving them a lead of their own.

An Unofficial Rose seems to be Miss Murdoch's homage to the Victorian novel. The ingredients are there: the objectified characters, the formal symbols of art and money, the religious undertones, the quasi-Jamesian dialectic and dialogue, the conflict between freedom and discipline, etc. The "unofficial rose" is one that grows wild as opposed to one that is cultivated. Tension will arise between the "roses" that give themselves up to their passions and those that admit only discipline for fear of passion. The models are Jamesian, *The Wings of the Dove* and *The Golden Bowl,* for example. The Golden Bowl here is a Tintoretto, owned by Hugh Peronett: a connection to an older world, while at the same time its monetary value immerses it in a newer.

With the sale of the painting, Randall, Hugh's son, can run off with Lindsay Rimmer, herself a little golden object of calculating love and affection. This is the central action, and around it revolves one set of manipulations after another. Each person appears to test his notion of freedom against moral decisions he must make, and simultaneously he finds that moral decisions have become choices fraught with self-interest. This dialectic works out at various levels, with the cultivated roses, the basis of the Peronett money, never too distant. In various guises, the roses are art, God, love, family, discipline, limitation. Of course, the unofficial rose is a "miracle of nature" and "owed nothing to the hand of man."

In the center of this play between man and nature is Emma Sands, a literary lion in the James manner, who acts as a kind of Prospero. She arranges and rearranges, controls all in the past and present. Jamesian, Olympian, Imperial, she directs human freedom, in the style of Fowles's Magus. There is no question that Iris Murdoch has created objective characters and that twists and turns in the plot have their valid explanation in human motivation. But the whole is less impressive than the filigree work, and too much energy is dissipated in sheer cleverness. Scope is sacrificed to witty solutions. Eventually, Miss Murdoch violates her own rules and does not give her characters the rope they need; for she indulges in what must either rise to satire or flatten out to allegory.

In *The Unicorn,* the last of these three books, one finds Miss Murdoch exploring the Gothic tradition, the Brontës and Le Fanu in particular, Jane Austen's *Northanger Abbey,* Hardy's dark tragedies. The landscape is particularly forbidding and ungiving: it is ever present as a restriction on freedom rather than a romantic expression of self. The threat of Nature provides an inflexible background for people who live by enslaving each other. Marian Taylor (a virgin Mary), the companion of Hannah Crean-Smith, visits Gaze Castle, where each character has in him elements of the harsh, brutal landscape. Such elements are expressed in Iris Murdoch's typical symbols of sexual dislocation or eccentricity, here homosexual, lesbian, sadistic, masochistic, etc. At the bottom of this Sadean human pyramid is Hannah, somewhat deranged, the victim who receives all their gifts of pain, cruelty, and abnormality.

Every attempt to gain freedom for Hannah only drives her further into captivity. Each attempt on Marian's part to bring salvation in unforeseen ways makes Hannah's situation more untenable; Marian's final interference drowns her at the moment that she would be free of her tormentors.

The novel has the interest of a gloomy, storm-ridden landscape. Locale, as well as situation, recalls a medieval scene, Childe Roland, the helpless girl guarded by dragon(s), the virgin imprisoned by sadistic priests or aristocrats, the innocent victim weighed down with the sins of others. The mythical one-horned creature of the title is the emblem of chastity and faultlessness; it can be tamed only by the innocent, and consequently evades capture. Hannah is the unicorn at bay: but in Miss Murdoch's handling, the single horn often becomes the twin horns of the cuckold.

The novel has interest only on its own terms. As soon as one attempts to question lines and ideas, the book becomes intellectual camp. Too many statements and ideas are hung on people incapable of sustaining them. Innocence victimized in a remote castle and the innocent figure testing her captors' sense of freedom: both notions seem ponderous in a novel that is as tongue-in-cheek as *Northanger Abbey*. Though her manner is sustained, Iris Murdoch does not succeed in pulling together the conceptual part of her argument, that people must lose themselves to achieve love, to allow love to penetrate. These concepts, fine in themselves, do not mesh with the sexual episodes, which are like intertwined arms and legs in jujitsu practice. Freedom, mind, and sex are at odds with the Gothic setting. Too many dark elements are loaded on to a witty frame. For all its expertness of construction and dialogue, *The Unicorn* is only intermittently satisfactory intellectual sport; it is, unfortunately, a portent of much of Miss Murdoch's work in the later 1960's.

Alan Sillitoe

Since *The General* (1960) and *Key to the Door* (1961), Alan Sillitoe has been working on a trilogy of novels built around the working-class protagonists Frank Hawley and Albert Handley, of which the first two have appeared, *The Death of William Posters* (1965) and *Tree on Fire* (1967), with the third expected in 1972–73. The two novels recall the best of Sillitoe, his work in *The Loneliness of the Long-Distance Runner,* and they also revive a question which most contemporary English writers have treated as if it were settled, that of class, class distinctions, class hatred. Sillitoe is excellent at catching the sharp, acrid hatred that the working classes feel for those born to power and position. And while hatred is not the noblest of passions, it does become, in the hands of a good writer, a matter of individual consciousness, indeed a point of definition and identity, an existential coordinate.

Sillitoe is not interested in the "New People," as represented by Fowles's Clegg in *The Collector,* who is caught between aspirations and stands for nothing. Sillitoe's working class represents a different culture and different tastes from those of the leisure class, and its aspirations are often based on hard-headedness, violence, anger. The working class, Sillitoe feels, is at least occasionally capable of good faith, while the other classes are not, not even sporadically.

The first novel of the trilogy, *The Death of William Posters,* takes its name from the legendary William Posters, an eternal fugitive, the man who refused to remain in one place and stabilize. He is for Frank Hawley a model, running from family, job, security, and moderation toward some open-ended form of self-consciousness. Hawley is evidently an extension of Arthur Seaton of *Saturday Night,* although more mature and less of a heel. In fact, although Hawley does appear connected to the earlier Seaton, Sillitoe has moved beyond anger and dissolution toward some understanding of the anguished, tortured underground man who seeks reciprocated love while resisting its stabilizing force. Put another way, Hawley yearns for an impossible love in which his strong sense of the working class is not lost and in which there is still potential growth. The novels take the form of an odyssey, with Hawley a modern Ulysses, moving from England to Algeria to fight in the rebellion, and then returning to England to rejoin his Penelope and Telemachus, the quasi-faithful Myra and his son Mark.

Hawley dominates the first volume, and his friend, the painter Albert Handley, is the focus of the second, with large sections devoted to Frank in Algeria. Sillitoe's evident point is to see the working-class artist, Handley, still in England, and the working-class revolutionary, Hawley, in Algeria. Their names show that they are to be thought of as doubles. Together, they indicate the possibilities of a working-class revolution, the theme that occupies the political center of the second book in the trilogy. But more important is the novelistic sense of the second volume, its wit, and, above all, Sillitoe's creation of Handley. He superficially recalls Cary's Gulley Jimson, the romantic artist who structures his life on splashes of color; but Jimson, despite his admirers, was too clearly the artist straining to cut a "sorry" figure. Handley, on the other hand, is very much part of the scene, and Sillitoe succeeds in the extremely difficult task of making us feel that Handley *is* an artist.

In nearly every respect, Handley convinces, from his rages which boil up from seemingly minor causes, to his championing of revolutionary movements. Also, Sillitoe makes him intelligent, not illogical and incoherent because he is artist. Near the end of *A Tree on Fire,* Handley says: " 'What I'm talking about is the common quest for spiritual energy that you get from the idea of revolution.' "

Revolution itself is tied firmly to the symbol of a particular tree, which a French plane in Algeria repeatedly bombs with napalm. The tree is desecrated, burned to the ground: "It burned in a circle of fire, and the longer Frank watched, the more surprised he was that the tree should take so long to be consumed." The tree is both the symbol of Algeria and Yggdrasill, the Norse Tree of the Universe. Its three roots spread out to wells, which sustain it even while it is being threatened; it denotes both wisdom and substance. In the Algerian tree, a man lies dead, killed by the impact of the bomb, a human being holding on, even in death, to the tree of life. Here, in this symbol, one has Sillitoe's vision, first of Algeria and then of all those who seek fulfillment in the desert.

Sillitoe appears to be almost the only contemporary English author of stature who takes working-class political ideas seriously and tries to see beyond the democratic well-being of England to world movements. Unlike Doris Lessing, who in her later fiction has recoiled politically, Sillitoe refuses to be disillusioned because he feels the working class has a reservoir of energy that can be directed toward violent change. Unlike Doris Lessing, he seeks alternatives—at the end of *A Tree on Fire,* in a commune—that involve struggling against mass destruction and denying an apocalyptic end. Albert Handley becomes a successful and sought-after painter, but he nurses his rage, is true to his anger, refuses to bend. An infuriating man in his fluctuations of behavior, he is trying himself against Dostoyevsky's challenge: if one wishes to achieve consciousness, one must confront the terrible loneliness and emptiness within. Like the long-distance runner, one must freely throw aside all external support.

And, wonder of wonders! the novels are not grim; the second is, in fact, extremely witty. Handley's family has the eccentricity and wit of people acting naturally, the type of thing Powell and Waugh felt was possible only with the upper middle class. The Handley family is completely mobilized for the revolution, with arms, a vicious watchdog, sons trained as insurrectionists, a deranged uncle at the headphones picking up messages from the world; now one family, later the whole country. Sillitoe has consolidated his political vision with his artistic aims: after a deadening flatness of language in some of his earlier books, his current prose is fully up to his ideas. While some episodes run on too long or do not quite achieve their intended lyricism, there is little question that this trilogy is turning into a considerable achievement.

C. P. Snow

With *Last Things* (1970), C. P. Snow ended his sequence *Strangers and Brothers,* an eleven-volume chronicle of England since the beginning of the First World War. Unlike Doris Lessing's *Children of Violence* and Anthony Powell's *Dance to the Music of Time,* Snow's series lost its impetus long before the final three volumes appeared. Although *Last Things* (encompassing the years 1965–68) is a nostalgic, occasionally touching farewell to both the series and the era, neither it nor the earlier two—*Corridors of Power* (1965 [1955–58]) and *The Sleep of Reason* (1968 [1963])—adds appreciably to our understanding of England in the second third of the century or to a deeper comprehension of Lewis Eliot, Snow's perpetual narrator.

In all three, Snow tells us things we already know; our reactions to change are more rapid and accurate than those of his major characters. In many ways, indeed, Snow has cheated us. For Eliot has not developed, has not responded with any of the intelligence we were led to expect from the earlier novels; in fact, has become an insufferable bore, really unintelligent. All this Snow presents without irony or even distance.

There is, as the final title indicates, a sense of exhaustion in this fiction, as though fiction itself along with everything else has become outmoded. F. R. Leavis's fierce attack on Snow at the beginning of the decade was an expression of a fear that literature would lose its religious fervor in the hands of such a popular figure, the "new man" of public affairs, reason, and science who was dabbling in the arts. Snow's career confirms Leavis's fears, for he became an internationally known figure outside his literary achievement, entering the Labour Government with the rank of a Cabinet member and later being made Baron Snow. In his numerous public statements, Snow invoked technological know-how as a way toward progress, speaking in terms of social movements, political solutions, economic support, but never in tones favoring the literary or artistic imagination.* His penultimate novel, *The Sleep of Reason,* seems to be his antidote to the forces of frenzy and illogic that possess people and governments.

All this has little to do with fiction; clearly, Snow had begun to use his novels as moral outposts. *Corridors of Power* is a tale of decent men working out seemingly insoluble problems. Snow is persuaded that the twin maidens, reason and decency, can resolve basic human discord. However, he offers up a poorly understood moral lesson. For if anything is true, it is that reason and decency rarely mediate in political differences; more often, self-interest or barely disguised nationalism functions. Surely, the novelist must strive to penetrate to other motives. Decency is too often a veneer; for a writer to accept it unquestioningly is to parade his own virginity or blindly accept technological progress.

Snow prefaces *The Sleep of Reason* with an epigraph from

---

* Snow's service in the government was somewhat equivocal, for Labour under Harold Wilson compromised on many issues concerning American military power, including Vietnam, while Snow personally attacked American intervention in Southeast Asia; a clear indication of unresolved conflict between private belief and public ambition. To compare Snow to Jean-Paul Sartre is instructive, for both are more interested in issues than in literature; but can anyone imagine Sartre holding an official post in de Gaulle's or Pompidou's government?

Goya's *Caprichos,* to the effect that "The sleep of reason produces monsters." The sleep of reason, here, is embodied in certain ghastly murders of children committed by warped youths, murders involving terror, torture, sadism, perversion of every type. But surely a novelist handling such inflammatory material—the "Moor Murders," familiar from news reports of the actual events—would have to be intense, insistent, psychological to his fingertips. Instead, Snow comes on flat and rational in a prose that besides being cliché-ridden has lost all vigor and tension. It is a prose that ends rather than creates for the reader. The description at the beginning of the novel and throughout sounds as nonchalant as a travelogue about surfing in New Zealand. Snow is capable of more, as *The Light and the Dark* and *The Conscience of the Rich* remind us, but fiction has become secondary, even bothersome, for him.

Parts of *Last Things* show vestiges of Snow's novelistic sense. After a very gauche beginning, it settles into a sometimes moving "final word," as Lewis Eliot suffers a cardiac arrest, stares down the corridor to death, but lives and waits for the second and final arrest. Snow is best here not when he tries to chronicle England's generation gap, about which he and Eliot appear to comprehend nothing, but when he defines the nature of mortality, the sense of the past, one's awareness of finality. The cardiac arrest isolates Eliot, because he must wait alone: "When one is as alone as one can get, there's still no end." But the end is in sight, just as Eliot sees the end of *his* England. The country has, as it were, also suffered an arrest, and the party system, the tempo of political life, the nature of the government itself must somehow change to meet new demands and new pressures. Whether intended or not, cardiac arrest symbolizes a political watershed, somewhat like those four houses in Doris Lessing's *Four-Gated City.*

If Eliot confronts mortality, so does the roster of old Snow gladiators; virtually all the Cambridge Fellows from *The Masters* have already died or die in this volume. Near the end, we hear the final service for Francis Getliffe, and the others die in other ways. Walter Luke, for example, is Lord Luke of Salcombe. Eliot only dimly grants, speaking for Snow, that ideals have been forfeited with the temptations of power, that personal ambition involves destructive compromise and devilish hypocrisy, and finally, that the pull of the irrational is stronger than all our plans and patterns.

Without adding anything appreciable to our knowledge of men or events, the last volume cleaves to Snow's original theme of *Strangers and Brothers,* although in a curiously ironic fashion. Near the end of his life and at the end of the decade, Eliot senses that men have never been more strange to each other, and that any ideal of brotherhood is distant indeed, is perhaps even a twisted ideal. There lies the irony, if Snow had cared to see it. About all he can say, however, is that the end is not in sight so long as there is consciousness. In this paradoxical way, Snow's last word is the humanist's reliance on individual awareness, and with that surely F. R. Leavis can have little disagreement.

Muriel Spark

Up to *The Mandelbaum Gate,* Muriel Spark's books have been slender, more suitable as "entertainments" than as serious fiction. * Her earlier novels moved perkily along surfaces but tended to elude deeper readings, although Miss Spark has always been earnest beneath her sense of play. In *The Mandelbaum Gate* (1965), she brought her wit to bear on serious matters. She attempted much, perhaps because spiritually she felt close to the materials of this novel. Amid the conflict between Israel and the Arabs and its inevitable intrigues, she set a number of characters desperately trying to reach some sense of "the other," that is, of something beyond themselves.

For Muriel Spark, the "other" may take many forms, but the real "other" is one's awareness of God's presence, and everything else is ultimately a variation or a manifestation of this sense. Here,

---

* Since *The Ballad of Peckham Rye,* in 1960, her fiction has included: *The Bachelors* (1960), *The Prime of Miss Jean Brodie* (1961), *The Girls of Slender Means* (1963); after *The Mandelbaum Gate,* she published *Collected Stories, I* (1968) and *The Public Image* (1968).

Barbara Vaughan is the central character who must find this awareness: her mother is Jewish, her father Catholic. Split by heritage like Miss Spark herself, she undertakes a pilgrimage in the Holy Land, a quest paralleling Jesus' wanderings, to seek her true identity and gain wholeness. A spinster of thirty-seven, Barbara will marry an archaeologist, Harry Clegg, if he can obtain an annulment; the twists and turns of this device fill the interstices of the novel, even though Barbara has already resolved (martyr-like?) to marry him whether or not he obtains the annulment. Harry is really a nonentity in this conflict, devoured by Barbara's Catholicism.

The scenic background is a divided Jerusalem represented by the Mandelbaum Gate, with Jordanian police, paranoiac about Israeli spies, on one side, and methodical Israeli officials on the other, taking security precautions but careful not to discourage tourism. The situation is ripe for humor, and there is no question that Miss Spark has played up many farcical aspects of the conflict, especially when handling the Arabs and certain religious dilemmas. But one must view the novel whole, to see if the serious religious elements coalesce with the human beings who embody them; if there is even a possibility for (1) an annulment, (2) a pilgrimage paralleling that of Jesus, (3) Middle East intrigue, and (4) cool English diplomats to come together effectively. Despite her desire for martyrdom, Barbara Vaughan is self-righteous, not even potentially intense. Despite his heroism, Freddy Hamilton, an English diplomat, is frivolous. Surface is all.

The situations are too often of the schoolboy variety: the lesbian overtones between Barbara and the headmistress Ricky, the Arabs (Waugh's Armenians) who will sell anything and anyone, the Arab girl who combines shrewdness and intelligence with terrible naïveté, the English diplomats who mope around uselessly but who have terrific courage when the chips are down, the quest for religious faith overcoming secular temptations, and the convolutions of the annulment, almost as involved as one of Yeats's gyres. The conception contains too many clichés, too many issues that have long since been resolved in books and journalism.

Yet Miss Spark ekes even more out of these sequences. For against the conspiratorial foreground is the playing out of the Eichmann trial. Evidently, she uses the trial as an example of Israeli efficiency, of Israeli sense of purpose, to contrast with the flounderings of the characters who are still seeking individual consciousness. This presumes Israel has found its consciousness, unlike Eichmann, who disguised his banality with bureaucratic efficiency. But the Eichmann parallel never really becomes clear. The real import is that something monstrous and momentous is being played out at *that* level, and if Miss Spark's novel were deeply significant it would somehow have had to attain the intensity of conflict suggested by the Eichmann trial. Compared with the swirling anger and hate of that event, Miss Spark's characters appear frivolous even as they enter their own version of Jesus' Passion.

Perhaps the chief disappointment of the novel comes from Miss Spark's assumption that the "Passion," modern version, can be of interest presented in the secular forms of her art. Perhaps the last novel to handle this premise convincingly was Graham Greene's *The Power and the Glory;* but Greene, like Conrad and Dostoyevsky before him, has been a man more obsessed with running than finding. Muriel Spark is not passionate in this way, although her characters call for a passionate commitment beyond words. Greene conveyed his obsession with pungent, brutal language and sharp images; Miss Spark winds in and out wittily. His whisky priest is a man forced to seek and regain faith by a desire to survive; her Barbara Vaughan is a spiritual dilettante who makes a pest of herself. She recalls the fiancée in *Heart of Darkness* whom Kurtz left behind in Brussels.

The most successful creations in the book are the Ramdez family, two generations of Arabs on the make for money, power, survival. Suzi is a marvelous mixture of Scheherazade and peasant; while Abdul, who tries to peddle his father's insurance, has achieved consciousness—as a liar, cheat, confidence man, and charmer. The father, Old Joe, who sexually turns on Ricky, the masculine schoolmistress, does what he can with insurance, real estate, investments, and white-slaving. Dramatically setting off Barbara, who seeks an annulment while also seeking the way of Jesus, the Arab Ramdezes show up the weakness of the plotting. For if the English in Jordan do finally see the irrational underside of their lives, then the resolution of the novel must take account of their experiences. But it does not. These elements, which should become integral parts of them, remain disparate, discrete; passions are unattended and discontinuous. And that gigantic theme of Eichmann in Jerusalem somehow becomes pretentious, a false fictional usage in which the novel borrows from life without being up to the momentousness of life. We possibly dislike being reminded once again that messy life is always greater than symmetrical fiction, but Miss Spark's novel makes us reject the artwork for the thing it represents, and that can only mean that the artwork has missed the mark.

Angus Wilson

In *The Old Men at the Zoo* (1961), Angus Wilson writes about the administration of a zoo in terms reminiscent of Snow's descriptions of Whitehall Street. Wilson's sick elephants and butting giraffes are analogous to Snow's bureau heads and administrators, and the way the keepers handle each species determines their own futures. Wilson, however, has tried much more. He has attempted to place the London Zoo, with all its comic implications, against the background of an atomic war. His aim evidently is to demonstrate that decisions for immediate survival must be made despite potential destruction. As in Snow's novels, man appears in his setting as a creature who has a duty to perform no matter what the circumstances, even the dubious job of evacuating zoo animals after an atomic attack.

There is a sense of the apocalypse in this theme as well as in several of the scenes: No doubt Wilson, like many of his grimmer contemporaries, sensed that the decade was opening ominously. Only shortly afterward, as if programmed, the United States and Russia entertained a nuclear facedown over missiles in Cuba. In a chapter facetiously entitled "A Good Old, Rare Old, Armageddon," there is an apocalyptic ending to the zoo, an explosion followed by the escape of dozens of beasts:

. . . the Old Zoo was in flames and from it came the agonizing screams and roars of hippos, rhinos, zebras, apes and trumpeting elephants. The roof had gone from the eagle house and high above it great condors, vultures and golden eagles were circling and spiralling up into the sky. The trees were filled with chattering parakeets, and among the beds of broken, bruised flowers lay the little bodies of a hundred multi-coloured tropical birds; for the aviary had been shattered into a thousand pieces. Here and there men were writhing on the turf. In the floodlight the pools of blood stared in technicolour red against an emerald grass. (p. 276)

Yet this is apocalypse with a difference, a kind of campy final ending to Noah's hopes. This apocalypse occurs in a novel that opens with a zookeeper being kicked repeatedly in the groin by a sick giraffe. This image, funny to everyone but the keeper, is as necessary to the novel as is the nuclear attack that disperses zoo beasts into the jungles of human beasts: Wilson may be suggesting final things in terms of a medieval bestiary, but without the ideological connotations of a modern political allegory, like *Animal Farm*. Wilson's own habitat for many years was the British Museum; since institutional personnel do not differ greatly, a curator of antiques is—allowing for differences of detail—not too far removed from a keeper of insects or birds. We can imagine Wilson, deep within the museum's dusty recesses, turning his colleagues into Regents Park exhibits.

The only ambivalence in the novel occurs in Simon Carter, Wilson's protagonist and narrator. Carter is the prototypical administrator, recognized both for his considerable talents and for his irony. In the course of the novel, Carter—whose wit provides depths unimagined in Snow's Lewis Eliot—undergoes unbearable strains; at one point he chooses his administrative duties at the sacrifice of his family. The pressures, however, are rarely seen or felt; they are rarely there. Once again, Wilson appears correct in all the details, but careless of the large conception. Carter, so central to both the serious and the comic halves of the novel, has no texture, even though the reader expects it of him. When a narrator reveals so little of himself, intensity is dissipated, the novel flattens; and we recognize that the heart of the book is the London Zoo, its marvelously unself-conscious keepers, its administrative bickering, its "office politics" where the danger is not a raging division chief but a sick giraffe who uses his hoofs indiscriminately.

Wilson's work in the sixties is difficult to see whole, much as Iris Murdoch's novels of the same period appear to move in several directions. Early on, *The Old Men at the Zoo* seemed to have a somewhat clearer *tonal* line than the early stories and than *Anglo-Saxon Attitudes,* a distinct break from the overwritten and over-stuffed *The Middle Age of Mrs. Eliot.* But with *Late Call* (1964) and *No Laughing Matter* (1967), Wilson moved into something rather different, the latter being a chronicle, almost a Galsworthian novel, although wittier, more irreverent. *No Laughing Matter,* a huge, rambling affair, is an attempt to follow a family in England for fifty years of this century, from before the Great War to the year the novel was published. One difficulty is that Wilson makes the family move in step with events rather than providing thematic development in the family itself.

There are eight Matthewses, including the parents, and all of them move in their own directions, providing an umbrella-like structure of upper-middle-class Englishmen and women who some-how survive the terrible years of this century. One Matthews is a Communist, another an actor, a third a prancing homosexual, a fourth something else. The father is a failed writer, the mother a frustrated, vindictive woman. As they grow, develop, mature, and age, they are worn down by events, by the political activity of the thirties, the disillusionment with ideological commitments, the ad-justments of the postwar years, the advent of the American influ-ence.

Since *Old Men,* Wilson's style appears to have picked up many of Virginia Woolf's mannerisms. One recalls bits and pieces of *The Years, The Waves, To the Lighthouse;* and yet little of the book catches on, perhaps because the family seems rudderless and this lack of direction does not have substance, does not become thematic. After 200,000 words, there is no sense of resolution to what one has read, no sense of its being social comedy, political tragedy, family chronicling; no sense that the lives of the charac-ters, however well phrased and presented, have become anything more than the author's own, well-directed words. This is, in one sense, a novelist's novel. Not necessarily the most felicitous of forms, a novelist's novel revels in its ability to fulfill skillfully a difficult technical assignment. Eight characters against a background of fifty years of a most complex century—the task is itself imposing, involving a sense of both panorama and detail, history and character, plot and theme, narrative and scene. The model is something like *War and Peace,* although war is itself distant, a portent rather than an actuality.

Wilson does not appear secure within his very great talent. A technical and verbal facility has replaced idea; an intense and deep conception of the material has given way to a flitting around among characters and events. In a sense, *No Laughing Matter* is the obverse of *The Middle Age of Mrs. Eliot,* in which intensity and depth were indeed evident but they underlay a character whose movements were too circumscribed for all the energy expended on her. This failure is all the more curious because Wilson is so clearly a "thick" novelist writing from sharp insight into people and events, with an ever-ready eye for detail, full of the sense of how people merge with their backgrounds, how they fit into their clothes, their houses, and their nightmares.

Two "New" Novelists:
John Fowles and Anthony Burgess

John Fowles (b. 1926)

Like Iris Murdoch, John Fowles tries to find, in the bizarre and the extraordinary, suitable metaphors for our current attitudes and styles. And like Miss Murdoch, he appears to feel that such metaphors can be found in our sexual practices, as we posture and couple while we seek salvation. Both writers also speak about love, or the search for love, while at the same time seeming to be fascinated by sadism, deprivation, love-longing (rather than fulfillment), voyeurism, and the other terms and tones that have become part of our ordinary contemporary equipment.

It was surely to break out of this cycle that Mr. Fowles wrote

The French Lieutenant's Woman (1969), a novel that moves back one hundred years in time and history. By setting the book in 1867, during the Golden Age of Victorianism, Fowles could "slow up" sexual activity. As he comments, the novelist in 1867 could write about love as a kind of ballet, while in 1970 the preliminaries pass rapidly into bed practices and the writer loses the sense of male-female relationships. We have all noted how in fiction the Victorians enjoyed areas of exploration in human relationships that are no longer available to us; by disguising or hiding behind feeling, they allowed for artifice, and artifice gave the writer mystery, ambiguity, special tones.

But Fowles is sufficiently continuous and unified as a writer so that even this excursion into Victorianism is held together by his previous preoccupations in both *The Collector* (1963) and *The Magus* (1965). Those two earlier books are, in fact, more interesting than the later venture, although perhaps more flawed. *The Collector,* in particular, while it did not enjoy the underground student success of *The Magus,* is a novel of considerable achievement, its chief quality being its insistency, a quality not often found in contemporary English novelists. This insistency in Fowles recalls Thomas Hardy's peculiarly urgent composition of people fixed by predisposition and events and held in their unrelenting grip. Put another way, this quality embodies a sense of destiny, an inexorable fate, what we find in early George Eliot and in Joseph Conrad, all linked tonally by the intensity of their vision.

Such a vision we find in *The Collector.* Inevitably, the book appears to be an intense statement of class feeling: a lower-class lottery winner imprisons a well-educated art student with whom he has secretly fallen in love. *The Collector* is the type of novel that at first appears deep but narrow; however, in retrospect broadens without losing psychological depth. Feeling is always attached to class. Miranda and Ferdinand—her Caliban—are isolated, like the characters in *The Tempest;* or, in *Robinson Crusoe,* where Miranda would have been Friday. Ironically, the jailer and his prisoner celebrate the "brave new world" that Miranda describes in Shakespeare, but this "new world" results in her falling ill and dying, while he stands by helpless. For Ferdinand is a harbinger of a new class that has neither taste nor feeling. He is leaden and clogged (his last name is Clegg). The New People are the economic under-dogs whom liberals have always championed; but the newly risen are never meek and grateful, are instead politically and socially massive and ready to impose their tasteless values.

All this is intensely ironic because Miranda has always been a well-wisher of lower-class seekers after power. Now, in their repre-sentative's company, she finds them deplorable—impotent, as Fer-dinand is, voyeurs, and physically revolting. In a literal sense, Miranda becomes a captive of the new values, the bad furnishings, the tasteless art objects, the pathetic attempts at smart decoration, the inability to enter into any kind of aesthetic experience. This representative of the "new society," she finds, can offer her every material comfort, convenience, indulgence of her needs and whims —but it is an impotent society which Ferdinand represents, eco-nomic progress based on shame of feeling. One is reminded of Godard's *Alphaville,* made within a year of *The Collector,* in which all displays of feeling are punished by public execution, with spec-tators applauding politely as though at a tennis match. Clegg's in-ability to feel is part of his prudishness; he places restrictions on anything that falls outside of his lower-class materialism.

Drenched in class—and Miranda feels considerable guilt about her detestation of Clegg—the novel is a good indicator of social problems working themselves out in a quiet, secretive, conspirato-rial way. The emerging New People, and those who imitate them, have rejected every value that Miranda embraces as life-giving. Based on sadism, the narrative works out in a conflict between life-in-death and death-in-life. Ferdinand is humanistically dead, but sudden money keeps him alive, indeed makes him emperor of his small kingdom. He can enslave, impose, dictate, and then look on, even pity and allow concessions. He has, with his hatred of the ruling classes in art and politics, reversed the roles. His desire for Miranda, which he cannot consummate sexually, is clearly a need to humiliate. Offering slavish devotion, he creates only discomfort, hatred, fear—all of which he can confront because he has money. By controlling Miranda, he gains revenge on every slight he has suffered—and continues to suffer—as a result of class.

Fowles has found in this version of the literature of enclosure a fine, working metaphor for the shrinking sense of England—diminishing to a crazy member of the lower class confronting his real and imagined oppressors in a small cottage in Sussex. So convincing is the metaphor, however, that the large sections devoted to Miranda's life before she was captured weaken the novel; her story is not compelling precisely because it has little to do with class feeling. Fowles had an obvious problem—to create Miranda for the reader *before* her enslavement, as he had earlier created Ferdinand. A parallel problem was one of invention: how to keep the novel going once the initial interchanges between the two characters had been exhausted; or how to prevent the interchanges from being exhausted. Nevertheless, the real quality of the novel is defined by the steady shrinkage of the situation—so that, like *Alice in Wonderland,* the matter moves from larger elements to smaller and still smaller, from London to a village in Sussex, to a cottage, to a room in a basement, to a coffin.

The theme of persecution of the female, with the undertone of male sadism, appears to derive from Hardy. Fowles's Sussex, although only intermittently seen and then viewed only through Clegg's eyes, is a kind of modernization of Hardy's Wessex. While there is nothing substantial in the parallelism, both writers do create an atmosphere in which magic of a sort occurs, where a girl innocently comes under the power of an obsessed, compulsive individual who does not consciously intend harm, where individual will —the very stuff of the girl's assumptions—is thwarted by some malevolent power that extends from the persecutor back into literary history: to Beauty and the Beast, Robinson Crusoe and Friday, Caliban and Miranda.

Literary allusions, like those in *The French Lieutenant's Woman,* abound. Miranda sees herself, ironically, as Jane Austen's Emma or, alternately, as Marianne and Elinor of *Sense and Sensibility.* Seeing herself as one of the remaining "Few," as against a New Person like Clegg, she measures herself in terms of artistic reactions. Too young to have had much experience—except with the painter George Paston—she must relate herself to literary and artistic adventures.

From lepidopterous collections, Clegg moves to people, and like his butterflies Miranda must be mounted. Clegg's voyeurism, his desire for pornographic camera shots of his captive, his penchant for poses and objects—all these are the "New People" equivalent of Miranda's artistic experiences. His, however, are exterior: while she likes painting, he likes photography; while she worships a George Paston painted figure, he worships his photographs of her. The fact that he can relate only to things that are collected and mounted dramatizes his impotence, his prudishness, his inability to bring deep feeling to the surface. Anything uncollected or un-mounted is free, and therefore poses a threat to his own bound will.

The Collector succeeds, as I said above, because of its insistence on a few intense points. Whenever it wavers from its psychological intensity—even when it becomes a matter of class, art, and power —the novel diffuses its force. *The Magus,* Fowles's much more ambitious second novel, is also about "collectors" and focuses on another *Tempest*-like situation. In this novel, Conchis (with a soft "ch," pronounced either "conscious" or "conscience") is the Magus, the magician or confidence man, in a way like Prospero of *The Tempest.* Yet with each part of the novel prefaced by a quota-tion from Sade, with the Bosch-like figures of the various plays within plays, with the hints of *Othello* in the sporting between Lilly and Black Joe, with the sexual dislocations of voyeurism and vica-riousness, one sees that the nature of Fowles's landscape is not *The Tempest*'s. Fowles is again attempting to find metaphors for pres-ent dislocations. And he is again, like Thomas Hardy, testing the individual's free will against the deterministic power of another's will, or against the play of events. In fact, if we carry the idea to a further stage, Fowles's repetitious use of "collection" and "collec-tors" can be compared to Hardy's Immanent Will, or the will of the universe, as it baffles, frustrates, and bends the individual.

All this is of some interest. And Fowles's setting on a "magical" Greek island not too distant from Athens, together with the Magus from the Tarot deck, the discussions of telepathy, the intricate play-acting, the mysterious appearance of figures from the dark, the Gothic haunted house, the imperious Conchis—all these are typical of Fowles's creation of a separate world which has its own rules and laws.*

* Recalling Francis Barrett's *The Magus: A Complete System of Occult Phi-losophy* (London, 1801).

Yet despite the underground popularity of *The Magus,* the novel sprays its effects. The twists and turns of the plot, of Conchis's plans and machinations are too frequent, finally too uncompelling. Fowles's protagonist, Nicholas Urfe, is unprepossessing, somehow not worth all the attention and love bestowed upon him. It is, after all, a question of the author turning everything into role-playing, and perhaps the novel should be read as that, as a kind of campy theatrical farce. But even so, the parts do not fit, the characters are lost amid strategies, and one is left not with Orpheus Nicholas saying farewell to Eurydice Alison, but with a wicked gleam in the author's eye.

Anthony Burgess (John Anthony Burgess Wilson, b. 1917)

A Clockwork Orange (1962), Anthony Burgess's most original work, is almost as much a composite novel as Joyce's *Finnegans Wake,* one of Burgess's models. The most immediate sources of *Orange* are, obviously, Joyce's two experimental novels, especially in the compulsive word play, the mixing of languages (Russian and English in Burgess), the attempt to create a night-talk and a day-talk. Another evident source is Orwell's *1984,* which also develops a new vocabulary to describe a totalitarian mentality. The society in which Burgess's Alex lives, whether it is Alex cured or uncured, approximates Orwell's future state in which lack of emotion and violence are the two sides of a coin. At one point, in the event we missed the Orwellian note, Burgess speaks of Staja (State Jail) No. 84F.

If the atmosphere immediately recalls Orwell, it also partakes of the hermetically enclosed criminal world of John Gay's *Beggar's Opera,* or Brecht and Weill's *Threepenny Opera.* And the language has strange echoes of a little-remembered English novelist, Gerald Kersh, a minor-league Céline, whose hard-boiled material included a gangster's patois, a rapid and brutal wit, and a dogged persistence to avoid verbal clichés—in all of which Burgess excels.

Despite Stanley Edgar Hyman's praise of the novel, however, *A*

Clockwork Orange is caught in the tangle of its own nostalgic dialectic, much as Burgess's *Malayan Trilogy* is wistful about British imperialism at the same time as it bows to its passing. Burgess often hides behind a basically sentimental view of the world and its processes, all based on assumptions that the status quo is preferable to change, or, put another way, that since all change must lead to excess, the past is preferable.

The title of *A Clockwork Orange* refers to the attempt to impose on man a mechanical arrangement antithetical to his growth as a human being; it symbolizes, in brief, the idea that the machine is perfect, man imperfect. The fifteen-year-old narrator, Alex, is a "hooligan," a product of England's creeping socialism, who must be de-fused through a series of brain-washing sessions performed by the Reclamation Treatment. After this series, in which through drugs and films showing scenes of extreme violence the "bad is turned into the good," Alex is de-emotionalized. His devotion to music, which was the artistic manifestation of his violent character, is now lost; Bach and Beethoven, in fact, make him ill. He becomes emotionally neuter, in practice a typical member of a socialist society, according to Burgess. The transformation of Alex recalls Ken Kesey's use of the lobotomy in *One Flew over the Cuckoo's Nest,* although Kesey's Randle Patrick McMurphy never indulges in Alex's kind of meaningless violence.

Ideologically, then, Burgess's point is clear: that a technologically oriented society, specifically one based on socialist principles of mindless amelioration, in its overriding desire to change people will kill all emotion, good and bad, in the process. Burgess's invention of a "new language," based chiefly on Russian roots, is emblematic of this new society; but his satire of contemporary England is rarely as sharp as Kesey's of America because Burgess makes Alex mechanical before and after he is cured. That may well reflect actuality, but it leaves the novelist no place to go. Alex is damned either way, which may be a good political point, but it is one-dimensional in fiction. If Alex is sane only while under the influence of music, murderous and amoral without it, perhaps the cure is more important for social reasons than Alex's emotional life is necessary for him. The point is, at least, disputable.

That Burgess returns Alex to his previous state, that is, both to

his violence and to Beethoven's "Ode to Joy," indicates a wistful-
ness for a lost Eden, a past no longer recoverable, even when
affairs are imperfect and men are uncontrollable.* It is a strange
area for a novelist in the 1960's to exploit, but such ideas permeate
the best of Burgess's work, the *Malayan Trilogy, Enderby, Tremor
of Intent,* among others, and they make the parts always appear
stronger than the final result. The Malayan novels (*Time for a
Tiger,* 1956; *The Enemy in the Blanket,* 1958; *Beds in the East,*
1959) are witty, with memorable scenes and with a fine sense of
England's hopeless position as technological America begins to
move in, and Malayans, Indians, and Chinese grow more and more
murderous toward each other. But there is no idea behind the
trilogy except the fact of England's declining fortunes, along with a
rather wistful look at what was once decent and expedient amateur-
ism and a sentimental view of the do-good Victor Crabbe, one in a
long line of Burgess's Prufrocks.

One need only compare the Malayan novels with Conrad's *Heart
of Darkness* or Orwell's *Burmese Days* to see how an idea can
inform the work and how this idea must be worked out with irony.
The resounding lie that Marlow tells Kurtz's fiancée at the end of
the Conrad novella is a bitter irony that indicts what Marlow still
believes in. And Orwell's Flory, like Cain, is marked, fated; his
choices are themselves the measure of Orwell's wry irony. On the
contrary, Burgess comes on straight; his Crabbe (neither fish nor
fruit) is fumbling and decent, not even Forster's Fielding, without
particular growth or insight. Forces rage around him that he never
effectively internalizes, and he is not, despite Burgess's urging,
Quixote.

Somewhat comparably, *Enderby* (1963) and *Tremor of Intent*
(1966) are incomplete, somehow artistically starved despite Burgess's usual marvelous way with language—indeed Joycean in *En-*

* The English edition contains an additional seventh chapter in Part III, providing for the novel a symmetrical (magical!) seven chapters in each of the
three parts, the form of a perfectly worked out concerto. More importantly,
however, the final chapter of the English edition tries to "resolve" Alex's
conflicts by turning him toward respectability: a future of work, wife, and
children. But in no real sense does this chapter settle the central dilemma of
the novel; by making Alex appear to "grow up," it simply evades the problem
by suggesting an unmotivated and unforeseen direction to his behavior.

derby—and his witty manner of charting eccentricities as normal and normalities as eccentricities. The first half of *Enderby*—the lavatory poet, one might call him—is successful, until the idea drops off and the North African episodes pile on without regard for the inner tensions of the main character himself. *Tremor of Intent* is clearly imitation Graham Greene and Joseph Conrad, with its tortured secret agent, its attempt to raise spying to an existential plane, its scenes of confession, moral dilemma, and temptation, all rolled into a James Bond thriller. Burgess is very much taken with food and drink, the whole scene of belching, farting, elimination, so that most individuals are a plumber's dream. But these digestive processes are rarely part of anything larger; except for Enderby, Burgess's characters have not regressed; they are not seeking alternate modes of being in food, and they are not, symbolically, ingesting their father in order to acquire his power.

Because there is almost no psychological process commensurate with all the physical activity, the characters are one-dimensional or interchangeable, despite Burgess's verbal play, his attention to detail, his acute sense of place and things. There is so much expert novel-making here that one wonders why his novels do not satisfy or, ultimately, do not tell us something we have not learned before. Surely, Burgess provides too much narration, conveys too much information, has too much going on all the time for the small amount finally revealed. There is no question that Burgess's fiction leaves little impression for so much expert effort, and the reason must be that the controlling ideas are not up to the richness and variety of the fill. Finally, we come to see that Burgess views psychological processes simplistically, and this shortcoming vitiates the kind of density that we have come to expect with verbal play and wit of such skill.

Acknowledgments

The author gratefully acknowledges use of copyrighted material from the following publications and publishers:

From *Murphy, Molloy, Malone Dies, The Unnamable,* by Samuel Beckett, to Grove Press.

From *The Alexandria Quartet,* by Lawrence Durrell, to E. P. Dutton & Co.

From *The Light and the Dark,* by C. P. Snow, to Charles Scribner's Sons.

From *The Confidential Agent, Brighton Rock, The Power and the Glory,* by Graham Greene, to The Viking Press.

From *Ivy Gripped the Steps, The House in Paris, The Death of the Heart, Bowen's Court,* by Elizabeth Bowen, to Alfred A. Knopf, Inc.

From *The Horse's Mouth,* by Joyce Cary, to Harper and Brothers.

From *Such, Such Were the Joys, Keep the Aspidistra Flying,* by George Orwell, to Harcourt, Brace & Co.

From *Officers and Gentlemen, Put Out More Flags, Brideshead Revisited,* by Evelyn Waugh, to Little, Brown & Co.

From *Party Going, Living,* by Henry Green, to The Viking Press.

From *Two Worlds and Their Ways, Bullivant and the Lambs,* by Ivy Compton-Burnett, to Alfred A. Knopf, Inc.

From *Lucky Jim,* by Kingsley Amis, to Doubleday & Co.

From *The Acceptance World, A Buyer's Market,* by Anthony Powell, to Little, Brown & Co.

From *Anglo-Saxon Attitudes,* by Angus Wilson, to The Viking Press.

From *Cards of Identity,* by Nigel Dennis, to The Vanguard Press.

From *Free Fall,* by William Golding, to Harcourt, Brace & Co.

I would also like to express especial appreciation to Professor Arthur Zeiger of the City College of New York for his careful reading of the manuscript and for his helpful suggestions.

Index